Back cover photographs courtesy of Larry Rana, Food and Nutrition Services, USDA.

Copyright © 1985 by
THE AVI PUBLISHING COMPANY, INC.
250 Post Road East
P.O. Box 831
Westport, Connecticut 06881

Library of Congress Cataloging in Publication Data

VanEgmond-Pannell, Dorothy.
    School foodservice.

    Bibliography: p.
    Includes index.
    1. School lunchrooms, cafeterias, etc.   I. Title.
TX945.V315   1985   642'.5   84–20382
ISBN   0–87055–463–8

ABCDE   3210987654

Printed in the United States of America

SCHOOL FOODSERVICE

Third Edition

Dorothy VanEgmond-Pannell
Director, School Foodservices
Fairfax County Public Schools, Virginia

VI PUBLISHING COMPANY, INC. WESTPORT, CONNECTICUT

SCHOOL FOODSERVICE

Third Edition

CONTENTS

PREFACE TO THIRD EDITION

The first edition of *School Foodservice* was published in 1974. Since then, there have been marked changes in school foodservice all across this country, and it has become a leading foodservice industry. Those changes have necessitated a complete revision of several sections of this book, particularly those on food production, menu planning, and equipment. Material on energy conservation has been added to the equipment section. Two additional chapters cover new aspects of school foodservice: Chapter 9, Promoting School Foodservice; and Chapter 12, Computerization.

With the growth of school foodservice has come an increased interest in learning more about the field, particularly among students in vocational schools and colleges. Feeding children in schools is a challenging and changing field, requiring better qualified people today than ever before.

I approached the writing of this book as a teacher and as a foodservice director. Thus, I have attempted to bring together information on training foodservice personnel and on operating a school foodservice. Much of the book is devoted to the organization and management of a school foodservice. Explanations of federal regulations are woven throughout this volume so that readers will understand how they influence school foodservice programs.

Many people have contributed to the three editions of this book. I wish especially to thank the staff at the Food and Nutrition Information Center of the National Agricultural Library in Beltsville, Maryland, and to thank the many people at the U.S. Department of Agriculture who furnished information and materials. Particularly helpful was the opportunity I had to be a part of the Nutrition and Technical Services staff at the U.S. Department of Agriculture on an Intragovernmental Personnel Agreement contract and to be a member of the National Child Nutrition Advisory Council.

My thanks also go to my colleagues and employer in the Fairfax County (VA) Public Schools; to Randy Altenberg of the Los Angeles School District for help with the personnel chapter; to Lyle Root, formerly of the Baltimore

County School District, who helped with the chapter on facilities and equipment; to John Cantwell of the U.S. Department of Agriculture for help with computerization; and to Larry Rana of the U.S. Department of Agriculture for his fine photography used throughout the book.

I gratefully acknowledge permission granted for the use of illustrations throughout the text. My special thanks and appreciation to my family, especially my husband, Jerry, for his patience and encouragement.

Dorothy VanEgmond-Pannell

RELATED AVI BOOKS

BATTER AND BREADING
Suderman and Cunningham
ENERGY MANAGEMENT IN FOODSERVICE
Unklesbay and Unklesbay
FOOD PRODUCTS FORMULARY SERIES, VOLS. I–IV
FOOD SERVICE SYSTEMS MANAGEMENT
Minor and Cichy
MENU PLANNING, 3rd Edition
Eckstein
L. J. Minor Foodservice Standards Series:
    VOL. 1   NUTRITIONAL STANDARDS
             Minor
    VOL. 2   SANITATION, SAFETY AND ENVIRONMENTAL STANDARDS
             Minor
    VOL. 3   BASIC ACCOUNTING STANDARDS
             Ninemeier and Schmidgall
    VOL. 4   EMPLOYEE MANAGEMENT STANDARDS
             McIntosh
PRACTICAL BAKING
Sultan
PRACTICAL BUSINESS RESEARCH METHODS
Blank
PRIVATE LABELS
Fitzell
PROCESSED MEATS, 2nd Edition
Pearson and Tauber
QUALITY CONTROL IN FOODSERVICE, Revised Edition
Thorner
STANDARDIZING FOODSERVICE FOR QUALITY AND EFFICIENCY
Tolve
THE PASTRY CHEF
Sultan

OVERVIEW AND HISTORY
OF SCHOOL FOODSERVICE

School foodservice—a $8.4 billion industry—is one of the world's largest foodservice businesses. During 1983, under the regulations of the National School Lunch Program 4.7 billion nutritious meals were served to an average 23.3 million students daily. In addition, sales of a la carte items in schools were valued at a billion dollars and are growing. There has been a tremendous growth in school foodservice since 1946 when an average 4.5 million children ate their lunches at school, at an annual cost of $231 million. This growth started with passage of the National School Lunch Act in 1946. In many communities, the school foodservice has grown from a soup kitchen to a fully equipped facility serving a nutritious lunch, breakfast, snacks, a la carte items, and, in some cases, meals for the elderly as well as for children. Participation in school food programs peaked in 1979–1980. School enrollment decreases and the drastic federal budget cuts of the early 1980s have caused a decline in participation since then.

All public and some nonprofit private elementary and secondary schools and any public or nonprofit child-care institution that maintains children in residence and operates principally for the care of children are eligible to participate in the National School Lunch Program. In order for a private school to participate in the program its tuition must be less than a stipulated amount. Many private schools that qualify and some public schools have chosen to operate without federal controls and funds. The number of public schools participating increased 22% between 1971 and 1980, when 92% of the public schools participated. The number of children served free or reduced-price lunches doubled between 1970 and 1974, and almost tripled by 1979. Then the decline of the 1980s started. By 1983, the number of schools (public and private) serving lunch under the National School Lunch Program was down to 90,360, a decline of 3,975 since 1979. Four million children dropped out of the program between 1980 and 1983.

The growth in school lunch programs during the 1970s can be attributed to increases in federal funding that were legislated as a result of public concern about hunger in the United States. Senator George McGovern's Committee on Nutrition and Human Needs and the White House Conference on Food, Nutrition, and Health focused attention on the problem of hunger, as did such books as *Their Daily Bread* and *Hunger U.S.A.* Groups such as the United League of Women, American School Food Service Association, Children's Foundation, and American Dietetic Association and individuals including Senators Hubert Humphrey (MN) and Allen Ellender (LA), Congressman Carl Perkins (KY), Dr. John Perryman, Dr. Jean Mayer, and Dr. Josephine Martin, also were influential in stimulating public concern and action. However, the 1980s have been characterized by declines in funding, stricter federal regulations (including the requirement that applications for free and reduced-price meals include social security numbers and that some applications be verified), and more audits by state and federal agencies. These changes started during the Carter administration and continued during the Reagan administration.

Thirty years ago many schools found themselves feeding free lunches out of funds from the paying student. Since there is no such thing as a free lunch, someone had to pay for it. If the paying student paid 25¢ in 1963, one can imagine how difficult it was to pay the cost of preparing two lunches (one being free) out of that 25¢ with a federal cash reimbursement of only 4¢ and commodities valued at another 6¢. Making students work for their lunches, scrutinizing free-lunch applications, and serving a different lunch to the free-lunchers all sound inhumane, but the lack of funds forced adoption of such practices in some parts of the country. It was a matter of pure survival for the school lunch programs.

Foodservice administrators in 1970 had hopes of feeding all children but were fearing revenue sharing by 1978. In the early 1980s, there were threats that school lunches would become a welfare program. Congressman Carl Perkins (KY) in March 1971 first introduced a bill to establish a universal foodservice and nutrition education program for children. How much would a universal feeding program cost the federal government? Estimates are outdated by the time they are compiled.

Federal funds currently pay about 56% of the total cost of the school lunch program (Table 1.1). State and local governments put in roughly 18% and the remaining 26% comes from student payments. The cost of preparing a lunch rose steadily between the spring of 1973 and 1979 when prices of food sky-rocketed. Some estimate that the cost per lunch will average more than $4 by the end of fiscal year 1989.

Operating a school foodservice that serves 20,000 lunches and 2000 breakfasts daily takes a qualified businessperson with a strong background in management, nutrition, and foods, and with much patience to interpret the detailed federal rules and regulations that govern the operation. Prepar-

TABLE 1.1. Source of Income per Lunch (Cash Payment and Commodities) under the National School Lunch Program, National Average

Time Period	Federal Contribution (¢) by Category of Lunches				State and Local Contribution (¢)
	Free	Reduced-Price	Paid	Commodities (all categories)	
1968	13.5	13.5	13.5		13.7
1969	14.1	14.1	14.1		14.1
1970	15.9	15.9	15.9		15.3
1971	21.1	21.1	21.1		15.4
1972	27.2	27.2	27.2		15.3
7/1973	55.00	45.00	8.00	7.00	17.3
11/1973	55.00	45.00	10.00	7.00	17.3
1/1974	57.75	47.75	10.50	7.00	20.00
7/1974	60.50	50.50	11.00	10.00[1]	20.00
1/1975	64.25	54.25	11.75	10.00	20.00
7/1975	66.75	56.75	12.25	11.00	20.90
1/1976	69.25	59.25	12.50	11.00	20.90
7/1976	71.50	61.50	13.00	11.75	22.30
1/1977	73.25	63.25	13.25	11.75	22.30
7/1977	77.00	67.00	14.00	12.75	NA[2]
1/1978	79.50	69.50	14.50	12.75	NA
7/1978	83.50	73.50	15.25	13.75	NA
1/1979	87.25	77.25[3]	15.75	13.75	NA
7/1979	93.25	83.25[3]	17.00	15.75	NA
1/1980	97.25	87.25[3]	17.75	15.75	NA
7/1980	102.00	92.00[3]	18.50	15.50	NA
1/1981	99.50	79.50	16.00	13.50	NA
7/1981	109.25	89.25	17.75	11.00	NA
9/1981	109.25	69.25	10.50	11.00	NA
7/1982	115.00	75.00	11.00	11.50	NA
7/1983	120.25	80.25	11.50	11.50	NA
7/1984	125.50	85.50	12.00	11.75	NA

Source: Based on *Fiscal Year 1947–1971 Report and Yearly Fact Sheets, 1976 Annual Statistical Review,* and *1983 Annual Historical Reviews,* Food and Nutrition Service, U.S. Department of Agriculture.
Note: Student payments are not shown since they varied from school to school.
[1] Before fiscal year 1975 commodity distribution rates were not specified by legislation.
[2] States were not required to furnish this information to USDA after 1977.
[3] Between Jan. 1, 1979, and Dec. 31, 1980, the rate could be up to 10¢ less than indicated depending upon state pricing policies.

ing and serving a nutritionally balanced lunch that costs $1.46 for food, labor, and other operating costs, and for which 15¢ of the income is in the form of USDA-donated foods takes good management and in some cases much ingenuity.

The dedication of school foodservice workers, primarily mothers in the early years, has been responsible for the growth and endurance of a sound nutritional program. It is an exciting, challenging business with student customers who keep management on its toes. The attitude "that's all you get; take it or don't be so choosy," if it ever was prevalent, has been replaced with a desire to please even the fussiest customer.

So much has happened during the last 15 years in school foodservice that perhaps one should concentrate on that period. However, a brief—but more complete—history follows. Many publications that trace the history of feeding programs in schools are available. The handiest are *The National School Lunch Program: Background and Development* (Gunderson 1971), on which I have relied heavily in relating this history; the National School Lunch Act of 1946, as amended (see Appendix III); the Child Nutrition Act of 1966, as amended (see Appendix II); and the *Annual Historical Review: Food and Nutrition Programs*, published by USDA. After reviewing the history of school foodservice, I examine in more detail several parts of the federally subsidized programs and then take a look at recent developments during the 1980s and what lies ahead. The glossary of terms that follow will be helpful to someone new to school foodservice and the federal legislation regarding the program.

GLOSSARY OF TERMS

Many acronyms are used in the context of school foodservice and generally they refer to federal legislation and regulations. Some of the most frequently used acronyms and other terms are included here for easy reference. The following is adapted from American School Food Service Association (n.d.).

ADA.   Average daily attendance.

ADP.   Average daily participation.

AIMS.   Assessment, improvement, and monitoring system; management improvement system to be used in the National School Lunch Program.

Amend.   To change a bill or regulation or part of a bill or regulation.

Appropriation.   Money allocated by the federal government for various child nutrition programs.

Audit.   System used to evaluate operation of Child Nutrition Programs for compliance with laws and regulations.

Audit trail.   System for tracing federal funds to determine if they were used for the purpose intended.

Authorizing committee.   Specific committee in the House of Representatives (Education and Labor) or in the Senate (Agriculture, Nutrition, and Forestry) that is concerned with child nutrition legislation.

Bill.   New legislation introduced in the House or Senate.

Bloc grant.   Specified amount of money that is not earmarked for specific programs.

Cash in lieu. Monies issued for purchase of foods instead of donated commodities.

Cash reimbursement rates. Monies received for serving meals that meet the federal meal requirements.

CLOC. Commodity letter of credit issued for purchase of specified foods instead of donated commodities.

CNA. Child Nutrition Act of 1966.

CND. Child Nutrition Division, FNS, USDA.

CNP. Child Nutrition Programs.

Comment period. Amount of time (number of days) given by USDA for interested persons to comment on proposed or interim regulations.

Commodity only school. Schools not participating in the National School Lunch Program but receive commodities for a nonprofit lunch program.

Congressional hearings. Opportunity for interested persons and/or organizations to present testimony before a Congressional committee.

Congressional Record. Verbatim account of happenings on the floors of the House and Senate. Issued daily when Congress is in session. Available in most libraries.

Continuing resolution. Resolution adopted by the House and Senate that would continue funding for various programs for a specified period of time if new legislation has not been adopted by the end of the fiscal year.

Cost of obtaining food. Costs related to obtaining agricultural commodities and other foods for consumption in the program.

Department. Functions of the administrative branch of the government are administered by various departments, i.e., Department of Agriculture.

Distribution agency. State, federal, or private agency distributing donated commodities.

Donated commodities or donated foods. Agricultural food items made available by the Department of Agriculture to Child Nutrition Programs.

Federal Register, Document that provides a uniform system for making available to the public regulations (proposed, interim, and final) and legal notices issued by federal agencies.

FNS. Food and Nutrition Services.

FNSRO. Food and Nutrition Service Regional Office.

Food Distribution Agency. Agency in state government responsible for commodity distribution.

Food stamps. Coupons used for increasing the food purchasing power of eligible households.

Free meals. Meals served at no cost to the recipient.

FSEA. Food Service Equipment Assistance.

Full funding. There will be no cut in reimbursement rates from previous year's rate.

FY. Refers to federal government's fiscal year beginning October 1 and ending September 30.

GAO. Government Accounting Office. Audits each department of the federal government.

Equipment. Articles and physical resources, other than land or buildings, used for such purposes as receiving, storing, preparing, transporting, or serving food.

Escalator clause. Automatic increase or decrease of reimbursement rate.

HR. Bills introduced in the House of Representatives are identified by HR before the bill number.

Income eligibility. Range of income within which students qualify for free or reduced-price meal.

Indirect cost. Those costs that cannot be directly identified because amount is prorated across several programs, i.e., electricity.

Interim regulations. Rule or regulation that has the effect of a final rule or regulation until the comment period is ended and final rule or regulation is published.

Lame Duck Session. Congress continuing in session during the period between election and swearing in of new members of Congress.

Law. (1) Bill that has been passed by both Houses of Congress and signed by the President. (2) Bill may also become law without the President's signature if not signed within 10 working days after receipt.

Lobbying. Group seeking to influence the passage or defeat of legislation or attempting to create a climate of favorable opinion toward legislation.

Lunch. Meal which meets the lunch pattern for specified age groups of children.

Majority party. Political party (Democratic or Republican) having the most members in either House.

Management companies. Commercial enterprise that contracts with a school board to operate foodservice programs.

Mandate. Legislation and/or regulation that demands something be done.

Mark up. The amending of a bill according to information obtained at a hearing or at the request of committee members.

Matching requirements. Federal funds must be matched by state funds as follows: (1) Three parts state or local money (including student payments) to one part Section 4 funds for paid meals, and (2) 10% of the product of all Section 4 funds multiplied by three.

Middle income. Income above what is defined as poverty level. Upper level may vary with economy of the nation.

Minority party. Political party (Democratic or Republican) having fewer members in either House.

Minority report. Any member of the committee who wishes to do so may submit a report setting forth his individual views. Sometimes a group of committee members will join in submitting a minority report even though they are not all from the same political party.

National Advisory Council for Child Nutrition Programs. Council appointed by Secretary of Agriculture. Its purpose is to make a continuing study of the operation of programs included in the National School Lunch Act and Child Nutrition Act of 1966.

Needs assessment (NET Program). Systematic process for delineating the scope, extent (quantity), reach, and success of any current nutrition education activities, including those relating to (1) methods and materials available inside and outside the classroom; (2) training of teachers in the principles of nutrition and nutrition education strategies, methods, and techniques; (3) training of school foodservice personnel in the principles and practices of foodservice management; and (4) compilation of existing data relative to factors impacting on nutrition education and training, such as statistics on child health and competency levels achieved by foodservice personnel.

NET. Nutrition Education and Training.

Nonprofit lunch program. Foodservice program maintained by a school for the benefit of children. All income from which is used solely for the operation or improvement of the foodservice.

Nonsubstitutable. Term used in commodity processing that requires only the donated commodity to be used.

NSLA. National School Lunch Act as amended.

NSLP. National School Lunch Program.

OA. Office of Audit, USDA.

Offer vs. serve. Students must be offered a complete meal but students may select three of the five items offered.

OI. Office of Investigation, USDA.

OIG. Office, Inspector General.

OMB. Office, Management and Budget.

On-site preparation. Food prepared in individual school kitchens.

P.A.C. Political Action Committee. Organization formed by an association which solicits funds for contribution to candidates for public office.

Paid meals. Refers to meals sold to children other than free and reduced-price meals.

Part 210. National school lunch program regulations.

Part 215. Special milk program regulations.

Part 220. School breakfast program regulations.

Part 225. Summer foodservice program regulations.

Part 226. Child-care program regulations.

Part 227. Nutrition education and training program regulations.

Part 230. Foodservice equipment assistance regulations.

Part 240.　Cash in lieu of commodities regulations.

Part 245.　Determining eligibility for free/reduced-price meals and free milk in schools regulations.

Part 250.　General regulations and policies—food distribution.

Participation.　Number of students eating meals or taking part in the special milk program.

Performance funding.　Guaranteed federal reimbursement for every meal that meets the requirements in school lunch and school breakfast programs.

PL.　Public law.

Plate waste.　Food taken but not eaten.

Pocket veto.　A bill does not become a law without the President's signature if the Congress adjourns before the bill is returned to Congress.

Private, nonprofit schools.　All schools other than public schools that do not operate for profit.

Processing contracts.　Agreement entered into by state or USDA to turn donated commodities into another or similar product; i.e., hamburger into hamburger patties.

Proposed regulations.　Regulations written for public comments; they are not enforceable.

Reauthorization.　Programs which have been authorized for a specific period of time, at the end of this time, may be continued by legislation that would reauthorize the program.

Rebate system.　Method by which the Education Agency or School Food Authority receive cash from the processor to cover cost of commodities in foods they have purchased.

Reconciliation bill.　Refers to the budget bill reported out of a conference committee that is a compromise between House and Senate budget bills.

Reduced-price meals.　Meals served to students who do not qualify because of family income for free meals and do not need to pay full charges.

Regulations.　Instructions for implementing public laws.

Reimbursement.　Financial assistance received from the federal government for meals served that meet federal requirements. Amount received is based on type of meal served.

Revenue sharing.　Consolidation of federal funds for several federal programs.

RFP.　Request for proposal by USDA.

S.　The S proceeds the number in all bills introduced in the Senate.

SAE.　State administrative expense.

Satellite foodservice.　Food prepared and transported from one school to other schools.

SBP.　School Breakfast Program.

School Lunch Pattern.　Formerly called the Type A Pattern. Made up of foods and portion sizes required by USDA regulations.

School year.   Period from July 1 to June 30 as defined.

SEA.   State Education Agency.

Section 4 funds.   Refers to federal funds appropriated for all lunches; usually called general assistance funds (NSLA).

Section 11 funds.   Refers to federal funds appropriated for free and/or reduced-price meals; usually called special assistance funds (NSLA).

Section 32 commodities.   Refers to commodities purchased by funds received by the Secretary from 30% of the custom receipts.

SF.   School food (NSLA).

SFA.   School Food Authority.

SFP.   School Food Program.

SFSP.   Summer Food Service Program (NSLA).

SMP.   Special Milk Program (CNA).

SPD.   School Programs Division of FNS, USDA.

Standard deductions.   Amount applied to income poverty guidelines to determine eligibility for free/reduced-price meals in lieu of hardship provision formerly allowed. This became effective January 1, 1981.

State Advisory Council for Commodity Distribution.   Council composed of representatives from schools in the state that participate in the school lunch program. Purpose is to advise the state agency as to the manner of selection and distribution of commodity assistance.

State agency.   That agency in the state that has jurisdiction over Child Nutrition Programs.

Subsidy.   Monetary or commodity assistance given by USDA to school foodservice programs.

Testimony.   Written statement stating an official position on legislation or regulations concerning Child Nutrition Programs presented before Congressional committees in Washington or in the field.

The Department.   Refers to USDA.

Type A Pattern.   See School Lunch Pattern.

Universal Food and Nutrition Program.   Lunch and/or breakfast offered to all children free or at a reduced price.

USDA.   U.S. Department of Agriculture.

YAC.   Youth Advisory Council.

HISTORICAL DEVELOPMENT

The Beginnings: 1853 to 1939

The Children's Aid Society of New York ran in 1853 one of the first recorded programs for serving meals to students. Philadelphia, Milwaukee, Boston, and other cities were serving lunches at some of their schools as early as 1853. Two books, *Poverty* (Hunter 1904) and *The Bitter Cry of the*

Children (Spargo 1906), brought to public attention the hunger and malnutrition that existed in this country. Hunter estimated that at least ten million persons were living in poverty in 1904. He observed that poverty's misery falls most heavily upon children. Hunter also estimated that in New York City alone 60,000 to 70,000 children "often arrived at school hungry and unfitted to do well the work required." Spargo described case after case of deplorable poverty in New York City. He pointed out that the country in which these people fondly dreamed their Utopia might be realized had given them instead, as Fourier prophesied, "poverty through plethora." What Spargo wrote in 1906 might well apply to the 1960s:

> The poverty problem is today the supreme challenge to our national conscience and instincts of self-preservation, and its saddest and most alarming feature is the suffering and doom it imposes upon the children.

The groups feeding children at lunch in the early 1900s were primarily volunteer groups. Soon, however, many schools all over the country assumed responsibility for serving lunches. In 1921 Chicago claimed it had "the most intensive school lunch system in America." All its high schools and 60 elementary schools were serving lunch as a responsibility of the Chicago Board of Education, which had started this program as early as 1910. The dining rooms and menus of those early programs bore little resemblance of those of today. The lunchroom in 1913 in Lower Merion (PA) was described by Cronan (1962) as "under the main stairway. The everyday menu consisted of soup, sandwiches, beans and ice cream."

By 1918, lunch of some type was being provided in schools in approximately one-quarter of the larger cities. It could hardly be compared to today's "Type A" lunch and most often was a cold lunch. A health officer in Pinellas County (FL), who knew that milk is valuable to children, started by placing a large white cow on the playground as an advertisement for his milk program. He was so pleased with the results that a bowl of hot soup was added to go with the milk.

School lunch programs expanded during the Depression when, for the first time, federal funds were appropriated for such programs. The first federal funds came from the Reconstruction Finance Corporation in 1932 and 1933. These paid labor costs for preparing school lunches in several towns in southwestern Missouri. By 1934 the funding had been extended to 39 states under the Civil Work Administration and the Federal Emergency Relief Administration. Congress passed a bill in 1935 that permitted 30% of the receipts from duties collected under the custom laws during each calendar year to be used to purchase surplus foods for use in school lunch programs and for needy families (Fig. 1.1).

The Works Progress Administration (WPA), created in 1935, assigned women in needy areas to jobs in the school lunch program. This resulted in school lunch programs becoming relatively organized and supervised by

FIG. 1.1. Early school lunches often consisted only of soup and milk.
Courtesy of U.S. Dept. of Agriculture.

each state. Some standardization of menus and recipes and procedures resulted. By 1941 the WPA program was operating in all states, the District of Columbia, and Puerto Rico. Some 23,000 schools were serving an average of nearly 2 million lunches daily and employing more than 64,000 persons (Fig. 1.2).

Growth from 1941 to 1960

In 1942 the surplus foods and federal funds were being used by 78,841 schools to serve some type of food to over 5 million children. The federal funds that year were used to purchase $21 million worth of food for the schools. According to Gunderson (1971), the food was available to a school if the school administration signed an agreement with the state distributing agency with the following provisions:

1. That the commodities would be used for preparation of school lunches on the school premises.
2. That the commodities would not be sold or exchanged.
3. That the food purchases would not be discontinued or curtailed because of the receipt of surplus foods.
4. That the program would not be operated for profit.
5. That the children who could not pay for their meals would not be

FIG. 1.2. Menus were expanded to include a sandwich, soup, milk, and fruit. *Courtesy of U.S. Dept. of Agriculture.*

segregated or discriminated against and would not be identified to their peers.

6. That proper warehousing would be provided and proper accounting would be rendered for all foods received.

The foods came directly from the farms to the schools. It meant a lot of perishables at one time. A superintendent in North Carolina remembered receiving a train carload of cabbages on the Tuesday before the Thanksgiving holidays. The weather was warm and by the following week the classroom used to store the cabbage was reeking with the odor of rotten cabbage.

An improvement in children's nutrition was noticed by educators and parents (Fig. 1.3). By 1943 lunch programs in 92,916 schools served 6 million children and employed many people. The effects of World War II were felt in every part of the country and especially in school lunchrooms. The number of schools with lunch programs declined to 34,064. Federal assistance was cut and commodities were no longer available. WPA workers were not available to help in school lunchrooms but were now employed to produce the supplies needed for the war. However, Congress amended Section 32 of the Agricultural Act of 1935 in 1944 to make money directly available to school districts for maintaining school lunch and special milk programs. The lunch program had become so much a part of the child's school day that it was not destroyed but temporarily diverted.

By 1946 school food programs had rebounded and even surpassed the

FIG. 1.3. In 1942 children could buy milk by the bottle at a reduced price at a settlement house in New York City's Lower East Side.
Courtesy of School Lunch Journal.

peak size attained before World War II. However, the uncertainty of federal funding and other forms of assistance made many school administrators cautious about instituting such programs in their schools.

The end of World War II did much to spur on school lunch programs. General Hershey, in a statement about malnutrition among the armed forces and how this jeopardized national security, did much to bring the importance of good nutritious food to the attention of Congress. Jobs were needed again. Agriculture was flourishing. Money previously spent on war was available. In June 1946, President Harry S. Truman signed into law the National School Lunch Act, (PL 79–396) as enacted by Congress (Fig. 1.4). The law is published in its entirety in Appendix I and is discussed in more detail later in this chapter.

The number of children participating in school lunch programs grew steadily throughout the 1950s from 8.6 million in 1950 to 14.0 million in 1960. The number of free or reduced-price lunches served fell during the early 1950s, but then recovered during the last years of the decade. There was little legislative activity or public interest concerning school food programs in this period.

Professional organizations passed resolutions supporting the policy that all students should have lunch at school. Committees were created by

FIG. 1.4. The National School Lunch Act was signed into law on June 4, 1946, by President Harry S. Truman (seated). Witnesses were (left to right): Rep. Clarence Cannon (MO); Clinton Anderson, Secretary of Agriculture; Rep. Malcolm Tarver (GA); Sen. Richard Russell (GA); Sen. Allen Ellender (LA); Rep. Clifford Hope (KS); Sen. George Aiken (VT); Rep. Ron Flanagan (WV); Nathan Koenig, Assistant to the Secretary of Agriculture; Paul Stark, Director of the Food Distribution Division, USDA; Robert Shields, Administrator, Product and Marketing Administration, USDA; and N. E. Dodd, Undersecretary of Agriculture. *Courtesy of School Lunch Journal.*

Congress to study the problems of hunger and manlutrition. *Let Them Eat Promises* (Kotz 1969) described the politics involved in the federal programs thus far established for feeding the hungry. Churches and volunteer groups in many cities found a cause to work for, and lunches soon were being served in schools that had never had a foodservice.

Poverty Rediscovered: The 1960s

Focus was placed upon poverty again in the middle 1960s, bringing new legislation and new interest in nutrition (Fig. 1.5). The Economic Opportunity Act of 1964 established programs that fed the preschool-age children in Head Start programs. Also, the Elementary and Secondary Education Act of 1965 provided funds (under Title I) to be used for school foodservices in deprived areas.

Concern about the nutritional status of children in the United States was caused by the reports of the Household Food Consumption Survey of 1965–

FIG. 1.5. By 1960 complete school lunches were being served in more than 45% of all schools with the aid of federal funds and commodity donations.
Courtesy of Prince George's County (MD) Public Schools.

66, which showed a definite decrease in nutritional intake during the previous 10 years. The Child Nutrition Act of 1966 (PL 89–642) provided funds to initiate new programs. Included under this act was the continuation of the Special Milk Program, which had previously been designated as Type C lunch under the National School Lunch Act and later under PL 85–478. The Child Nutrition Act also provided for a pilot breakfast program, for funds to purchase school foodservice equipment in low-income areas, and for state administrative expenses. USDA was designated as the one agency with authority over the program.

In 1968 several groups brought national attention to poverty with the stories they told. The Committee on School Lunch Participation published *Their Daily Bread* (Fairfax 1968) in which poverty was identified as one of the main reasons for unrest in America. Discrimination against children who were receiving free and reduced-price lunches was brought to light. That same year the Citizens Board of Inquiry into Hunger and Malnutrition in the United States (1968) focused on poverty in their book, *Hunger, USA*. The Board was critical of the school lunch program as it was being administered and blamed agricultural policies for restricting and limiting the growth of the program. The Board declared that 280 counties in the United States needed emergency assistance to alleviate hunger. CBS television's documentary "Hunger in America" brought the hunger that existed in America to the attention of the average American, and the response was immediate.

The general acceptance of the program was attested to when Congress passed PL 87–780, which stated that "the seven-day period beginning on the second Sunday of October in each year is hereby designated as National School Lunch Week, and the President is requested to issue annually a proclamation calling on the people of the United States to observe such a week with appropriate ceremonies and activities."

The concern about hunger stimulated passage of legislation in 1968 that authorized funds for foodservices for some summer programs and extended the breakfast program. The President sent a message to Congress in May 1969 urging legislation that would eliminate hunger and malnutrition. It was not until fiscal year 1969 that the free-lunch program was actually funded. Prior to this, the formula for apportionment of federal funds to the states had only increased the funding slightly as the number of free lunches increased. The higher reimbursement rates still did not provide adequate funds until 1969 when money to provide free and reduced-price meals, in addition to the regular child foodservice programs, was allocated. The funds were a boost to needy children (Table 1.2) and quickly resulted in significant increases in the number of free or reduced-price meals served. The President's White House Conference on Food, Nutrition, and Health of 1969 recommended that the school lunch program be expanded to provide free lunch (and breakfast when needed) to all children through the secondary school years.

Even though funding was available, many school districts still were cautious about entering the program. Also, many school buildings in inner cities did not have proper facilities. It took time for remodeling if funds were made available on the local level. Industry was now involved and new ideas of how to feed students a meal even if kitchen facilities were not available resulted in heat-and-serve type lunches, engineered foods, Vit-A-lunches, and other new feeding concepts.

Universality and the 1970s

The beginning of the 1970s looked very bright for school feeding programs with enactment of important new pieces of legislation and the introduction of the Universal Food Service and Nutrition Education Program for children by Carl Perkins (KY) in the House of Representatives and by Hubert Humphrey (MN) in the Senate.

Amendments to the National School Lunch Act and the Child Nutrition Act in 1970 clarified the responsibilities related to providing free and reduced-price meals, revised the program's matching payment requirements, strengthened the nutrition training and education benefits of the program, and provided for special assistance to the states on the basis of family income. Discrimination against children receiving free and reduced-price meals was declared unlawful. The 14th Amendment to the United States Constitution was used to bring law suits against school districts in at least nine states having no lunches at school. The Children's Foundation became active in looking out for the welfare of children. The federal government has its own monitoring agencies. The Office of Inspector General (OIG) in coordination with the Office of General Counsel and the Department of Justice seek to detect illegal practices by auditing 1% of the programs. Their objectives are to determine if free and reduced-price lunches are being served to all needy children, if their anonymity is being protected, and if proper controls on the receipt and disbursement of funds are being used.

In August 1979 auditors from the Office of the Inspector General reviewed 2,842 lunches in 22 school districts and found that 70% did not meet the minimum meal requirements. Earlier that year 171 of 488 meals sampled in one school district did not meet minimum meal requirements. These findings pointed up two broad problems: inadequate, vague requirements and guidance and ineffective or complete lack of monitoring.

The seventies were years of much legislation, amending and reamending the school lunch and breakfast programs. The most stabilizing action was the escalating clause which helped assure that funding would increase in accordance with the food-away-from-home-cost index. The funding had grown from $100 million in 1946 to more than $3.7 billion in 1980.

The number of schools participating in the National School Lunch Program increased steadily, with the largest increase between 1970 and 1971. The number of free and reduced-price lunches doubled (Table 1.2). In 1979 it was estimated that 85% of those in need of free lunches were receiving them. The laws passed in 1970 and 1971 (PL 91–248, PL 92–32, and PL 92–153) were forceful in that they contained the funding necessary to put them into action. Thousands of inner-city schools were able to convert rooms into kitchens and buy the equipment needed for preparing and serving food with the funds made available. Children from families with an income at or less than 125% of the poverty level were eligible to receive free meals, and those with an income between 125 and 195% of the poverty level were eligible to receive reduced-price meals. A few schools had such high percentages of free meals that it was more economical to operate a "universally" free program, paying for those who did not qualify for free lunches with local funds.

Also, in 1972 the quantity of USDA-donated foods distributed was far less than expected. Only a little over half of the funds appropriated were spent, because of the high cost and limited amounts of available surpluses. The purpose of USDA-donated foods was to help remove surpluses from the market and to support commodity prices. By 1972 the purpose of USDA-

	No. Schools		Rate of	No. Children		Rate of
Fiscal Year	Total in U.S.[2]	Participating in N.S.L.P.[3]	Participation (%)	Total Enrollment[2]	Participating in N.S.L.P.[3]	Participation (%)
1947	188,077	44,537	23.7	26,606,077	6,596,633	24.8
1948	188,077	44,542	23.7	26,606,077	6,594,952	24.8
1949	168,985	47,803	28.3	26,982,687	7,631,764	28.3
1950	168,985	54,157	32.0	27,525,345	8,596,765	31.2
1951	164,091	54,436	33.2	28,065,023	9,471,704	33.7
1952	164,091	55,663	33.9	29,059,023	10,220,720	35.2
1953	154,900	56,851	36.7	29,690,331	10,740,018	36.2
1954	154,900	56,337	36.4	30,998,048	11,117,567	35.9
1955	149,562	58,458	39.1	34,029,035	12,030,970	35.4
1956	149,562	56,140	37.5	35,636,445	11,552,663	32.4
1957	141,004	57,261	40.6	36,656,246	11,683,736	31.9
1958	141,004	59,929	42.5	38,364,195	12,601,228	32.8
1959	137,836	61,033	44.3	39,480,239	13,294,368	33.7
1960	137,836	62,325	45.2	40,664,042	14,078,149	34.6
1961	128,757	63,961	49.7	42,204,978	14,751,546	35.0
1962	128,757	64,447	50.1	43,415,735	15,552,706	35.8
1963	125,703	66,715	53.1	45,194,438	16,400,458	36.3
1964	125,703	68,526	54.5	46,935,514	17,547,843	37.4
1965	122,101	70,132	57.4	48,151,723	18,666,270	38.8
1966	122,101	70,597	57.8	49,676,224	19,781,074	39.8
1967	116,666	72,944	62.5	50,509,016	20,237,423	40.1
1968	116,666	71,983	61.7	51,245,895	20,614,410	40.2
1969	116,307	74,861	64.4	51,733,867	22,078,808	42.7
1970	116,307	75,593	65.0	52,100,765	23,127,222	44.4
1971	113,626	79,924	70.3	51,982,123	24,639,663	47.4
1972	98,502	83,333	84.6	52,000,000	24,900,000	56.6
1973	101,386	86,381	85.2	51,400,000	25,200,000	57.5
1974	101,365	87,579	86.4	51,400,000	25,000,000	56.3
1975	101,508	88,921	87.6	51,000,000	25,300,000	56.6
1976	100,141	89,426	89.3	50,500,000	25,900,000	57.4
1977	101,654	91,285	89.8	50,100,000	26,700,000	59.3
1978	100,973	93,097	92.2	48,900,000	27,100,000	55.4
1979	102,533	94,335	91.6	48,600,000	27,400,000	56.3
1980	102,530	94,178	91.7	48,000,000	27,000,000	56.2
1981	101,500	92,914	91.6	46,700,000	26,800,000	57.4
1982	100,500	91,151	91.3	45,000,000	23,000,000	50.9
1983	99,560	90,360	91.0	44,500,000	23,100,000	51.7

Source: Food and Nutrition Service, U.S. Dept. of Agriculture.

[1] Data for Type C lunches are included for FY 1947 through FY 1959, except for cost per lunch which is computed on Type A lunches only for all years.

[2] Includes District of Columbia, Puerto Rico and Virgin Islands; Alaska as a territory prior to Statehood in FY 1959; Hawaii as a territory prior to Statehood in FY 1960; Guam beginning in FY 1957; American Samoa beginning in FY 1963. Number of schools and

dary Schools, Number of Lunches, and Income per Lunch—Fiscal Years 1947–1983

No. Lunches[1]			Rate of Free or Reduced (%)	Avg. Contribution to Lunch (¢)			
Average Served Daily[3]	Total	Free or Reduced		Federal	State & Local	Children's Payments	Total
6,016,129	910,926,717	109,352,390	12.0	9.3	5.6	15.5	30.4
6,014,596	972,008,521	123,306,846	12.7	11.5	7.2	18.3	37.0
6,960,169	1,119,094,198	165,454,817	14.8	10.9	7.2	18.1	36.2
7,840,250	1,275,923,146	212,193,369	16.6	12.1	7.4	17.7	37.2
8,638,194	1,393,145,667	177,654,075	12.8	10.7	7.5	18.7	36.9
9,321,297	1,489,890,214	169,621,882	11.4	8.3	8.2	20.4	36.9
9,794,896	1,583,638,073	167,378,873	10.6	10.6	8.5	21.7	40.8
10,139,221	1,661,403,101	173,340,769	10.4	12.9	8.5	21.8	43.2
10,972,245	1,806,586,577	189,878,731	10.5	10.0	8.3	22.1	40.4
10,536,029	1,726,598,923	181,005,485	10.5	11.2	8.6	23.4	43.2
10,655,567	1,771,179,627	186,014,151	10.5	13.0	8.8	23.7	45.5
11,492,320	1,882,570,199	202,881,028	10.8	9.3	9.7	24.2	43.2
12,124,464	2,008,685,185	211,822,563	10.5	10.2	10.2	25.3	45.7
12,839,272	2,142,312,115	217,192,652	10.1	10.5	10.3	25.9	46.7
13,453,410	2,264,989,097	228,059,654	10.1	10.0	10.1	26.3	46.4
14,184,068	2,415,269,937	240,135,558	9.9	11.6	10.2	26.6	48.4
14,957,218	2,552,744,662	245,731,540	9.6	11.3	9.9	27.2	48.4
16,003,633	2,696,471,800	266,076,086	9.9	11.7	10.0	27.5	49.2
17,023,638	2,892,260,684	285,839,648	9.9	13.9	10.1	27.6	51.6
18,040,330	3,093,120,784	336,017,462	10.9	10.2	10.7	27.6	48.5
18,456,530	3,147,004,666	384,814,451	12.2	10.7	12.7	29.4	52.8
18,800,342	3,217,886,186	417,078,904	13.0	13.5	13.7	30.9	58.1
20,135,873	3,368,155,438	507,705,712	15.1	14.1	14.1	30.9	59.1
20,887,870	3,565,092,824	738,541,361	20.7	15.9	15.3	31.0	62.2
22,260,092	3,848,301,437	1,005,691,831	26.1	21.1	15.4	28.3	64.8
22,900,000	3,972,100,000	1,285,300,000	32.4	26.5	15.5	27.2	69.2
23,000,000	4,008,800,000	1,402,400,000	35.0	30.2	17.3	28.0	75.5
23,000,000	3,981,600,000	1,478,100,000	37.1	35.2	20.0	29.5	84.7
23,200,000	4,063,000,000	1,637,900,000	40.3	42.0	20.9	32.2	95.1
23,432,000	4,170,900,000	1,766,800,000	42.4	47.4	25.2	30.1	102.7
23,870,000	4,249,000,000	1,906,100,000	44.9	49.9	22.6	30.4	102.9
24,109,000	4,291,500,000	1,907,700,000	44.5	56.7	NA[4]	NA	NA
24,594,000	4,377,800,000	1,911,500,000	43.7	61.5	NA	NA	NA
24,522,000	4,365,000,000	1,958,900,000	45.1	70.8	NA	NA	NA
24,340,000	4,357,300,000	1,901,300,000	43.7	61.5	NA	NA	NA
24,500,000	4,386,200,000	1,978,300,000	45.1	73.3	23.7	31.9	128.9
23,560,000	4,217,900,000	2,052,100,000	48.6	78.9	26.7	34.6	140.3
20,980,000	3,755,000,000	1,883,300,000	50.2	78.8	36.0	41.2	155.9
21,220,000	3,798,400,000	1,962,400,000	51.7	85.0	NA	NA	NA

total enrollment source: U.S. Department of Health, Education, and Welfare. Total schools in United States are compiled biennially. Private schools are partially estimated in all years.

[3]Peak month nationally. Children participating in N.S.L.P. includes an adjustment for absenteeism based on information supplied by Office of Education on attendance rates.

[4]Since 1977 states have not been required to furnish this information to USDA.

donated foods was questionable. The unspent funds were appropriated in cash to the school districts in the spring of 1973 (PL 93–13).

Starting in August 1979 federal regulations required that school food authorities (school districts) promote activities that involve children and parents in their foodservice programs. These activities, such as menu planning, promoting the program, enhancing the eating environment, have brought many positive changes.

The economy had tremendous impacts on the programs, with the cost of lunch increasing by 70% between 1970 and 1977. The Fair Labor Standards Amendments of 1977 called for a minimum wage of $2.65 per hour, with $2.90 in 1979, $3.10 in 1980, and $3.35 in 1981. Union strikes closed foodservices temporarily in several large cities. During the decade school enrollment fell by about 4 million students; however, participation grew by 4 million to reach a participation rate of 54%. The number of free lunches increased from 21% in 1970 to 45% in 1984.

Competition. A new challenge was placed on the administrators of the National School Lunch Program, who had no experience at competition, when foodservice management companies were made eligible to receive commodities and cash reimbursement in school programs. Foodservice companies had been operating in a few schools for more than 28 years, but previously had not been eligible for federal funds since they were profit making. The next challenge, a surprise to many in school foodservice, was passage of PL 92–433 in 1972. This law opened schools to competitive food operations, as stated in Section 7:

> Such regulations shall not prohibit the sales of competitive foods in food service facilities or areas during the time of service of food under this Act or the National School Lunch Act if the proceeds from the sales of such foods will inure to the benefit of the schools or of organizations of students approved by the schools.

School administrators, school foodservice leaders, parents, and Congressmen spoke out against the amendment. Perryman (1972) called it "the most permissive legislation in the 26-year history of school food service." Senator Edward Kennedy (1972) voiced his concerns about the "pressures which may now be placed on our local school officials to permit the sale of food items that will directly compete with the school lunch and breakfast programs." Senator Edward Brooke (1972) wrote "I realize the valuable role that the present school lunch program plays in insuring that students be afforded diets that are high in nutritional value, ... The results of Section 7 could be both nutritionally and financially harmful to students, parents, and foodservice programs through the country." The American Medical Association also supported the school lunch program's nutritious foods and disapproved of the availability of confections and soft drinks on school premises. In the spring of 1973 new bills were introduced to rescind the opening of the doors to competitive foods; years of public comments and hearings followed on what foods should and what foods should not be made available for sale, and when. Finally in 1980 the "competitive foods" regulations were issued (discussed later in this chapter).

Residential Child-Care Services.   In 1975 the National School Lunch Act was amended to extend the definition of a "school" to include any public or nonprofit private child-care institution that maintains children in residence; operates principally for the care of children; and, if private, is licensed to provide residential child-care services under the appropriate licensing code by the state or local level of government. Therefore, children in homes for the mentally retarded, emotionally disturbed, and physically handicapped became eligible to participate in the National School Lunch Program, extending the ages from infancy to 21.

Plate Waste.   During the seventies reports on plate waste in school foodservices made the headlines on television and in leading newspapers across the country. Plate waste was found to be high among elementary children, particularly in schools serving frozen, preplated meals. The publicity started bringing about many changes: (1) offering of choices and more variety, (2) improvement in food quality, (3) new meal patterns, which allow for portions to be varied according to the age of the child, and (4) new attitudes among those in the school foodservice business which view the child more as a customer rather than as a lucky recipient.

The plate waste publicity also marked the start of USDA studies done under contract by outside firms. The studies became so numerous and involved so much money that it took a large staff at USDA to monitor them. Congress continued to ask for more studies, taking a large chunk of federal dollars each year; too often the studies were not used.

NATIONAL SCHOOL LUNCH ACT OF 1946

The philosophy and purposes behind the National School Lunch Act of 1946 (Appendix I) are stated in Section 2 of the law:

SECTION 2. It is hereby declared to be the policy of Congress, as a measure of national security to safeguard the health and well-being of the Nation's children and to encourage the domestic consumption of nutritious agricultural commodities and other food, by assisting the States, through grants-in-aid and other means, in providing an adequate supply of foods and other facilities for the establishment, maintenance, operation, and expansion of nonprofit school-lunch programs.

Surplus Foods

The second objective of the law—to provide markets for agricultural production and a larger share of the national income to farmers—certainly was an important factor in its passage. The school lunch program provided a ready and desirable outlet for disposing of surplus crop products. The state education agency and individual schools in any state participating in the National School Lunch Program agreed that participating schools would

1. serve lunches which meet minimum nutritional requirements prescribed by the Secretary of Agriculture;
2. serve meals without cost or at a reduced cost to children who were determined by local school authorities to be unable to pay the full cost of the lunch;
3. make no discrimination against any child because of his inability to pay the full price of the lunch;
4. operate on a nonprofit basis;
5. utilize foods declared by the Secretary as being in abundance;
6. utilize free commodities as donated by the Secretary; and
7. maintain records of receipts and expenditures and submit this report to the State agency as required.

Definition of Lunch Types and Reimbursement

The minimum nutritional requirements were defined in 1946 by the Secretary for three types of lunches: Type A, Type B, and Type C. Type A lunch was defined as containing:

½ pt of fluid whole milk[1]
Protein-rich food consisting of one of the following or a combination: 2 oz (edible portion as served) of lean meat, poultry, or fish; or 2 oz of cheese; or 1 egg; or ½ cup of cooked dry beans or peas; or 4 Tbsp of peanut butter
¾ cup serving of two or more vegetables or fruits, or both
1 portion or serving of bread, cornbread, biscuits, rolls, muffins, etc., made of whole-grain or enriched meal or flour
2 tsp of butter or fortified margarine[2]

Type B lunches contained smaller quantities of the components in the Type A lunch and were served primarily in those schools with inadequate cooking facilities. Type C lunches consisted only of ½ pt of fluid whole milk served as a beverage.

The cash reimbursements, established by the Secretary of Agriculture, were a maximum of 9¢ for a Type A lunch, 6¢ for a Type B lunch, and 2¢ for a Type C lunch. Each state was to receive money on the basis of school lunch participation in the state and the per capita income of the state. The

---

[1]Milk requirement was relaxed to include chocolate milk, skim milk, and buttermilk as well as whole milk and changed again to more stringent requirements.
[2]Later reduced to 1 tsp of butter or fortified margarine, and later eliminated.

federal funds were to be supplemented with state funds. From 1947 through 1950 the federal funds were to be matched dollar for dollar, and then progressively the state was to take a greater share of the financing. The child's payment for lunch was included in the state's matching funds and contributed the greatest part of the matching funds. When the per capita income of a state was less than the average per capita income in the United States, the matching funds were reduced. In addition to the cash reimbursement, commodity donations were provided by Section 416 of the Agricultural Act of 1949 and Section 32 of the Agricultural Act of 1935.

Changes in the Law

The National School Lunch Act has been amended numerous times since its passage in 1946. Appendixes II and III contain the Child Nutrition Act of 1966 and the National School Lunch Act, respectively, as amended. Some 16 or more laws directly or indirectly affect the feeding programs in schools, and several agencies other than USDA are involved in administering these laws. The regulations are stiff and in many instances states have been unable to utilize all the money alloted under the laws, not because of lack of need, but because of the restrictions placed on its use.

USDA-DONATED FOODS

Foods are purchased by the USDA with funds made available under Section 6 of the National School Lunch Act, Section 32 of Public Law 320, and Section 416 of the Agricultural Act of 1949. Approximately 18% of the food used in preparing a lunch is a USDA-donated commodity.

Section 32 of the 1935 Agricultural Act authorizes the Secretary of USDA to buy surplus "nonbasic" perishable commodities. The purpose is to support farmers' income when market prices are down, to encourage exports, and to encourage domestic consumption. The Secretary of Agriculture determines what constitutes a surplus and which commodities may be purchased under Section 32. These items normally are meats, poultry, fruits, and vegetables. Section 32 is financed by a permanent appropriation from U.S. customs receipts.

Section 416 of the 1949 Agriculture Act authorizes purchase of foods under "price support" programs. Congress determines the prices at which USDA will purchase basic, nonperishable commodities such as wheat, rice, dairy products, soybeans, peanuts, and corn. These purchases are governed by the Commodity Credit Corporation. Section 6 of the National School Lunch Act requires USDA to purchase a minimum level of commodities. Starting in the 1980 school year states were required to set up advisory

TABLE 1.3. **Contributions to National School Lunch Program**

	Federal Contributions ($)					
	Cash			Donated Commodities[1]		
Fiscal Year	Section 4	Section 11	Section 32	Sec. 32 & 416	Section 6	Total
1947	62,338,155	—	—	2,312,479	5,735,269	70,385,903
1948	54,000,000	—	—	19,340,561	13,439,329	86,778,890
1949	58,875,000	—	—	21,550,031	14,474,763	94,899,794
1950	64,565,000	—	—	38,504,934	16,684,026	119,753,960
1951	68,275,000	—	—	34,836,455	15,089,210	118,200,665
1952	66,320,000	—	—	16,582,743	15,590,016	98,492,759
1953	67,185,000	—	—	51,724,476	14,744,071	133,653,547
1954	67,266,000	—	—	94,217,791	14,826,278	176,310,069
1955	69,142,000	—	—	70,305,837	12,830,253	152,278,090
1956	67,145,648	—	—	99,946,204	14,802,020	181,893,872
1957	83,915,000	—	—	131,072,002	14,659,931	230,546,933
1958	83,830,000	—	—	75,961,833	14,802,256	174,594,089
1959	93,890,000	—	—	66,821,691	42,669,843	203,381,534
1960	93,814,400	—	—	70,915,823	61,108,847	225,839,070
1961	93,746,304	—	—	71,623,432	61,080,734	226,450,470
1962	98,760,000	—	—	113,026,690	69,074,090	280,860,780
1963	108,600,000	—	—	120,970,681	58,875,807	288,446,488
1964	120,810,000	—	—	135,660,411	59,270,071	315,740,482
1965	130,435,000	—	—	212,949,375	59,458,642	402,843,017
1966	139,090,000	2,000,000	—	116,849,780	58,006,289	315,946,069
1967	147,685,000	2,000,000	—	130,418,911	57,938,924	338,042,835
1968	154,947,000	4,807,199	—	220,455,672	55,520,976	435,730,847
1969	162,041,000	10,000,000	31,754,686	207,790,939	64,165,362	475,751,987
1970	168,034,775	44,603,745	87,619,690	200,758,518	64,434,166	565,450,894
1971	224,710,499	202,798,419	104,682,578	214,877,594	64,306,096	811,375,186
1972	225,700,000	237,000,000	276,100,000	312,100,000[2]	—	1,050,900,000
1973	225,700,000	236,800,000	419,700,000	328,500,000	—	1,210,700,000
1974	409,000,000	255,600,000	420,000,000	316,100,000	—	1,401,400,000
1975	463,400,000	825,600,000		418,300,000	—	1,707,300,000
1976	516,000,000	963,400,000		456,400,000	—	1,935,800,000
1977	561,300,000	1,112,700,000		501,400,000	—	2,175,400,000
1978	619,200,000	1,205,600,000		558,000,000	57,600,000[3]	2,440,400,000
1979	685,100,000	1,314,000,000		675,300,000	69,600,000	2,744,000,000
1980	771,900,000	1,524,100,000		772,500,000	132,00,000	3,200,500,000
1981	708,000,000	1,689,200,000		578,900,000	316,300,000	3,292,400,000
1982	421,100,000	1,770,200,000		420,700,000	339,900,000	2,951,900,000
1983	446,600,000	1,954,600,000		410,800,000	379,200,000	3,514,100,000

Source: Food and Nutrition Service, U.S. Dept. of Agriculture.
[1]Value is cost to federal government.
[2]Sections 32, 416, and 6 are shown as one figure starting with 1972.

councils to let USDA know what kinds of donated foods their schools can use. The councils meet at least once a year to discuss which commodities their schools like best, as well as new products they want.

Donated foods may or may not be processed. Fresh fruits are even shipped across the United States. These foods are packaged and delivered to receiving points inside the state. The school districts are usually responsible

and Value of USDA Commodities—Fiscal Years 1947–1983

	State & Local Contributions ($)			Value of Food ($)		
Children's Payments	State & Local Governments	Other	Total	Total	Local Purchase	% Local (of Total)
112,540,000	20,616,000	17,532,000	150,688,000	136,696,026	128,648,278	94.1
138,282,000	29,052,000	22,674,000	190,008,000	175,592,098	142,813,208	81.3
158,553,000	35,418,000	23,887,000	217,858,000	204,267,052	168,242,258	82.4
177,336,000	39,000,000	31,553,000	247,889,000	236,341,759	181,152,799	76.6
207,213,000	46,477,000	32,627,000	286,317,000	263,436,309	213,510,644	81.0
242,370,000	54,418,000	38,457,000	335,245,000	281,714,016	249,541,257	88.6
275,926,000	57,162,000	46,380,000	379,468,000	331,257,279	264,788,732	79.9
303,276,000	62,962,000	51,782,000	418,020,000	387,380,392	278,336,323	71.9
336,362,000	68,991,000	53,908,000	459,261,000	407,148,099	324,012,009	79.6
377,212,000	65,427,000	72,335,000	514,974,000	482,139,449	367,391,225	76.2
418,151,000	71,671,000	83,651,000	573,473,000	587,453,989	440,822,056	75.2
453,227,000	83,623,000	98,018,000	634,868,000	559,926,193	469,162,104	83.8
505,083,000	90,478,000	113,203,000	708,764,000	618,535,992	509,044,458	82.3
555,707,000	92,608,000	127,522,000	775,837,000	671,513,132	539,488,462	80.3
594,840,000	94,943,000	134,898,000	824,681,000	714,585,141	581,880,975	81.4
642,374,000	93,920,000	151,519,000	887,813,000	780,895,494	598,794,714	76.7
694,030,000	97,076,000	156,377,000	947,483,000	825,978,443	646,131,955	78.2
741,856,000	103,260,000	166,323,000	1,011,439,000	884,948,482	690,018,000	78.0
797,572,000	113,682,000	178,700,000	1,089,954,000	979,351,017	706,943,000	72.2
852,773,000	122,004,000	210,380,000	1,185,157,000	986,447,833	811,591,764	82.3
925,018,113	146,527,947	253,965,941	1,325,512,001	1,061,876,791	873,518,956	82.3
995,756,029	161,972,891	278,551,294	1,436,280,214	1,143,999,085	808,022,437	75.9
1,041,241,376	154,979,002	320,276,653	1,516,497,031	1,232,247,012	880,200,711	77.9
1,104,959,419	185,056,427	361,594,582	1,651,610,428	1,276,296,310	1,011,103,626	79.2
1,090,209,734	216,377,796	376,943,927	1,683,531,457	1,411,696,309	1,132,512,619	80.2
1,080,400,000	616,000,000	1,050,900,000	2,747,300,000	1,562,800,000	1,250,700,000	80.0
1,123,700,000	692,700,000	1,210,700,000	3,027,100,000	1,666,100,000	1,408,400,000	84.5
1,174,000,000	797,000,000	1,401,000,000	3,372,400,000	1,931,300,000	1,615,200,000	83.6
1,308,500,000	848,800,000	1,705,700,000	3,863,000,000	2,239,300,000	1,827,700,000	81.6
1,310,000,000	930,000,000	1,893,500,000	4,133,500,000	2,264,100,000	1,850,000,000	81.7
1,290,000,000	960,000,000	2,120,200,000	4,370,200,000	2,392,200,000	1,850,000,000	77.3
NA[4]	NA[4]	2,433,600,000	NA[5]	NA[5]	NA[5]	NA[5]
NA	NA	2,693,500,000	NA	NA	NA	NA
1,399,500,000	1,039,100,000	3,102,000,000	NA	NA	NA	NA
1,460,300,000	1,125,600,000	NA	NA	NA	NA	NA
1,547,000,000	1,351,000,000	NA	NA	NA	NA	NA
NA	NA	NA	NA	NA	NA	NA

[3] "Bonus" commodities were made available starting in 1978. Section 6 funds are not included in these figures for 1978–1983.
[4] Since 1977 states have not been required to furnish this information to USDA.
[5] Not available.

for picking up commodities at a designated pick-up area and distributing them to the individual schools.

By 1982 several states had organized the distribution of commodities through commercial food distributors, who receive the commodities at their warehouses. School districts receive the commodities as ordered or needed, along with other foods they purchase. The price for these services range from 90¢ to $1.50 or more per case. In most states large school districts with central warehouses are allowed the option of receiving commodities directly or through commercial distributors. Also, some school districts provide storage and distribution services at a fee to other school districts.

The quantity of donated commodities that is purchased each year depends on the federal budget and the entitlement for each lunch. The entitlement level is set each year by USDA. Foods valued at that level are purchased and provided to the state distributing agency for distribution to each school district based on the number of lunches served. For example, the entitlement per lunch in 1982 through 1984 was 11.5¢.

In spite of the distribution of surplus commodities to schools and other agencies, the stored quantities of some items have grown. The cost for storage alone in 1983 was $377.9 million. The surpluses included 1 million tons of rice, 18 million bushels of wheat, 431 million bushels of corn, 53 million pounds of honey, 715 million pounds of butter, 1.8 billion pounds of dry milk, and 1.1 billion pounds of cheese. Some of these foods were designated as "bonus" foods and made available to schools and other agencies in addition to their entitlement (Table 1.3). This was done to encourage greater use of surplus foods. However, products were not moved out of storage as fast as new products were moved into storage. During 1982–1984 large quantities of surplus foods were distributed to low-income people.

Processing USDA-Donated Foods

As high labor costs and a lack of skilled labor changed traditional food preparation, more school districts started using prepared items or convenience foods, such as bakery bread, hamburger patties and turkey rolls. Many school districts have found that frozen cherries, whole turkeys, hard-wheat flour, nonfat dry milk, shortening, and rolled wheat—all USDA-donated commodities—were sometimes a problem to utilize. One solution to this problem has been the processing of commodities into foods ready for use or more acceptable for use in the schools.

As far back as 1958 a few school districts had donated commodities processed or repackaged by industry into a different end product. Pennsylvania was one of the pioneer states in commodity processing. Since 1969, when written instructions were issued by the Food Distribution Office of USDA, many more school districts started having the commodities processed. Prior to 1969 the contracts for processing donated foods had to be approved by USDA, but in that year the state distributing agents were given authority to approve the contracts. In some cases the donated foods are shipped directly to a factory for processing for which the school district pays the cost. By 1983 states had processing contracts with over 500 companies. Cheese and flour are the largest items converted under these contracts.

In June 1983 regulations were published in the Federal Register establishing a National Commodity Processing (NCP) system. These regulations permitted agreements between USDA and processors to convert *bonus* commodities only into various end products. Under these agreements, a company like Pillsbury can market products nationwide and not have to have a different contract with each state distribution agency. The NCP system has streamlined the process for the processors, as well as the schools, and made the end products available in all states. Affiliated Food Processors (AFP) handles a considerable amount of the end products through a computerized tracking system, called C.A.T.S. (Commodity Accountability Tracking System).

The NCP system is expected to solve many of the problems with "rebates" and "discounts" for school districts. However, the system would work best if *all* commodities were included, thus avoiding the problem of using bonus commodities and nonbonus commodities in the same products. As it is today, bonus commodities may be handled under the NCP system, but nonbonus commodities must be handled under state processing contracts (state by state). The Secretary of Agriculture has the authority to determine which commodities are eligible for distribution under the NCP system. When this system is changed to include all commodities, the next question might be why not let school districts have "letters-of-credits" to purchase commodity foods under more competitive conditions and locally.

Alternatives to the USDA-Donated Commodity Program

Though local school districts usually agree that the quality of most USDA-donated foods is excellent, they often have little advance notice of when foods will be received. Lack of storage facilities, particularly for frozen foods, lack of skilled labor, high labor costs, food likes and dislikes of the locale, and not being able to plan ahead are a few of the problems facing school foodservice administrators when using donated commodities.

During the 1978–1979 school year eight school districts took part in a 1-year pilot program and received all cash from USDA's budget for their lunch programs in place of donated foods. The study confirmed that schools could get more out of the money and serve lunches that cost less if they received cash and no commodities. While USDA was still analyzing data, the National Frozen Food Association issued a report prepared by Kansas State University of the pilot projects reporting a potential annual savings of $162 million.

During the spring of 1980 the "voucher" system, or "letter of credit" system, was promoted by the National Frozen Food Association and many foodservice directors. Under this arrangement schools would receive "letters of credit" for particular foods. Congressmen listened with interest and passed legislation to fund a national study. Foreseen problems of getting quick reaction when a particular food needed to be removed from the market, bookkeeping difficulties, and assuring fair prices would be charged were concerns. Ninety school districts participated in the 3-year study: 30 letter-of-credit sites, 30 cash sites, and 30 control commodity sites. The impact of the different systems on school districts and on the stocks of surplus foods will be carefully analyzed.

VARIED MEAL PATTERNS REPLACE TYPE A

The Type A meal pattern lasted 35 years with only three changes. By the 1970s, nutritionists were saying that the pattern was out-of-date and was not keeping pace with today's eating practices and life styles. Frequent criticisms were that the Type A pattern was not responsive to the protein contributions of food components of both meat and milk and that the pattern did not take into consideration the nutritional needs of children of different ages. In 1977 proposed changes in the meal pattern and other regulations were published in the Federal Register for comment. After field testing and public comment the USDA published the regulations in two parts. The interim regulations issued in August 1979 included the following provisions:

1. Expansion of bread alternates to include rice and pasta
2. Requirement that schools offer unflavored lowfat, skim, or buttermilk
3. Requirement that schools devise a program of student involvement
4. Requirement that schools devise a program of parent involvement
5. Recommendations that schools not offering a choice of meat/meat alternate each day serve no one meat alternate or form of meat more than three times per week; that fat, sugar, and salt be kept at moderate levels; and that menus should include several foods containing iron each day, vitamin A-rich foods at least twice a week, and vitamin C-rich foods several times weekly

On May 16, 1980, the final regulations were released, dropping the "Type A" name and simply calling the new patterns "School Lunch Meal Patterns." These regulations called for

1. varying portion sizes for children of various ages;
2. allowing schools to serve lunch to children age 1 to 5 years at two service periods;

3. increasing the required quantities of two meat alternates[1]—eggs and dry beans/peas—to be nutritionally equivalent to meat and the other meat alternates; and
4. changing the bread requirement to specify the number of servings required by week and to increase the total number of servings required.

The new school lunch meal patterns (see Chapter 2) offer much flexibility, as discussed in detail in *Menu Planning Guide for School Food Service* (U.S. Dept. of Agriculture 1983).

BREAKFAST PROGRAM

The federally supported School Breakfast Program was created on a pilot basis by Congress in 1966 (PL 89–642) when $7.5 million was spent. The program was focussed primarily on schools in poor areas and where children had to travel long distances to reach school. In 1968 Congress seemingly removed the program from the pilot status but it was not declared permanent by Congress until 1975. In 1972 the program was expanded, making all schools wishing to apply eligible (PL 92–153). The funds are primarily from Section 4 of the Child Nutrition Act and Section 32 of the Agricultural Adjustment Act of 1935. It is apportioned to all states according to participation and the economic need of the state.

From 752 schools on a pilot basis in 1967 when 80,232 breakfasts were served, the breakfast program grew to include 34,200 schools serving 3.8 million children in 1981. As of May 1984, breakfast was being served at 34,400 schools to 3.4 million children daily. The program grew in spite of temporary freezes on new programs in 1969, and in spite of a number of problems, such as (1) lack of guidelines and regulations for operating the program; (2) inadequate funding; (3) uncertainty about the future of the program and its permanency; (4) requirement that detailed reports and records be kept; (5) convincing those who question the value of breakfast program; (6) scheduling of breakfast.

A report entitled *If We Had Ham, We Could Have Ham and Eggs* (Food Research and Action Center 1972) cited the problems that the pilot program faced with cost and in convincing administrators of a need for a breakfast program. Some resistance occurred because some administrators felt that parents were responsible for breakfast and not the school. Testimonials from school nurses, principals, and teachers all over the country praised the breakfast program. Many related its positive effects; increased classroom performance, improved behavior, and increased attendance. Tes-

---

[1]Revised in August 1982 to original quantities.

timony at Senate hearings, as recorded in the Congressional Record, indicated that the breakfast program led to ". . . improved attendance records, improved behavior, and alertness throughout the morning, less drowsiness due to hunger and of course improved performance and marks as a result of this program." The Food Research and Action Center and the Dwyer, Elias, and Warren (1973) studies pointed out the important part the breakfast program could play in eradicating hunger in this nation. In 1979 Congress instructed USDA to institute an outreach breakfast-promoting activity, and extended the breakfast program to public and private residential child-care institutions.

After Congress made the School Breakfast Program a permanent program in 1975, it was expected to flourish. However, that was not to be the case. USDA-donated commodities were eliminated for breakfast in 1980, and the following year the cash reimbursement was shaved (Table 1.4). Yearly there are threats of funding cuts in the program.

Schools can qualify for extra federal funds if they are in the "specially needy" or "severe need" category. To qualify a school must serve 40% or more of its lunches free or at a reduced price, or be required by their state to serve breakfast. At one time five states (New York, Ohio, Texas, Michigan, and Massachusetts) mandated breakfast programs under certain conditions. Texas, for example, required breakfast programs in all schools in which 10% or more of the students were eligible for free or reduced-price breakfasts.

Much research has supported the value of breakfast. Nutritionists have often declared breakfast as the most important meal of the day. The nutrients missed by skipping a meal, particularly breakfast, are not usually regained, leaving the day's consumption below the Recommended Dietary Allowances. The Iowa Breakfast Studies indicated that children who were hungry could not perform to their full potential in the classroom and had trouble concentrating and paying attention. Research done by the University of Maryland has shown that dietary Vitamin C is more frequently adequate for children participating in the school breakfast program than for those not participating.

TABLE 1.4.   Breakfast Cash Reimbursement Rates

Basic Rates	1980–1981	1981–1982	1983–1984	1984–1985
Paid	$0.1475	$0.0825	$0.09	$0.095
Free	0.520	0.57	0.6275	0.655
Reduced-Price	0.425	0.285	0.3275	0.355
Severe Needy Rates:				
Free	0.6275	0.685	0.735	0.7875
Reduced-Price	0.575	0.385	0.435	0.4875

The National Evaluation of School Nutrition Program Final Report, a large federally funded study, found that children who ate breakfast were substantially better nourished than those who skipped breakfast (U.S. Dept. of Agriculture 1983). The *Report* estimated that the more than 600,000 students who currently skip breakfast would eat it if a breakfast program were available in their schools. However, the study found no relationship between breakfast program participation and children's height or weight. When the foods served at school were compared to alternative breakfasts, the school breakfast was superior only in milk-related nutrients. As a matter of fact, the school breakfast provided less vitamin A, vitamin B_6, and iron than the breakfasts eaten by nonparticipants. These findings have caused many to recommend that the breakfast meal pattern be examined and improved.

Breakfast Meal Requirements

The breakfast pattern was set by the Secretary of Agriculture to include as a minimum:

½ pt of fluid milk
½ cup of fruit or vegetable or fruit juice or vegetable juice
1 slice of whole grain or enriched bread or an equivalent serving of biscuits, muffins, rolls, etc., or ¾ cup or 1 ounce, whichever is less, of whole-grain, enriched, or fortified cereal
A meat or meat alternate as often as is practicable

Many nutritionists and school foodservice administrators have felt from the outset that the minimum breakfast in USDA regulations is inadequate nutritionally. Some have contended that a meat or meat alternate should be a requirement, not a recommendation. Therefore, some states have added these as a requirement in administering the program locally where reimbursement rates covered the added costs. The lack of funds to pay for staff during the pilot stages of the program also encouraged the use of high-carbohydrate breakfasts that required little or no preparation. Schools without facilities served the "engineered cake" or formulated grain-fruit product and milk, which met the vitamin requirements through fortification and took the place of fruit and cereal in the breakfast. This practice could encourage poor food habits, it was argued. In 1978, at the request of Senators Talmadge, Stennis, and Allen, the General Accounting Office evaluated USDA's proposal to ban the formulated grain-fruit product and milk breakfast. Because of the cost of providing breakfast and the lack of facilities, it was determined that to ban the formulated grain-fruit product and milk would mean many schools would have to discontinue the breakfast program (see Table 1.5). The question became "is the formulated grain-fruit product and milk breakfast better than no breakfast at all?"

TABLE 1.5. Average Cost per Breakfast
in 1977–1978

School District	Food	Nonfood	Total Cost
Cleveland, OH	$0.279	$0.2264	$0.5054
Long Beach, CA	0.2576	0.3501	0.6077
Tucson, AZ	0.164	0.3692	0.8607
New York, NY	0.2599	0.2927	0.5526

SPECIAL MILK PROGRAM

The Special Milk Program subsidized milk purchased by children in excess of the number of half pints served as a part of the lunch and breakfast. For example, if school purchased milk for $0.071 per half pint in 1972, a child might pay $0.04 and the federal subsidy would be $0.04. The program was available for "nonprofit schools of high school grade and under and

FIG. 1.6. The Special Milk Program was considered by some to be competitive with the School Lunch Program.
Courtesy of Fairfax County (VA) Public Schools and U.S. Dept. of Agriculture.

nonprofit nursery schools, childcare centers, settlement houses, summer camps, and similar nonprofit institutions devoted to the care and training of children." The annual consumption of milk in 1946–1947 was 228 million half pints; by 1969–1970 consumption had grown to 2.7 billion half pints, but it fell to 1.9 billion half pints in 1980. Between 1978 and 1979 more than 2000 schools dropped the program; frequent changes in regulations and the record keeping required caused many school districts to discontinue the milk program.

Appropriation of federal funds for the Special Milk Program was uncertain on many occasions after funds were first authorized in 1954. In 1966 the program was made part of the Child Nutrition Act, and funds were appropriated until June 1970. With free lunches being funded and growing rapidly, the President and Congress asked if special milk funds were still needed (Fig. 1.6). Many people wondered if the program would be continued, as it was funded hesitantly year by year throughout the 1970s. In 1980 funding was drastically cut, and the following year it was completely eliminated. Many foodservice managers and directors supported elimination of the milk program because they thought it diverted income from the lunch program and even added to plate waste.

ASSESSMENT, IMPROVEMENT, AND MONITORING SYSTEM

The Assessment, Improvement, and Monitoring System (AIMS) is a system that guides state agencies in their review and audit of local school foodservices. Rules for this new approach to assuring that federal regulations are being carried out were issued in September 1980 and became effective in January 1981. School districts are checked on the following five performance standards:

1. Applications for free and reduced-price meals—to determine if correctly approved or denied
2. Number of free and reduced-price meals claimed for reimbursement—to determine if the number of children and currently approved applications by category and days of service claimed are correct
3. System for counting and recording reimbursable meals—to determine if it yields correct claims
4. Required food components—to determine if meals claimed contain the required foods as specified in the relevant meal pattern
5. Meals claimed for federal reimbursement—to determine if costs are allowable and are documented by acceptable and reviewable records

Reviews by the state agency are required once every 4 years; reviews of large school districts are done every 2 years. A state agency will review, as a minimum, the first four standards listed above and follow up when errors are found. Sanctions may be taken after the first review if the state agency thinks they are warranted. Sanctions are required on standards 2, 3, and 4 after the second (follow-up) review if corrections have not been made. Emphasis under this system is on corrective action.

If a state agency uses the audit method, they must assess a claim against districts any time a violation is uncovered.

COMPETITIVE FOODS

Competitive foods regulations were issued in 1980 after a couple of years of public comment and legal battles led by candy and cola manufacturers. The final guidelines placed limits on the sale of only a few foods. The four categories of restricted foods are soda water; water ices; chewing gum; and certain candies, including hard candies, such as jellies, gums, marshmallow candies, fondants, licorice, and spun candies. These foods have to contain only 5% or more of the Recommended Daily Allowance for one of the eight basic nutrients per 100 kilocalories or per serving. Those eight basic nutrients are protein, vitamin A, ascorbic acid, niacin, riboflavin, thiamine, calcium, and iron.

The regulation was overturned by a judge in early 1984 in a suit brought by the National Soft Drink Association. The judge said the Secretary of Agriculture had "overstepped his authority." The regulations had restricted sales of the nonnutritional foods throughout the school. The judge ruled that the Secretary could regulate only in the school cafeteria area. This overturn would allow the sale of sodas, etc. everywhere else but in the school cafeteria.

A comment period to this change in authority was provided in May 1984. The federal competitive foods regulation will probably be eliminated. Each state and local school district will have to establish restrictions if any are to exist.

THE EARLY 1980s

The federal budget cuts of the early 1980s had a dramatic impact on child nutrition programs. The cuts, which started in January 1981, represented the first decrease in funding of school food programs since 1966. The Budget Reconciliation Act passed in August 1981 meant further budget cuts, effective immediately.

Table 1.6 illustrates the severity of the 1981 cuts in federal funding and then their leveling off. Some fear that the subsidy for paying children will be

TABLE 1.6. Federal Contributions to National School Lunch Program during the Early 1980s

Type of Funding	August 1980–December 1980			January 1981–July 1981			August 1981–July 1982			August 1983–July 1984		
	Paid	Free	Reduced	Paid	Free	Reduced	Paid	Free	Reduced	Paid	Free	Reduced
National School Lunch Program												
Federal Cash	$0.185	$1.020	$0.920	$0.16	$0.995	$0.795	$0.105	$1.0925	$0.6925	$0.115	$1.2025	$0.8025
Federal Commodities	0.1575	0.1575	0.1575	0.135	0.135	0.135	0.11	0.11	0.11	0.11	0.11	0.11
Bonus Commodities	0.061[1]	0.061[1]	0.061	0.061[1]	0.061[1]	0.061[1]	0.02[2]	0.02[2]	0.02[2]	0.02–0.25[3]	0.02–0.25[3]	0.02–0.25[3]
Total	$0.4025	$1.2375	$1.1375	$0.355	$1.190	$0.990	$0.235	$1.2225	$0.8225	$0.245–0.475	$1.3325–1.5625	$0.9325–1.1625

[1] Estimated dollar value, dependent on how much the local school used of grain products, dairy products, peanut products and shortening.
[2] Estimated dollar value, dependent on how much the local school used of dairy products.
[3] Unlimited quantities of bonus dairy products were available.

TABLE 1.7. Percentage of Lunches Served Free and at Reduced Prices in Some of the Largest School Districts—1983

School District	Percentage of Lunches Served	
	Free	Reduced-Price
New York City Public Schools	88	6
Los Angeles County Schools	72	6
Chicago Public Schools	88	3
Hillsborough County Schools	48.6	7.4
Detroit Public Schools	86.3	2.3
Houston Independent Schools	66.5	7.4
Memphis Schools	80	3
Philadelphia Schools	93	4
Dallas Public Schools	70	10

the first to go if the federal deficit makes it necessary to further reduce social programs in the late 1980s. The prices charged students were increased from 5¢ to as much as 30¢, but as of 1984 the subsidy had not been eliminated. As had been the experience before, participation in school lunch programs decreased when the price charged increased. Because of high unemployment and the poor economy, the number of students qualifying for free or reduced-price meals increased (Table 1.2). In 1984, 45% of the lunches served under the National School Lunch Program were free lunches and 6% were reduced-price lunches. In many big cities these percentages were even higher (Table 1.7).

Along with the budget cuts, there were some changes in program regulations. One change was that the "offer versus served" distinction was extended first to senior high schools, then to elementary schools as a local option. In the past, all components of the meal had to be *served* to elementary students in order for meals to qualify for reimbursement, although high school students simply had to be *offered* all components. Those school districts opting to extend "offer versus served" to the elementary level, found it reduced plate waste and in turn cost (Fig. 1.7). At a time when costs were increasing, this was a real plus.

Another change in the regulations was the requirement that the social security numbers of parents be included in the applications for free and reduced-price lunches. Some people refused to give this information and were lost from the free and reduced-price roles. In the fall of 1983, verification of information on the applications became a requirement. Even though only 3% had to be verified the first year, the time this took was a problem for local school districts with a high percentage of free and reduced-price meals. The percent to be verified was decreased to $1\frac{1}{2}$% the following year.

School lunch made national headlines again—this time over "catsup being a vegetable." The issue arose because, in an effort to reduce costs and make meal patterns more flexible, USDA proposed crediting more foods, for example, allowing tofu to count as a meat/meat alternate and items like catsup to count as a vegetable. The news media picked up on this and blew it out of proportion. The proposed meal and crediting changes were withdrawn, unfortunately, and not reissued. Some of the changes were needed.

Not all the changes were bad. Students were more likely to be treated as customers by foodservice personnel than in earlier years. More choices and variety were seen in menus. Economy measures were put into place across the country. Managers of school lunch programs became very conscious of cost per serving and per item, of waste, and of time. They became better managers.

And it is good they did because as labor costs and other expenses continued to rise, many school lunch programs experienced financial problems. Local and state funding was tighter, and school lunch programs were often

FIG. 1.7. Before 1981 elementary students had to be served all parts of the lunch for their meal to qualify for reimbursement.
Courtesy of Fairfax County (VA) Public Schools and U.S. Dept. of Agriculture.

charged for fringe benefits and other costs that they had never had to absorb before. Educational budgets were feeling the cuts of 1981 in several ways.

Further complicating the situation were President Reagan's New Federalism proposals, which were sent yearly to Congress as proposed legislation. If ever enacted into law and reflected in the federal budget, these proposals might lead to termination of the National School Lunch Program. According to the New Federalism concept, funds for such a program would be given to the states with few stipulations. In addition, the funds to be given would be less than needed, with the idea that states would supplement federal funds with state revenues. Lobbying by the American School Food Service Association and other groups, such as the School Board Association, was instrumental in preventing adoption by Congress of the New Federalism proposals during the early 1980s.

President Reagan's 1984 budget *proposed*

1. creating a general nutrition assistance bloc grant that would cover the breakfast, child-care and summer feeding programs;
2. requiring food stamp offices to determine eligibility for free and reduced-price lunches;

3. delaying for 6 months the updating of annual reimbursement rates (before 1981, the rates were updated twice a year);
4. eliminating the Nutrition Education and Training (NET) Program;
5. indexing for inflation the cost of reduced-price lunches, thereby lowering reimbursement to schools.

Again in the 1985 budget, President Reagan proposed the bloc grant, eliminating NET, and indexing for the reduced-price lunch. Many think of this as "the calm" election year, and fear what cuts will be proposed the next four years.

The late 1980s will bring many changes in the operation of school food-services. Food and labor costs are increasing faster than can be dealt with. Energy costs will cause conservation to spread and will place more de-mands on the equipment manufacturers to provide energy efficient equip-ment. Use of computers in the kitchen, as well as in the manager's office, will provide unlimited possibilities.

THE FUTURE: 1988–2000

In 1982 the Census Bureau issued population projections through the year 2000, which will have a direct impact on the school lunch market. The number of births in 1981, for example, was 3.6 million and is projected to increase through 1988 to 3.9 million births a year before declining again. The "baby boom" of the 1950s, with its 4 million births per year, is not expected to happen again in the United States. The median age of Americans is projected to be 36.3 years in the year 2000, up from the median age of 31.2 years in 1984.

This projected composition of the population (Table 1.8) is important in planning for the year 2000. For example, the high-school-age population will be down, while the intermediate-age population will be up. The age group between 40 and 64 years will be much larger. Persons in this age

TABLE 1.8.   Age Composition of U.S. Population in 1982 and 2000

Age Group	1982 % of Total	1982 Number	2000 % of Total	2000 Number
65 and Over	11.6%	26,833,000	13.1%	35,036,000
40–64	24.5%	56,930,000	30.9	89,688,000
20–39	33.2%	77,077,000	28.1	75,249,000
15–19	8.5%	19,829,000	7.1	18,950,000
5–14	14.6%	33,959,000	14.3	38,277,000
Under 5	7.5%	17,370,000	6.5	17,624,000

Source: Census Bureau.

group will change careers several times during their lifetime and will fill adult education classes in the evenings. The service of food to this age group in evening adult education classes and to those over 65 in group-type housing will be potential markets. School foodservice operations could become "community nutrition" foodservice centers, serving not only school-age children but adults of all ages.

Projecting the future of school foodservice is difficult since the federal budget and the economy will have so much affect on school lunch programs. However, we can be sure that school foodservice will continue to be a political football, facing recurring federal cuts, last minute funding approvals, and threats of more cuts and audits. The continual changes in regulations, the need for more training and guidance materials, the political influence on the guidance materials, and more complicated accountability will make the manager's job harder. A letter-of-credit system is likely to replace USDA-donated foods. Verification of information on applications for free and reduced-price meals will reduce the number served, and more school districts will pull out of the National School Lunch Program unless the program regulations are relaxed. Some of the fast-food chains will compete for the business of large high schools in affluent areas, as they are looking for new investments and ways of expanding their operations. The prices they charge and the limited menus they offer will probably be problems to overcome.

The future of school foodservice depends largely on the legislation passed next. Lobbyists, from apple growers to carbonated drink vendors, from the American Dietetic Association to the National Restaurant Association, will plead yearly for changing or maintaining the directions of school foodservices. School foodservice has become as much a part of a school day as English and will stay in one form or another. For so many years it was slow to change, and now it has the flexibility to change, for progress.

BIBLIOGRAPHY

AMERICAN MEDICAL ASSOCIATION COUNCIL ON FOODS and NUTRITION. 1972. A Council statement; confections and soft drinks in schools. School Foodservice J. 26(10): 26.
AMERICAN SCHOOL FOOD SERVICE ASSOCIATION. (n.d.). Glossary of Terms. ASFSA, Denver, CO.
ANON. 1971. In the beginning . . . more beginning. School Lunch J. 25(6): 18–30.
BARD, B. 1968. The School Lunchroom: Time of Trial. John Wiley & Sons, New York.
BRIGGS, H. L. and CONSTANCE C. HART. 1931. From basket lunches to cafeterias—a story of progress. Nation's Schools 8:51–55.
BROOKE, E. 1972. Letter to the editor. School Foodservice J. 16(10):24.
CITIZEN'S BOARD OF INQUIRY INTO HUNGER AND MALNUTRITION OF THE U.S. 1968. Hunger, U.S.A. Beacon Press, Boston.
CRONAN, MARION. 1962. The School Lunch. Chas. A. Bennett Co., Peoria, IL.
DWYER, J. T., M. F. ELIAS, and J. H. WARREN. 1973. Effects of an experimental breakfast program on behavior in the late morning. Master's Thesis, Harvard School of Public Health, Cambridge, MA.

FAIRFAX, JEAN. 1968. Their Daily Bread. Committee on School Lunch Participation. McNelley-Rudd Printing Service, Atlanta, GA.

FOOD AND NUTRITION SERVICE. 1970. Chronological Legislative History of Child Nutrition Programs. U.S. Dept. Agr., Washington, DC.

FOOD RESEARCH AND ACTION CENTER. 1972. If We Had Ham, We Could Have Ham and Eggs . . . If We Had Eggs: A Study of the National School Breakfast Program. Gazette Press, Yonkers, NY.

FOOD RESEARCH AND ACTION CENTER. 1983. Doing More with Less. Food Research and Action Center, Washington, DC.

FORD, WILLARD STANLEY. 1926. Some Administrative Problems of the High School Cafeteria., Columbia University, New York.

GUNDERSON, G. W. (ed). 1971. The National School Lunch Program: Background and Development. FNS 63. U.S. Dept. Agr., U.S. Govt. Printing Office, Washington, DC.

HUNTER, R. 1904. Poverty. (Reprinted 1965. Poverty: Social Conscience in the Progressive Era.) Harper & Row, New York.

KENNEDY, E. 1972. Letter to the editor. School Foodservice J. 26(10):24.

KOTZ, N. 1969. Let Them Eat Promises: The Politics of Hunger in America. Prentice-Hall, Englewood Cliffs, NJ.

PERRYMAN, J. 1972. Log of the executive director. School Foodservice J. 26(10):18.

POLLITT, ERNESTO, MITCHELL GOISOVITZ, and MARITA GARGIULO. 1978. Educational benefits of the United States School Feeding Program: a critical review of the literature. American J of Public Health, 68(5):477–481.

POPKIN, BARRY M. 1982. The National Evaluation of School Lunch and Breakfast. University of North Carolina, Chapel Hill.

READ, M.S. 1973. Malnutrition, hunger, and behavior. J. Am. Dietet. Assoc. 63:379–385.

SANDSTROM, M. M. 1959. School lunches. Yearbook of Agriculture. U.S. Dept. Agr., U.S. Govt. Printing Office. Washington, DC.

SPARGO, J. 1906. The Bitter Cry of the Children. Macmillan, New York.

TUTTLE, D. 1962. Iowa Breakfast Studies, University of Iowa. Cereal Institute, Chicago.

U.S. COMPTROLLER GENERAL. 1977. Report to the Congress—summary of a report. The National School Lunch Program—Is it Working? U.S. General Accounting Office, Washington, DC.

U.S. DEPARTMENT OF AGRICULTURE. 1976. Annual Statistical Review Food and Nutrition Programs, Fiscal Year 1976. U.S. Govt. Printing Office, Washington, DC.

U.S. DEPARTMENT OF AGRICULTURE. 1980. Factors Influencing School and Student Participation in the School Breakfast Program, 1977–78. U.S. Govt. Printing Office, Washington, DC.

U.S. DEPARTMENT OF AGRICULTURE. 1982. Annual Historical Review of FNS Programs. U.S. Govt. Printing Office, Washington, DC.

U.S. DEPARTMENT OF AGRICULTURE. 1983. The National Evaluation of School Nutrition Programs. Vols. I, II, and Executive Summary. System Development Corporation, Santa Monica, CA.

U.S. DEPARTMENT OF INTERIOR. 1921. Bureau of Education Bull. 37. Washington, DC.

U.S. GENERAL ACCOUNTING OFFICE. 1980. Major Factors Inhibit Expansion of the School Breakfast Program. U.S. General Accounting Office, Washington, DC.

MENU PLANNING

The menu is the single most controlling factor in a foodservice operation. It would be ideal if the kitchen layout were planned around the menus and the equipment purchased for the menus to be prepared; however, this is seldom the case. Certainly menus should be planned before food is purchased, before the labor needs are determined, and before the price of the meal to the clientele is decided. Planning menus requires a great deal of knowledge about the operation. Consequently, when planning menus the following should be considered: (1) nutritional needs; (2) food preferences; (3) compliance with federal regulations; (4) whether standard or choice menus will be used; (5) the amount of money available; (6) equipment in the kitchen; (7) staff—the number of employees and their skill; (8) type of service; (9) food supply and USDA-donated foods; (10) season and climate; and (11) aesthetics. These topics are discussed in turn, then aids to menu planning and breakfast menu planning are considered.

NUTRITIONAL NEEDS

School foodservices use the USDA meal patterns (Table 2.1) in planning nutritional needs; however, a few school systems have tried computing the nutrients themselves. During the 1970s the Computer Assisted Nutrient Standard (CANS) system was tested and liked by some school districts, such as San Diego, California. The computer software was programmed in FORTRAN, which limited its use. Another attempt at planning menus by nutrients was initiated by USDA in the 1980s at the request of several school districts. This time the computer software was developed for the microcomputer in BASIC. (See Chapter 12 for more on use of computers in school foodservice.) With the increased use of computers, the new approach, called Nutrient Standard Menu Planning, developed by USDA has become

TABLE 2.1.   School Lunch Patterns for Various Age/Grade Groups

Components	Minimum Quantities				Recommended Quantities[2]	Specific Requirements
	Preschool		Grades K–3	Grades 4–12[1]	Grades 7–12	
	Ages 1–2 (Group I)	Ages 3–4 (Group II)	Ages 5–8 (Group III)	Age 9 & Over (Group IV)	Age 12 & Over (Group V)	
Meat or Meat Alternate: A serving of one of the following or a combination to give an equivalent quantity:						• Must be served in the main dish or the main dish and one other menu item.
Lean meat, poultry, or fish (edible portion as served)	1 oz	1½ oz	1½ oz	2 oz	3 oz	• Vegetable protein products, cheese alternate products, and enriched macaroni with fortified protein may be used to meet part of the meat/meat alternate requirement. Fact sheets on each of these alternate foods give detailed instructions for use.
Cheese	1 oz	1½ oz	1½ oz	2 oz	3 oz	
Large egg(s)	½	¾	¾	1	1½	
Cooked dry beans or peas	¼ cup	⅜ cup	⅜ cup	½ cup	¾ cup	
Peanut butter	2 Tbsp	3 Tbsp	3 Tbsp	4 Tbsp	6 Tbsp	
Vegetable and/or Fruit: Two or more servings of vegetable or fruit or both to total	½ cup	½ cup	½ cup	¾ cup	¾ cup	• No more than one-half of the total requirement may be met with full-strength fruit or vegetable juice. • Cooked dry beans or peas may be used as a meat alternate or as a vegetable but not as both in the same meal.
Bread or Bread Alternate: Servings of bread or bread alternate A serving is: • 1 slice of whole-grain or enriched bread • A whole-grain or enriched biscuit, roll, muffin, etc. • ½ cup of cooked whole-grain or enriched rice, macaroni, noodles, whole-grain or enriched pasta products, or other cereal grains such as bulgur or corn grits • A combination of any of the above	5/week	8/week	8/week	8/week	10/week	• At least ½ serving of bread or an equivalent quantity of bread alternate for Group I, and 1 serving for Groups II–V, must be served daily. • Enriched macaroni with fortified protein may be used as a meat alternate or as a bread alternate but not as both in the same meal. Note: *Food Buying Guide for Child Nutrition Programs,* PA-1331 (USDA 1984) provides the information for the minimum weight of a serving.
Milk: A serving of fluid milk	¾ cup (6 fl oz)	¾ cup (6 fl oz)	½ pint (8 fl oz)	½ pint (8 fl oz)	½ pint (8 fl oz)	At least one of the following forms of milk must be offered: • Unflavored lowfat milk • Unflavored skim milk • Unflavored buttermilk Note: This requirement does not prohibit offering other milks, such as whole milk or flavored milk, along with one or more of the above.

Source: National School Lunch Program, Food and Nutrition Service, U.S. Dept. of Agriculture (1983a).
[1]Group IV is the one meal pattern which will satisfy all requirements if no portion size adjustments are made. USDA recommends, but does not require, that you adjust portions by age/grade group to better meet the food and nutritional needs of children according to their ages. If you adjust portions, Groups I–IV are minimum requirements for the age/grade groups specified. If you do *not* adjust portions, the Group IV portions are the portions to serve all children.
[2]Group V specifies recommended, not required, quantities for students 12 years and older. These students may request smaller portions, but not smaller than those specified in Group IV.

more feasible. It is discussed later in this section. The lunch should contribute a minimum of one-third the Recommended Daily Allowances, which are discussed in more detail in Chapter 3. When using USDA meal patterns, the menu planner may refer to *Food Buying Guide for Child Nutrition Programs* (U.S. Dept. of Agriculture 1984), which provides the yields of food by purchased units and is a companion to *Menu Planning Guide for School Food Service* (U.S. Dept. of Agriculture 1983a).

The meat/meat alternate in the menu may be made up of a combination of foods. The meal requirement specifies the following:

Grades K–3 Group III	Grades 4–12 Group IV
1½ oz meat or 1½ oz cheese or ¾ egg or ⅜ cup cooked dry beans/peas or 3 Tbsp peanut butter	2 oz meat or 2 oz cheese or 1 egg or ½ cup cooked dry beans/peas or 4 Tbsp peanut butter

Commercially prepared combination foods, such as chicken pot pies, may be used if the amount of meat is known. Other meat alternates, such as the eggs used in a cake or bread, peanut butter in cookies, or cheese in a sauce can be counted toward meeting the protein needs. Two menu items are the maximum number that may be used to meet the meat/meat alternate requirement. For example, in a menu consisting of spaghetti with meat and cheese sauce, tossed salad, French bread with butter, chocolate brownies, and milk, the combined contribution to the meat/meat alternate requirement is

ground beef	11 lb	(5.6 serving/lb)	61 2-oz servings meat
cheese	3 lb	(8 serving/lb)	24 2-oz servings meat alternate
eggs	15	(1 egg/serving)	15 2-oz servings meat alternate
			100 2-oz servings for Group IV

Using protein-fortified enriched macaroni, spaghetti, and other noodles in combination with meat, poultry, fish, or cheese to meet one-half of the minimum requirement is a way of stretching the food dollar. Also, vegetable protein products can be used to meet up to 30% of the requirement; however, most cooks have found that 15% with 85% meat is a more desirable ratio. For example:

6 lb dry textured vegetable protein (10% moisture and 50% protein)
9 lb water
Yields: 15 lb hydrated product
Combined with: 85 lb meat
Yields: 100 lb mixture

Recipes will need some alteration when vegetable protein is used. FNS Notice 219 from the USDA is very helpful in making the adjustments.

The vegetable/fruit requirement must be met with at least two sources. Minimum quantities are ½ cup for students in grades K–3 (ages 5–8, Group III) and ¾ cup for those in grades 4–12 (ages 9 and over, Group IV).

The vegetables used in the main dish (such as tomato products used in spaghetti) may be counted in meeting this requirement. Full-strength fruit or vegetable juice can be counted toward meeting up to one-half of the vegetable/fruit requirement. Large combination salads, if they contain at least ¾ cup of two or more vegetables and/or fruits in combination with meat or meat alternates, such as a chef salad or a salad bar arrangement, meet the full requirement. The challenge is to offer fruits and vegetables the students will eat.

Pies, cakes, cookies, brownies, etc., are considered additional foods for energy. But pizza crust, pasta, rice, as well as breads made with enriched or whole grain, can be counted toward meeting the bread requirement.

Butter or fortified margarine may be used in cooking or as a spread on bread. Since 1975 there has not been a butter–margarine requirement.

The milk requirement is a serving (½ pint or 8 fl oz) of fluid milk. At least one of the following forms of milk must be offered: unflavored lowfat milk, unflavored skim milk, and unflavored buttermilk. Other milks, either flavored or unflavored, may be offered as a choice. To satisfy the meal requirement, milkshakes must contain ½ pint of fluid milk meeting state or local standards for fluid milk. These standards vary from state to state and should be checked with the proper state agency. Assuring that ½ pint of fluid milk is present in a milkshake requires close monitoring.

Foods in addition to those needed to meet the meal patterns are desirable for older children whose energy needs are greater than those satisfied by the meal patterns. Children 6 to 8 years old frequently find that the meal patterns provide more food than they can eat. Additional foods may be undesirable for these children.

Nutrient Standard Menu Planning

Schools must be approved by state agencies in order to use the nutrient standard rather than the meal pattern system of menu planning. A rather extensive pilot program using this new system was begun in 1983. The increased availability of computers in schools makes nutrient standard menu planning a viable alternative to meal pattern planning.

The nutrient standards specified by USDA are shown in Table 2.2 and represent about one-third of the daily allowances for calories and seven nutrients—protein, iron, calcium, vitamin A, thiamine, riboflavin, and vitamin C. School lunches are expected to meet these standards on the average over a week's time.

Lunches can exceed the nutrient standards, but should not be below them. Use of standardized USDA recipes is essential unless a school system wishes to calculate the nutrient content of its own recipes. Also, ½ pint milk must be served daily, whereas under "offer versus served" milk only has to be "offered." This is confusing to everybody.

There are basically three steps in nutrient standard menu planning: (1)

TABLE 2.2. Nutrient Standards for the National School Lunch Program[1]

ood energy[2]	570	calories
rotein	13	grams
alcium	330	milligrams
itamin A	1300	international units
on	4.7	milligrams
hiamin	0.40	milligrams
iboflavin	0.47	milligrams
itamin C	17	milligrams

[1] The standards are one-third of the Recommended Dietary Allowances (1980) interpolated from two RDA age groups, children 7–10 years old and the mean of males and females 11–14 years old. School lunches are expected to meet the nutrient standards averaged over a week. Menus planned using the nutrient standards must included a minimum of three menu items, one of which in ½ pint of fluid milk.

[2] The food-energy standard is based on the minimum of the Recommended Dietary Allowances range for the specified sex–age groups.

Source: U.S. Dept. of Agriculture (1983b).

determining the edible part and nutritive value of foods used in school lunches; (2) calculating the nutrient content of recipes and creating a recipe file; and (3) calculating the average nutrient content of lunches served during a school week and comparing that to the USDA nutrient standards.

When using nutrient standards to plan menus, one realizes the need for the Recommended Dietary Allowances to be more exact and perhaps not so generous. USDA has available a "Computer Coding Manual" that is helpful in planning menus using the nutrient standard approach.

FOOD PREFERENCES

Food preferences are instilled in people at an early age and are slow to be changed. Regional food habits should be considered in menu planning. Menus served in the New England states may include Boston baked beans and brown bread, whereas in the South the menu may include regional favorites such as candied yams, black-eyed peas, and hominy grits. However, regional foods are not as popular among today's students as they once were. The universal favorites seem to be hamburgers, spaghetti with meat sauce, pizza, and sandwiches.

Black Americans enjoy soul foods, and these preferences should be considered in planning menus. In communities with a large foreign population, the food preferences may be different from other communities in the same region. It is important that menus be planned to reflect the regional, racial, religious, and nationality preferences of the groups to be served.

There are also fads in food as in dress and these should be capitalized on when planning menus. These fads change quickly and it takes close communication with students to keep up with the changes. If menus include foods that the students like, there will be greater participation, less plate waste, and better morale. Food means many different things to people, as pointed out by Roundtree (1949): "Food is eaten for enjoyment, for emotional release, for social prestige, and for attention, adverse or otherwise. Food is refused because of such unconscious emotions as the pleasure of paining others and showing self-assertion."

What a person will accept and what he prefers are two different things. Some menus that are merely acceptable can be used, but most of the menus should actually be preferred in order to keep the students happy. It is possible to do this and still serve a nutritious meal. Certainly it is desirable to encourage students to try new foods or different foods, but putting them on a menu and serving them seldom does this without the aid of nutrition education. When nutrition education is being taught, much can be done with new, different combinations of foods and greater variety can be offered.

COMPLIANCE WITH FEDERAL REGULATIONS

The meal requirements for school food programs are numerous and are coupled with many more recommendations. Refer to the *Menu Planning Guide for School Food Service* (U.S. Dept. of Agriculture 1983a) for detailed discussions. Regulations do allow for certain variations in the food components of the basic meal patterns on an experimental basis and individual children are unable to consume certain foods for medical reasons. Also, religious, economic, ethnic, and physical needs have been accepted as reasons for approving variations from the basic meal requirements; however, these exceptions must be granted by the Food and Nutrition Service, USDA.

As discussed in Chapter 1, schools are now required only to *offer* all parts of the meal pattern to students in elementary and junior high schools, whereas before 1981 all parts had to be *served* in order for meals to qualify for reimbursement. Whether "to offer" or "to serve" in elementary and intermediate schools is a local decision. Federal regulations require that "offer versus served" be carried out in senior high schools. It may be extended to elementary and junior high schools at the discretion of local school food authorities. In "offer versus served," school lunch programs must offer all five food items in the school meal patterns. Students must choose at least three of the five items for their lunch to be reimbursable as a lunch. This should be kept in mind when planning go-togethers, particularly for how the foods will be served.

STANDARD AND CHOICE MENUS

Standard Menus

A standard menu is a set menu meeting all the meal requirements without any choice. This type of menu is commonly used in elementary schools

FIG. 2.1.   Before 1980, the standard, no-choice menu was most common in elementary schools.
Courtesy of Fairfax County (VA) Public Schools and U.S. Dept. of Agriculture.

where the administration is often concerned about the amount of time needed to serve the children. Younger students may take too much time in choosing from several items offered. The advantages of using a standard menu are (1) greater productivity and lower labor cost, (2) faster moving lines, (3) less equipment needed, and (4) ease in determining quantities of food needed.

It is impossible to plan one menu that all students will like. Also, older students object to someone else deciding what they will eat. Therefore, standard menu is more acceptable in elementary schools than in secondary schools.

The menu variety is, or should be, more limited when a standard (no-choice) menu is served (Fig. 2.1). Unpopular items will cause fewer students to eat. The foods included in a standard menu should be liked by at least 50% of the students.

Multiple-Choice Menus

Choice menus take careful planning and are more difficult to produce, but have several advantages: (1) the number of lunches served usually increases; (2) plate waste decreases; (3) students complain less; (4) there is greater opportunity to meet students' nutritional requirements; and (5) more variety can be offered.

When parts of a menu are offered for students to make some choices, it
may be referred to as a multiple-choice menu. For example,

> Salisbury steak
> Mashed potatoes—gravy
> Choice: Buttered spinach or orange juice
> Hot rolls and butter
> Choice: Gelatin dessert or brownies
> Choice: Lowfat milk or chocolate milk

Care must be taken in offering choices within the meal pattern, since *all*
combinations possible must meet the nutritional requirements. In the above
menu, potato chips cannot be offered as a choice with mashed potatoes,
because potato chips are not considered a vegetable. However, buttered
spinach and orange juice can be offered as a choice. Any of the combinations in the sample menu will meet the meal pattern.

Another consideration in planning a choice menu is that serving time will
be increased, but with careful planning it can be kept at a minumum. For
example, if the choices are tossed salad and tomato juice, each can be
served in individual serving dishes, so the student can pick up his choice
without having to be waited on by a foodservice worker. In the sample
menu, each of the choices can be made without individualized service,
since only one choice item goes on the plate. One plate can be ready with
spinach and another without.

Offering choices is particularly desirable when a less popular item is on
the menu. This also will make it possible to increase the variety (see Table
2.3). Though it appears that students would be happy with hamburgers
every day, this is seldom the case. Studies have shown that one's desire for a
food diminishes after having eaten it, and even a popular food will become
less appealing after continued repeating, particularly if the person does not
make the choice of repeating. Since vegetables are the least preferred food

TABLE 2.3. Knox County (TN) Schools' Cycle Menus Offer Choices of Main Dishes

Monday	Tuesday	Wednesday	Thursday	Friday
1–1	1–2	1–3	1–4	1–5
Fish with cheese on bun	Taco (2)	Chicken	Pizza casserole	Hamburger
Hot dog with chili	Hamburger	Pork Bar-B-Q sandwich	Hamburger	Club cheese sandwich
Potato	Salad with lettuce, tomato,	Potato	Salad choice	Potato
Vegetable salad	cheese	Green peas with pimento or	Fried okra	Bean salad
Fruit salad	Potato	onions	Carrot and raisin salad	Baked apples
	Corn	Beet salad	Hot rolls	
	Applesauce	Hot rolls		
2–1	2–2	2–3	2–4	2–5
Steak with gravy	Pizza	Turkey	Spaghetti	Hamburger with french fries
Hot dog with chili	Hamburger	Ham sandwich	Hamburger	Meat salad on lettuce with slices of
Sauerkraut	Tossed salad	Sweet potatoes	Tossed salad	pears, pineapple, tomato
Potato	Corn	Lima beans	Green beans	Crackers
Green beans	Applesauce	Broccoli	Applesauce	Jello
Hot rolls		Hot rolls	French bread	

Note: Fresh fruit, fruit juice, and 2% milk are available daily. Any menu item can be purchased a la carte.

for most students, a choice of vegetables can lessen plate waste and in turn help meet the nutritional goals. It is common for people to complain about food. The complaints seem to be less when a choice of well-prepared food is offered. When an individual makes the decision of what he will eat, he tends to be less critical than when he does not have a choice. With multiple-choice menus, as many choices can be offered as the cafeteria staff can handle. A choice of main dishes may be offered without slowing the line if one of each choice is dished up and ready at all times to be picked up by the student. When there are two or more choice items to go on the plate, it will be necessary to dish the food up on request of each student. This will slow the speed of the serving line and increase the labor cost per meal served.

Multiple Menus

Multiple menus contain more than one entire menu that students may select. This may be accomplished with two entirely different fixed menus, such as

Grilled cheese sandwich	Sliced beef and gravy
Tomato soup	Whipped potatoes
Potato chips	Buttered green peas
Fresh fruit cup	Hot rolls Butter
Milk	Milk

These two menus might be referred to as the "soup and sandwich" line and the "regular" lunch line. Some school foodservices have been able to serve multiple menus with four or more choices successfully. However, this seems extreme. The same can be accomplished with fewer choices within the menu multiple. When choices are offered, additional time is needed in preparation, which means more labor. The "soup and sandwich" or "speed line" has been very successful in secondary schools. It is desirable to have more than one serving line when multiple menus are offered, though it is possible to manage them on one line. One of the menus can be a rather routine, fixed menu with few changes. Students like the security of knowing what to expect. The speed line might have the following components:

Soup of the day:	Monday—Tomato
	Tuesday—Vegetable
	Wednesday—Chili
	Thursday—Tomato
	Friday—Chicken noodle
Sandwich	Hamburger or fishburger
	Peanut butter and jelly or cheese
French fries or Salad	
Milk	

The dessert can be sold extra. Though this menu offers little variety, it may make a large number of students happy. The regular lunch line menu can offer more variety. Again, the goal is to serve a nutritional lunch that will be eaten. The nutritional value is there even if the variety is not.

Since many teenage girls are concerned with their weight and their calorie needs are less than the athletic teenage boy's needs, it may be desirable to offer—as part of a multiple menu—a salad plate that meets the meal lunch patterns. Two examples are shown in Table 2.4.

Len Fredrick, former director of the Las Vegas School District Food Service in the 1970s, was well known for his "combo" lunch. The combo was made up of one of 15 a la carte hot and cold sandwiches, an order of french fries or a tossed salad, and a super shake or milk. The combo met the federal meal requirements, Fredrick claimed.

The choices in a multiple menu can be planned so that the preparation is not too difficult. For example, when turkey and dressing are served on the regular menu, turkey salad is on the salad plate or in a sandwich on the sandwich line. When planning choices, the amount of labor needed for preparation and serving must be considered. There are also usually more leftovers and waste when choices are offered. This can be expensive if the use of leftovers is not considered in the planning. Ease in the preparation and serving of choices of desserts is possible by offering choices like chilled canned fruit and cake with a variety of icings. Chilled canned fruit takes very little time to apportion, and a basic yellow cake can be used with various icings. When offering a meat dish or any dish requiring much preparation, the other choice can be one needing little preparation, such as frozen fish squares or ground beef patties, which require only cooking.

TABLE 2.4. Two Diet Menus

	Quantities[1]			Quantities[1]	
	K–3	4–12		K–3	4–12
Chef salad with Julienne	½ cup	¾ cup	Grated cheese or	1½ oz	2 oz
ham and cheese or	1½ oz	2 oz	cottage cheese		
hard-cooked egg	¾	1	Peach and pineapple	½ cup	¾ cup
Salad dressing			slices[2]		
Hot roll with butter[3]	1 oz roll	1 oz roll	Lettuce leaves[2]	⅛ cup	¼ cup
Choice of milk	½ pt	½ pt	Slice of Italian bread	1½ oz	1½ oz
			with butter[3]		
			Choice of milk	½ pt	½ pt

[1]Quantities are given only for those items that contribute toward meeting the meal requirements.

[2]The amounts of fruits and lettuce indicated more than meet the meal requirement for fruit/vegetable. The fruit portion could be decreased.

[3]The bread requirement of 8 servings per week is difficult to meet with diet menus if portions are not increased or croutons are not added to the chef salad.

Salad Bars

With the popularity of self-service during the late 1970s and 1980s in fast-food operations, schools have found it simple to promote salad bars, and with much success. The salad bar is being used to provide a complete lunch, fixings for a sandwich, and a salad with a meal. To assure that all federal meal requirements are met, careful supervision may be necessary. Large combination vegetable and/or fruit salads, containing at least ¾ cup of two or more vegetables and/or fruits, are considered as two or more servings and will meet the full vegetable/fruit requirement. Consider the following when setting up a salad bar:

1. Meat and meat alternates are the most expensive part of the meal and preportioning will help assure that the correct amount is served or taken.
2. Eight servings per week of bread and bread alternate may be slightly difficult to serve on the salad bar. Croutons, pasta products, and crackers add variety and help meet the bread requirement.
3. A cashier should be stationed at the end of the salad bar where the tray can be checked to assure all components of the meal patterns are on the tray. Students do not have to take all foods under "offer versus served."

Suggested Salad Bar Offerings. A great many foods can be offered at a salad bar. The suggestions here provide guidance in selecting foods that will meet the meal requirements and be appealing.

Offer at least four of the following daily for a variety of colors, shapes, and textures:

Bean sprouts	Cucumber slices
Chick peas	Broccoli flowerettes
Cauliflower flowerettes	Celery, chunks or chopped
Sauerkraut	Spinach leaves
Radishes, sliced or whole	Three-bean salad
Julienne beets	Green peas with onions
Carrots, sliced or grated	Beans, green, wax, or kidney
Tomatoes, cherry or wedges	Pickle chips, dill or sweet
Green pepper, rings or slices	

Offer at least three of the following daily. Proportion to assure the meat/meat alternate meal requirement is met. (If "offer versus served" is being carried out the meat/meat alternate does not have to be proportioned.):

Cheese, grated or cubed
Eggs, sliced or wedged
Cottage cheese
Chicken, tuna, or egg salad
Julienne ham
Julienne roast beef
Julienne salami

Julienne turkey
Macaroni salad (made with pro-
 tein-fortified macaroni)
Three-bean salad (made with
 dry beans/peas)
Combination of the above

Offer one of the following daily:

Peaches, diced or
 sliced
Pears, diced or sliced
Pineapple

Orange wedges
Apple slices or
 applesauce
Melon pieces

Fruit cup
Grapes
Raisins

Offer at least eight servings of bread weekly:

Sliced breads and rolls,
 enriched or
 whole grain
Crackers

Soft pretzels
Croutons
Bread sticks

Muffins
Pasta products

Offer at least two salad dressings each day.

FIG. 2.2. A taco salad bar can provide all the components of the meal pattern.

FIG. 2.3. Salad bar items should be kept cold and displayed attractively.

As in other types of foodservice operations, variety is needed in the offerings at a salad bar. A number of specialty salad bars have been successfully used. These include a (1) taco salad bar (Fig. 2.2); (2) potato bar serving large baked potatoes with various toppings; (3) sandwich bar with pita pocket bread to be filled by students; (4) fruit and cheese bar offering fresh and canned fruits; (5) deli bar with choice of meats and cheese served by the ounce; (6) breakfast bar with cereal in a salad bowl with toppings; and (7) dessert bar serving ice cream with toppings or cake with toppings.

There are many attractive pieces of equipment for salad bars, however, some schools have successfully turned a regular serving line into a salad bar. The important thing is that the food be kept cold—for sanitation reasons as well as for customer appeal (Fig. 2.3).

THE AMOUNT OF MONEY AVAILABLE

In order to operate a sound foodservice, the amount of money that is available to be spent on food must be known. It should never be a guessing game, hoping there will be enough income at the end of the month to cover the cost. Recipe and menu costing are discussed in Chapter 11. Determining labor cost is far easier than determining food cost. Waste and price increases in food make it difficult to project how much the served food will cost.

Perhaps the best start, in determining the amount of money that can be spent for food, is to determine the income received for each lunch served. In most instances this can be determined by adding together the sources of income (Table 2.5).

No formula can be applied to every situation. The cost of labor is higher in some parts of the country than others, as is the price of food. If many

TABLE 2.5. Determining the Income
for School Lunches

Source of Income	Sample Amount ($)
Student's payment for lunch	0.85
Federal reimbursement	0.12
State reimbursement (if any)	0.06
County or city funds (if any)	0.02
Donations (if any)	
Value of USDA commodities	0.16
Total income	$1.21

prepared foods are used, the food cost will be higher but the labor cost should be lower. The formula most frequently applicable for on-site preparation is 50 to 55% of the income used for food, 35 to 40% of the income used for labor, and 5 to 10% for miscellaneous items such as paper needs and detergents and other indirect costs.

Assuming that 55% of the income is available for food and the total income per lunch is $1.21, then 66¢ can be used for food. The cost of the ½ pint of milk, a relatively constant figure, could be subtracted first. If the milk costs 13¢, this would leave 53¢ to cover all the other foods in the menu. If the cost of one menu is greater than the amount of money available, the next day's menu can be under, so that it evens out.

EQUIPMENT IN THE KITCHEN

It would be ideal if the equipment were selected to fit the menus planned; however, in many cases the lack of equipment or the existing equipment determines what can be on the menu. If oven space is limited, a menu that includes cake, yeast rolls, and baked potatoes may be physically impossible. The number and size of mixers will determine how many mixed items are possible on a single menu. If a deep-fat fryer is not available, french fries will need to be of a type that can be browned in the oven, and fried chicken will need a different type of batter than that used in deep-fat frying. The serving utensils and dishes may also be controlling factors in menu planning.

STAFF—THE NUMBER OF EMPLOYEES AND THEIR SKILL

If foodservice is staffed closely, the number of foods requiring extensive preparation will need to be limited. A balance in the amount of preparation required is desirable, so that the workload is not almost impossible one day and very light the next. Also, overloading one employee should be avoided. For example, strawberry shortcake and yeast rolls may overload the baker if they are prepared the same day. Menus that require a lot of last-minute preparation should be avoided.

The skills and abilities of personnel may limit the menus. On-the-job training can help develop skills, but in most cases a less elaborate dish that does not require unfamiliar skills may be the solution. Using some prepared foods—such as dehydrated potato flakes instead of fresh potatoes for mashed potatoes, preportioned hamburger patties instead of making the patties out of meat purchased in bulk, and cakes from mixes—can make it possible to get the variety of food desired; and in many cases a better quality results than when inexperienced or rushed personnel are preparing it. A comparison of the labor involved in using commercially baked cookies, using frozen cookie dough, and making cookies from scratch has persuaded many foodservice directors and managers that they cannot afford to pay the labor costs needed to prepare labor-intensive items like cookies from scratch. More and more mixes, preportioned items, precooked foods, frozen doughs, and bakery products are being used to reduce labor cost. A comparison should be made to determine if there is really a savings to the individual operation before increasing the use of convenience foods. Too often the labor cost is not reduced, and the cost of food increases when convenience foods are used.

TYPE OF SERVICE

When food is prepared and served in the same location, a greater variety of foods can often be planned in the menus than when the food is taken to other locations to be served. In the latter case, certain foods may have to be eliminated from the menu because they do not transport well or because there may be danger of high bacterial counts. Foods that contain eggs, mayonnaise, or poultry, especially when in mixed dishes, should be handled with great care and kept at a temperature below 45°F or above 150°F at all times and served at these temperatures. If it is not possible to keep hot foods at 150°F or above and keep cold foods at 45°F or colder, combination dishes with protein-rich foods in them should be eliminated from the menu. Bacterial growth is discussed in detail in Chapter 10.

Though most school foodservices use cafeteria-style service, some classes eat family style. When students eat in their classrooms, in common areas, or in other such locations, soups and juices may have to be omitted from the menu. However, all of these factors may have little effect on the menu when the employees are determined to overcome them or serve the food in spite of them.

FOOD SUPPLY AND USDA-DONATED FOODS

The availability of food will limit menus. The frequency of deliveries and storage space in the kitchen may also enter into menu planning. A small school located some distance from a city may find the availability of foods very limited.

For school foodservices participating in the National School Lunch Program, there is an additional factor that has to be considered when planning menus—USDA-donated foods. In order to get the full value of the commodities issued by USDA and keep the price of the lunch to the students as low as possible, it is necessary to utilize the USDA-donated foods. This may be the greatest challenge of menu planning—particularly when the donated food is very unpopular with the students or is very difficult to prepare. For the most part, USDA-donated foods are of top quality and, for most conventional on-site preparations, can be used in the menus.

Donated food can be used in numerous ways and the ingenuity of the personnel can mean great savings in the food budget. Some donated foods are out of the ordinary or unfamiliar to the students. Nutrition education may be needed to make the students familiar with the food. For example, canned purple plums and fresh cranberries are unfamiliar foods to children in some parts of the country. Also, the irregular distribution of donated foods may require sudden menu changes or flexibility in menus. The donated foods should be treated as if they were purchased from funds in the local budget—that is, utilized effectively.

Processing of USDA-donated foods into other more usable products will increase their utilization (see discussion in Chapter 1). For example, frozen whole turkeys have limited use in planning favored lunches. Processing by a commercial manufacturer can convert the turkey into turkey ham, nuggets, hot dogs, and other variety meats, all of which can easily be used in school foodservices.

SEASON AND CLIMATE

People tend to want heavier, hotter foods in cold weather; cool salads, gelatin desserts, and cold sliced meats are more appealing in the hot summer. Chili will not go over as well in summer as when snow is on the ground.

The seasons also affect the cost of purchased food. Corn-on-the-cob is very expensive in March, whereas in August and September when it is in season, the prices are lower. It is helpful to have a list of foods with the seasons when they are most plentiful when planning the menu (Table 2.6). The seasonal availability of foods in California, Hawaii, and Florida may not correspond with that in the middle and eastern states.

TABLE 2.6. Average Monthly Availability of Selected Fresh Fruits and Vegetables

Food	Jan. (%)	Feb. (%)	Mar. (%)	Apr. (%)	May (%)	June (%)	July (%)	Aug. (%)	Sept. (%)	Oct. (%)	Nov. (%)	Dec. (%)	Annual Total (million lb)
Apples	10	9	10	9	8	5	3	4	9	12	10	11	3,470
Apricots	—	—	—	—	11	60	27	2	—	—	—	—	24
Asparagus	—	6	28	31	20	10	—	—	1	1	1	—	100
Avocados	9	7	8	8	8	7	7	8	7	9	11	11	170
Bananas	8	8	10	9	8	8	7	7	7	8	9	9	3,845
Blueberries	—	—	—	—	1	26	43	28	2	—	—	—	33
Broccoli	10	9	12	9	9	7	5	5	7	9	9	9	102
Cabbage	10	8	9	9	9	9	8	7	7	8	8	8	1,900
Cantaloupe	—	—	3	4	10	20	25	22	11	4	1	—	1,410
Carrots	10	9	10	9	8	7	7	7	7	9	9	8	1,455
Celery	9	8	9	8	8	8	8	7	7	8	10	10	1,548
Cherries	—	—	—	—	11	41	43	5	—	—	—	—	123
Corn	3	2	4	7	16	17	16	14	8	5	5	3	1,600
Cranberries	—	—	—	—	—	—	—	—	8	26	48	18	38
Cucumbers	7	5	6	7	11	12	12	9	8	8	8	7	664
Grapes	4	3	3	3	2	6	11	17	18	15	10	8	474
Honeydew	1	1	3	5	7	12	10	20	22	15	3	1	310
Lettuce	8	7	9	9	9	9	9	9	8	8	8	7	4,620
Nectarines	—	—	—	—	1	19	36	30	12	—	—	—	160
Onions, green	7	6	8	10	11	10	10	8	7	7	7	7	178
Oranges, all	11	12	13	11	10	7	5	4	4	5	8	10	3,240
Parsley	8	7	9	7	7	8	7	8	8	9	11	11	83
Peaches	—	—	—	—	6	17	31	29	15	15	—	—	1,020
Pears	7	7	7	6	4	2	4	13	16	17	10	7	490
Peppers, sweet	8	7	8	7	8	10	11	9	9	8	8	7	558
Pineapples	7	7	11	10	12	12	9	7	6	5	7	7	173
Plums	—	—	—	—	1	15	33	32	15	2	—	—	280
Potatoes	9	8	9	8	9	8	8	8	8	9	8	8	11,726
Radishes	8	8	10	11	11	8	8	7	6	6	9	8	243
Spinach	9	9	11	9	9	8	7	6	7	8	8	9	61
Squash	8	6	6	7	8	9	10	9	9	11	10	7	376
Strawberries	3	5	8	18	29	16	7	5	4	2	1	2	372
Sweet potatoes	9	8	8	7	5	3	3	5	9	11	19	13	854
Tangerines	21	8	7	4	2	—	—	—	—	5	20	32	270
Tomatoes	7	6	8	8	11	11	11	9	7	8	7	7	2,530
Turnips and rutabagas	12	10	10	8	6	4	4	6	7	11	13	9	186
Watermelons	—	—	1	3	10	28	31	20	5	1	—	—	2,860

Source: U.S. Dept. of Agriculture (1983a). Figures are based on 5 years of statistics.

Holidays and special occasions should be taken into account when menus are planned. Serving foods traditionally served on holidays in the area (region) will create festivity and be appreciated by students of all ages. Starting in January, there are many holidays that lend themselves to special dishes or to decorating common foods. Education Week, National School Lunch Week, United Nations Day, and special days in the school, such as a championship football game and French Week, are occasions that give the foodservice an opportunity to participate in the school's activities.

AESTHETICS

"People eat with their eyes" is a saying that is very true. A meal can be nutritionally adequate and contain favorite foods, but if it is not attractively served and visually appealing, it may not be eaten. When planning meals with "eye appeal," the planner will use some basic principles used by an artist in obtaining good design. The list of rules or principles seems long and perhaps too involved at first, but after practice they become automatic. Variety plays an important part in eye appeal—variety in color, shapes, flavors, textures, and temperatures.

Color Combinations

A colorless menu with all white food is uninteresting and pale looking. Sliced turkey, mashed potatoes, cauliflower, and vanilla pudding with milk make a very unattractive plate. But sliced turkey, candied yams, green beans or broccoli, and lemon pudding with a cherry on top and milk make a very beautiful, colorful plate and will stimulate the appetite. Perhaps a more popular version would be thinly sliced turkey on a sesame seed bun, potato rounds, sliced tomatoes and lettuce leaf, choice of vanilla and lemon puddings with topping and cherry, and milk.

Variety of Foods

Avoid the use of the same food in more than one dish. When apple juice or applesauce is on the menu, the addition of apple pie lacks variety; whereas, cherry pie or peach pie would add the needed variety.

Texture

Texture refers to the way the food feels in the mouth—soft, crisp, smooth, hard, chewy. Variety in texture is desirable, and a good rule is to plan a soft or smooth food, crisp food, and a hard food into each menu for interest in texture. Creamed chicken, mashed potatoes, rosy applesauce, chocolate pudding, and milk would all have basically the same feel in the mouth, whereas a menu of chicken nuggets with honey or barbecue sauce, green beans, fresh apple, hot roll, and milk would give the variety in texture desired.

Shape

Variety in the form in which food is presented plays a big part in eye appeal. A menu of all square shapes lacks variety in shape (for example, fish square, hash brown potatoes, cole slaw, cornbread square, and cake square). A variety of shapes, such as a combination of diced, squares, circles, and strips, is more appealing. The use of the scoop for portion control may result in too many "mounds." Portioning of food can limit variety in shapes and the scoop should not be used for more than two items.

Flavors

Flavors that are combined should offer variety. Highly seasoned foods should be combined with foods of mild flavor. A good example of this is traditional "go-togethers": cranberries with turkey; tartar sauce with fish squares; mint jelly with lamb; and spaghetti with tossed green salad. The basic flavors are sweet, sour, salty, and bitter. A combination of spicy foods with bland ones, of sweet foods and sour foods, with a balance of the flavors is desirable.

Consistency

Consistency refers to the degree of firmness or density of foods. Foods with sauces should not be combined with foods that are runny, but rather with foods that are firm. Children prefer firm foods and generally dislike combination or casserole items. If the main dish is a casserole-type dish then the vegetable should not be a mixture. Plain foods add balance when combined with casserole dishes. Variety in the way the food is prepared can be exploited by the menu planner. Fried, baked, broiled, steamed, boiled, and raw foods offer variety when a combination of two or more methods of preparation is used.

AIDS TO MENU PLANNING

Successful menu planning takes time, concentration, reference materials, and knowledge. Menus should be planned far enough ahead so that orders can be placed and received. It is poor management to plan the menu by the day, depending on what is on hand. Other school foodservices' menus can be useful as guides and provide ideas. As a matter of fact, McDonald's and Pizza Hut have made the food choices of student-age customers more universally the same.

Reference materials that can be helpful in planning menus are *A Menu Planning Guide for School Food Service* (U.S. Dept. of Agriculture 1983a), *Food Buying Guide for Child Nutrition Programs* (U.S. Dept. of Agriculture 1984), recipes, past records, and a list of commodities to be used and an inventory of what is on hand.

Plan menus at least 2 weeks in advance. Start by selecting a meat or meat alternate for each day, then select the vegetables and fruits to go with the main dish. Add the breads, butter, and milk and additional foods as desired.

Lunch Pattern	MONDAY	PORTION SIZE		TUESDAY	PORTION SIZE	
		Group	Group		Group	Group
Meat and Meat Alternate						
Vegetable and Fruit						
Bread and Bread Alternate						
Milk						
Other Foods						
	WEDNESDAY	PORTION SIZE		THURSDAY	PORTION SIZE	
Meat and Meat Alternate						
Vegetable and Fruit						
Bread and Bread Alternate						
Milk						
Other Foods						
	FRIDAY	PORTION SIZE				
Meat and Meat Alternate						
Vegetable and Fruit						
Bread and Bread Alternate						
Milk						
Other Foods						

FIG. 2.4. Sample menu-planning worksheet is geared to lunch meal patterns. *Courtesy of U.S. Dept. of Agriculture.*

A menu-planning worksheet used by many school foodservices is shown in Fig. 2.4. Before a menu is used, it should be set aside for a period of time and then reviewed to catch errors or problems. A checklist that is helpful in reviewing menus is shown in Fig. 2.5.

When menus are planned, it is a good idea to indicate on the menus the

	Yes	No

Nutrition:
1. Do all menus meet meal requirements?
2. Is a vitamin C-rich food included frequently?
3. Is a vitamin A-rich food included twice a week?
4. Is an iron-rich food included frequently?
5. Is bread requirement for the week met?

Physical Aspects:
6. Has the inventory of what is on hand been considered in planning?
7. Is the equipment adequate to prepare each menu?
8. Is the work load among workers balanced?
9. Do the menus fit the skills of the employees?

Aesthetics:
10. Are the lunches planned with good color contrast?
11. Do the lunches have foods of both mild and strong or pronounced flavors?
12. Are there varieties in shape of foods?
13. Do the meals contain something crisp and something soft? Something hot? Something cold?
14. Are most of the foods and food combinations familiar to the children and liked?
15. Have holidays been considered in the preparation?

Other Considerations:
16. Have ways of using USDA-donated foods been included in the lunches?
17. Are lunches planned in order that some preparation can be done the day before?
18. Have the lunches been planned in keeping with the season of the year?
19. Has excessive use of foods high in fats been avoided?
20. Is there a balance in the week between low-cost and high-cost meals?
21. Is a lowfat milk offered?
22. Are the menus within the food budget?
23. Is the menu acceptable to the students?

FIG. 2.5. A checklist is a great help in weekly menu planning.

sources of the recipes that will be used in preparing the foods and the serving sizes. For example:

Spaghetti with meat sauce	Tossed green salad	Apple crisp
USDA, D-30	USDA, E-18	School recipe
¾ to 1 cup serving	½ cup	⅓ cup

This information becomes more important when the planner is not the person who will be in charge of the food preparation. When menus are planned by someone other than the one in charge of preparation, it is important that notes of explanation be given.

Student Committee

Good communication with students is necessary to accomplish the goals of school feeding. The adults planning menus may like scalloped tomatoes, okra gumbo, and tuna casserole, but these may be unfamiliar or unpopular foods with students. Student committees containing a good representation of the cultural and social groups within the student population can be used effectively in planning menus. The committee might consist of students, teachers, parents, school board members, the foodservice manager, and the foodservice administrator. The committee can act as adviser in menu planning, testing new foods, testing recipes, selecting qualities of foods to be purchased, and suggesting policy changes.

Surveys and polls conducted by student leaders can give valuable information to menu planners. Student complaints and comments should be listened to and action taken to improve situations. Students should be thought of as "customers."

Elementary-age students enjoy menu planning. A class studying food units will be excited about planning a school menu. It is a good opportunity for making them feel a part of the planning. And it affords an opportunity for teaching nutrition and telling the school lunch story.

Cycle Menus

One of the greatest aids to successful menu planning is the use of cycle menus. These are a set of menus carefully planned to be rotated over a certain period of time. The menus are used consecutively and repeated. Not only do cycle menus save time, but they make it possible to forecast what foods will be needed over an entire year with fair accuracy. This is very important information for bid buying (see Chapter 7). Cycle menus also make the scheduling of work easier (see Chapter 6). Their use makes it possible to standardize preparation and enables personnel to become more experienced. If cycle menus are taken a few steps further, food orders for the cycles, work schedules for the cycles, and quantities to be prepared can all be planned once and these become cycle food orders, cycle work schedules, and cycle preparation information to be reused or rotated with the menus. It may be possible to buy foods in larger quantities if there is an advantage to doing so and if storage is available.

For school lunch programs where the students are captive customers, cycle menus have to be long enough and contain enough variety, so the cycle does not become too monotonous and repetitious. However, at some ages repetition can be positive and quite desirable: "It's Friday, it must be pizza" may appeal to some students.

Cycle menus can be of any length. Two- to 5-week cycles, with 10 to 25

Set I	Sept 6	Oct 11	Nov 15	Dec 27	Jan 31	Mar 6	Apr 10	May 15
Set II	Sept 13	Oct 18	Nov 22	Jan 3	Feb 7	Mar 13	Apr 17	May 22
Set III	Sept 20	Oct 25	Nov 29	Jan 10	Feb 14	Mar 20	Apr 24	May 29
Set IV	Sept 27	Nov 1	Dec 6	Jan 17	Feb 21	Mar 27	May 1	June 5
Set V	Oct 4	Nov 8	Dec 13	Jan 24	Feb 28	Apr 13	May 8	June 12

FIG. 2.6. Menus for the entire school year can be easily scheduled with 5 sets of cycle menus.

menus to be rotated, are very workable and satisfactory. Each of the 5-day or week of menus is called a "set" to be numbered and charted as to the week of the year the "set" is to be served (Fig. 2.6).

A cycle of 3 weeks to be used over a 3-month period or for a season can solve the seasonal food problem. This would mean a fall cycle, winter cycle, spring cycle, and if needed a summer cycle. Cycles longer than 6 weeks lose their purpose and advantages. The number of menus in the cycle is determined by how many different entrees or main dishes are to be served. To determine how long a cycle a school system needs, list all the main dishes to be served, as illustrated in Table 2.7. Put three stars beside the most popular

TABLE 2.7.   Sample List of Main Dishes/Sandwiches for a Cycle Menu

Spaghetti with meat sauce***
Lasagne
Pizza***
Burritos with cheese/meat sauce
Tacos with refried beans and cheese
Fried chicken**
Chili con carne (alternate)[1]
Barbecued chicken
Turkey nuggets** with honey and barbecue sauce
Batter fried fish

Hamburgers***
Fishburgers**
Hot dogs**
Steak sub***
Grilled cheese sandwich*
Peanut butter and jelly sandwich
Hoagies or submarines**
Meat ball sub
Barbecue on bun**
Pizzaburger***
Ham and cheese sandwich
Sliced turkey sandwich
Roast beef sandwich
Baked ham (alternate)
Tuna salad (alternate)
Fried fish (alternate)

***indicates that this is a popular menu to be repeated in the cycle up to three times.
  **indicates this is a popular menu to be repeated up to two times.
[1](alternate) indicates an item may be too unpopular, too expensive, seasonal, or too difficult in preparation to repeat often. It can be shown as an alternate on the cycle and repeated every other time the cycle comes up to be served.
    *indicates this is economical or is a government commodity and is to be repeated once.

dishes, two stars by the next popular, and one star by the main dishes that warrant repeating because they are abundant, are USDA-donated commodities, or are economical.

From this list 10 to 25 menus can be planned. The alternates are used to add variety. Ground beef is in so many popular foods that special attention needs to be given so that ground beef does not appear more than three times per week, and preferably only twice. More frequent serving will cause the children to feel that only ground beef is being served. A good rule to follow in planning a week of menus is to use two beef meals, one fish or pork meal, one poultry meal, and one meat alternate.

Some dishes may be wanted on the menus but are seasonal, too expensive, not popular enough, or too hard to prepare to be repeated as often as the cycle itself. In this case, these dishes can be made alternate menus.

Cycle menus are planned as you would plan a standard week's menu, but there is one additional step—checking the adjoining menus. It is wise to lay the sets of menus out in such a fashion that they can be seen as a whole. Make sure that repeats are not too close; particularly check the Friday and the following Monday's menu and the last menu in the cycle and the first menu of the cycle.

If cycle menus are to be used by the planner or planners there is much that may not need explaining. However, if cycle menus are to be followed by other food managers who were not a part of the planning, as in large centralized systems where perhaps as many as 100 different school cafeterias are to use them, then much explanation is needed. Notes should be made at the side or bottom of the menu sets. Recipe numbers or recipe sources should be given; if recipes are not available to all that will use the cycle, recipes should be furnished with the menus. The size of servings should be indicated since the menus should have been planned to meet the nutritional needs of the children.

Disadvantages of the cycle menus are that they can be monotonous if the menus are not carefully planned and if the cycle is not long enough. Other disadvantages may be that USDA-donated foods are often unknown to the planner at the time the menus are planned; cycle menus can be too expensive if seasonal foods are not taken into consideration; holidays and special occasions may not be included in the cycles. There are, however, some solutions to these disadvantages.

Frequency Charts. A frequency chart lists the number of times foods appear on the menu. Frequency charts can indicate meats, vegetables, breads, fruits, and desserts, and at a glance repeats of foods can easily be seen (Figs. 2.7 and 2.8). If a food is repeated frequently, the question should be asked, Is this a popular food? If not, Why is it being repeated? The completed chart is valuable in determining the quantities of meats, certain vegetables, etc., that will be used during the cycle or year. This information is useful and needed in estimating quantities to buy.

Item	Set I					Set II					Set III					Set IV				
	M	T	W	T	F	M	T	W	T	F	M	T	W	T	F	M	T	W	T	F
Ground beef Spaghetti Meat balls Lasagne Chili Tacos Burritos Hamburgers																				
Roast beef																				
Chicken Fried BBQ Turkey Nugget																				
Fish, batter fried Fishburgers Hot dogs Luncheon meat Ham Tuna																				
Cheese Grilled Pizza																				

FIG. 2.7. Frequency charts, such as this one for meat and meat-alternate foods for a 4-week cycle menu, are useful in planning and help avoid monotonous repetition of particular foods.

Monotony. Monotony or repetition of unpopular menus can be avoided. For example, if on a 4-week cycle, meat loaf or chili con carne is to be put on the menu, but because of unpopularity or expense, it is undesirable to repeat every 4 weeks (or as frequent as the menu cycle repeats), then show as a "Manager's Choice: Meat Loaf or Chili Con Carne." Then meat loaf could be served every other time the menu is repeated.

USDA-Donated Foods. Cycle menus should be made flexible and general, not too specific. Changes should be made when need be, although not too frequently because then the menus lose their importance as a guide. If a menu calls for green vegetable rather than specifying green peas, the manager can use what is available or preferred, giving a variety of ways

Item	Set I					Set II					Set III					Set IV				
	M	T	W	T	F	M	T	W	T	F	M	T	W	T	F	M	T	W	T	F
Canned																				
Beans, green																				
Beans, lima																				
Beans, kidney																				
Corn																				
Potatoes, dehydrated																				
Sauerkraut																				
Carrots																				
Tomatoes																				
Pork 'n beans																				
Frozen																				
French fries																				
Hash brown potatoes																				
Mixed vegetables																				
Spinach																				
Peas																				
Broccoli																				
Fresh																				
Tossed salad																				
Cole slaw																				
Celery sticks																				
Tomatoes																				

FIG. 2.8. Sample frequency chart for vegetables for a 4-week cycle menu.

vegetables can be prepared. Also, USDA-donated foods can usually be utilized soon after arrival. By putting "a variety of fruit" or "choice of fruit," the manager can utlilize the USDA-donated commodities that are available.

Holiday Menus. Holiday menus can be attached to the cycle menus to be used on the appropriate dates. By blocking out the cycle to see when each holiday falls, it is possible to arrange to celebrate various occasions. For example, if cake is on the Valentine's Day menu or pie is on George Washington's Birthday, cherries can be used instead without having to change the entire menu.

Seasonal Foods. Notes or footnotes to a menu can provide additional information about what foods to use. For example, sliced tomatoes may be used on a hamburger when tomatoes are in season; pickle and onions, when tomatoes are out of season. The use of general terms, such as "green vegetable of the day", "soup of the day," "choice of salads," and "fruit," give the menu user enough flexibility to include seasonal foods as they become available.

Leftovers. Unused leftovers are very expensive. In planning menus it should be kept in mind that leftovers must be used within 36 hours. Leftovers may be changed slightly and offered as a choice the next day. Some leftovers may be frozen for use the next time this food appears on the menu.

BREAKFAST MENU PLANNING

The USDA regulations specify that a federally subsidized breakfast shall consist of a minimum of

½ pt of fluid milk as a beverage, or on cereal or a part used for both purposes

½ cup of fruit or vegetable or fruit juice or vegetable juice

1 serving of whole-grain or enriched bread, biscuits, rolls, muffins, etc.; or ¾-cup serving (or 1 ounce, whichever is less) of whole-grain or enriched or fortified cereal

It is recommended that a meat/meat alternate (such as an egg, meat, cheese, or peanut butter) be added when practical. Most nutritionists feel that a protein-rich food should be a part of the minimum requirement or served at least twice a week. Additional foods—such as potatoes, bacon, donuts, butter or fortified margarine, jellies, jams, honey, and syrup—may be added to help satisfy appetites.

TABLE 2.8. Sample Breakfast Menus

Monday	Tuesday	Wednesday	Thursday	Friday
Orange juice (½ cup) School-made sweet roll (1 to 2) ½ pt milk	Applesauce (½ cup) Hash-browned potatoes with chopped ham Toast and jelly ½ pt milk	Orange juice (½ cup) Open-face grilled cheese sandwich ½ pt milk	Apple juice (½ cup) Cream chipped beef on toast ½ pt milk	Pineapple juice (½ cup) Scrambled eggs Toast and jelly ½ pt milk
Sliced banana Cold cereal Whole wheat donut ½ pt milk	Orange juice Soft-boiled egg Toast and jelly ½ pt milk	Apple juice French toast ½ pt milk	Orange juice Cooked oatmeal Cinnamon toast ½ pt milk	Applesauce Link sausage Toast and jelly ½ pt milk

The same basic guides discussed for planning lunch menus can be applied to planning breakfast menus. The menus should be planned 2 to 4 weeks in advance. Cycle menus consisting of 1 to 3 weeks of menus are usually adequate. Menus should have variety and provide contrast in textures and flavors. Sample menus are given in Table 2.8.

SUMMARY

Menu planning is a complicated job and controls many parts of the foodservice operation. What are the goals in planning menus? The nutritionists would like primary emphasis on serving a variety of nutritional foods and introducing new foods. However, simply putting nutritious food on the menu does not accomplish the goal. Menus should be planned around what the children will eat and not what the planner likes. Unless there is close cooperation between the cafeteria and teachers, with new foods introduced in the classroom and the cafeteria viewed as laboratory, a new food may end up as plate waste. With "offer versus served" it is no longer necessary to force children to take food they do not plan to eat.

When a food is known as unpopular "but nutritious" an alternate food, more popular and almost equally nutritious, should be offered as a choice. Unpopular menus can affect participation; there is often a definite correlation between what the menu is and how many students buy lunch. For example, a school that serves 450 meals when a popular menu is offered may well serve only 250 meals if the menu is unpopular. Since staffing is usually determined by the average number of meals served daily, large fluctuations from the average cause many problems for the staff. Low participation caused by unpopular menus also leads to financial losses. The best solution is to rework or possibly discard unpopular menus.

BIBLIOGRAPHY

ANON. 1964. Guide to Average Monthly Availability of 88 Fresh Fruits and Vegetables. United Fresh Fruit and Vegetable Assoc., Washington, DC.
ANON. 1972a. In behalf of breakfast. School Foodservice J. 26(1):33–41.
ANON. 1972b. Notebook on soy. School Foodservice J. 26(7):51–84.
BARKER, L. M. 1982. The Psychobiology of Human Food Selection. AVI Publishing Co., Westport, CT.
ECKSTEIN, ELEANOR F. 1967. Menu planning by computer: The random approach. J. Am. Dietet. Assoc. 51:529.
ECKSTEIN, ELEANOR F. 1978. Menu Planning. 2nd edition. AVI Publishing Co., Westport, CT.
FREDRICK, L. 1977. Fast Food Gets an "A" in School Lunch. Cahner Books International, Boston.
FOOD RESEARCH AND ACTION CENTER. 1972. If We Had Ham, We Could Have Ham and Eggs . . . If We Had Eggs: A Study of the National School Breakfast Program. Gazette Press, Yonkers, NY.

Bibliography

69

HARPER, J. M. and G. R. JANSEN. 1979. Comparison of Type A and NSM Menus in the National School Lunch Program. Colorado State University, Fort Collins.

HARPER, J. M. and G. R. JANSEN. 1979. Pilot Study to Compare Type A Lunches with Alternative Subsidized Lunches among High School Students. Colorado State University, Fort Collins.

PENNINGTON, J. and A. THOMPSON. 1976. Dietary Nutrient Guide. AVI Publishing Co., Westport, CT.

ROUNDTREE, J. 1949. The human factor in nutrition study. J. Home Economics *41:*433.

SCHNAKENBERG, D. D. 1976. The Impact of Novel Military Feeding Systems on Dining Hall Attendance, Plate Waste, Food Selection and Nutrient Intake. Letterman Army Institute of Research, San Francisco.

SKEABECK, ANNE. 1974. "Why won't some teenagers eat?" School Foodservice Journal, *28*(1):52–55.

U.S. DEPT. OF AGRICULTURE. 1971. Quantity Recipes for Type A School Lunches. U.S. Govt. Printing Office, Washington, DC.

U.S. DEPT. OF AGRICULTURE. 1983a. Menu Planning Guide for School Food Service. PA 1260. U.S. Govt. Printing Office, Washington, DC.

U.S. DEPT. OF AGRICULTURE. 1983b. Nutrient Standard Menu Planning Computer Coding Manual. U.S. Govt. Printing Office, Washington, DC.

U.S. DEPT. OF AGRICULTURE. 1984. Food buying guide for Child Nutrition Programs. PA 1331. U.S. Govt. Printing Office, Washington, DC.

WEST, B. B., G. S. SHUGART, and M. F. WILSON. 1978. Food for Fifty. 6th edition. John Wiley & Sons, New York.

WEST, B., L. WOOD, V. HARGER, and G. SHUGART. 1977. Food Service in Institutions. 6th edition. John Wiley & Sons, New York.

WYMAN, JUNE R. 1972. Teenagers and food. Food and Nutrition *12*(1):2,3–5. U.S. Govt. Printing Office, Washington, DC.

NUTRITION

". . . to safeguard the health and well-being of the Nation's children . . ."

Foodservices in institutions, such as schools, hospitals, and college residence halls, cater to a captive audience and therefore should feel a special obligation to serve nutritious foods. School foodservices were established on the premise that they would aid in maintaining a good nutritional status in healthy children and improving the nutritional status when the need exists. Therefore, those who plan menus for a school foodservice should have an understanding of nutritional requirements for children from the age 5 through 18. And those preparing the food must know the characteristics of vitamins and minerals in order to conserve them during preparation.

In order to eliminate hunger and malnutrition in the United States, good food habits need to be taught to students at home and through programs in nutrition education. Unless a student is taught to like nutritious foods and to understand his body's needs, he may often turn away from the well-balanced meal to snack foods. These snack foods are usually high in carbohydrates and fats. Poor eating habits, not the lack of food, are the primary reason for malnutrition in this country.

Nutrients are chemical compounds needed for good health, for building and repairing body tissues, for regulating body processes, for normal growth, and for providing energy needs. There is a great variety of foods year-round in this country to furnish all the nutrients needed. Therefore, the challenge is to get students to eat foods that contain the nutrients needed.

People require different amounts of food depending on their age, sex, activity, and size. Some bodies can utilize food better than others. However, when more food is eaten than the body requires, it is stored in the form of fat.

The characteristics of well-nourished people are (1) strong bones, muscles, and teeth; (2) healthy skin and blood; (3) feeling good; (4) enough energy for everyday activities; and (5) radiant and vigorous appearance. Poor nutrition or malnutrition occurs when too little food is eaten or the

70

wrong kinds of food are eaten. When this happens, children may grow slowly or not at all; may have bowed bones and enlarged joints; may have dry, flaky, and rough skin; may have inflamed eyes, dry hair, decayed teeth, anemia, and nervous disorders, and be listless and tired.

Food, when eaten, is digested and then absorbed from the digestive tract. Nutrients in food are classified into six main groups: protein, fats, carbohydrates, minerals, vitamins, and water. No one of these nutrients acts completely independently of the others. Protein, carbohydrates, and fats furnish the energy needed, which is measured in calories. A calorie is defined as the amount of heat it takes to raise the temperature of a kilogram of water 1°C.

Nutrient density is a concept that compares the number of calories and the quantities of nutrients in a food. It is particularly valuable when one is trying to cut down on calories. For example, potato chips are high in calories and low in nutrients and, thus, are less nutrient dense than an apple. This is important to remember when planning menus for small children.

MAJOR NUTRIENTS

Protein

Protein is abundant in this country. It is found in meats, poultry, eggs, fish, dairy products, fruits, vegetables, legumes, and cereal products. However, protein from animals is superior to that from plants because it contains a greater number of amino acids. Proteins are made up of 20 amino acids, but many sources of protein lack some of the amino acids. However, a combination of animal and plant protein sources is very satisfactory.

The functions of protein in the body are to (1) build and maintain body tissues, (2) provide energy, (3) regulate body processes, and (4) build resistance to disease. Protein is not stored in the body; therefore, it is essential that good sources of protein be eaten daily. Any excess protein in the body is used for energy. People with extreme protein deficiency may exhibit poor muscle tone and posture, lowered resistance to disease, slow recovery from illnesses, stunted growth, and anemia.

Fats and Carbohydrates

Fats and carbohydrates are important sources of energy. Some foods high in fat are butter, margarine, oil, shortening, fat meat, cream, chocolate, nuts, and cheese. Fats are a more concentrated source of energy than are carbohydrates and protein. Fats also function in the body by carrying fat soluble vitamins and supplying essential unsaturated fatty acids. The average lunch provides 35–38% of its calories from fat.

Carbohydrates are simply sugars and starches. Foods that are classified as high in carbohydrates are honey, syrup, molasses, sugars, dried fruits, cereal products, and starches. It is recommended that 60–65% of the calories come from complex carbohydrates, such as grain and vegetables. Special emphasis should be put on reducing fat in the diet. In 1979 USDA issued recommendations for decreasing the fats, sugars, and salt in school lunches.

Minerals

Minerals are needed only in small quantities but perform very important jobs in the body. Minerals make up a large part of the body's bones and teeth. Not all the minerals present in the body are known to be essential. Calcium, iron, and phosphorus are three minerals that are essential and may be deficient in a diet if foods are not carefully chosen.

Calcium. The primary source of calcium is milk and milk products. Leafy green vegetables and fish also contribute to calcium needs. However, vitamin D must be present in the body for efficient absorption of calcium. Calcium needs are greater during the growing years; however, the requirement for calcium continues through life.

The functions of calcium in the body are to (1) build bones and teeth, (2) regulate the heart, (3) aid in blood coagulation, and (4) regulate nerves and muscles to react normally. Deficiencies of calcium may cause poorly formed bones and teeth and slow clotting of blood.

Iron. According to a nationwide study by the USDA of nutrients in school lunches, more lunches were deficient in iron than any other nutrient. Iron is needed for forming red blood cells and other body cells and for carrying oxygen to the body tissues. Therefore, the quantity of iron needed depends upon the individual's sex and age, with females requiring more iron than males. If one lacks adequate quantities of iron, nutritional anemia may result; this is characterized by shortness of breath, dizziness, pale skin, gastric disturbances, and a feeling of weakness.

Small amounts of iron are found in a wide variety of foods, such as lean muscle meats, liver, fish, poultry, dry beans, molasses, and many dark green vegetables. The extent to which the body can make use of iron in foods depends not only on the quantity but also on the source and the presence of other foods that are eaten in the same meal. Since no one food or group of foods furnishes large quantities of iron, it is important that cereals and breads be enriched with iron. Foods rich in iron are listed in the pamphlet *Menu Planning Guide for School Food Service* (U.S. Dept. of Agriculture 1983) and are shown in Table 3.1.

TABLE 3.1. Iron-Rich Foods

Vegetables	Fruits	Breads (Enriched or Whole-Grain)	Cereals and Cereal Products (Enriched or Whole-Grain)	Miscellaneous
paragus	Apples (canned)	Biscuits	Bulgur	Dry beans
ans (canned)	Apricots (canned)	Boston brown bread	Noodles	Dry peas
green, lima, wax	Berries	Cornbread	macaroni, spaghetti	Eggs
rk green leafy	Cherries (canned)	Loaf	Rice	Meats
beet greens, chard, collards, endive,	Dried fruits	Muffins	Rolled wheat and oats	especially liver and
escarole, kale, mustard greens, spinach,	apricots, dates, figs,	Rolls		other organ meats
turnip greens	peaches, prunes, raisins			Peanut butter
her dark green	Grapes (canned)			Turkey
broccoli, Brussels sprouts				Shellfish
as				
green, immature and cowpeas,				
mmature seed				
uash (winter)				
veet potatoes				
matoes (canned)				
mato juice, paste, puree, sauce				

Phosphorus. Phosphorus is usually adequate in diets containing enough iron since many iron-rich foods are also good sources of phosphorus. Phosphorus is fundamental in the building of bones and teeth.

Iodine. Iodine is usually in adequate supply in nongoitrous regions without particularly having to watch the diet. In some areas of the country, iodized salt can aid in supplying the small quantity of iodine needed to help the thyroid gland function properly.

Vitamins

Vitamins are chemical compounds found in foods and are known to be essential to good health. There are over 20 vitamins believed to be important for optimal health. Letters of the alphabet have been used to differentiate some vitamins in addition to their chemical names. Vitamins are classified as either water soluble or fat soluble. Since preparation of food can destroy some vitamins, it is very important for those who prepare food to know how to retain the vitamins in food. This is discussed further in Chapter 8.

Vitamin A. Vitamin A is present in animal sources, such as liver, egg yolks, butter, whole milk, cheese, and cream. Also, the body can convert carotene into vitamin A. Carotene is the yellow pigment found in yellow and orange fruits and vegetables and is also present in dark green vegetables. Therefore, "dark green and deep yellow" fruits and vegetables are good sources of vitamin A, as shown in Table 3.2.

The functions of vitamin A in the body are to (1) promote growth, (2) help eyes adjust to dim lights, (3) maintain a healthy lining in the digestive tract, and (4) promote healthy skin. Symptoms of vitamin A deficiency

74   🕄 Nutrition

TABLE 3.2.   Foods Rich in Vitamin A and Carotene

Vegetables	Fruits

Good Source:

Beet greens	Apricots
Broccoli	Cantaloupe
Carrots	Mangoes
Chard, Swiss	Papayas
Chicory greens	Purple plums (canned)
Chili peppers, red	
Collards	
Cress, garden	
Dandelion greens	
Kale	
Mixed vegetables	
Mustard greens	
Peas and carrots	
Peppers, sweet, red	
Pumpkin	
Spinach	
Squash, winter	
Sweet potatoes	
Turnip greens	

Fair Source:

Asparagus, green	Cherries, red sour
Chili peppers, green (fresh)	Nectarines
Endive, curly	Peaches (except canned)
Escarole	Prunes
Tomatoes	
Tomato juice or reconstituted paste or puree	
Vegetable juice cocktail	

include retarded growth, dry eyelids, reddened eyes, night blindness, lowered resistance to infection, and poor teeth formation. However, excesses of vitamin A can be detrimental, causing enlarged liver and spleen, loss of hair, lack of appetite, and headaches.

Since mineral oil reduces the absorption of carotene and vitamin A, it should not be combined with foods. Vitamin A, which is fat soluble, is stored in the body and is not easily destroyed in the preparation of food. Studies of the lunches served in schools across the country have shown that the vitamin A nutritional goals are usually met. However, it is recommended that a good source of vitamin A be included in menus every other day; along with the daily consumption of butter, milk, and other foods which help meet the requirement.

B Vitamins.   Thiamine (B_1), riboflavin (B_2 or G), and niacin (nicotine acid) are the best known of the eleven B vitamins.

Thiamine. Thiamine is a water-soluble vitamin which is present in both plant and animal sources. However, the amounts present are relatively small. Cereal grains contribute the greatest part of the thiamine in our diets, and we depend on the enrichment of cereals and grain products to put thiamine back into the products after refining. Meats, poultry, fish, and some dairy products also contribute small quantities of thiamine.

The functions of thiamine in the body are (1) to promote normal appetite and digestion, (2) to help convert carbohydrates to energy, and (3) to help the heart, nerves, and muscles function properly. Deficiency of thiamine causes poor appetite and poor digestion, listlessness and fatigue, retarded growth, and nervousness.

Riboflavin. Riboflavin is a water-soluble vitamin that is highly unstable. It is widely distributed in foods with liver being an excellent source. About 80% of the riboflavin in the diet is concentrated in milk, meat, poultry, fish, and cereal products. Egg yolks and green leafy vegetables are also rich sources of riboflavin.

The functions of riboflavin in the body are to (1) promote vitality, (2) aid in converting carbohydrates into energy, (3) increase resistance to infection, (4) help maintain good vision and healthy clear eyes, and (5) build healthy skin and mouth tissue. A riboflavin deficiency may cause eyes to be oversensitive to light and blurred vision. Cracks may appear in the corners of the mouth and the tongue may become inflamed.

Niacin. Niacin, like vitamin A, occurs in two forms. Tryptophan, an amino acid found in protein-rich foods, can be converted in the body to niacin. Niacin as such is present in poultry, fish, meats, enriched flours, and cereal products. Niacin is water soluble, but is much more stable than riboflavin and thiamine.

The functions of niacin in the body are to (1) help convert fuel foods into energy, (2) promote healthy skin, (3) help the nervous system function, (4) aid in digestion, and (5) prevent and cure pellagra. Niacin deficiency causes mental depression and nervousness, disgestive disturbances, and rough, inflamed skin.

Vitamin C. Vitamin C is frequently called by its chemical name, ascorbic acid. It is the most unstable of the vitamins. Being water soluble, it can be destroyed by heat and light. Much care should be taken in preparing and serving vitamin C-rich foods. The handling of these foods is discussed in Chapter 8.

Citrus fruits, tomatoes, and dark green leafy vegetables are some of the best sources of ascorbic acid. Only a small amount is stored by the body; therefore, a good source of this vitamin is needed daily in the diet. Some of the best sources of ascorbic acid are listed in *Menu Planning Guide for*

School Food Service (U.S. Dept. of Agriculture 1983) and are presented in Table 3.3.

The functions of vitamin C in the body are to (1) promote healthy gums, (2) help build resistance to infection, (3) promote healing of wounds, (4) help in proper utilization of iron, (5) help build and maintain bones, tissues, and blood, and (6) prevent scurvy. A deficiency of ascorbic acid in the body may cause weakened bones, tendency to bruise and bleed easily, and swollen and painful joints. Scurvy is the disease caused in extreme cases of deficiency of ascorbic acid.

Many vitamin C-rich foods are unpopular with most students. Either they are not familiar with these foods or dislike their taste. More than 90% of the vitamin C in the diet is found in fruits and vegetables, and unfortunately the largest plate waste seems to occur with fruits and vegetables. Nutrition education can do much to correct this.

TABLE 3.3. Foods Rich in Vitamin C

Vegetables	Fruits
Good Source:	
Broccoli	Acerola
Brussels sprouts	Acerola juice
Cauliflower	Grapefruit
Chili peppers, red and green	Grapefruit juice
Collards	Grapefruit-orange juice
Cress, garden	Guavas
Kale	Kumquats
Kohlrabi	Mangoes
Mustard greens	Orange juice
Peppers, sweet, red and green	Oranges
	Papayas
	Pineapple juice
	Strawberries
	Tangerine juice
	Tangerines
Fair Source:	
Asparagus	Cantaloupe
Cabbage	Honeydew melon
Dandelion greens	Raspberries, red
Okra	Tangelo juice
Potatoes (baked, boiled or steamed)	Tangelos
Rutabagas	
Sauerkraut	
Spinach	
Sweet potatoes (except canned in syrup)	
Tomatoes	
Tomato juice or reconstituted paste or puree	
Turnip greens	
Turnips	

One of the best means of motivating students to eat fruits and vegetables in recent years has been to provide a salad bar. Since vitamin C is not stored in sufficient amounts in the body, it is important to include a source of vitamin C that students *will* eat in the menus. A choice of more than one source of vitamin C will increase the possible consumption. For example, offer a choice of buttered spinach and chilled orange juice, or a choice of sweet potatoes and white potatoes.

Vitamin D. Vitamin D is needed for the absorption of calcium. A severe deficiency of vitamin D may result in rickets. Milk fortified with vitamin D is the most reliable source of vitamin D in most school menus. One half-pint of fortified milk furnishes at least three-fourths of the required vitamin D, or approximately 100 I.U. Also, the sterols of the skin are changed into vitamin D through the exposure of the skin to sunlight.

Too much vitamin D over long periods of time can cause loss of appetite, nausea, weakness, and even kidney failure.

NUTRITIONAL REQUIREMENTS AND RECOMMENDATIONS

Several groups have published recommendations and standards that provide guidance in planning nutritious meals and in evaluating the quality of diets. Some of these guidelines are designed primarily for the general public, while others are of particular interest to those in school foodservices.

Dietary Guidelines for Americans

In February 1980 the U.S. Department of Agriculture and the U.S. Department of Health and Human Services (formerly Department of Health, Education and Welfare) issued a set of dietary guidelines for Americans in the publication *Nutrition and Your Health.* The guidelines concentrated on decreasing the consumption of fat, refined sugar, and sodium (salt). Most nutritionists agreed with these objectives. However, lobbyists for various food industries challenged the guidelines and questioned whether the typical consumption of fat, refined sugar, and salt by Americans is harmful. Despite the political controversy surrounding the guidelines, they have brought national attention to the consumption, and possible overconsumption by many, of fat, refined sugar, and sodium.

The new school lunch meal requirements issued by USDA in 1980 were designed to provide less fat than had the earlier meal patterns. This was done by adding the requirement that lowfat milk be offered and dropping the requirement that butter or margarine be included in the menu. The new meal patterns are discussed in detail later in this section.

TABLE 3.4A. Recommended Dietary Allowances Revised 1980[a]. Food al

Category	Age (years)	Weight (kg)	Weight (lb)	Height (cm)	Height (in)	Protein (g)	Fat-Soluble Vitamins Vitamin A (µg R.E.)[b]	Vitamin D (µg)[c]	Vitamin E (mg α T.E.)[d]	Water-Soluble Vitam Vitamin C (mg)	Thiam (mg
Infants	0.0–0.5	6	13	60	24	kg × 2.2	420	10	3	35	0.3
	0.5–1.0	9	20	71	28	kg × 2.0	400	10	4	35	0.5
Children	1–3	13	29	90	35	23	400	10	5	45	0.7
	4–6	20	44	112	44	30	500	10	6	45	0.9
	7–10	28	62	132	52	34	700	10	7	45	1.2
Males	11–14	45	99	157	62	45	1000	10	8	50	1.4
	15–18	66	145	176	69	56	1000	10	10	60	1.4
	19–22	70	154	177	70	56	1000	7.5	10	60	1.5
	23–50	70	154	178	70	56	1000	5	10	60	1.4
	51+	70	154	178	70	56	1000	5	10	60	1.2
Females	11–14	46	101	157	62	46	800	10	8	50	1.1
	15–18	55	120	163	64	46	800	10	8	60	1.1
	19–22	55	120	163	64	44	800	7.5	8	60	1.1
	23–50	55	120	163	64	44	800	5	8	60	1.0
	51+	55	120	163	64	44	800	5	8	60	1.0
Pregnant						+30	+200	+5	+2	+20	+0.4
Lactating						+20	+400	+5	+3	+40	+0.5

Note: Designed for the maintenance of good nutrition of practically all healthy people in the United States.

[a]The allowances are intended to provide for individual variations among most normal persons a they live in the United States under usual environmental stress. Diets should be based on a variet of common foods in order to provide other nutrients for which human requirements have been less well defined:

[b]Retinol equivalents: 1 retinol equivalent = 1 µg retinol or 6 µg β-carotene.

[c]As cholecalciferol: 10 µg cholecalciferol = 400 I.U. vitamin D.

[d]α-tocopherol equivalents: 1 mg d-α-tocopherol = 1 α T.E.

[e]1 N.E. (niacin equivalent) = 1 mg niacin or 60 mg dietary tryptophan.

TABLE 3.4B. Estimated Safe and Adequate Daily Dietary

Category	Age (years)	Vitamins Vitamin K (µg)	Biotin (mg)	Pantothenic Acid (mg)	Trace Elements[b] Copper (mg)	Manganese (mg)
Infants	0–0.5	12	35	2	0.5–0.7	0.5–0.7
	0.5–1	10–20	50	3	0.7–1.0	0.7–1.0
Children and Adolescents	1–3	15–30	65	3	1.0–1.5	1.0–1.5
	4–6	20–40	85	3–4	1.5–2.0	1.5–2.0
	7–10	30–60	120	4–5	2.0–2.5	2.0–3.0
	11+	50–100	100–200	4–7	2.0–3.0	2.5–5.0
Adults		70–140	100–200	4–7	2.0–3.0	2.5–5.0

Source: from Recommended Dietary Allowances, Revised 1980. Food and Nutrition Board, National Academy of Sciences–National Research Council, Washington, DC.

[a]Because there is less information on which to base allowances, these figures are not given in the main table of the RDA and are provided here in the form of ranges of recommended intakes.

utrition Board, National Academy of Sciences–National Research Council

Water-Soluble Vitamins					Minerals					
boflavin (mg)	Niacin (mg N.E.)^e	Vitamin B$_6$ (mg)	Folacin^f (μg)	Vitamin B$_{12}$ (μg)	Calcium (mg)	Phosphorus (mg)	Magnesium (mg)	Iron (mg)	Zinc (mg)	Iodine (μg)
0.4	6	0.3	30	0.5g	360	240	50	10	3	40
0.6	8	0.6	45	1.5	540	360	70	15	5	50
0.8	9	0.9	100	2.0	800	800	150	15	10	70
1.0	11	1.3	200	2.5	800	800	200	10	10	90
1.4	16	1.6	300	3.0	800	800	250	10	10	120
1.6	18	1.8	400	3.0	1200	1200	350	18	15	150
1.7	18	2.0	400	3.0	1200	1200	400	18	15	150
1.7	19	2.2	400	3.0	800	800	350	10	15	150
1.6	18	2.2	400	3.0	800	800	350	10	15	150
1.4	16	2.2	400	3.0	800	800	350	10	15	150
1.3	15	1.8	400	3.0	1200	1200	300	18	15	150
1.3	14	2.0	400	3.0	1200	1200	300	18	15	150
1.3	14	2.0	400	3.0	800	800	300	18	15	150
1.2	13	2.0	400	3.0	800	800	300	18	15	150
1.2	13	2.0	400	3.0	800	800	300	10	15	150
+0.3	+2	+0.6	+400	+1.0	+400	+400	+150	h	+5	+25
+0.5	+5	+0.5	+100	+1.0	+400	+400	+150	h	+10	+50

^fThe folacin allowances refer to dietary sources as determined by *Lactobacillus casei* assay ter treatment with enzymes ("conjugases") to make polyglutamyl forms of the vitamin available to e test organism.

^gThe RDA for vitamin B$_{12}$ in infants is based on average concentration of the vitamin in human ilk. The allowances after weaning are based on energy intake (as recommended by the American cademy of Pediatrics) and consideration of other factors, such as initial absorption.

^hThe increased requirement during pregnancy cannot be met by the iron content of habitual merican diets or by the existing iron stores of many women; therefore, the use of 30 to 60 mg pplemental iron is recommended. Iron needs during lactation are not substantially different from ose of nonpregnant women, but continued supplementation of the mother for 2 to 3 months after rturition is advisable in order to replenish stores depleted by pregnancy.

Intakes of Additional Selected Vitamins and Minerals^a

Trace Elements^b				Electrolytes		
Fluoride (mg)	Chromium (mg)	Selenium (mg)	Molybdenum (mg)	Sodium (mg)	Potassium (mg)	Chloride (mg)
0.1–0.5	0.01–0.04	0.01–0.04	0.03–0.06	115–350	350–925	275–700
0.2–1.0	0.02–0.06	0.03–0.06	0.04–0.08	250–750	425–1275	400–1200
0.5–1.5	0.02–0.08	0.02–0.08	0.05–0.1	325–975	550–1650	500–1500
1.0–2.5	0.03–0.12	0.03–0.12	0.06–0.15	450–1350	775–2325	700–2100
1.5–2.5	0.05–0.2	0.05–0.2	0.1–0.3	600–1800	1000–3000	925–2775
1.5–2.5	0.05–0.2	0.05–0.2	0.15–0.5	900–2700	1525–4575	1400–4200
1.5–4.0	0.05–0.2	0.05–0.2	0.15–0.5	1100–3300	1875–5625	1700–5100

^bSince the toxic levels for many trace elements may be only several times usual intakes, the upper levels for the trace elements given in this table should not be habitually exceeded.

80   Nutrition

Recommended Daily Dietary Allowances

The Food and Nutrition Board in 1940 developed the Recommended
Daily Dietary Allowances (RDAs), which are the quantities of specific nutrients needed by men, women, children, and infants and became the dietary standard in the United States. Though first published in 1943, the list
of RDAs has been revised eight times (Tables 3.4A and B). The nutrients
recommended are based on research started before the turn of the century.
The recommended allowances include the actual requirement for each
nutrient plus a safety factor.

The Five Food Groups

The Five Food Groups, still referred to by many as the Basic Four, is a
simple guide prepared by the Institute of Home Economics and based on
the Recommended Daily Dietary Allowances. This guide is most useful to
the average person in meeting recommended requirements without having
much knowledge of nutrition. The Basic Four Groups were reduced from
the Seven Basic Food Groups and are easily remembered as the Milk Group,
Meat Group, Vegetable and Fruit Group, and Bread and Cereal Group. In
1980 the fifth group, fats and sugars, was added. By using the number of
servings suggested in each group, one can plan an adequate menu that will
supply most of the nutrients needed.

Type A Lunch Pattern

The Type A pattern was established as a part of the guidelines of the
National School Lunch Act. Like the Five Food Groups, it provided a simplified way of planning nutritionally adequate meals. Before 1980, most
schools participating in the National School Lunch Program planned their
menus using the Type A lunch pattern, which provided approximately one-
third of the Recommended Daily Dietary Allowances for a student between
the ages of 10 and 12 years. However, as discussed in Chapter 2, some
schools have recently begun menu planning based directly on nutrient
standards and the nutritive content of foods. In 1983–1984, some 30 school
districts were part of a study to determine the acceptability of menus
planned using this method.

The Type A lunch pattern as amended includes

½ pt fluid milk as a beverage
2 oz edible portion of lean meat, poultry or fish, 2 oz cheese, 1 egg, ½
    cup cooked dry beans or dry peas, 4 Tbsp of peanut butter, or an
    equivalent quantity of any combination of the above listed foods
¾ cup serving of 2 or more vegetables or fruits, or both
1 serving of whole grain or enriched bread

The guidance materials point out that foods rich in iron, vitamin A and vitamin C must be included to assure that the nutritional goals are met. Following studies in 1968 by USDA, the butter or margarine requirement was lowered from 2 teaspoons to 1 teaspoon. In 1975 the butter requirement was eliminated.

An Ad Hoc Committee (1969) appointed by the Secretary of Agriculture to study the school lunch program recommended, among other things, that

Any program that can present evidence of its ability to consistently meet one-third RDA by a combination of ordinary foods differing from the Type A pattern should be authorized to do so and the resultant meals should be eligible for reimbursement from federal funds. Ethnic, economic and other considerations may make a variety of patterns desirable and should be given consideration in the formulation of program regulations.

Many nutritionists felt that the Type A lunch pattern was out of date and did not meet the needs of today's children at different ages. Nutritional analyses of actual lunches showed some B vitamins lacking in the menus and the publicity about plate waste during the 1970s pointed up a real need for

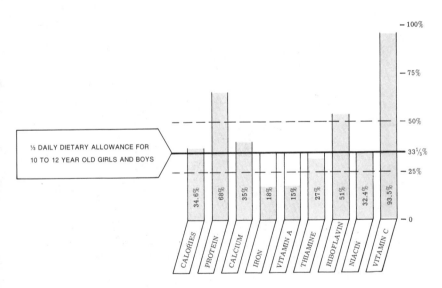

FIG. 3.1. Nutrient analysis of a typical school lunch. When daily dietary allowances are different for girls and boys, the greater requirement is used. Menu is listed below.

Menu	Size Serving
Fish Square	3.6 oz cooked
on Bun	1
Buttered Potatoes	½ cup
Red and Green Cole Slaw	⅓ cup
Cake with Chocolate Icing	1 serving
Milk	½ pt

change. Older children were complaining that the lunch did not provide enough food to meet their needs. See Figs. 3.1, 3.2, and 3.3 for analyses of three sample menus.

New Meal Patterns

In 1977 a complete revision of the Type A lunch pattern was published in the Federal Register for comment and suggestions. The proposed changes would have added many requirements, but many of those were not included in the final form of the new meal patterns which were released in

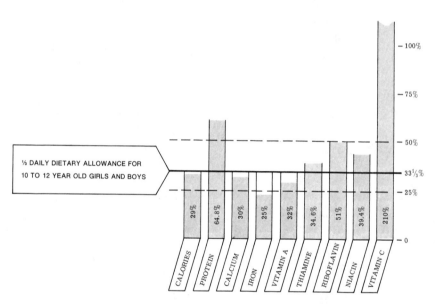

FIG. 3.2. Nutrient analysis of a typical school lunch. When daily dietary allowances are different for girls and boys, the greater requirement is used. Menu is listed below.

Menu	Size Serving
Hamburger Pattie	2 oz
on Bun	1
French Fries	½ cup
Catsup	1 Tbsp
Sliced Tomato	1 slice
Orange Juice	½ cup
Butter Cookie	2
Milk	½ pt

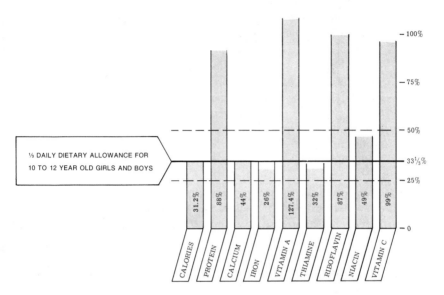

FIG. 3.3. Nutrient analysis of a typical school lunch. When daily dietary allowances are different for boys and girls, the greater requirement is used. Menu is listed below.

Menu	Size Serving
Fried Chicken	1 leg
Potato Salad	½ cup
Cooked Spinach	⅓ cup
Hot Roll	1 serving
Butter	1 tsp
Vanilla Pudding	½ cup
Milk	½ pt

two steps. The interim regulations were introduced in 1979, followed by the final regulations and the new meal patterns in the spring of 1980. These were revised in 1982.

The new meal patterns dropped the name "Type A" and are simply known as the school lunch meal patterns (see Table 2.1). They clearly state what the minimum portion sizes are to be for five different age/grade groups. The regulations had for many years encouraged variations in portion size to adjust for the differing needs of children of various ages; however, many state agencies did not allow the smaller quantities to be served. Determining how much to serve should no longer be a problem and there is much flexibility. The following features of the new meal patterns and the accompanying regulations should be noted:

1. Minimum quantities of the four lunch components (five foods) are stated for five age/grade groups.
2. Preschoolers can be served in two seatings.
3. If one does choose to serve the larger portions of Group V, smaller portions should be made available for those who prefer less; however, minimum quantities for that age/grade must be offered.
4. All age groups must be offered all four components (five foods, at the minimum quality specified) in order to meet the meal requirements.
5. "Offer versus served" is *required* in high schools but may be extended to other age groups.
6. The bread alternates were expanded to include enriched or whole-grain rice, macaroni, noodles, and other pasta.
7. The bread requirement of one serving a day was extended to include a minimum requirement for the week, making the weight, or amount, of the bread and bread alternate important.
8. The cottage cheese requirement was increased to more nearly equal the protein value of meats and other meat alternates.
9. The milk requirement was clarified by stating that unflavored or flavored whole milk may be offered as a choice but at least one of the following milks must be made available: unflavored fluid lowfat milk, unflavored skim milk, or buttermilk.
10. Choices of a variety of foods should be offered children to better meet their needs, appeal to their likes, and introduce them to new foods.
11. It is recommended that iron-rich foods be offered frequently, as well as foods high in vitamins A and C.
12. It is recommended that the quantity of fat, salt, and sugar be controlled.
13. Students and parents are required to be involved in the foodservice activities.

There are many points to consider when using the meal patterns and planning menus. The goals are to assure that the nutritional needs of the children are met and realistically within the other restrictions and with foods that students will eat.

The milk requirement of the meal pattern can be met by offering at least one of the following forms of fluid milk: unflavored lowfat milk, unflavored skim milk, or unflavored buttermilk. Choice of whole milk or chocolate milk is encouraged. Some nutritionists frown on using chocolate-flavored milk because of the increased carbohydrates and additional calories. However, in some schools milk consumption has increased when flavored milk was offered in addition to plain milk (Fig. 3.4). Many teenage girls, along with the American Dietetic Association, were pleased when the milk guidelines were changed in 1979 to require a lowfat milk be offered. However, when

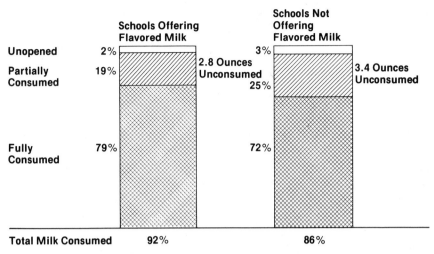

Total Milk Consumed   92%   86%

FIG. 3.4. In 1975 a USDA study showed a higher percentage of milk was consumed in schools that served chocolate milk than in those serving only white milk.

the nutritive content of plain whole, chocolate-flavored whole milk, and skim milk are compared (Table 3.5), one can see that the vitamin A content of skim milk is considerably less. Since the daily calcium requirement for a 10- to 12-year-old boy or girl is 1.2 grams, the ½ pt of milk provides only about 80% of the goal of supplying one-third the requirement; thus, other sources of calcium should be provided to supplement the milk.

Protein-rich foods are expensive and may consume one-third or more of the food dollar. For economy reasons a combination of meat, poultry, or fish and one of the less expensive meat alternates such as eggs, dry beans or peas, and peanut butter may be used in meeting the nutritional needs. The use of soy protein to meet a part of the protein requirement is a practical solution to rising food costs and to the possible shortage of meats anticipated 10 to 20 years from now. Since USDA approved the use of soy protein to meet up to 30% of the protein requirement, there has been a noticeable increase in the number of different brands of the product available on the

TABLE 3.5. Nutritional Comparison of Milks

1 Cup Serving (250 ml or ½ pt)	Calories	Protein (gm)	Calcium (gm)	Iron (mg)	Vitamin A (I.U.)	Thiamine (mg)	Riboflavin (mg)	Niacin (mg)	Vitamin C (mg)
Milk									
Whole	160	9.0	0.29	0.10	350	0.08	0.42	2.25	2.0
Skim	90	9.0	0.30	0.10	10	0.10	0.44	2.25	2.0
Chocolate whole milk	215	9.0	0.28	0.50	325	0.08	0.40	2.30	2.5
Chocolate drink skim milk	190	9.0	0.27	0.50	200	0.10	0.41	2.30	2.5

Source: Food and Nutrition Services, U.S. Dept. of Agriculture (1978).

market. Nutritionists question the long-range effects of using vegetable protein products in diets.

Since the meal patterns are designed to meet the nutritional needs of children of all ages, it is desirable to adjust the portions to meet the needs of a younger and an older child. The USDA has given definite guidelines on portion sizes, which are shown in Table 2.1.

NUTRITIONAL BENEFITS OF SCHOOL LUNCH

In 1966, 1970, 1972, and 1975 samples of lunches from different parts of the United States were analyzed for vitamins and other nutrients. On the average, the lunches served exceeded the goal of one-third of the 1968 Recommended Dietary Allowances for thiamine, riboflavin, niacin, vitamin D, and vitamin B_{12} for children 10 to 12 years of age. Riboflavin was in all cases in excess of the goal. Laboratory analyses were not made for vitamin C. Vitamin B_6, vitamin A, vitamin D, and thiamine were most often short of the goals. Other studies have shown that the school lunches have not achieved the goal for iron. The new meal patterns should better meet the goals, particularly for the B vitamins.

At the request of Congress, a study of the National School Lunch Program was initiated in 1979. The first results of this evaluation were released in April 1983 (Wellisch et al. 1983). Surveys were conducted of a nationally representative sample of 290 public schools with approximately 6500 students in grades 1–12. Students who participated in the lunch program, compared with those who did not, were eating higher-quality lunches that have the following characteristics.

- Higher in energy
- Higher in vitamin A
- Higher in vitamin B_6
- Higher in calcium
- Higher in magnesium
- Lower in vitamin C

The study confirmed that the school lunch program delivers benefits to those who participate in it, especially to poor students. However, the school breakfast program did not fare so well. Compared with alternative breakfasts, school breakfasts were superior only in milk-related nutrients. The breakfast program meal pattern is at fault.

In 1982 the University of North Carolina completed a regional research project that showed participants in school lunch and breakfast programs had significantly better nutrition and health than nonparticipants. For example, students between the ages of 6 and 11 who ate the school lunch consumed 70% more vitamin A, 6% more energy, and 20% more calcium, iron, and vitamins B_6 and C than did those who did not eat the school lunch. Teenagers, also, showed marked increases in daily consumption of eight essential nutrients compared with nonparticipants.

NUTRITION EDUCATION

Nutrition education should go hand in hand with a students feeding program aimed at meeting the nutritional needs of its customers. Funds were for a short time available for local programs in nutrition education. The Nutrition Education and Training Program was first funded by PL 95–177 in 1977 and much credit goes to Senator Hubert Humphrey for this. The program provides funds to states to encourage effective dissemination of nutrition information to children, to train foodservice workers, and to train teachers to teach nutrition. In 1978 the states received $26 million or 50¢ per child. However, beginning in 1979 the funding was cut each year until only $5 million was appropriated in 1982, 1983, 1984, and 1985.

Nutritional labeling laws have increased the interest in nutrition. The public is beginning to realize that malnutrition can and does exist in this land of plenty due to a lack of knowledge, not a lack of food. Nutrition education can provide a person with the necessary information to choose

FIG. 3.5.   School foodservice, as part of the total education of students, can be a model laboratory-classroom for nutrition education and related subjects.

foods needed to build a healthy body. The goals, however, are to change poor food behavior and habits. Therefore, nutrition education should attempt to bring about behavioral change. It is easier to establish good food habits than to change or modify food habits already established.

As pointed out by the White House Conference on Food and Nutrition in 1969, there has been a lack of interest in nutrition education for the past 20 years. Everyone leaving it to someone else to teach nutrition has often meant that only those students taking home economics have been reached. It has been realized that nutrition will have to become a part of the curriculum in order to assure that it is taught (Fig. 3.5). Parents need to be reached since the early impressions and attitudes toward food are often lasting ones. Television provides an excellent means for reaching parents and the small child during the very impressionable years.

With vending machines carrying a range of tempting snack foods, commercial foodservices with a concern for profits, and rising costs of nutritious foods becoming factors in school feeding, nutrition education is essential. The school foodservice program should provide a model laboratory-classroom for nutrition education in the years ahead.

BIBLIOGRAPHY

AD HOC COMMITTEE. 1969. Recommendations of Ad Hoc Committee on Nutrition Standards for School Lunch and Other Child Feeding Programs. U.S. Govt. Printing Office, Washington, DC.
AMERICAN ACADEMY OF PEDIATRICS. 1979. Pediatric Nutrition Handbook. American Academy of Pediatrics, Evanston, IL.
BETTELHEIM, B. 1972. Why school lunch fails. School Foodservice J. 26(3):36–39.
CALLAHAN, D. L. 1971. Focus on nutrition—you can't teach a hungry child. Part II. School Foodservice J. 26(8):25.
DWYER, J. T., M. F. ELIAS, and J. H. WARREN. 1973. Effects of an experimental breakfast program on behavior in the late morning. Master's Thesis, Harvard School of Public Health, Cambridge, MA.
FEINGOLD, B. F. 1974. Why Your Child Is Hyperactive. Random House, New York.
FOOD AND NUTRITION BOARD. 1980. Recommended Dietary Allowances. 9th edition. Natl. Res. Council, Natl. Acad. of Sci., Washington, DC.
GUTHRIE, H. A. 1977. Effect of a flavored milk option in a school lunch program. J. Am. Dietet. Assoc. 71(1):35–40.
HERBERT, V. 1981. Nutrition Cultism Facts and Fictions. George F. Stickley Co., Philadelphia.
HILL, M. M. 1968. Nutrition and the type A lunch. Nutrition Program News. U.S. Dept. Agr., U.S. Govt. Printing Office, Washington, DC.
LABUZA, T. P. 1977. Food and Your Well-Being. AVI Publishing Co., Westport, CT.
LEVERTON, R. M. 1965. Food Becomes You. 3rd edition. Iowa State Univ. Press, Ames.
LOWENBERG, M. E., E. P. NEIGE, T. HUNTER, E. D. WILSON, J. R. SAVAGE, and J. L. LUBAWSKI. 1968. Food and Man. John Wiley & Sons, New York.
McWILLIAMS, M. 1980. Nutrition for the Growing Years. 3rd edition. John Wiley & Sons, New York.
MURPHY, E. W., P. C. KOONS, and L. PAGE. 1969. Vitamin content of type A school lunches. J. Am. Dietet. Assoc. 55(4):378.
NATIONAL NUTRITION CONSORTIUM. 1975. Nutrition Labeling. The National Nutrition Consortium, Inc., Bethesda, MD.

PENNINGTON, J. A. 1976. Dietary Nutrient Guide. AVI Publishing Co., Westport, CT.

POLLITT, E., M. GOSOVITZ, and M. GARGUILO. 1978. Educational benefits of the United States school feeding program: A critical review of the literature. Amer. J. of Public Health 68(5):477–481.

READ, M.S. 1973. Malnutrition, hunger, and behavior. J. Am. Dietet. Assoc. 63:379–385.

ROBINSON, C. H. 1978. Fundamentals of Normal Nutrition 3rd edition. Macmillan, New York.

U.S. COMPTROLLER GENERAL. 1981. Report to the Congress. Efforts to Improve School Lunch Programs—Are They Paying Off? U.S. General Accounting Office, Washington, DC.

U.S. DEPT. OF AGRICULTURE. 1975. Nutritive Value of American Foods in Common Units. U.S. Govt. Printing Office, Washington, DC.

U.S. DEPT. OF AGRICULTURE. 1983. Menu Planning Guide for School Food Service. U.S. Govt. Printing Office, Washington, DC.

U.S. DEPT. OF AGRICULTURE & HEALTH, EDUCATION & WELFARE. 1980. Nutrition and Your Health: Dietary Guidelines for Americans. U.S. Govt. Printing Office, Washington, DC.

U.S. DEPT. OF HEALTH, EDUCATION & WELFARE. 1979. Healthy People, the Surgeon General's Report on Health Promotion and Disease Prevention Background Papers. U.S. Govt. Printing Office, Washington, DC.

U.S. OFFICE OF TECHNOLOGY ASSESSMENT. 1978. Nutrition Research Alternatives. U.S. Govt. Printing Office, Washington, DC.

WELLISCH, J. B., S. D. HANES, L. A. JORDAN, K. M. MAURER, and J. A. VERMBERSCH. 1983. The National Evaluation of School Nutrition Programs. Final Report—Executive Summary, Vols. 1 and 2. System Development Corporation, Santa Monica, CA.

WHITE, P. and N. SELVEIG. 1972. Chocolate milk vs whole milk in school lunch programs. J. American Dietet. Assoc., 62:220.

WILLETT, R. 1972. The dramatic age of nutrition. Food Management 7(1):54–67.

WILSON, E.D., K. H. FISHER, and M. E. FUQUA. 1975. Principles of Nutrition. John Wiley & Sons, New York.

ORGANIZATION MANAGEMENT

As school foodservices grew from "soup kitchens" to full-fledged businesses, it became necessary for them to become more and more organized. School foodservices are now competing with commercial firms for business within schools in many parts of the country and have had to become more accountable and very cost-conscious. A successful operation must operate on sound business principles—well organized and well managed. This is particularly true in the food industry, from large chain operations to a small sandwich bar. Each year 50% of the new commercial restaurants that open fail, and another 25% fail by the end of the third year. The food industry is a business of fragile intangibles. The basic principles of management are the same for restaurants, hospitals, residence halls, and school foodservices. The larger the foodservice operation, the more complex the organization becomes. School foodservices range from those in small individual schools serving less than 100 to those in centralized city and county units with 250–600 schools serving 100,000–500,000 meals per day.

PURPOSE AND PRINCIPLES OF ORGANIZATIONS

The purpose of an organization dealing with manpower is, according to West *et al.* (1977), "to accomplish with the efforts of people some basic purpose or objective with the greatest efficiency, maximum economy, and minimum effort, and to provide for the personal development of the people working in the organization."

For an organization to function effectively and to grow, it must utilize all resources—people, materials, and facilities—to their fullest. The most important of the resources is people. To be effective, an organization must provide for the people to be utilized to their fullest capabilities. To accomplish this, the organization must operate under some general principles:

1. A clear line of authority exists and is understood by the employees.

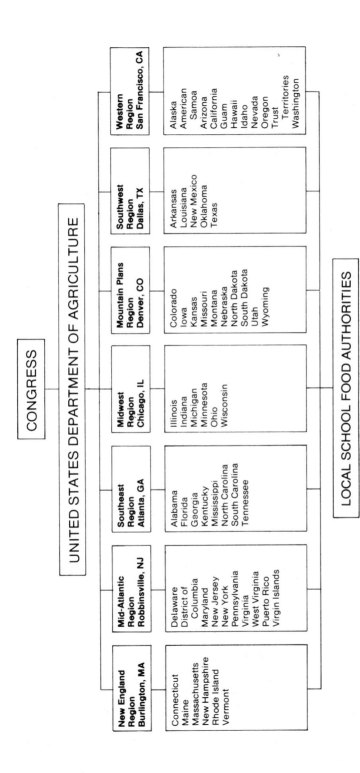

FIG. 4.1. Organizational chart showing responsibility for administration of the National School Lunch Program.

2. Objectives and goals are set and used as a measurement of success.
3. Responsibilities are clearly identified for each member of the organization.
4. Leadership is effective.
5. The necessary materials and equipment are available.

One of the very basic questions to be asked about any organization may be "Who decides there is one?" In the case of the National School Lunch Program, the laws start with Congress. The responsibility for administering the program is given to the Department of Agriculture. The Department of Agriculture administers the program through seven regional offices (Fig. 4.1). At the local level, the board of education is the overall governing body that enters into an agreement with the state education agency to carry out federal and state rules and regulations concerning school food programs. The agreement is made in order to receive federal and state cash reimbursement and USDA donated foods. The sample organization chart in Fig. 4.2 shows how a state's line of authority may be established. Foodservice is located within the state department of education in all states; however, that is about all the different states have in common. A typical delegation of authority in local school systems is shown in Fig. 4.3.

A detailed organizational chart should show the positions in an organization (and the current occupants), the responsibilities of the various positions, and the relationship among departments and services. Positions with

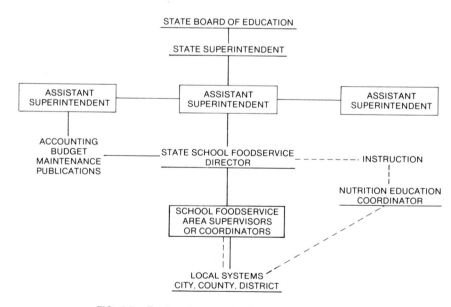

FIG. 4.2. Foodservice organizational chart—state level.

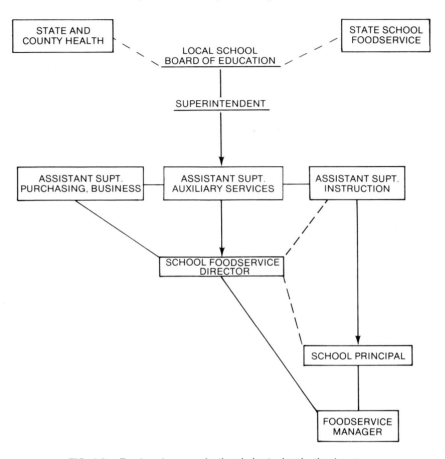

FIG. 4.3. Foodservice organizational chart—local school system.

the greatest authority are shown at the top of the chart with those with the least authority at the bottom. The line of authority is best shown and understood when displayed in the form shown in the examples (Figs. 4.2–4.5). It is important that each person in an organization knows to whom he or she is responsible and who is responsible to him or her.

For a school foodservice to function effectively within a centralized unit or in individual units, the *foodservice* needs to be an established part of the school system. If the board of education, which establishes policy, puts the responsibility for management and sale of all food and beverages under the school foodservice division, the program is more likely to be successful. The advantages of centralization are lost if authority and responsibility are not also centralized. Sometimes foodservice management fails because operational authority is divided. The foodservice management is merely a consul-

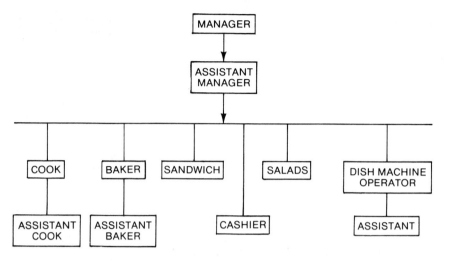

FIG. 4.4. Organizational chart for a large secondary school (single unit) with a la carte sales.

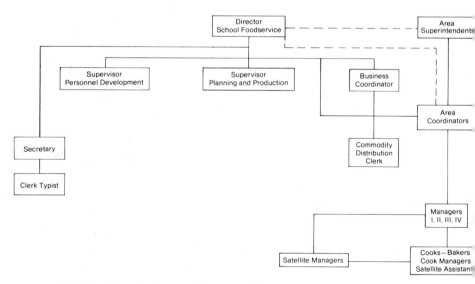

FIG. 4.5. Example of a well-structured school foodservice with 8 area coordinators for 168 managers.
Courtesy of Dade County (FL) Public Schools, School Foodservice.

tant when authority becomes divided. It cannot be held responsible for the successes or failures if the *authority* for carrying out policies, rules, and regulations has not been given with the *responsibility.*

OBJECTIVES OF MANAGEMENT

Management is responsible for planning, directing, and controlling the foodservice in a sound financial manner and for serving good, nutritious food as a part of the educational system. Management should (1) set the standards; (2) develop the objectives and goals; (3) make the policies; (4) do the planning and organizing; (5) communicate with the workers, the public, the parents, the school administration, and the board of education; (6) control quality of food; (7) control costs; (8) carry out the objectives and goals; (9) supervise and direct; (10) evaluate; (11) teach and encourage the growth of the foodservice workers; and (12) look out for the foodservice's welfare.

Standards are needed as a point of reference—as a means of evaluating. How can the cook know if he is doing a good job? How does the manager know if he is managing well? How does the director know if the foodservice is doing a good job? There are several measurements of the success of a school foodservice: comments from customers; percentage of participation (number served is some indication of customer satisfaction); cost per meal; number of meals produced per labor-hour; morale among employees; and the ratio of income to expenditures. These can be tools of measurement if there is a reference point, or standard, by which to evaluate each item. The director can look at each of the school foodservice units and evaluate it on the basis of objectives, goals, and standards.

Although specific objectives and goals may differ from school to school, five important general objectives should be adopted by all foodservices:

1. Operate the program on a sound financial basis within the budget.
2. Serve good quality, nutritious food to all students.
3. Teach good food habits.
4. Meet the needs of the students in a satisfying way.
5. Give employees an opportunity for personal development.

The objectives, goals, and standards of a school foodservice should be set by the people involved—the staff, the students, the administration and the board of education. All may have different aims or measurements of success. The dietitian-oriented food director may be mostly concerned about serving nutritious food, whereas students may not like the food served or may be tired of it and want changes, more choices, or different foods. The administration and board of education may be most concerned about whether the foodservice has a deficit. The objectives of a foodservice have to be a realistic combination of those of all involved.

JOB ANALYSIS, DESCRIPTION, AND SPECIFICATION

Once the basic plan of an organizational chart has been established and the line of authority is set, then it is important to analyze each job. A job analysis is used by management in preparing a job description and specification for each position.

Job Analysis

A job analysis is a look at the whole job: what the duties are; qualifications required; promotions possible; physical conditions of the work; and salary and fringe benefits. An outline for preparing a detailed job analysis is given below.

Job Analysis Outline

I. Title
   A. Code number
   B. Job definition
II. Duties
   A. Regular or daily duties
   B. Periodic duties (weekly, monthly, etc.)
   C. Occasional duties
III. Minimum Starting Requirements for Position
   A. Education
      1. Read, write, and speak English
      2. Elementary school—8 grades
      3. 1–2 years high school
      4. 3–4 years high school
      5. High school and some special training
      6. Partial college, 1–2 years
   B. Special training
      1. Pre-job training necessary
      2. On-the-job training needed
      3. Additional training recommended for advancement
   C. Experience
      1. Minimum required to enter occupation

    2. Related experience in other occupations
    3. Experience desirable to enter occupation
  D. Personal Qualifications
    1. Age range
    2. Physical size and strength desired
    3. Skills essential to performance on the job
  E. Other
    1. Certificate, such as health
    2. License
    3. Union membership
    4. Civil service examination
    5. Minimum score on standardized test
IV. Ways of Entering
  A. Public and special employment services
  B. Apprenticeship
  C. Other methods
V. Equipment and Materials Used
  A. Kinds of equipment and materials used
  B. Safety risks
  C. Equipment and uniform to be supplied by the worker
VI. Responsibility of the Worker
  A. Supervising work of others
  B. Independent judgment required
VII. Conditions of Work
  A. Hours
    1. Regular hours
    2. Amount and frequency of overtime
    3. Vacations with or without pay
    4. Regulations
      a. Local, state, federal
      b. Union
  B. Regularity of employment
  C. Physical demands: amount of time spent standing, walking, sitting, lifting, etc.
  D. Physical conditions of surroundings: heat, air conditioning, noise
  E. Contact with others: alone, few others, many others
VIII. Advancement
  A. Lines of promotion
  B. Opportunity for advancement
  C. Related occupations
    1. Occupations to which the job may lead
    2. Occupations from which one may transfer

IX. Earnings
   A. Basis for pay
      1. Amount of payment determined by hour, piecework, day, week, or month
      2. Frequency of payment, e.g., weekly, monthly
   B. Average pay for a beginner
   C. Average pay for a highly skilled worker
   D. Benefits
      1. Pensions
      2. Social security
      3. Unemployment insurance
      4. Sick leave
      5. Workmen's compensation
   E. Rewards and satisfactions in addition to monetary rewards

Job Description

A job description is a general description of the job, which provides management and the employees a mutual understanding of what the job entails. An example follows:

Job Description Sample

Job title: Foodservice Assistant
Grade step: II
Job definition: Prepare the main dish and vegetables.
General duties: Responsible for the preparation of the main dish and cooked vegetables. Is to prepare food for the serving line and keep all foods on the serving line at lunchtime. Responsible for the cleaning and maintaining of the small equipment, washing of pots and pans when needed. Will help with the general preparation and serving of food and the cleaning.
Requirements: Must be able to read and write English, to do simple arithmetic, be able to follow oral and written direction. Must have the capacity to grasp and adjust to new and changing situations. Manual dexterity and ability to work under pressure are desirable. Must be neat in appearance and is required to wear uniform-type clothing, hairnet or cap covering on hair, comfortable shoes. Health certificate is required.
Tools and equipment: Scales for weighing ingredients and portion control, mixer, ovens, ranges, steam cookers, steam-jacketed kettle, fryer, food chopper, meat slicer, vertical-cutter-mixer.
Working conditions: Work an average of 35 hours per week, Monday through Friday with school holidays, for ten months a year. Kitchen is well lighted, ventilated, and comfortable. Much standing on feet and some lifting are required.

Supervision: Responsible to the School Foodservice Manager. Gives supervision in large operations to an assistant cook.

Personal requirements: High school education or equivalency test. At least 1 year experience in foodservice preparation.

Job Specification

A job specification is a combination of a job analysis and description. It is used primarily in interviewing and selecting the person for a specific position. It is important for the prospective employee to know what a job entails, what clothes to wear, hours of work, and what will be expected of him before accepting the position. For example:

Job Specification Sample

Job title: Foodservice Assistant
Grade step: II
Department: Foodservice
Supervised by: Foodservice Manager
Job summary: Prepares main dish and vegetables
Education: High school education or equivalency test. Must be able to speak, read, and understand English. A test score of 50 or above required on "Knowledge Test."
Experience: 1 year previous experience in foodservice.
Health requirement: Recent health certificate.
Personal: Male or female, neat, clean, wears uniform.
Reference: Personal, two previous employees.
Hours: 7:30 a.m. to 2:30 p.m., Monday through Friday. School holidays, 30-minute lunch breaks.
Wage code: II-a.
Fringe benefits: Insurance, health, life; lunch; retirement; personal leave days; sick leave days.
Possible promotions: To assistant foodservice manager or cook–manager.

STATE ADMINISTRATIVE STAFF

There are no official guidelines for the administrative staffs on the state, county, or city levels. The responsibilities, authority, and salary of the state director and staff differ significantly from one state to another. State directors have realized this and asked time and again that job descriptions be developed by one of the governing agents as models. This is an area in which surveys, studies, and recommendations are needed. In general, the state director and staff are responsible for the following:

1. Providing leadership to school foodservices in the state
2. Interpreting relevant legislation, policies, rules, and regulations of federal agencies
3. Instructing, informing, and teaching school foodservice workers within the state
4. Representing the state in school foodservices matters
5. Providing accounting systems for reporting to the federal agency
6. Claiming, collecting, and distributing federal funds to the schools in the state
7. Administering and evaluating school foodservice programs

The state staff's responsibilities and the way they are carried out vary, as to their function within the state, the number on the staff, and the qualifications of that staff.

CENTRALIZED ADMINISTRATION

More and more school foodservices are operating yearly under a centralized organization. Counties, cities, and districts may organize under a board of education and have a group of schools under the control of one administration. When foodservice administration is centralized, a director or supervisor of foodservices is usually appointed to work under the general direction of the superintendent of schools or school business administrator. This person is responsible for working with the school managers in the units. The degree of control that central administration has over the school foodservices may vary from little control with only the financial aspects being centralized to very rigid control. Centralized planning may include planning menus, purchasing on bid, warehousing, fiscal control, and personnel. Many advantages can result from centralization of foodservice administration: more qualified leadership can be afforded; more purchasing power is obtained; better organization and management is possible; principals spend less time tied up with foodservice matters. All result in significant savings.

Local Director and Supervisor

The administrative staff on the local level may or may not have official guidelines, depending on the state and the school district. Many recommendations have been made in speeches by leaders and by task force groups in committee meeting reports, but little has been published. Task force groups and leaders, such as Josephine Martin, have recommended that "a foodservice specialist is needed for each 20 foodservice programs; this formula allows the specialist to devote a minimum of 4 hours individualized help per month to each program." This specialist is most frequently called a "supervisor." Supervisor is defined by Spriegal *et al.* (1957) as: ". . . any person who is responsible (1) for the conduct of others in the achievement of a particular task; (2) for the maintenance of quality standards; (3) for the protection and care of materials; and (4) for services to be rendered to those under his control."

Some school systems call the head administrator of school foodservice a *director.* The director of a county or city school foodservice, according to the American School Foodservice Certification Committee, is "one who plans, organizes, directs, administers the foodservice program in a school system according to policies established by the Board of Education." In smaller systems the director and supervisor may be one and the same. Ordinarily a director is employed when the system becomes complex and consists of more than 30 programs. Regardless of the size of the system, a director should have as a minimum qualification a Master's degree in foodservice administration or in related fields with a strong background in business. The larger the system and responsibility, the more experience, leadership, and education may be desired. As a part of an educational program, the director of foodservice should ideally be not only a business person but also an educator.

The *supervisor* or *coordinator,* is under the director, if there is one, in the line of authority. A supervisor is responsible for evaluating the programs, and aiding and generally directing the individual foodservice units. He or she works directly with the school foodservice units. The minimum qualifications for a supervisor should be a baccalaureate degree in foods. The larger the system and the more supervisors there are in the system, the more specialized they may be. For example, in the Dade County (FL) schools the director is assisted by a business coordinator, supervisor of planning and production, supervisor of personnel and development training, and eight area foodservice coordinators (Fig. 4.5).

An *assistant to the supervisor* is a term used for the position just below the supervisor but of the supervisory category. The assistant to the supervisor is responsible to the supervisor and/or director for evaluating, supervising, training, aiding, and carrying out the policies and objectives of the foodservice. The greatest part of this person's time is spent in individual schools. A minimum of a high school education and at least five or more years experience as a successful, outstanding manager of a school foodservice should be required. A college degree is most desirable for an assistant to the supervisor. However, a person with less education but with good training and experience in actual management can work very effectively with managers and workers in the schools.

Supervision is needed for effective administration of a foodservice program. A supervisor or an assistant supervisor for every 20 schools is a realistic level of control (Table 4.1).

TABLE 4.1. Administrative Staffing Guide
for School Foodservice

No. School Foodservices	Director	Supervisor or Coordinator	Assistant to Supervisor
1–15		1	
16–30		1	1
31–40		1	1
41–60	1	1	2
61–80	1	1	3
81–100	1	2	4
101–125	1	2	5
126–150	1	2	6
151–175	1	3	7
176–200	1	4	9
201–225	1	4	10

The amount of time that administrative staff can spend in the schools is an important consideration. The director will have less time than other staff due to the administrative demands on him or her. A minimum of 20% of the director's time should be spent in school foodservices. An assistant to the supervisor should be in the schools 75% of the time; whereas the supervisor, due to special assignments, may be limited to 50% of the time in actual supervision.

The line of authority is usually as shown in Fig. 4.3. The reason the principal is put into the line of authority over the manager is that the manager of foodservices should be considered a member of the school's staff. The manager should receive directions from the school foodservice supervisor working with the principal.

Good sound leadership from the director and supervisors is necessary for progress and success of the program. Some of the characteristics of a good administrative leader are the following:

1. Stimulates leadership within the group.
2. Builds morale.
3. Develops cooperation.
4. Disciplines when needed.
5. Has knowledge and understanding of human nature.
6. Delegates responsibility and authority.
7. Has the ability to make decisions.
8. Instructs subordinates properly.
9. Listens to others' ideas.
10. Has high expectations of employees.

The attitude of the director and other leaders has a significant influence on the people they supervise and their accomplishments. Workers respect a leader who informs the staff of policies, of what is expected of them, maintains set standards, and disciplines those who do not abide by those standards. A leader should maintain good working conditions, represent and support workers with management, have a good attitude and boost morale, and have good public relations. It is desirable for a leader to encourage workers to think, to give suggestions, and then give recognition to those who deserve it. A leader should make decisions carefully and stand by the decision, accept the responsibility for workers, and impartially promote workers when merited. More and better work is obtained by praising employees at the right time than by criticizing them. Employees must want to do the job if their efforts are to produce good results.

There are basically three styles of manager: (1) authoritarian—one who gives orders, dictator; (2) laissez-faire—one who gives free-rein; (3) democratic—one who leads through cooperative means and through encouraging participative management. Democratic management produces more creativity, ingenuity, and involvement among employees. Participative management requires trust and confidence between workers and management. It is a means of increasing the involvement of workers in the decision-making processes that directly affect their lives.

Good work should be recognized, and poor work deserves constructive criticism. Employees deserve to be trained, to be guided, and to have a clear understanding of what is expected of them. The job description, followed by work schedules, can give the guidance and understanding of what is expected of them.

School foodservice needs more qualified people to fill management positions. In 1972 the American School Foodservice Association conducted a survey which indicated that of the 16,530 school districts in the United States that were participating in the National School Lunch Program, only 1461 school districts had educationally qualified supervisors, that is, supervisors with degrees in the foodservice field.

School Foodservice Manager

A manager has the responsibility for the administration of the unit school and works under the school system's foodservice director or the school principal. In a decentralized system, a manager may be responsible for all the planning, purchasing, and staffing as well as other tasks. The duties and responsibilities of a manager in a centralized system include the following:

1. Carrying out the rules and regulations of federal and state agencies and of the local board of education
2. Preparing and serving food that meets the nutritional needs of the students: prepare the food in a safe and sanitary way; prepare appetizing and attractive food in the correct quantities and of high quality;

use standardized recipes and procedures; and serve standardized portions

3. Managing personnel in a way to help prevent grievances and undesirable situations: promote teamwork and efficient production; provide on-the-job training and means of growth for employees; provide a safe and pleasant atmosphere in which to work; plan and assign work of the employees by means of outlining duties and work scheduling

4. Purchasing food and supplies in the quality and quantity needed. Checking, receiving, and storing food and other items properly

5. Promoting good public relations with the students, faculty, and parents. Assist in offering nutrition education to the students

6. Maintaining a sanitary foodservice: make sure that employees have had health examinations and are healthy; promote high standards of sanitation and comply with the local and state health regulations and codes of sanitation

7. Controlling the financial management within the budget: prepare and maintain accurate and adequate records of the income and expenditures, and the number of meals served

8. Evaluating the operation and correcting deficiencies

To carry out all of these responsibilities, a manager must have training and experience. The manager must be able to perform all the jobs in the foodservice; have a knowledge of nutrition and menu planning, food cost control, and personnel management; and must know and understand the importance of good sanitation. The manager must have a knowledge of the general care and operation of all the equipment in the kitchen. The booklet *School Food Service Workers Other than the Director and Supervisor* (Am. School Food Service Assoc. and Assoc. Business Officials, n.d.) lists the following qualifications for a manager:

1. Graduation from high school
2. Knowledge of nutritional requirements for children and youth
3. Knowledge of basic menu planning based on the nutritional requirements of the Type A lunch pattern and other types of school foodservice and on other factors (flavor, texture, temperature, color, shape or form, and attractive servings)
4. Knowledge of menu planning work sheets
5. Knowledge of purchasing procedures
6. Personal cleanliness
7. Sanitary practices in food preparation
8. Knowledge of training programs for accident prevention and use of safety precautions
9. Experience in use of standardized recipes and methods of quantity food preparation which retain nutritive values

10. Experience in keeping accurate records of food cost control, recipe costing, menu costing, inventories, participation records, labor cost control, and profit and loss

11. Ability to organize and manage a school foodservice program, which includes in-service training program on personnel relations, work schedules, and policies relating to the school foodservice program

12. Ability to work with others in a pleasant and cooperative manner

To obtain people with these qualifications, a school foodservice nearly always has to train its own employees or work closely with the local comunity college, vocational or technical training center, and universities for this purpose. The basic knowledge may be obtained through courses, but experience as an assistant to a manager is desirable to become competent in carrying out all the responsibilities.

BIBLIOGRAPHY

AM. SCHOOL FOOD SERVICE ASSOC. and ASSOC. BUSINESS OFFICIALS. 1965. The school food service director. Bull. 3. Am. School Food Service Assoc., Denver, CO.
AM. SCHOOL FOOD SERVICE ASSOC. and ASSOC. BUSINESS OFFICIALS. (n.d.) School food service workers other than the director and supervisor. Am. School Food Service Assoc., Denver, CO.
ANON. 1972. State directors cost out school meals. School Foodservice J. 26(7):22.
BELASCO, J. A., D. R. HAMPTON, and K. F. PRICE. 1975. Management Today. John Wiley & Sons, Inc., New York.
CLOYD, F. 1972. Guide to foodservice management. Institutions Volume Feeding Magazine, Chicago, IL.
COLEMAN, J. 1970. Instructor's Guide: Management of Food Service. Florida Dept. Educ., Tallahassee.
CUMMINGS, T. G. and E. MOLLOY. 1977. Improving Productivity and the Quality of Work Life. Praeger Publishers, New York.
DONNELLY, J. H., Jr., J. L. GIBSON, and J. M. IVANCEVICH. 1975. Fundamentals of Management. 2nd edition. Business Publication, Dallas, TX.
DRUCKER, P. F. 1974. Management. Harper & Row, New York.
ESHBACH, C. E. 1979. Foodservice Management. 3rd edition. CBI Publishing Co., Boston.
FRANCIS, D. and D. YOUNG. 1979. Improving Work Groups: A Practical Manual for Team Building. University Associates, San Diego, CA.
JUN, JONG S. and E. N. DYOTM. 1973. Tomorrow's Organizations: Challenges and Strategies. Scott, Foresman and Company, Glenview, IL.
HANNI, R. B. 1968. Development of evaluative procedure for assessing operational-efficiency of school food service. Ph.D. Thesis, Ball State Univ., Muncie, IN.
KAHRL, W. 1973. Planning and Operating a Successful Food Service Operation. Chain Store Age Books, New York.
MALI, P. 1972. Managing by Objectives. John Wiley & Sons, Inc., New York.
NICHOLSON, R. H. 1966. Centralization trends in school lunch systems. Proceeding from Association of School Business Officials. The Association, Evanston, IL.
SISK, H. L. 1974. Management and Organization. 3rd edition. Southwestern Publishing Co., Cincinnati.
SPRIEGEL, W. R., E. SCHULTZ, and W. B. SPRIEGEL. 1957. Elements of Supervision. 2nd edition. John Wiley & Sons, New York.

STOKES, J. W. 1973. How to Manage a Restaurant or Institutional Food Service. 2nd edition. Wm. C. Brown Co., Dubuque, IA. and Forestry. U.S. Govt. Printing Office, Washington, DC.

U.S. SENATE, 92ND CONGRESS. 1971. Hearing before the Committee of Agriculture.

WEST, B., L. WOOD, V. HARGER, and G. SHUGART. 1977. Food Service in Institutions. 6th edition. John Wiley & Sons, New York.

ZABKA, J. R. 1971. Personnel Management and Human Relations. ITT Educational Services, New York.

PERSONNEL MANAGEMENT

Managing people is one of the most challenging of all the jobs of an administrator or supervisor. The people in an operation—their attitudes, abilities, desires, and interests—influence the success or failure of the operation. Management sets the standards but must depend on its employees to carry them out. *Personnel management* can be defined simply as the directing of people in carrying out the jobs to be done.

Why do people want to work at a certain place? Money may come to mind. However, surveys have shown that money is low on the list of reasons for wanting to work at a certain job. Five of the main reasons employees list for being happy with a job are (1) security; (2) feeling of belonging; (3) good supervision; (4) opportunity for promotion; (5) job satisfaction—the job is interesting, challenging, and provides a feeling of accomplishment. The turnover rate for school foodservice is relatively low (11% nationwide) compared with that in other types of foodservice, such as the fast-food industry (165%).

"How much labor is enough?" is a difficult question to answer. Some foodservices may be staffed with twice the labor-hours that are really needed to carry out the job and still complain "we need more help." Low productivity and unplanned work may be the main reason for such a situation. To staff a foodservice properly may require more than a staffing guideline. To obtain high productivity in a foodservice usually requires a combination of several of the following: time and motion studies, planned work schedules, finding more efficient ways of carrying out each job, purchasing laborsaving equipment, rearranging equipment, changing menus and serving periods, and motivating employees.

STAFFING

Lunch Programs

No magic formula can be used for staffing all foodservices. The type of employees needed and the labor-hours will differ for numerous reasons from one operation to another. Management has to set and enforce reasonable limitations on the number of labor-hours permitted. However, training employees well and making changes that increase their efficiency will lead to higher productivity in most operations.

Factors Influencing Amount of Labor Needed. Some of the factors that should be considered in determining the number of employees and the number of labor-hours needed in a particular foodservice are discussed here.

Foodservice system used. Labor needs are different for kitchens with on-site preparation, finishing kitchens, central kitchen operations, etc.

Number of meals served. In smaller operations (serving under 200 meals) labor cost is a higher percentage of total costs than it is in larger operations serving 400 or more meals. The larger the operation, the higher productivity should be.

Menus. A no-choice lunch menu takes fewer labor-hours than a choice menu. A la carte service and preparation require additional labor-hours. Breakfast menus usually require less preparation, therefore fewer labor hours, than lunch menus.

Type of food used. Whether food is purchased already prepared or partially prepared or is prepared from scratch in the foodservice kitchen greatly influences the labor needs of an operation. A hamburger menu could be prepared using ground beef in bulk, frozen hamburger patties, or precooked hamburger patties. The more-prepared purchased food is, the more it costs; but less labor should be involved in using it. When a commercial bakery bakes breads and other baked goods for a foodservice, the food cost goes up and the labor cost should go down: it should not require the same number of labor-hours if the baking is done by the commercial bakery. Use of preplated frozen dinners, frozen entrees, preportioned foods, precooked foods, and other forms of prepared food will have an effect on labor needs. The number of labor-hours has to be decreased as convenience items are used more. The greatest pitfall in using convenience items, which usually cost more but require less labor in preparation, is that management does not cut the labor. Therefore, the cost of food goes up but the labor cost stays the same, and a deficit results.

Number and length of lunch periods. Most staffing formulas are based on three 30-minute lunch periods. When the lunch periods are 45 to 60 minutes or there are more of them, additional labor-hours are usually required to handle preparation before lunch and after-lunch cleanup and pre-preparation.

Kind and arrangement of equipment. Labor-saving equipment can make for higher productivity and labor economy. A conveyor dishwasher in a foodservice serving 350 to 400 meals will wash the dishes in less time and the operator's time can be better utilized than is possible with a door-type dishwasher. The arrangement of equipment in an efficient manner can ensure higher productivity. A spacious, spread-out kitchen will mean additional labor-hours and a lot of wasted steps for the employees. A more compact kitchen with efficiently arranged equipment cost less to build and can be operated with less labor than an overly spacious kitchen.

Number of serving lines.   One serving line requires from one to three people serving the food, depending on the menu, and a cashier. Two lines may require twice the number of people to cover the stations at serving time. In order to have the number of people needed at serving time, some employees may work only 2 or 3 hours as needed.

Experience and training of employees.   The training and years experience of employees influences their productivity. However, perhaps "training" of employees rather than "experience" is more important because the employee's prior experience may have involved inefficient work methods.

Supervision.   The ability of a manager to assign duties and train employees will determine, in large part, the staff needed.

Type of dishes used.   When all disposable dishes (single use) are used, the labor-hours needed should be approximately one-half hour less per 100 lunches than needed if reuseable dishes are used and machine washed. If the amount of labor cannot be reduced proportionately as the cost of disposables increase, an unbalanced budget may result.

How Much Is Enough?   The guidelines published by many of the states' school foodservices show an average of 13 to 20 meals per labor-hour. West *et al.* (1977) recommend 12 to 14 lunches per labor-hour. Wynn (1973) in Broward County, Florida, has found that using a positive approach ("How many meals can we produce with a certain number of labor hours?") has resulted in very high productivity. The county averages 16 meals per labor-hour and has set 12 meals per labor-hour as its minimum goal in schools using a dishwashing machine and 13 meals per labor-hour in schools using disposables. Training has increased their productivity, also. The school foodservice in Fairfax County, Virginia, has increased productivity from 9 meals per labor-hour to an average of 16.5 in less than 10 years.

With wages and fringe benefit costs having increased threefold in the last 10 years, it is essential to increase productivity by using some convenience food items and labor-saving equipment. The staffing guidelines shown in Table 5.1 have worked successfully in hundreds of school foodservices. They are suitable for a self-contained unit, where the menu choice is limited, some labor-saving devices are available, dishwashing is done, and some but not all bread is baked on the premises.

TABLE 5.1. Staffing Guidelines
for School Lunch Program[1]

Number Lunches Served	Meals per Labor Hour	Total Hours
Up to 100	9½	9–11
101–150	10	10–15
151–200	11	15–17
201–250	12	17–20
251–300	13	20–22
301–350	14	22–25
351–400	14	25–29
401–450	14	29–32
451–500	14	32–35
501–550	15	35–36
551–600	15	36–40
601–700	16	40–43
701–800	16	43–50
801+	18	50+

[1] These recommendations do not include hours for breakfast, a la carte, or dinner.

Distribution of Labor-Hours. The number of labor-hours available should be distributed throughout the work day according to need (e.g., to provide enough people at serving time). A combination of part-time and full-time workers is usually the most efficient way of staffing a foodservice. One-meal-a-day school foodservices do not need cooks and bakers for 8 hours. It may be necessary for the manager of a large school foodservice to work 8 hours per day, but seldom is any other employee needed for more than 6 hours. The productivity of foodservice workers is greatest during the first 6 hours and declines after that. Also, school foodservices in most of the country draw their labor force from "housewife-mothers" who make excellent workers, but who may want a job that permits them to be home when their children get home from school. Students have been successfully used in many school districts at serving time. Because of higher transportation costs, many adults will not come to work for 2 hours. High school students can work, if their class schedules permit 1 or 2 hours and be paid accordingly.

Breaking down the labor hours and distributing them wisely over the work day will require some experimenting with adjusting of employees' arrival and departure times. Wynn (1973) states that in an elementary school "no one except the manager needs to arrive more than 3 hours before serving time." In distributing the labor-hours available, the number of employees needed at serving time should be decided first. For example, in a school foodservice serving 300 lunches per day, four or five people are needed at serving time: two servers, one cashier, a dish-machine operator, and one person backing up the line. According to Table 5.2, this size opera-

TABLE 5.2. Staffing Guide for School Foodservice Serving 300 Lunches[1]

Position	Hours
Manager (backup)	6½
Cook (Cashier)	6[2]
Baker (serve on line)	5[2]
Dishmachine operator and serve on line	3½
	21

[1]Based on 14½ meals per labor-hour.
[2]Fifteen minutes for break is included in this time. The employees eat lunch on their own time.

tion would require 20–22 hours of labor. A possible distribution of labor hours among different employees is shown in Table 5.2.

An operation that serves 500 lunches would require 36 to 40 labor-hours according to the staffing guide. If the school had two serving lines with three lunch periods (11:30, 12:00, and 12:30), the distribution of hours could be as shown in Table 5.3. The 6 hours assigned to the cook are needed in this size operation.

School foodservices should be conscious of how much time is spent in preparation and cleanup. The more skilled employees should be utilized in preparation, and the less skilled employees for cleanup.

Labor Cost. The labor cost in a foodservice where food is prepared on-site and served with use of limited convenience foods and few dispos-

TABLE 5.3. Staffing Guide for School Foodservice Serving 600 Lunches[1]

Position	Arrival/Departure[2]	Total Hours[3]	Assignment at Serving Time
Manager	7:30–2:30	6½	Supervision
Cook	8:00–2:30	6	Line I backup
Assistant cook	8:30–2:30	5½	Line II backup
Baker/Desserts	8:00–2:00	5½	Serving, Line I
Salads, etc.	9:00–2:00	4½	Serving, Line II
Cashier (Head)	10:30–2:30	3½	Line I cashier
Cashier	11:00–1:30	2	Line II cashier
Dishroom	9:30–2:30	4½	Dishwashing
		38	

[1]Based on 16 meals per labor-hour.
[2]Ten minutes for break is on work time. Employees' lunch (30 minutes) is on their own time but is included in arrival/departure times shown.
[3]Hours paid.

ables should average between 30 and 35% of the income. As pointed out previously, the more convenience foods and disposables used, the lower the percentage of income that can be spent on labor. Staffing and labor cost must be correlated. How much it would cost to staff according to the guidelines in Table 5.1 will depend on the wages and fringe benefits paid. In order to determine if the recommended staffing is within the labor cost that can be afforded, multiply the anticipated income by 30% and 35% to obtain the allowable dollar range. Take the average wages per hour and multiply by the number of labor-hours (from Table 5.1). Then compare this figure with the 30 to 35% of the anticipated income. See the following example:

Calculation of Anticipated Income per Day

Elementary school serving 300–325 lunches and charging 90¢ per lunch.

Served:
250 Paid

250 paid lunches @ $0.90	$225.00
250 lunches @ $0.12 federal reimbursement	30.00

50 Free

50 free lunches @ $1.10 federal reimbursement	55.00
50 free lunches @ $0.10 state reimbursement	5.00

10 Reduced

10 reduced-price lunches @ $0.70 federal reimbursement	7.00
10 reduced-price lunches @ $0.40	4.00
A la carte sales	12.25
Value of USDA-donated food @ $0.15 per child	
× 310 children	46.50

10 Adult

10 adult lunches @ $1.40	14.00
Anticipated income per day	$398.75

Calculation of Allowable Labor Cost per Day

At 30% of income ($398.75 × 0.30)	$119.63
At 35% of income ($398.75 × 0.35)	139.56

Calculation of Labor Cost Based on 15 Meals per Labor-Hour

Staffed with 21 hours and with average wages of $5.00 per hour (includes manager) plus 25% fringe benefits.

Cost for 21 hours @ $5.00	$105.00
Fringe benefits ($105.00 × 0.25)	26.25
Total labor cost	$131.25

In this example, the calculated labor cost is within the allowable range of 30 to 35% of anticipated income. However, if the income or productivity (meals per labor-hour) were significantly less, this would not be the case and adjustments would have to be made in the operation. For example, foodservices serving under 200 meals with no additional income from a la carte sales are likely to have labor costs that are more than 35% of the income. In most cases they should become finishing kitchens or be co-managed. The larger the operation, the greater productivity should be. A centralized preparation kitchen will have higher productivity as the volume increases and more labor-saving equipment is made available. In Los Angeles and Corpus Christie centralized preparation is taken a step further: the food is preplated in the central kitchen, eliminating the need for many labor-hours in the kitchen where the food is to be served.

A La Carte Staffing

Many secondary schools and some elementary schools sell food separately or in addition to the regular meals. Staffing of a la carte service varies depending on the number of items offered and preparation to be done. When the foods being sold a la carte are prepared on the premises, the labor needs and costs are greater but the food cost lower than they would be if prepared items are bought and sold.

Two different methods may be used to arrive at a staffing. Using a labor cost of 25 to 35% of the income is workable in most situations. Use 25% of the income for labor cost when the food is all prepared items and requires no preparation, only recording and selling. A labor cost of 30% of income is reasonable when some preparation is required; this percentage increases as the food cost decreases and the amount of labor needed increases. For example:

$220 a la carte income (sale for the day)
$220 × 0.30 (30%) = $66.00 can be spent on labor

To determine how many hours can be used, divide $66.00 by the average wages and fringe benefits paid:

$66.00 ÷ $4.20 per hour = 15.7 hours

Suppose the school in the previous example, which served 300–325 complete lunches per day, also offered a la carte items with sales of $220 per day. The total staffing would be 36 labor-hours: 21 for the regular lunches and 15 for the a la carte service.

Another method to use is to convert all food sales (in addition to regular lunches) to the equivalent of work as preparing the lunches (Table 5.4). The formula of $1.50 equal to 1 meal is based on the time needed in preparing and serving a la carte foods: that is, it takes approximately the

TABLE 5.4. Converting a la
Carte Food Sales to Meals
per Labor-Hour

Sales	Equivalent Number of Lunches
$ 1.50	1
30.00	20
60.00	40
75.00	50
100.00	67
150.00	100

same amount of time to prepare and serve $1.50 worth of a la carte items as one lunch. This formula should be adjusted to fit the individual situation. If the a la carte or other food sales are purchased prepared items, then the labor needs will be less. The above formula assumes some preparation is done in the kitchen, such as making salads, sandwiches, and soup, and mixing juices.

Breakfast Staffing

The amount of labor needed for a breakfast program depends on the number of meals served and how much preparation is necessary (Table 5.5). When the menu consists of "engineered cake" and ½ pt of milk, hardly any labor is needed. Volunteer labor could certainly be used. Labor cost can be kept at a minimum by using foods that can be prepared with the lunch the day before. Dovetailing the preparation and cleanup of breakfast with that of lunch reduces the labor needs. Using disposables instead of dishwashing may be an advantage if the labor is needed for only a short time and is unavailable for that short a time.

With a relatively simple breakfast such as the federal guidelines would provide (½ pt milk, ½ cup fruit or vegetable or fruit juice or vegetable juice, and serving of cereal or bread with protein-rich foods when budgets best allow) the staffing that seems to work best is based on 20 to 30 meals per labor-hour.

Scheduling of Work. With careful planning and preparation, ½ to ¾ hour should be adequate for preparing most breakfasts for serving. Serving usually takes less than 15 minutes and cleanup requires ½ to 1 hour. An example of scheduling of work for breakfast follows:

Menu

Orange juice (½ cup)
Scrambled egg (1)
Cinnamon toast (1 slice)
Milk (½ pt)

Number served: 50
Employees: 1½-hour employee (7:30 to 9:00): Person in charge of breakfast
1-hour employee (7:45 to 8:45): Assistant

Time	Person in Charge of Breakfast	Assistant
7:30	Turn oven on Pour juice in disposable cups	
7:45	Prepare scrambled eggs	Prepare cinnamon toast
8:00	Set up line	Set up line
8:10	Serve breakfast	Serve breakfast
8:25	Cleanup	Cleanup Portion jelly for next day
8:45	Prepare records and reports	

The a la carte sale of juice, sweet rolls, cereal, milk, and other items on the menu, particularly in secondary schools, can add to income. Usually the

TABLE 5.5. Staffing Guide for School Breakfast Program

Number Breakfasts	Number Labor-Hours	Number Employees	Breakdown of Hours per Person
Up to 20	1	1	1
30	1½	1	1
40	2	2	1½ ½
50	2½	2	1 1½
75	3	2	1½ 1½
100	4	3	1½ 1½ 1
125	5	3	2 2 1
150	5–6	3	2 2 1–2

labor-hours assigned for breakfast are added to a part-time employee's hours; for example, a 4-hour employee may be assigned one additional hour for breakfast and become a 5-hour employee. Many foodservices are able to add a breakfast program without increasing labor-hours. If the foodservice is operating at a deficit or is overstaffed, this should certainly be considered. Also, this is a way of increasing productivity and encouraging better use of employees' time. Time and motion economy, pre-preparation, dovetailing (combining jobs), and good planning will result in a smooth operation with high productivity.

Any foodservice with a reasonably smooth operation can adjust to the addition of a breakfast program with little or no problems if the staffing recommendations given here are followed.

RECRUITING

Recruiting of employees is best done on a continuous basis. Preparing for a vacancy and being selective, rather than being forced to hire a person less qualified than desired because of immediate needs, is good personnel management. It may be a problem to find labor in one area, and thus there is a greater need for recruiting. In order to recruit, job descriptions (see Chapter 4) stating the required minimum standards for employment are needed.

Making people interested in the job, in the organization, in foodservice, and being known as a good employer can go a long ways toward self-perpetual recruiting. Using job titles that sound appealing can increase the desirability of the job: "cafeteria hostess," "dish-machine operator," and "cafeteria aide or assistant" have more appeal than "kitchen helper," "dishwasher," "pot washer," and "kitchen worker." Good public relations are also important for the foodservice. A story on the foodservice concerning the valuable service it provides to a community's children, employees' accomplishments, or other items of this nature in a local newspaper can make people interested and jobs more appealing. Some effective ways of recruiting follow.

Internal recruitment is good for employee morale. Whenever a position is available, it should be announced so that current employees have a chance to advance. Supervisors should encourage good workers to apply for a better position. Going outside to hire a new person when there are qualified people within a foodservice will kill incentive. Employees also can be a source of finding people who want a job. They can spread the news of job openings to friends, neighbors, and relatives. However, relatives of employees should not be employed in the same cafeteria.

Advertising through newspapers, trade journals, notices in public places, and over radio or television can get results. Many local papers and radio stations will carry public service announcements free of charge. Recruiting at high schools, vocational schools, and colleges can be very effective. Many schools have placement offices or a school newspaper, which can be used for recruiting. In some cases, the work can be instructional in nature and count toward laboratory experiences in vocational training programs.

Personnel management should have potential managers, cooks, and bakers lined up for promotion. The position of assistant manager can be utilized to train someone for a manager's position so that when a vacancy comes up, management does not desperately have to pick an untrained replacement. Training programs should include courses for people interested in management, with on-the-job-training under the direction of a good manager until a vacancy occurs. Most skilled cooks and bakers can teach others their skills. This prepares someone to assist them, to take their place if they are sick, and to be ready for promotion when an opening occurs. Training for promotion can often be done on an employee's own time. Adult education schools are often eager to help sponsor classes in this area. Recruiting outstanding people into the foodservice will result in a better program. Recruiting should mean looking ahead and having replacements ready.

APPLICATION AND INTERVIEW

The use of written job applications is mandatory regardless of the size of a foodservice operation. The application form should be simple and ask only questions that are pertinent, legal, and useful to the employer. Figure 5.1 shows a very simple form of application.

Applications usually ask for *references.* Checking these references can be very valuable and can help in making a better choice when hiring. If references are not checked, an application has lost much of its value. References are often checked by telephone, in which case a few simple questions about the applicant's honesty, attendance and punctuality, length of employment with company, quality of services, and reason for leaving will probably be adequate.

Turnover is expensive and careful hiring practices can cut down the amount of turnover. A *personal interview* with applicants provides them with a chance to see if they want the job and would like working for this foodservice; most importantly it gives management an opportunity to evaluate applicants' attitudes, interest, ability, and compatibility with other employees. The interview can help significantly in the selection of a qualified person. When a head cook or baker is interviewed, a test involving the interpretation of a recipe can help determine knowledge of food preparation, as well as the ability to read and write.

An interviewer should keep in mind the two purposes of an interview before employment: (1) to introduce applicants to the school foodservice,

CLASSIFIED EMPLOYMENT BRANCH

LOS ANGELES UNIFIED SCHOOL DISTRICT

APPLICATION

DO NOT WRITE IN THIS SPACE

EXACT NAME OF JOB YOU ARE APPLYING FOR

PLEASE ANSWER EVERY QUESTION BELOW RETURN THE APPLICATION AS SOON AS YOU HAVE COMPLETED IT ASK FOR HELP IN COMPLETING THE APPLICATION IF YOU NEED IT. PRINT IN INK OR TYPE. Your Social Security Number will be used for employment related identification purposes only.

PRINT YOUR NAME HERE

DATE	YOUR STREET ADDRESS	CITY	ZIP CODE
PHONE NUMBERS State Area Code (If not 213):	HOME	BUSINESS	SOCIAL SECURITY NUMBER

EDUCATION (CIRCLE HIGHEST GRADE COMPLETED)   7   8   9   10   11   12   AA   BA-BS   MA-MS

DATE COMPLETED

What other training or education have you had which might help you on this job?
For example: Have you taken any special courses? Do you speak, read, or write a language other than English?

LAST

WORK EXPERIENCE (PAID AND UNPAID) Start with the job you have now, or your last job, if you are not working now.
Check (√) this box ☐ if you do not want us to contact your present supervisor.

		EMPLOYMENT DATES	
1. EMPLOYER	ADDRESS	FROM:	TO:

YOUR JOB TITLE AND DUTIES

YOUR SUPERVISOR'S NAME	CHECK (√) ONE:	☐ FULL-TIME ☐ PART-TIME

		EMPLOYMENT DATES	
2. EMPLOYER	ADDRESS	FROM:	TO:

FIRST

YOUR JOB TITLE AND DUTIES

YOUR SUPERVISOR'S NAME	CHECK (√) ONE:	☐ FULL-TIME ☐ PART-TIME

		EMPLOYMENT DATES	
3. EMPLOYER	ADDRESS	FROM:	TO:

YOUR JOB TITLE AND DUTIES

YOUR SUPERVISOR'S NAME	CHECK (√) ONE:	☐ FULL-TIME ☐ PART-TIME

MIDDLE (MAIDEN)

Have you ever taken a test for a job with the Los Angeles Unified School District? ☐ Yes ☐ No
If yes, was the test on a tape recorder? ☐ Yes ☐ No
If the test is given in more than one place, (√) check the place you'd rather take it.
☐ South-Central L. A.   ☐ East L. A.   ☐ Harbor Area   ☐ West L. A.   ☐ Central L. A.   ☐ San Fernando Valley   ☐ Pacoima Area
IF YOU HAVE EVER WORKED FOR THE LOS ANGELES UNIFIED SCHOOL DISTRICT, COMPLETE THE FOLLOWING:

		EMPLOYMENT DATES	
YOUR EMPLOYEE NUMBER	PRESENT OR LAST JOB TITLE	FROM:	TO:

WHERE DID YOU WORK?	YOUR NAME WHEN YOU WORKED FOR US, IF DIFFERENT

IF YOU ARE NOT NOW EMPLOYED BY THE LOS ANGELES UNIFIED SCHOOL DISTRICT STATE REASON FOR LEAVING

ALL OF THE ANSWERS ON THIS APPLICATION ARE TRUE
TO THE BEST OF MY KNOWLEDGE (SIGNATURE) ——▶

DO NOT WRITE BELOW THIS LINE

FIG. 5.1. Sample application of employment.
Courtesy of Los Angeles Unified School District, School Foodservice.

kind of work, pay scale, fringe benefits, hours, personal leave, etc.; and (2) to enable the interviewer to evaluate whether applicants are qualified to do the job, would fit into the organization, and has the appropriate attitude toward the work. When a management position for a foodservice is being filled, the objective of the interview is a little more complex. The interviewer is then interested in the applicant's ability to direct others, knowledge of the overall operation of a foodservice, personality characteristics important to the job, and overall qualifications. It is best if two or more persons interview an applicant, particularly for management; then a pooled judgment is possible and usually more reliable.

Conducting an Interview

Interviews should be conducted in privacy without interruptions, in a pleasant, comfortable situation. Since the applicant may be nervous, an "ice-breaking" question of mutual interest and unrelated to the job will help relax the applicant. The interviewer should be in charge of the interview. Questions should get the person talking and most questions should require more than a yes or no answer. Some typical questions that can be used in interviewing an applicant are the following:

1. Have you had any experience in cooking and serving food to large numbers of people? Do you like to cook?
2. What do you see yourself doing 5 years from now?
3. How would you describe yourself?
4. What really motivates you to do your best?
5. Why should I hire you? What do you think you will contribute to the program?
6. How do you work under pressure?
7. Why do you want to work for school foodservice?
8. Where have you worked before? Which jobs did you like best? Which did you like least? Why? If the applicant has had no previous work experience, you may refer back to high school, and ask, "What was your best subject?"
9. Do you know of anything that will prevent you from being at work regularly and on time?
10. Does our starting salary meet your current needs?
11. What courses have you taken in high school or college pertaining to foodservice?
12. Do you have any questions about the job?

Questions should be limited to those that are relevant and legal. The Equal Opportunity Law (Title VII of the Civil Rights Act of 1964) prohibits an employer from discriminating against job applicants because of race, color, sex, religion, or national origin. Questions related to political beliefs, age, marital status, dependent status, sexual preference, and handicaps that are not job restrictive should not be asked. An employer could be subject to a discrimination complaint if such questions are asked. A conscious attempt should be made to hire, at all levels of the organization, employees who are representative of the sex and ethnic balance of the community's labor force.

A written application and personal interview may be sufficient for evaluating an applicant for a supervisory position whose past experience can be checked and educational background is verified by college transcripts. Written tests are an added tool for evaluating a person's qualifications and ability for management. Such a test should question basic knowledge needed for carrying out the job. The overall qualifications the interviewer is looking for with the application, references, test, and interview include the following:

1. Physical—good health, not overweight, walks easily, good sight and hearing; someone who can work at the speed desired, free from infectious diseases and skin conditions. (These are all best determined through a pysical examination.)
2. Education—ability to read, write, and comprehend simple directions is essential for all positions in foodservice. The greater the responsibility, the more education desirable.
3. Personal appearance—clean, well-groomed, cheerful, direct, alert, and interest in the position offered.

When there are a number of applicants for a position, the evaluation of the interview, the application, the references, and the test become more important. In all fairness to applicants, these tools for evaluation should be weighed on the same scale. A rating chart may be very helpful. Assign a numerical rating to each qualification; for example, education might be assigned 1 point for less than 6th grade education, 2 points for 6th to 9th grade education, 3 points for 10th to 12th grade education, 4 points for high school diploma, 5 points 1 year college, 6 points 2 years college, 7 points 3 years college, 8 points bachelor's degree, etc.

EMPLOYMENT POLICIES

Contracts

Employees feel much more secure and more responsible when they have a signed contract. However, most school districts simply notify employees of their assignment and salary for a coming year; within a specified time an employee must notify the school if he or she does not plan to accept the position. Contracts in the true sense of the word are uncommon. Civil service procedures do protect the employee.

Performance Reviews

The first 4 to 12 months of employment may be a probationary period in which the worker is evaluated; at the end of this predetermined period, the employee is given a written evaluation (Fig. 5.2). Based on this evaluation, the employee may be dismissed, given an extended probationary period if his performance is in doubt, or made a permanent employee. The first evaluation or performance review is the most important; however, another evaluation should be done 4 to 6 months later and yearly thereafter.

The task of rating employees is very difficult and can be unpleasant. It is easier to give a good or excellent rating than to tell someone he is not doing the job well. A performance rating can be very valuable and should be carefully done and written with the employee fully aware of the evaluation. The employee's signature and the evaluator's signature should appear on the evaluation.

Performance reviews or evaluations should be used in making decisions about salary increases, promotions, transfers, lay-offs, and dismissals. Too often, length of service is the prime criterion for promotion. The ability of a person, not age or years of service, is a better criterion. Foodservices would do well to follow the trend of the eighties and base reward on merit.

Performance of managers and supervisors should be reviewed and evaluated too. They are appraised on entirely different standards than other employees, that is, on the quality of work and quantity of work they get done through others. Evaluations of managers and supervisors should be based on the following considerations:

1. Employee turnover, problems with employees, morale of employees who work under the person
2. Standards of sanitation—health department checks
3. Quality of food and service—customer satisfaction and income, percent of participation
4. Profit and loss of the foodservice—sound financial situation
5. Personal appearance, public relations
6. Absenteeism and tardiness
7. Efficiency in carrying out the rules and regulations of the system and duties of the job

Performance indicators should be established for each position. The measurements are basically in four areas:

- Quantity—how much someone produces
- Quality—how well it is done
- Timeliness—how long it took
- Cost—at what cost

PERFORMANCE EVALUATION FOR CAFETERIA MANAGERS
FOOD SERVICES BRANCH — LOS ANGELES UNIFIED SCHOOL DISTRICT

Last Name	First Name	Employee Number

Job Title	School or Other Work Location

Report for .... to .... Indicate dates during which employee is being evaluated.
(Date)   (Date)

If "Below Work Performance Standards" is checked, please see Paragraph 5 on the reverse side of this form.

Exceeds Work Performance Standards
Meets Work Performance Standards
Below Work Performance Standards

Comments Made by Supervisor

1. SUPERVISORY ABILITY ☐ ☐ ☐

a. Organizing and scheduling staff work   a. ☐ ☐ ☐
b. Training and instructing staff   b. ☐ ☐ ☐
c. Dealing with staff fairly and impartially   c. ☐ ☐ ☐
d. Maintaining staff adherence to rules and regulations   d. ☐ ☐ ☐
e. Ensuring use of standard recipes and menus, meal component requirements, and principles of good nutrition   e. ☐ ☐ ☐
f. Ensuring use of approved price and portion schedules   f. ☐ ☐ ☐
g. Maintaining attractive food appearance and merchandising   g. ☐ ☐ ☐
h. Menu planning, including student and community involvement   h. ☐ ☐ ☐
i. Ordering, storing and inventorying of food supplies   i. ☐ ☐ ☐
j. Maintaining records, reports, and monetary and ticket controls   j. ☐ ☐ ☐
k. Ensuring good housekeeping, sanitary and safety practices   k. ☐ ☐ ☐
l. Controlling labor and food costs   l. ☐ ☐ ☐
m. Maintaining cafeteria security   m. ☐ ☐ ☐
n. Assuring proper equipment use and energy conservation   n. ☐ ☐ ☐

2. WORK HABITS ☐ ☐ ☐

a. Maintaining a good attendance and punctuality record   a. ☐ ☐ ☐
b. Complying with oral and written instructions   b. ☐ ☐ ☐
c. Keeping supervisors informed of major work problems   c. ☐ ☐ ☐
d. Adaptability to emergencies and new situations   d. ☐ ☐ ☐
e. Willingness to undertake additional needed training   e. ☐ ☐ ☐

3. RELATIONSHIPS WITH OTHERS ☐ ☐ ☐

a. Other classified employees, faculty, and supervisors   a. ☐ ☐ ☐
b. Pupils   b. ☐ ☐ ☐
c. Parents and community representatives   c. ☐ ☐ ☐

4. OVERALL WORK PERFORMANCE ☐ ☐ ☐

Signature of Site Administrator	Date

Signature of Area Food Services Supervisor	Date

It is understood that, in signing the Performance Evaluation Form, the employee acknowledges having seen and discussed the report. The employee's signature does not necessarily imply agreement with the conclusions of the supervisor. If desired, the employee may attach a written statement.

Signature of Employee

(OVER)

122

INSTRUCTIONS FOR PREPARING PERFORMANCE EVALUATION FORMS
FOR CAFETERIA MANAGERS

1. An evaluation must be completed and discussed with each permanent employee at least once a year, prior to the closing of the regular school year in June.

2. The evaluation is to be completed by the employee's immediate supervisor *and* technical supervisor. In most cases, this is the site administrator in charge of the cafeteria and the school's Area Food Services Supervisor. The evaluation can be prepared and served jointly or separately, depending upon the wishes of the site administrator.

3. The employee's evaluation is recorded by placing a check mark ($\sqrt{}$) in the appropriate box opposite the factor being evaluated. Evaluations are to be based on observation or knowledge, and not on unsubstantiated or undocumented charges or rumors. No evaluation may be based on derogatory materials in the employee's personnel file unless the employee has been given prior notice of and an opportunity to review and attach his or her comments to such material.

The supervisor shall:

a. Discuss the written evaluation with the employee.

b. Review with the employee the duties of his/her current job, job performance standards, and how well the employee meets those standards.

c. Sign the performance evaluation form and obtain the signature of the employee or a witness.

d. Give the employee a copy of the completed form. If the employee has left the work location, forward the employee's copy to the local Classified Personnel Office, requesting that it be mailed to the employee.

e. Send the original copy of the performance evaluation to the Classified Selection Section, Business Services Center, by school mail.

f. Retain the triplicate copy for school files.

USE OF COLUMNS AND ADDITIONAL FORMS

4. **Meets or Exceeds Work Performance Standards.** A check in either of these columns indicates that the employee's work is satisfactory or better. If the employee's work is truly exceptional and worthy of special notice and commendation, a Notice of Outstanding Work Performance (Form 80.21) should be used.

5. **Below Work Performance Standards.** If any factor is rated below work performance standards, the following must be included in the **Comments** box:

a. A statement of the problem or concern.

b. The desired improvement and suggestions on how to improve.

Continued failure of the employee to show improvement should lead to preparation of a Notice of Unsatisfactory Service (Form 5302).

6. An employee who disagrees with the evaluation should contact the Head Office of the Food Services Branch.

FIG. 5.2. Performance evaluation form for foodservice managers.
Courtesy of Los Angeles Unified School District, School Foodservice.

Pay Scales

The pay scale for jobs in a foodservice should be comparable to other jobs in the community requiring similar skills. State labor laws, minimum wage laws, and local laws also will influence the pay scale. Pay increases should be worked out in steps and grades to give an incentive and to keep the morale of employees high. Most employees want to feel they are being paid what other persons are being paid for the same job with the same or comparable qualifications. People are happier or more content with their jobs if they know what kind of raise to expect, what they have to do to obtain it, and when they can expect to obtain it.

A manager of a foodservice should be paid on the basis of how many meals are served, the size of the operation, years of experience, formal education completed, number of state-approved courses completed, and performance. Some foodservice units use the total income of the operation to determine the rate of pay a manager will receive. This should be correlated with the profit and the quality of the operation. Some school systems use the salary scales of the instructional staff as a basis for determining salaries of foodservice managers. Certainly if a manager has an education equal to that of a teacher, the responsibility of a manager warrants such a pay scale.

Promotions

Foodservice employees should expect opportunities for growth and reasonable chances for promotion. The possibility of promotion to a position that has more responsibility and pays more is an incentive to perform better. Therefore, fairness in promotions is essential. Merit is of prime importance in promotion; however, the length of service should be used when there is a choice between two people of equal qualifications and equal quality of performance. Midwest City-Del City (OK) School Foodservice promotes to a higher classification or an increased number of hours depending upon job performance, tenure and training, willingness to work the number of hours and time of day required, and attitude toward job and ability to work with people.

Resignations

Resignation occurs when an employee voluntarily decides to give up his or her job. It is good administrative policy to require that resignations be submitted in writing. This written resignation will prevent any misunderstanding and will become a part of the employee's permanent personnel record. The person should be interviewed to find out the reasons for leaving. If the reasons are related to the job, the employer should want to be aware of these and correct them. Reasonable notice of resignation should be expected by the employer. "Reasonable" will depend on the cause for resignation, but under ordinary circumstances a 2-week notice is adequate.

Fair Employment Practices

What do the phrases "fair employment practices" and "equal employment opportunities" mean to a foodservice manager? They are embodied in many laws administered by the federal government and prohibit discrimination against a person because of race, color, religion, nationality, or sex. A manager should be very careful that these laws are not broken when handling personnel problems.

"Affirmative action" refers to a law that encourages recruitment, employment, and training of minorities. Also, the Equal Pay Act of 1963, which is administered by the Labor Department's National Labor Relations Board, requires equal pay for women for equal work. These fair employment regulations are especially important to the school foodservices that handle their own personnel duties. If there are unions involved, Title VII of the 1964 Civil Rights Act has power over fair employment practices.

Employee Handbook

Communication is the single most important way of preventing misunderstandings and avoiding unhappy employees. The policies of an organization should be known to its employees. A written handbook is desirable and can prevent misinformation. The handbook does not have to be an elaborate publication, but it should inform employees of the policies regarding (1) promotion, (2) termination, (3) leaves of absence, (4) pay scale, (5) overtime pay, (6) holidays, (7) pay periods, (8) personal or annual leave, (9) sick leave, (10) health benefits, (11) insurances, (12) workmen's compensation, (13) transfers, (14) demotions, (15) grievances, (16) dress code, (17) health certificate or tuberculosis test requirements, (18) retirement, and any other policies or benefits that the employee would be interested in.

Personnel Records

The application, references, test results, and interview evaluation are all a part of an employee's personnel record, as is each performance review. Correspondence concerning an employee's work and any actions taken concerning promotions, leaves of absence, etc., should become part of the record. This record should be kept for at least 10 years after an employee

Name_____ S. S. Number_____

Home Address_____ Telephone No._____

_____

Date Employed_____ Position_____

Rate of Pay_____ Place Assigned_____

Raises and Changes:

Date	Salary Increase	Step/Grade Change	Place of Assignment

Leave of Absence_____ Returned_____

Termination_____ Reason_____

Comments:

FIG. 5.3. Sample personnel record that can be kept on 5 × 8 inch cards or entered into the computer for quick, easy reference on all active personnel.

has left for reference purposes. For managements convenience, an active personnel file should be made, possibly using 5 × 8 inch cards for pertinent information (Fig. 5.3).

Orientation of New Employees

New employees are almost always ill-at-ease. They need to be informed of the rules and know what is expected of them. An informative talk with the manager should let new employees know the hours of work, coffee breaks, lunch breaks, rules and regulations, use of the time sheet, whom they are responsible to and whom they can ask questions of, location of washroom and toilet facilities, and the philosophy of the foodservice. An introduction to fellow employees and a friendly reception from them should be expected. New employees should be shown the kitchen, storerooms, dining room, and given a tour of the operation with explanations about the equipment. Any equipment that is dangerous and perhaps unfamiliar to new employees should be explained and demonstrated and its safety features pointed out. Systematic job training should begin at this point. Detailed work schedules (see Chapter 6) should be given to employees and step-by-step instructions should be given about what they are to do and how. If the manager does not do the training, then the training should be planned and the employee put under the guidance of an experienced employee.

The personnel handbook or policy manual should be explained to all new employees. A more detailed explanation and discussion of the foodservice traditions, aims, and policies should be given employees as their training period continues. The objective of this orientation period is to challenge their interest and encourage them to learn.

TRAINING PROGRAMS

Management owes it to its employees to provide opportunities for their personal development. There are many advantages to be realized from good training programs: (1) reduction in labor turnover; (2) less absenteeism; (3) fewer accidents; (4) lower production costs; (5) better morale of employees; (6) greater job satisfaction and fewer complaints and grievances; (7) higher rate of productivity; (8) better sanitation practices; and (9) lower food cost and less waste.

Group training saves time, and the group acts as a stimulus for individuals to approach new topics. It is important to use well-trained teachers and not fellow workers. The group will accept a certain amount of instruction from a fellow worker but not much. An able instructor can stimulate and inspire employees to want to learn. It is important to develop the individual as well as help him or her master routine skills.

The American School Food Service Association has set certification standards, which are administered by the School Food Service Foundation. The
Foundation encourages the expansion of foodservice courses being offered.
The standards are set as guides for each state for making courses available,
issuing certification, and compensating the advancement. A few states have
required certification programs. Since 1960, Mississippi's State Department
of Education has required that all school foodservice managers be certified.
The certificates are valid for a period of 1 year but can be renewed for 3-
year periods by completing a Basic II Course of Study offered by an approved school lunch institute.

North Carolina's Department of Public Instruction has developed a series
of six training courses in cooperation with the Department of Community
Colleges. Instruction is presented via television with classroom instruction
provided by community colleges and technical institutes throughout the
state. The courses are designed for 30 hours of instruction, and on completion the trainee is awarded a certificate from the institute. Pay increments
are recommended to local boards of education. The state legislature passed
a bill in 1971 that requires local foodservice supervisors to attend one of the
three supervisor's workshops sponsored by the state yearly.

California has made many training opportunities available to foodservice
employees. Many other states offer similar training programs. Also, universities and colleges, adult education classes, and technical institutes offer
school foodservice courses. For example, Purdue University offers several
correspondence courses with college credit that are very appropriate for
school foodservice employees. An outstanding collection of materials—
audio and visual aids—useful in teaching such courses is housed at the Food
and Nutrition Information and Education Materials Center, National Agriculture Library in Beltsville, Maryland.

In late 1970 federal funds were made available to states and local districts
through the Nutrition Education and Training Program (PL 95–166) for
training of foodservice employees. The need for these funds was pointed
out by the Inspector General's Office with the audits that were done in the
late 1970s. The funds made it possible for all states to offer training to their
foodservice employees; these programs were continued even after federal
funds were cut.

PERSONNEL PROBLEMS

One person can be a very destructive force on group spirit. Management
can hope by careful selection processes to select workers who will build
morale and can work well with others. However, this is sometimes not the
case.

Experienced management is often able to observe symptoms of problems and forestall any serious difficulties among staff members. Upward and downward communication are the most important steps to running a smooth operation. When employees are informed and involved in decision-making, a feeling of belonging and togetherness will occur. When employees do have complaints, a manager should listen very carefully. If an argument has occurred between employees, it is usually advisable to let the employees get over their emotional upset and then gather all the facts from all individuals involved.

Personnel problems can often be prevented if there is a definite line of authority, a definite field of responsibility, work schedules, clear, concise instructions, adequate supervision, and good working conditions. If a problem does arise, management should consider how to prevent it from happening again. Often a problem occurs when management has failed to discipline or correct one or more of the workers but rather "let it ride." Action should be taken, in the form of a talk with the employee about the problem and what you expect him or her to do to correct it. Tardiness, frequent absences, wasting time, excessive talking, spreading rumors, gossiping, stealing, refusing to obey orders, drinking liquor or taking narcotics on the job, having a hangover, and using foul language are all behaviors that warrant a manager discussing the problem with an employee.

Managers should avoid losing their temper when handling these matters. Other pitfalls to avoid are idle threats, bluffing, using profanity, humiliating a worker in front of others, scolding a worker publicly, striking a worker, and being sarcastic or apologetic. "Quality circles" (discussed in Chapter 6) and "nominal group techniques" are two more formalized means of letting employees be heard. These methods can have positive effects with the younger employees coming into the work force.

Disciplining Employees

When an employee is not carrying out the duties of the job or when personnel problems are being caused by his or her behavior, it is the responsibility of the supervisor or manager to counsel or discipline the employee in some way. Disciplining an employee may involve oral warning, demerits on the employee's record, a separate (isolated) job, less desirable work assignment, being sent home for the day, restricted chances for promotion, suspension, or dismissal. The method used will depend on the seriousness of the situation and the policy of the operation.

There are some points to remember when counseling and disciplining an employee:

1. Wait until you and the employee have had a chance to cool down if anger and excitement has been displayed.
2. Talk with the employee in private. It is embarrassing to be reprimanded in front of other employees.

3. If you criticize the employee's performance, do not compare it with another employee's performance.
4. Allow the employee an opportunity to tell his side of the story or to explain his performance.
5. Discuss ways of improving and changes that will need to be brought about. The employee should then be given time to improve. It may be advisable to put what action is to be taken in writing.

For the sake of all employees, a manager or supervisor must use fair disciplinary measures. It is an important part of personnel management. Employees desire to work in a climate that encourages cooperation and high morale. One employee with an attitude of resentment, sullenness, or uncooperative behavior can destroy the morale of others and keep a whole group of employees upset. An unsigned employee survey might help an employer uncover the reasons for poor morale and personnel problems.

When disciplining is necessary, an interview or talk with the employee should be the first step in solving the problem. If this fails to correct the problem, then transfer, demotion or suspension, or dismissal may be appropriate.

Transfer

In a centralized school system a transfer of an employee from one unit to another may solve a personnel problem. This is particularly true if a personality clash is the cause of the problem. Some people cannot work peacefully together. If the employee has references showing he is capable of being a good worker, the reason for the present problems should be analyzed to determine if a transfer is recommended. However, the employee should be made aware of why he is being transferred to another school and that the transfer represents a second chance to perform adequately.

Demotion/Suspension

In some cases demotion of a person to a less important position may be the desired action when a personnel problem occurs. An employee should be warned of this possibility before the actual demotion is made. This method of discipline may be most suitable when an employee does not take on the responsibilities of the position very well or is unable to give orders to those under him satisfactorily.

Suspension or time off from the job without pay may be appropriate action for an employee with excessive absenteeism or tardiness. This may work especially well with less mature employees.

Dismissal

Dismissal occurs when a person leaves a job involuntarily. Studies have shown that the most frequent reasons for dismissal are inability to get along with others and unsatisfactory work. It is only natural that all people do not get along, and if there is a personality conflict, it is usually wise to make some type of change. If a person has undesirable traits such that he cannot work in a "people" oriented job, he or she should be dismissed. It is only fair to warn an employee if his job performance or attitude at work is unsatisfactory. A talk in private about this, with a chance for the employee to correct the problem, is good policy. The way an unsatisfied employee is treated, even one disliked by the other employees, has an effect on the morale of the employees and may cause insecurity among them if they feel they may be dismissed without adequate warning.

For the personnel records, for future reference, and just to be safe any warning about unsatisfactory work and what is to be done to correct it and the time allowed for an outcome should be in writing. The larger the system and the more employees, the more important this policy is. Dismissals are unpleasant, usually have a defensive air about them, and should be handled by a mature person.

Dismissals on the spot in the fit of anger should be avoided. If managers have this authority, they may act in an irrational way when angered. Reasons for dismissal, which should be written in the employee handbook, include the following:

1. Excessive absence and tardiness
2. Unsatisfactory performance and inablility to perform the tasks assigned
3. Proven dishonesty
4. Conviction of a job-related crime
5. Insubordination, discourteous conduct, and disobedience
6. Drinking alcoholic beverages or taking narcotics on the job or being under the influence on the job
7. Accepting gratuities from suppliers
8. Violating administrative rules and regulations
9. Immoral or unethical conduct that affects the work
10. Inability to work with others

A dismissal should be recorded in a written notification form. The employee to be dismissed should be given a final interview in which the reasons for the dismissal are reviewed. Strong points of the employee should also be brought out. If the employer feels he can recommend this person for another position, the employee should be told this and perhaps helped in obtaining another position. All dismissed employees should have a chance to express themselves and a right to appeal if they feel they have been treated unjustly.

UNIONS

Employees have the right, under the Federal Labor Management Relations Act of 1947, to form, join, or assist a union. Any foodservice is subject to becoming unionized. A union will recruit employees until it has gained the necessary membership to become recognized. As soon as management becomes aware of union activity in its organization, it should prepare for the relationship with the union. When the union has sufficient members, it will demand consultation or meetings with management. Each of the steps in the process of unionization entails detailed procedures and legal requirements. Experts in the field can be of tremendous assistance and advise management on the legal aspects.

A union generally drafts a contract for management's consideration. This draft can include anything from already established practices to some outrageous non-negotiable items. Sooner or later contract negotiations come about. It is usually not advisable for top management to be present during the actual negotiations, because once it has spoken the negotiations take on a degree of finality. Negotiations usually require some give and take by both sides to arrive at a document that both sides can live with.

A contract between a union and management is a binding agreement. It usually gives a union the right to protect the workers' rights, help solve their problems, enforce the agreement (contract), recruit new members, and work with management. Management retains the right to manage but, with a contract, has another party looking over its shoulder. However, there can be advantages to a contract that does spell out who can do what and under what conditions. Dismissing someone who has broken provisions of a contract becomes a "business matter" and management may feel more action can be taken in this respect when there is a union than when there is not. Written reports and good records of actions taken in regard to employees become more important and essential when an organization is unionized.

BIBLIOGRAPHY

BEACH, D. S. 1975. Personnel: The Management of People at Work. 3rd edition. Macmillan, New York.
BENDER, R. and D. VANEGMOND-PANNELL. 1982. Successful change for productive growth. School Food Service J. 36(8):100–102.
BLACK, J. M. 1970. How to Get Results from Interviewing. McGraw-Hill, New York.
BLAKE, R. R. and J. S. MOUTON. 1981. Productivity: The Human Side. AMACOM, American Management Assoc., New York.

CLOYD, F. 1972. Guide to Foodservice Management. Institutions Volume Feeding Magazine, Chicago.

CONNELLAN, T. K. 1978. How to Improve Human Performance: Behaviorism in Business and Industry. Harper & Row, New York.

FLIPPO, E. B. 1976. Principles of Personnel Management. 4th edition. McGraw-Hill, New York.

FRANCIS, D. and D. YOUNG. 1979. Improving Work Groups: A Practical Manual for Team Building. University Associates, San Diego, CA.

HARRIES, J. O., JR. 1976. Managing People at Work. John Wiley & Sons, New York.

HUGHES, C. L. 1976. Making Unions Unnecessary. Executive Enterprises Publications Co., New York.

HUNT, J. W. 1971. Employer's Guide to Labor Relations. The Bureau of National Affairs, Inc., Washington, DC.

KNOLL, A. P. 1976. Food Service Management—A Human Relations Approach. McGraw-Hill, New York.

SIEGEL, J. 1980. Personnel Testing under EEO. AMACOM, American Management Assoc., New York.

SWEENEY, N. R. 1980. Managing People: Techniques for Food Service Operators. Lebhar-Friedman Books, New York.

U.S. DEPT. OF AGRICULTURE. 1977. A Profile of School Food Service Personnel. U.S. Govt. Printing Office, Washington, DC.

WEST, B. B., L. WOOD, V. HARGER and G. SHUGART. 1977. Food Service in Institutions. 6th edition. John Wiley & Sons, New York.

WYNN, J. T. 1973. Staffing Broward County style. School Foodservice J. 27(1):44–54.

ZABKA, J. R. 1971. Personnel Management and Human Relations. ITT Educational Service, New York.

WORK PLANNING AND SIMPLIFICATION

According to the *Washington Post* in 1980, the United States ranked with Great Britain in having the lowest rate of productivity gains (27%) during the previous 10 years. In the same period, the productivity of Japanese workers increased by 107% and that of West Germanys by 70%. As a result of these findings, President Reagan and Congress established a White House Conference on Productivity. Its purpose was to study the decline in the U.S. rate of production since 1979.

The productivity, or output per hour, of American workers, grew at a fairly steady annual rate of 2.5% between 1948 and 1974. It remained almost flat for the next 4 years and then began to decline by about 1% yearly. The Conference on Productivity, convened in October 1983, identified a number of factors contributing to the recent decline in productivity, which is a serious matter and is a threat to the nation's economy. One of the biggest factors is the use of outdated, unautomated equipment in American factories and businesses, including school foodservice kitchens. The productivity of foodservice kitchens will remain level until kitchens are rid of bulky, unwieldy pieces of equipment. This is a major problem to be dealt with during the 1980s.

In the school kitchen organizing and planning the use of time are essential to improving efficiency. The purpose of personnel management should be effective utilization of human resources and staff time. The food industry is known to have very low productivity—40 to 45% of time yields useful work. Thus, if employees are making an average of $5.31 per hour ($4.25 plus $1.06 in fringe benefits), it is in effect costing $13.28 for an hour of useful labor. Planning the work with the conscious objective of improving employees' performance can increase productivity and result in a lower labor cost.

134

WORK PLANNING

The planning of work in any organization may take several forms. It may be no more than in informal understanding among employees about what each person does and agreement that everybody helps each other when need be. In more formal approaches to work planning, supervisors give verbal directions to employees about their work assignments or prepare written work schedules for the entire staff.

Written plans prevent misunderstanding and forgetting of assignments. A work plan should be made regardless of staff size, whether the staff consists of 2 or 22 people. A good work schedule is a written assignment of jobs; that is, someone is designated to do each specific job at a particular time until all jobs and duties are scheduled—daily, weekly, and monthly. Daily scheduling of the tasks in an operation is the heart of organizing time.

The purposes of work schedules are to inform employees of the work to be done, the responsibility of each employee and the sequence of each employee's duties with time requirements. Some of the advantages of using work schedules in a school foodservice are the following:

1. Saves time and energy. Setting deadlines will encourage speed. An employee making 50 sandwiches with no time limit probably will not finish as soon as an employee who is given a time limit.

2. Makes the job easier. Employees who know what to do next and do not have to constantly ask someone can do their jobs better, with less effort, and possibly dovetail some jobs.

3. Helps make a smooth, efficient operation. Efficiency is not obtained by close supervision.

4. Helps employees develop a sense of security and pride in their work. When specific work goals are set, the responsible employee can feel pride and accomplishment in fulfilling the goals and completing the job.

5. Reduces the possibility that a job will be left incomplete or undone. Scheduling helps assure that jobs will be done on time and that the food will be ready to serve on time. Jobs that are frequently left undone or forgotten include putting the condiments out, cutting butter, and filling napkin and straw dispensers; but yet it is important that they be done.

6. Distributes responsibilities and workload more evenly. Helps prevent the possible complaint that "she doesn't do her share."

7. Gives a manager more time to "manage" without the constant interruption of employees asking "what should I do now?"

8. Sets goals and benchmarks. Helps motivate employees and yields feelings of accomplishment and job satisfaction.

Of course, work schedules do not assure that the quality of the food served in a school will be better or that its nutritional value will be adequate, but they do help. They simply let all employees know what jobs they are responsible for and when the work must be done.

A properly staffed kitchen can seldom do the work required without being organized and planned. Delegating duties and responsibilities are important parts of foodservice management. Work schedules should be prepared ahead. The manager is responsible for preparing work schedules, though the staff can help divide the duties. The assignment of work should always be done by someone who knows both the operation and the workers' abilities.

When cycle menus are used, work schedules can be prepared and reused with slight changes, saving considerable time. In a centralized school district, work schedules can be standardized to some extent; this saves considerable time for each manager. Each manager, however, will still need to assign a specific person to each job.

Work schedules should include assignments for housekeeping and general cleaning. The cleaning chores that are done daily, weekly, and monthly can be standing assignments. Rotating some of the undesirable jobs may be advisable in some cases. Rotation of simple cleaning jobs works well, but with jobs that require skills, rotation is obviously not recommended. Efficiency and improvement come from experience and conscious efforts to improve, whereas rotating jobs tends to reduce employees' pride and feeling of responsibility and does not afford the chance for improvement and increased efficiency.

Pre-preparation for the next day's menu should be considered when a work schedule is planned. This requires that a manager look ahead and not consider just the jobs required for a particular day. When the menu requires little preparation, much time can be wasted unless the time is utilized in preparing for another day's menu. Work schedules should help distribute the workload more evenly, so that employees do not feel overworked on any particular day.

Preparing work schedules helps managers to determine the particular hours they need workers most. For example, a 4-hour worker may be needed more for serving and cleanup than during the morning preparation. Each person's work should be distributed evenly over the entire day or hours worked. A trained cook or baker should be utilized with a less skilled person assisting and cleaning up. Rest periods should be distributed over the day with a short break after every 2 to 3 hours of work.

Employees should eat a snack or lunch before the school lunch period. Their productivity during the peak serving time will be greater if they have already eaten. When employees eat lunch before serving it, the food can be tasted for seasoning, and adjustments made if need be. Also, this practice discourages employees from nibbling or eating while serving, prevents the nervousness that sometimes results from being hungry, results in less overeating by employees, and reduces the likelihood that employees will be sleepy and lack energy in the afternoon. In general, when employees eat before serving, shorter lunch breaks result.

Perhaps the most difficult part of developing written work schedules is putting a time limit on the jobs. Assigning too much work without giving sufficient time may result in an employee feeling pressured and even defeated before getting started. The aim is to get the work done in an organized manner in the time that is necessary. A schedule should help each employee to look ahead and should assure that everything is ready when needed. The person assigned to a particular job should also be responsible for completing the job, whenever possible. Following through with the completion of the job will result in more pride in the work.

The following points should be considered in preparing work schedules:

1. Assign a responsibility, if possible, to each person. Avoid assigning all "helping" jobs to the same person.
2. Determine the hours a person is to work based on job assignments.
3. Distribute the work load over the hours to be worked by each employee.
4. Put time limits on jobs. Avoid overloading one person and giving too little time within which to perform the tasks.
5. Give instructions when possible on work schedules to prevent need for questions.

Types of Work Schedules

Although many different work schedule forms are used by various food-services, there are basically three types of work schedules: individual, daily-unit, and organizational. Most managers do not have the time to prepare, on a daily basis, detailed individual work schedules. Therefore this type, though very desirable, is recommended only for new employees or when many changes are made in the daily procedure (Fig. 6.1).

A daily unit work schedule is recommended for most operations (Fig. 6.2). If employees are trained and generally know their responsibilities and how to carry them out, this type of work schedule works beautifully. In a large operation where the jobs are more specialized and each employee spends his or her time on basically the same job every day, it may not be necessary to use either an individual or daily unit work schedule; instead, an organizational work schedule may be used with individual assignments made daily (Fig. 6.3). This type of work schedule must be accompanied by daily assignments, or it will be of little value.

As a result of effective work scheduling, many operations are able to cut labor cost. Also, food cost may be cut by having employees make mixes, cookies, etc., rather than waste time during a part of the day. Effective

Schedule for: _____ Mary Dobson _____   Hours: _____ 8:00–1:00 _____

Serving time: _____ 11:30, 12:00 _____   Date: _____ Monday, April 2 _____

Position: _____ Baker _____

Menu: Hamburger on Bun
      Tater Tots
      Lettuce and Tomato Salad
      Chocolate Cake
      Milk

Time	Preparation	Number to Prepare for	Recipe	Directions
8:00	Prepare cake	250	C-28	2½ times recipe
9:00	Clean area			
9:30	Coffee break			
9:40	Make icing		C-26	2½ times recipe
10:15	Wash pots and pans			
10:30	Cut cake and ice			Cut cake 6 × 10, portion
	Portion up			onto "ice cream square"
11:00	Eat lunch			dish
11:20	Set up line with desserts			
11:30	Serve on line			
12:00	Serve on line			
12:20	Put fruit in refrigerator			4 cans fruit cocktail
	for tomorrow			3 cans sliced peaches
12:30	Wash dining room tables			2 cans USDA pineapple
12:45	Clean milk cooler			tidbits

FIG. 6.1. Daily individual work schedule.

organization means delegation of duties in such a way that manpower can be used more productively.

WORK SIMPLIFICATION

Foodservices in institutions typically have low productivity with much wasted effort and time. And yet, employees may be working harder than necessary due to inefficient and difficult methods of performing the job. Work simplification in a foodservice can improve productivity by 25% easily and result in more being done by fewer people.

Work simplification is defined as a conscious effort to find the easiest, quickest, and simplest way to perform useful work by avoiding and eliminating wasted work. It does not mean "working harder" or necessarily faster

Menu: Lasagne Casserole
Tossed Salad
Chilled Peach Halves
Buttered French Bread
Milk

Time	Manager (7 hr)	6-hr Assistant	5-hr Assistant	4-hr Assistant
7:30–8:00	Make coffee or tea for teachers			
8:00–8:30	Help with lasagne sauce	Prepare lasagne		
8:30–9:00	Lunch count—Tickets		Dip up fruit and refrigerate	
9:00–9:30				
9:30–10:00	Teacher's salads		Wash vegetables for salad	
10:00–10:30	Cut bread and butter	Prepare bread crumbs for fried chicken tomorrow		Cut up vegetables for salad
10:30–11:00	Eat lunch—	Eat lunch—	Put out desserts Eat lunch—	Set up line—napkins, straws, dishes
11:00–11:30	11:15 Put food on steam table	Put food on steam table	Wash pots and pans	Mix salad for first lunch
11:30–12:00	Cashier	Serving Set up for next line	Serving Help in dishroom	Back up line Dishroom
12:00–12:30	Serving	Serving Set up for next line	Cashier Help in dishroom	Back up line Dishroom
12:30–1:00	Serving	Serving Put away food	Cashier 10-min break	Back up line Dishroom
1:00–1:30	Count money—10-min break Help to clean tables	10-min break Clean tables	Clean steam table	Eat lunch
1:30–2:00	Prepare reports	Cleanup	↓	Clean dishroom
2:00–2:30	Place orders	↓		Help with kitchen cleanup
2:30–3:00	Take topping out of freezer and put in refrigerator for tomorrow			

FIG. 6.2.   Daily unit work schedule for an elementary school.

but "working smarter." It means eliminating the unnecessary. This may involve changing habits, equipment, materials, or arrangements. Habits or routines play an important part in workers' performance, and to perform in a way different than they are used to requires breaking the habit and replacing it with a new routine. It is not until the new routine becomes a habit that performance reaches peak efficiency. However, it may seem easier at first to employees to continue old patterns than to try something new.

The increased productivity that can result from training employees in work simplification can cut labor cost significantly, ensure safer and better working conditions, lessen employees' fatigue, make the quality of production better and more uniform, and result in higher wages. Some school districts have increased their productivity from 12 meals per labor-hour to 16–18 meals per labor-hour, and the primary factor in making this possible was training in work simplification.

Time	Manager (7 hr)	Cook (6 hr)	Ass't Cook (6 hr)	Baker (6 hr)	Salads (5½ hr)	Sandwich (6 h
7:30–8:00	Organizing day					
8:00–8:30	General supervision					
8:30–9:00	General supervision	Prepare ingredient for Main Dish	Prepare vegetables or helping cook	Baking breads and desserts	Prepare salads and juice or help ass't cook	Prepare sandwic for a la carte & help baker
9:00–9:30	General supervision					
9:30–10:00	General supervision	Special cleaning	Special cleaning Steamer and/or steam jacketed kettle	Special cleaning bake oven	Special cleaning salad refrigerator	Prepare dishroom and wash pots, pans and small equipment
10:00–10:30	General supervision	Preparation				
10:30–11:00			Eat lunch	Eat lunch	Eat lunch	
11:00–11:30	Eat lunch	Eat lunch	Prepare food for serving line		In charge of set up line 2	Eat lunch
11:30–12:00		Back up lines	Serving on line or Cashier	Serving on line or Cashier	Serving on line	Help on serving li dishroom
12:00–12:30	Lunch periods	Back up lines	Serving on line or Cashier	Serving on line or Cashier	Serving on line	Help on serving li dishroom
12:30–1:00		Back up lines	Serving on line or Cashier	Serving on line or Cashier	Serving on line	Help on serving li dishroom
1:00–1:30	Check leftovers and give instructions / 10 min break	Put away leftovers/ clean / 10 min break	Count money / 10 min break	Count money / 10 min break	Cleanup line 2 and put food away	10 min break / Prepare for tomorrow
1:30–2:00	Prepare bank deposit and reports	Prepare for tomorrow	Prepare for tomorrow	Prepare for tomorrow		
2:00–2:30	Check kitchen					
2:30–3:00	Prepare orders, etc.					

Time	A la Carte Snack Bar (4½ hr)	Snack Bar (4 hr)	Dish Machine Operator (4 hr)	Server (3½ hr)	Server (3 hr)
9:00–9:30	In charge of snack bar or a la carte				
9:30–10:00				Dishing up desserts	
10:00–10:30	Prepare sandwich	Prepare fruits, cakes, etc for snack bar	Prepare condiments (mustard, catsup, salad dressing)	Help baker	
10:30–11:00	Set up area	Prepare condiments (catsup, mustard)			
11:00–11:30	Eat lunch	Break / Set up a la carte	Eat lunch	Break	In charge of set up line
11:30–12:00					
12:00–12:30	A la carte or snack bar	A la carte or snack bar	Dishroom	Serving on line	Serving on line
12:30–1:00					
1:00–1:30	Put away food / Prepare records	Eat lunch	Break	Eat lunch	Eat lunch
1:30–2:00	10 min break / Prepare for tomorrow	Clean steam table or snack bar	Finish dishroom and clean up		Cleanup line 1
2:00–2:30		Refrigerate fruits, etc. & prepare for tomorrow	Put dishes away		
2:30–3:00					

FIG. 6.3. Organizational work schedule for a secondary school staffed with 55½ labor hours. Special individual instructions and assignments can be attached to the chart daily.

Motion Economy

The principles of motion economy described by Barnes (1968) and Kazarian (1979) should be utilized by more school foodservices to increase productivity. Motion economy can be divided into three principal segments: (1) hand and body motions, (2) work process or sequence, and (3) design of tools, equipment, and work place. Some principles of motion economy drawn from Barnes and Kazarian and examples of how they can be applied to school foodservices are given here.

1. Use both hands at the same time to do useful work when possible.
   Examples:
   a. Panning rolls—Pick up a roll in each hand and put onto the pan.
   b. Racking dishes—Pick up a plate in each hand to put into the dishwashing racks. Use both hands to take dishes out of the racks and stack.
   c. Serving the line—Pick plate up with one hand and bring mid-way to meet the food that has been dipped or picked up by the other hand. Put the fastest person at the beginning of the serving line to set the speed for the other workers.
2. Perform work in a rhythmic way.
   Examples:
   a. Cutting with French knife—Place French knife point on the cutting board and with other hand move the vegetable under the knife; rock the knife up and down cutting the vegetables and developing a rhythm.
   b. Natural rhythm—Stirring, racking dishes, panning biscuits, etc., can be done most effectively with natural rhythmic movements.
3. Use smooth, continuous, curved motions when possible rather than straight-line motions with sharp changes in direction. This could increase productivity by 25%.
   Examples:
   a. Wiping tables—When wiping tables use a wide archlike motion rather than a straight-line one.
   b. Mopping floors—Mopping in a circular motion from side-to-side is less tiring and easier than a push-and-pull, back-and-forth motion.
   c. Spreading sandwich fillings—A circular motion without lifting the tool is most efficient for spreading sandwich fillings on bread.
4. Use the fewest, shortest, and simplest motions.
   Examples:
   a. Use a 2-, 3-, or 4-inch wide pastry brush instead of a 1-inch brush for greasing pans, buttering bread, and putting mayonnaise on sandwiches. Use of the largest size practical can reduce the number of strokes fourfold.

b.   Use the largest measure practical, not multiples of a smaller one; for example, a 1-cup measure instead of 16 tablespoons and a quart measure instead of 4 cups. Use the correct size spoon, ladle, or scoop to portion with. Avoid dipping twice because it takes twice the time.

c.   Use wire whip for mixing flour and water.

5.   Use the available equipment that is *best* for the job. Examples:

   a.   Pastry bag—Use a pastry bag for stuffing celery, filling deviled eggs, weiners, potatoes and cream puffs, and for putting decorative mayonnaise, salad dressing or whipped cream on as toppings (Fig. 6.4).

   b.   Sifting and blending—Use wire-whip attachment on mixer to incorporate air and blend ingredients instead of sifting.

   c.   Dish machine—Wash all nonelectrical equipment or parts of equipment that are small enough to fit in the dish machine. Wash all small tools, pots, and pans that will fit in the dish machine.

   d.   Slicer attachment—Use slicer attachment on mixer for slicing potatoes, carrots, cucumbers, radishes, etc.

   e.   Grater attachment or vertical cutter-mixer (Fig. 6.5)—Use the grater attachment or the very fast vertical cutter-mixer for chopping carrots and cabbage for salad, for making bread crumbs, and grating cheese. When using the grater attachments, attach a plastic bag to the chute of the attachment so that the grated product goes directly into the bag for easy storing.

   f.   Food slicer—Use the automatic food slicer for slicing several tomatoes at a time (Fig. 6.6) and shredding lettuce. Make a chart of the dial settings for cutting French bread, ham, cheese (½-oz,

FIG. 6.4. Pastry bag can make job easier and take half the time.

FIG. 6.5. Making a tossed salad with this veritical cutter-mixer only takes 4 seconds.

1-oz, 2-oz portions), and other foods that are cut frequently. Place chart on wall over the machine.

g.　Portion scoops—Use portion scoops for filling muffin pans (No. 12 or 16), for cookies (No. 40), for sandwich fillings (No. 30 or 40), and portioning Salisbury steak patties (No. 10).

h.　Automatic timers—Use timers, not memory, to keep time.

i.　Scales—It is faster and more accurate to weigh ingredients than to measure them by volume.

j.　Change (money) counters—When large quantities of change are to be sorted, counted, and rolled for the bank, use of automatic counters is cost effective.

6.　Combine operations and eliminate all unnecessary parts of job. Examples:

a.　Cook in serving pans.

b.　Add dry milk to dry ingredients, then add water, eliminating reconstitution of milk.

c.　Congeal gelatin in souffle cup or dish in which it is to be served.

d.　Use one-bowl method of mixing cakes.

e.　Combine butter and spreads or peanut butter and jelly before spreading on bread for sandwiches.

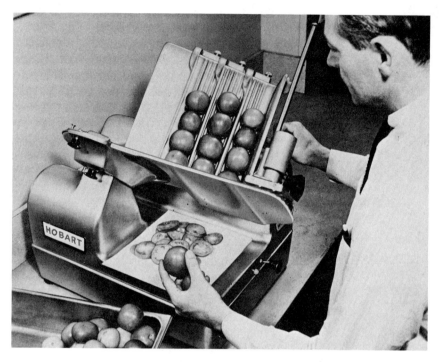

FIG. 6.6. Food slicer can make slicing tomatoes easier and quicker.

    f.   Roll biscuit dough in pan, then cut into squares or triangles. Approximately 9 lb of dough in an 18 × 26 inch pan cut 6 × 16 yields 96 biscuits.

    g.   Cut several stalks of celery at one time.

    h.   Roll pastry for cobbler in 18 × 26 inch sheet pan, then cut 8 × 10 and bake. Thicken juice from fruit with cornstarch, sugar, and spices; add precooked fruits (or canned fruits). Portion and top with pastry square. Saves time, pans, oven space, and is more attractive.

7.   Locate tools, materials, and supplies close to the point of use and in a definite place.

    Examples:

    a.   Serving tools—Store serving tools near the serving line.

    b.   Spices—Store spices most frequently used by baker in the baker's area; those used by cook in the cook's area.

    c.   Attachments—Store attachments for mixer with mixer.

    d.   Vegetables—Store vegetables near sink where they will be cleaned. Store food ready to be served near serving line.

    e.   Labeling—Label drawers for ease in locating tools. Label shelves in storeroom in categories in alphabetical order and coordinate the arrangement with the inventory sheet for ease in taking inventory.

   f.   Color coding—Use color coding of scoop handles, of labels, of forms, etc., to differentiate between different sizes or types.

   g.   Duplicaters—If a tool is needed frequently at more than one location, purchase a duplicate. This is particularly important with measuring spoons, cups, thermometers, and other small equipment.

8.   Arrange work, tools, and materials in sequence.

   Examples:

   a.   Work centers—Equipment should be arranged to avoid crisscrossing.

   b.   Portioning—The worker should arrange the item being portioned and the tools in such a way that it is not necessary to reach across or backtrack and that the work flows in sequence (Fig. 6.7).

   c.   Numbering directions—Directions for operating equipment or performing certain tasks can be numbered so that the sequence of necessary steps is clear.

9.   Arrange for physical conditions most conducive to work.

   Examples:

   a.   Lighting—35 footcandles on equipment; 35–50 footcandles on work surface.

   b.   Temperature at 75° to 80°F.

   c.   Relative humitidy at 50 to 60%.

   d.   Ventilation that will change air every 5 minutes.

   e.   Light-colored walls and ceiling without glare.

   f.   Working surface at the correct height (35–37 inch) for the worker.

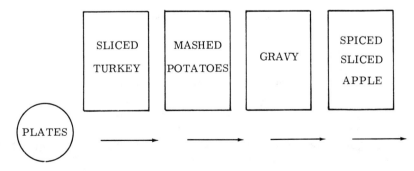

FIG. 6.7. The left hand picks up the plate, right hand dips, and the plate is passed to server on the right.

   g. High-backed stools at work table allow worker to alternate between standing and sitting during long jobs. This will improve circulation and is less tiring than staying in one position for a long time.

   h. Reduce noise and distractions.

   i. Allow 10-minute rest breaks after 2 hours of work.

10. Keep tools and equipment in good working condition.

   a. Have thermostat on ovens checked and calibrated every 3 to 6 months.

   b. Perform preventive maintenance checks yearly reducing down time considerably.

   c. Sharpen knives on a regular basis.

   d. Remove dust buildup from refrigeration coils with vacuum as often as needed.

11. Eliminate unnecessary walking and reaching, stretching, and bending. Examples:

   a. Use cart to carry supplies needed from storeroom to place of work. (Fig. 6.8)

   b. Put large equipment on wheels so it can be brought easily to the place of use.

   c. Take recipe or list of ingredients to the storeroom and fill many orders at one time. Typically, one person fills orders and delivers food from storeroom. At $4.00 per hour, it costs 32¢ for every 5 minutes used walking back and forth to the storeroom to get items.

   d. Use foot pedal controls and knee lever when possible.

   e. Put materials where they can be reached without stretching. The normal reach of most people is from 12 to 14 inches, and the maximum reach without stretching is from 22 to 24 inches. As a test, place a 25 pound bag of salt in the normal reach range and one in the maximum reach range. Lift one at a time with both hands. The one farther away seems much heavier and takes more energy to lift. Placing materials in the normal reach range of employees will make their jobs easier and less tiring.

12. Standardize procedures. Examples:

   a. Eliminate "to taste" directions in recipes by determining how much of an ingredient (such as salt or sugar) is needed and adding this information to the recipe. If a recipe calls for 8 minutes of cooking but in your equipment 10 minutes are required for proper results, then change the recipe.

   b. Put cartons of milk in the milk cooler the same way each time. It may not be necessary to count them daily.

13. Eliminate any body motion that is unproductive.

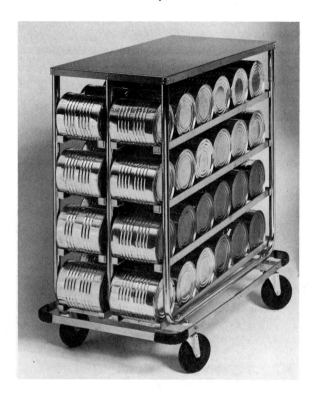

FIG. 6.8. Can-dispensing cart is an example of compact, accessible, mobile equipment that combines jobs.
Courtesy of Edlund Company, Inc.

14. Do not use hands for any work that can be done by other parts of the body.
15. Use force of gravity whenever possible.
    Examples:
    a. Let product drop through a chute to get to where it is to go.
    b. Place receiving pan lower than chopping board so chopped product can fall into receiving pan and not have to be lifted by worker.
16. Use the simplest way of performing a job.
    Examples:
    a. Use uncooked noodles in assembling lasagne casserole for baking (Table 6.1).
    b. Oven-frying many foods is easier.
    c. Use hands (clean or plastic gloves) for picking up rather than tongs, scoop, or other equipment when practical.
    d. Add oil to the water when cooking rice and pasta to prevent it from boiling over.

TABLE 6.1. Example of Job Simplification by Change That Eliminates Steps
in a Recipe for Lasagne Casserole

Ingredients	100 Portions Weight (lb)	(oz)	Measure	Method
Onions, chopped	1	2	3 cups	1. Cook onions in fat until onions are clear but not brown.
Oil or melted fat		4	½ cup	
Tomato puree			3¼ qt	2. Combine onions, puree, paste, water, sugar, and seasonings.
Tomato paste			2¼ qt	3. Season meat with salt and pepper. Brown lightly. Drain.
Water			2 gal.	
Sugar		1½	3 Tbsp	4. Combine meat, 6 lb of cheese and sauce.
Salt		2	3 Tbsp	5. Pour about 1 qt meat-cheese sauce in each of 4 greased baking pans (about 12 × 20 × 2 in.).
Worcestershire sauce			1½ Tbsp	
Garlic powder			1 Tbsp	
Ground beef	8			6. Cover with a layer of noodles. Repeat layers of sauce, noodles, and end with layer of sauce. Three layers of noodles (12) and 1 gal. of sauce per pan. Sprinkle 5 oz cheese on top of each pan.
Salt		2	3 Tbsp	
Pepper			1 tsp	
Cheese, shredded	7	4		7. Cover pans tightly with aluminum foil and bake 1 hr at 350°F (moderate oven).
Lasagne noodles (uncooked)	6			8. Let stand 15 to 30 min before removing aluminum foil. Then cut into servings.

e. Weighing all dry ingredients is more accurate and often faster than measuring by volume.

f. Shape rolls or biscuits or cookies in long roll and cut off appropriate amounts with dough cutter. Two rolls can be placed parallel to each other and cut at the same time with a knife.

g. Put cold water over hard-cooked eggs immediately after cooking for ease in removing shell.

h. Heat only enough liquid to dissolve gelatin and sugar and add cold or iced liquid for quick congealing.

i. Coat sides and bottom of pan in which gelatin is congealed for ease in removing it from the pan.

j. Fasten a plastic bag to the mouth of the shredder or grater to receive shredded vegetables or grated cheese.

k. Put oil rather than flour on stainless steel baker's table and rolling pin when rolling out biscuits, pastry, or rolls.

l. Have pot sink ready with soapy hot water to soak pans. Five minutes in the steamer will loosen hard cooked-on residue.

m. Cut small amounts of parsley with kitchen scissors.

n. Save time and oven space by placing hamburger patties three layers deep in pan. Separate each layer with a strip of aluminum foil just wide enough to cover each row of patties.

o.   Separate egg whites and yolks by breaking them through a small funnel. The whites go through but the yolks will not.

p.   Use large rubber scraper to remove batter from mixing bowl.

17. Schedule tasks to be done in slack time. All employees should be producing steadily at useful and productive tasks.

a.   Make mixes for cakes, biscuits, and puddings in "off hours" to store for future use.

b.   Grate cheese and store in 5-pound amounts in labeled plastic bags.

c.   Grind bread crumbs and store in labeled plastic bags.

d.   Prepare refrigerator cookies and store for future use (Table 6.2).

18. Question how all jobs are being done.

a.   Should different raw materials be used?

b.   Would partially preprocessed or preprocessed products be advisable?

c.   Can the frills be afforded?

d.   Would changing the forms or shapes of the finished products save time?

e.   Would changing the order of doing a job make it simpler? Example: Cutting cake into portions before frosting is a simpler order of doing the job.

f.   Can labor-saving machines be used?

Most jobs in a foodservice operation could probably be improved by rearranging or simplifying the way they are being done. To improve or simplify a job, it is necessary to analyze what is being done—by standing back and watching the job being performed and making notes on the movements made. Charting the flow of the work will point out unnecessary or awkward movements. Taking a motion picture of the job being performed can be most helpful. Then ask yourself what is being done and why? Is it really necessary to do the job that way? Work out simpler and better methods. Putting them into practice may be the hardest part of job simplification to accomplish.

There are three main parts to any job in a foodservice: (1) getting ready, (2) doing, and (3) cleaning up. The getting-ready time should be as short as possible and not be slowed down because the worker has to look for the necessary tools. The cleanup should go quickly. The important part of a job is the doing. Planning all parts of a job before starting to perform it saves time. Employees should ask any questions and get explanations of unfamiliar tasks, then collect all food and equipment needed for a job, before starting it.

Sandwich Assembly

A sandwich assembly incorporates many of the economy principles just mentioned (Fig. 6.9). The tools and materials are assembled in the best

150   Work Planning and Simplification

TABLE 6.2. Basic Cookie Recipe

Ingredients	2000 Portions			Method
	Weight			
	(lb)	(oz)	Measure	
Butter	8			1. Cream butter and sugar in mixer.
Sugar, granulated	6			
Sugar, light brown	4			
Flour, all-purpose	16			2. Combine dry ingredients.
Baking powder		12		
Salt		3		
Eggs			3 dozen	3. Add the eggs and vanilla to the butter and sugar mixture.
Vanilla			¾ cup	4. Gradually add the dry ingredients.
				5. Use the variations you desire (see below).
				6. Roll each one pound portion of dough to a 12 in. long roll (the width of wax paper).
				7. Wrap in wax paper and chill overnight, or wrap tightly with aluminum foil, label, and freeze.
				8. Slice on slicing machine set at 12 or thickness desired.
				9. Bake on greased baking sheet in 375°F oven for 7–10 min.

Variations: For making 6 kinds of cookies at one time, divide the dough into equal parts—about 6 lb in each part.
To each 6 lb add one of the following variations:
Peanut Butter Cookies: add 3 cups peanut butter.
Vanilla Cookies: as is.
Coconut Cookies: add 2 cups coconut.
Chocolate Cookies: add 1 cup cocoa and 3 Tbsp water.
Nut Cookies: add 2 cups finely chopped nuts.
Raisin Cookies: add 2 cups raisins.
Date Cookies: add 2 cups dates.
To make all one kind of cookies, add one of the following to the entire base dough:
Peanut Butter Cookies: add 1 gal. plus 2 cups peanut butter.
Vanilla Cookies: as is.
Coconut Cookies: add 3 qt of coconut.
Chocolate Cookies: add 6 cups cocoa and 1½ cups of water.
Nut Cookies: add 3 qt nuts.
Raisin Cookies: add 3 qt raisins.
Date Cookies: add 3 qt dates.

sequence and are within the maximum reach range; items used most often are within the normal reach range. Both hands are used to place the bread on the cutting board. A circular motion is used in spreading the mayonnaise on the bread with a pastry brush. Both hands are used to put the lettuce and meat on the bread and then the top slice of bread on.

To become more efficient at assembling sandwiches, try the following:

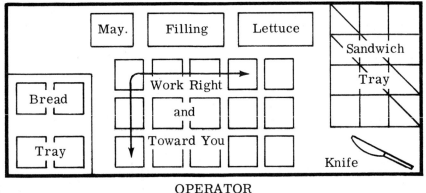

FIG. 6.9. The principles of motion economy are incorporated in this sandwich assembly arrangement.

1. Use both hands.
2. Have all supplies in front of you when you start.
3. Arrange supplies in the order to be used.
4. Use assembly-line production when more than one person is making sandwiches.
5. Leave bread in wrapper until ready to put on board to assemble.
6. Cut bread wrapper in half and turn down each half on a tray at assembly area; remove wrapper as bread is needed. (Have trash can near for discarding wrappers.)
7. Use spatula for spreading butter, mayonnaise, or fillings. Economize on motions—two strokes of the spatula should evenly distribute the spread to the edges of a slice of bread.
8. Use corresponding slices of bread (slices next to each other in loaf), as these make a more uniform sandwich.
9. Cut three to four sandwiches at one time.

USING QUALITY CIRCLES TO INCREASE PRODUCTIVITY

Quality circles, one form of quality control, can increase productivity and motivate employees to do a more efficient job. In the quality circle approach, a small number (around 10) of employees meet regularly to identify, analyze, and solve problems in production. The group needs to be taught elementary techniques of problem solving. The employees in the group will begin to really think about what they are doing and how they are doing it, and will begin to carefully plan their work assignments. The goal is for them to work more intelligently and correct inefficiencies. Much of the success of quality circles is due to improved employee morale. They motivate employees, encourage teamwork, and may result in employee recognition (perhaps increased pay). A study by A. T. Kearney, Inc., of 16 successful companies in 1981 showed that involving employees is one of the main keys to increased productivity.

The quality circle technique deserves to be tried in school foodservices. When you consider the benefits of raising productivity from 16 meals per labor-hour to 16½ or 17 meals per labor-hour, it is worth trying quality circles. Nippon Electric Company plant in Fuchu, Japan, doubled productivity in 3 years using this technique. The company's management attributes 25% of the increase in productivity to workers' input.

When employees are involved in the process of improving productivity and their ideas contribute to changes in an operation, they are more likely to accept and effectively implement new production methods. They can make it work with greater determination. If all employees become interested and do not feel that their jobs are in danger because of greater efficiency, a group effort can get significant results. If employees are made aware of the principles of motion economy and work simplifications, they can study their own movements and cut out unnecessary ones. In a class of foodservice workers studying work simplification several years ago in the Chapel Hill, North Carolina, schools, the class members demonstrated how they performed an operation. The others in the class offered improvements and new methods. Some of the members of the class said "it won't work" even before it was tried. However, each was asked to try the new methods during the next week. At the next weekly class, a stopwatch was used to test the new improved way against the old way. The group became very interested and suggested new, improved, simplified methods of performing several different jobs.

BIBLIOGRAPHY

AVERY, A. C. 1967. Work design and food service systems. J. Am. Dietet. Assoc. 51:148.
BARNES, R. M. 1968. Motion and Time Study: Design and Measurement of Work. 6th edition. John Wiley & Sons, New York.
CHAPPELL, V. M., B. J. CRAIG, R. L. SWENSON, and W. C. TURNER. 1975. Work productivity: getting the most for the time. School Foodservice J. 29(8):614.
COLEMAN, J. 1970. Instructor's Guide: Management of Food Service. Florida State Dept. of Education, Tallahassee.
CONNELLAN, T. K. 1978. How to Improve Human Performance: Behaviorism in Business and Industry. Harper & Row, New York.
CUMMINGS, T. G. and M. EDMONDS. 1977. Improving Productivity and the Quality of Work Life. Praeger, New York.
JOEL, R. 1977. Managing Productivity. Reston Publishing Co., Reston, VA.
KAZARIAN, E. A. 1979. Work Analysis and Design for Hotels, Restaurants and Institutions. 2nd edition. AVI Publishing Co., Westport, CT.

PEDDERSEN, R. B., A. C. AVERY, R. D. RICHARD, J. R. OSTENTON, and H. H. POPE. 1973. Increasing Productivity in Foodservice. CBI, Boston.

ROSS, J. E. and W. C. ROSS. 1982. Japanese Quality Circles and Productivity. Reston Publishing Co., Reston, VA.

STANTON, E. S. 1982. Reality-centered People Management. AMACOM, American Management Association, New York.

WELCH, J. M. and G. HOCKENBERRY. 1975. Everything you always wanted to know about work sampling. School Foodservice J. 29(1):71.

WEST, B., L. WOOD, V. HARGER, and G. SHUGART. 1977. Food Service in Institutions. 6th edition. John Wiley & Sons, New York.

WYNN, J. T. 1973. Staffing Broward County style. School Foodservice J. 27(1):44–54.

PURCHASING FOOD

Forty to 60% of the school foodservice dollar is spent for food. The range is broad due to the differences between the cost of food ingredients for "from scratch" cooking and that of "convenience" foods or pre-prepared foods. The labor costs should also show a correspondingly broad range. Also, purchasing practices can influence how much is spent on food and if there is a profit or a loss. Purchasing practices, additionally, determine the quality of food purchased.

Purchasing consists of more than merely ordering. "Purchasing" means that planning has gone into the ordering. Buying the *right product* in the *amounts needed* at the *time needed* within the *price that can be afforded* are, according to Lendal Kotschevar (1975), the challenges of purchasing.

The purchaser should have a knowledge of food and have contact with the customer in order to know what is needed, as well as the best sizes, or cuts and grades, or qualities desired. In large school systems where all purchasing is done through a purchasing agent, good communication between the agent and the foodservice personnel is necessary. Specifications should be written by foodservice personnel with the help of the purchasing department. It takes testing and comparison of products by foodservice staff to determine the best buy and best product for the job.

FACTORS INFLUENCING PURCHASING

The factors that influence what is to be purchased are the menu, food budget, labor cost and skill of personnel, season and availability of food, storage, number of meals, equipment available, the USDA-donated foods, and federal regulations. Each of these factors is discussed in turn.

Menu

The menu is the blueprint for purchasing. One should buy for the menu rather than planning the menu around what has been purchased. The menu should be planned, however, with a knowledge of what is available on the market and what can be afforded. Cycle menus make it possible to plan and purchase ahead.

Food Budget

The food budget will have considerable control over what is put on the menu and consequently what is purchased. Pre-costing menus can help prevent overspending. However, post-costing is essential since it is the actual cost that matters. The food budget can be divided among the components (foods) of the lunch. Thus ranges are set of how much of the food dollar is to be spent for meat and meat alternates, milk, vegetables, fruits, bread, and additional food; these help assure that total purchases are within the total budget. For example, if the income is $1.38, and if 50% of the money is budgeted for food, there will be 69¢ to use for food. This 69¢ can be further divided among the components of the lunch (Fig. 7.1).

Labor

The labor available and skill of the labor should be considered by a foodservice manager when deciding if fresh or frozen, mixes, preportioned

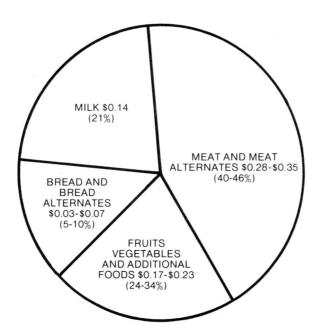

FIG. 7.1.   This sample food budget is based on an income of $1.38 per meal served with 50% (69¢) being used for food.

or bulk, pre-prepared or precooked products will be purchased. The cost of labor has increased so much in the last 10 years that more and more foodservices are purchasing prepared items and convenience foods. Factories are able to produce, on assembly lines with conveyor belts and automation, food for less than can a foodservice, particularly where productivity is low. The lack of skilled personnel also makes it necessary in many cases for foodservices to purchase prepared items, such as bakery products. When the use of convenience foods increases, the food cost will increase and a greater percentage of the dollar will be spent on food; consequently the percentage spent for labor will have to decrease.

Season and Availability

The price and quality of food is affected by the season and availability of food. Purchasing fresh bell peppers will cost considerably more in January than when they are in season. In January frozen green peppers or dehydrated green peppers could be a better buy and could be substituted for fresh ones in most instances. The time to put cantaloupe on the menu and on the purchasing list is May–August, when it's in season and widely available. Table 2.6, which shows the average monthly availability of fresh fruits and vegetables will be helpful in planning menus and purchases.

Storage

The type of storage needed and what is available should be considered when purchasing. Storage may determine the quantities purchased and how frequently deliveries will have to be made. Canned rather than frozen items must be purchased if temperatures of 0°F or below are not available for holding frozen food until time of use. The keeping ability of fresh fruits and vegetables determines how frequently they are purchased. The need for frozen storage has increased faster than the availability of frozen storage school foodservices and probably curtails the use of frozen foods.

Number of Meals

Naturally, the number of meals to be served and the volume of a la carte sales will determine the quantities needed. Usually these are projected figures based on past experience. Recipes may be used in determining quantities of some items, along with buying guides, such as the *Food Buying Guide for School Food Service* (U.S. Dept. of Agriculture 1984).

Equipment Available

The type and amount of equipment available also affect what foods should be purchased. For example, if a deep-fat fryer is not available, purchase frozen french fries that can be reconstituted in an oven. If a slicer is not available, purchase cheese and luncheon meat preportioned. When sufficient oven space is not available, it may be necessary to purchase bakery bread when other oven foods are being prepared.

In some cases, it may be economical to let equipment stand idle, reduce labor cost, and purchase commercially prepared foods. Careful analysis of the cost and quality of commercially prepared foods compared with those made from scratch is necessary.

Customers' Likes and Dislikes

Which style of barbecue do your customers prefer? There are so many different flavors of pudding, fruitsicles, hot dogs, chili, etc., how can foodservice managers be sure they are selecting the preferred? Taste parties are one of the best ways to get customer feedback. Otherwise, directors or managers who decide what to buy based on their own likes and dislikes or those of the staff may be catering to the wrong clientele. Smart buyers realize that it does not matter what they like but what the customers like that really matters. See Chapter 9 for details on how a taste party can help foodservice buyers.

Much also can be learned about food preferences by talking with students and watching plate waste. Ask why someone did not like the food. Often managers shy away from finding out.

USDA-Donated Foods

The commodities received by schools from the USDA will make considerable difference in what is purchased. The donated foods, which account for about 15–20% of the total food have to be worked into the menus and in some cases immediately (when the product is a fresh produce). To buy large quantities of canned and frozen items could be unwise unless the type and quantity of USDA-donated foods that may be received are known.

Processing Contracts

Can a product that you need be made with USDA-donated foods? This is only important if the product you want to purchase is made from foods you have or can get in large supply. Nearly 25% of the total USDA-donated commodities issued are being processed. Using these foods effectively in the manufacturing of prepared foods through processing agreements, for example, has contributed 5–8¢ to each food dollar in the schools in the state of New York and in Fairfax County, Virginia.

Forty-two state agencies have processing contracts with over 500 food companies. The purchaser can contact the state agency to see which companies have agreements that are approved. The National Commodity Processing contracts with companies have added another group of contracts, which are easier to use.

As long as the USDA-donated foods are continued, processing contracts should be utilized, particularly for any product containing grains and dairy products, such as bread, pizza, crackers, ice cream, burritos, and meat/fruit turnovers. Additionally, when a USDA-donated food is in a form that you cannot use, a processing contract can be very useful, or when you do not want to change the quality of the product you are using. For example, if students like the particular hamburger patty being used and it is a prepared patty, a processing agreement would allow the USDA-donated ground beef to be sent directly to the company for adding seasoning and forming into patties.

The requirement of using USDA-donated foods and having a processing agreement approved by the state agency or USDA should be written into bid specifications. It is important to have competitive bidding in the processing.

Federal Regulations

The federal regulations that affect what school foodservices purchase are many; a few of these are described here.

The School Lunch Patterns and Breakfast Pattern have much control on package size, portion sizes, and ingredients that go into products for school foodservices. The *Food Buying Guide for School Food Service* (1984) is an essential aid to determining yields of foods and how large the portion must be to contribute a specified amount to the meal requirements.

Enriched or whole-grain breads, pasta products, and rice are considered a bread or bread alternate. For pasta products to count as a meat alternate they must be fortified with protein.

Natural vegetable and fruit juices may count as a vegetable or fruit, but they can be counted for no more than one half of that requirement.

Unflavored fluid lowfat milk, skim milk, or buttermilk must be made available at lunch as a beverage. Flavored and whole milk may be offered as a choice too.

Some commercially prepared foods bear CN labels, which indicate they have been evaluated by USDA's Food and Nutrition Services to determine their contribution to the meal requirements and are certified by a Child Nutrition (CN) label. This label assures the purchaser of how much meat and meat alternate, vegetable, bread, etc., is in a specific size portion. The importance of knowing exactly what is in a product and having more than a sales representative's word was recognized after the audits in the late 1970s when many meals were shown as being deficient nutritionally, or of unknown quantities. A foodservice director needs to know what is in a commercially prepared meat product, for example, pizza or burrito. Does it contain 1 or 2 ounces of meat, a serving of bread, and ⅛ or ¼ cup of vegetable? The CN label provides some guarantee and will become extensively used as government programs are held more accountable and more prepared foods are used. Inspectors from the USDA or U.S. Department of Commerce check the products packaged under the label to assure the product does have what is stated on the label. The CN label, however, is limited primarily to meat and poultry products.

SUPPLIERS

For many school systems an important question is who to buy from—a broker, wholesale house, or manufacturing company. A wholesale house is the most frequently used supplier by school foodservices, though its markup is more than that of a manufacturer or broker. A wholesaler may average a 25% markup to cover the middleman's commissions, company profits, and service, particularly delivery, as needed. The fewer middlemen, the lower the cost.

A good business relationship with salesmen and jobbers can be very valuable to a purchaser. Salesmen and jobbers can be helpful and furnish information and promotional materials on new products on the market. However, nothing is free and the cost of these extras is built into the price a purchaser pays.

Kickbacks

Trading stamps, gifts of any type, and discounts or bid prices for purchases for home use should be discouraged and refused. There are many means that salesmen and company representatives can use to win favoritism. Accepting gifts and favors puts the purchaser in a position that can stand in the way of good, sound business practices.

Delivery Charges

Delivery charges are high. Each stop a company's truck makes costs the company. One company calculated it cost at least $25 per delivery stop. A purchaser should keep this in mind and should consider the cost. It will save both the purchaser and vendor money in the long run if a month's order can be delivered at one time rather than in four different trips on a weekly basis. Dividing business among too many vendors can also result in a high cost to the vendor and in turn to the purchaser as well as increase paper work in handling invoices. It is desirable to encourage competition among vendors, but the larger the volume of business with a single vendor, the better the price.

Special Services

Company representatives are frequently asked to exhibit at conventions or to advertise in state newsletters. Of course, such activities can be "written off as promotional costs," but when requests are numerous, the costs are added to the price of the products sold. Demonstrations of new products are valuable services, but must be considered in the costs. Door prizes, promotional materials, etc., are additional costs that must be considered when a company prices a product.

Charge Accounts

Charge accounts at local grocery stores should never be started by a school foodservice. Buying "family size" packages in quantity is very costly. Running out and using the local grocery store can become a habit—a bad habit—that should be replaced by good planning. Good management practices show up very strongly in purchasing practices.

CENTRALIZED PURCHASING AND STORAGE

Small foodservices are at a disadvantage when purchasing because of their lack of buying power; typically, they pay about 18% more for food than do large school districts. Centralized purchasing in large volume has many advantages including the following:

1. Better prices can be obtained.
2. The person purchasing can become more proficient and specialized.
3. Budget and fiscal controls are centralized.
4. Buying power is greater with volume.
5. Managers save time, as do salesmen who would otherwise have to call on each school.
6. Written specifications can be developed and competitive bid buying used, resulting in a greater degree of standardization.
7. Evaluation of the products received can be made frequently. More power for correcting errors and receiving credits for poor qualities delivered.

Some small school districts have combined their purchasing needs and effectively increased the volume, and, in turn, reduced the prices paid.

Some school systems use centralized storage facilities for storing supplies for several months. The goods then are distributed as needed to individual schools by the system's trucks and drivers. The purchase price of the goods to the system may be less when purchased in larger volume and delivered to one central location than if a wholesale house were to deliver to individual schools. This can mean a 10 to 15% savings in the purchase price. The question that must be answered is how much does it cost the school system to store and then to deliver goods from the central storage point to the individual schools? In some cases, it may cost more for the school system to store and distribute, than for the wholesaler to perform this service and charge for it. The savings possible will depend on how well organized and efficient the school system's distribution methods are.

TYPES OF PURCHASING

There are four basic types of purchasing: buying on the open market, buying on informal bid, buying on formal bid, and formula pricing. With open-market purchasing a purchaser buys from whomever he wishes and the prices may change from week to week. Open-market purchasing may be done over the telephone, or a salesman calls on the purchaser (manager) and takes orders. Informal bids are a type of gentleman's agreement, which is arrived at after two or three prices have been compared. Actually this method takes on many of the qualities of the formal bid except that no contract is signed. Formal bids are signed legal contracts between a purchaser and a vendor who agrees to supply an estimated quantity of items meeting written specifications at a certain price for a certain period of time. Formula pricing is rather new, but in an uncertain market it is favored by vendors.

Open Market

The open-market type of purchasing is used most frequently for purchasing fresh produce and often by small establishments, which do not have the buying power to use the informal or formal bid methods. When the open market is used, prices should be compared among at least two or three companies and more if the time and the vendors are available. The greatest disadvantage to open-market buying is the time required to compare prices and the problems that may result from oral commitments. However, the time spent on checking prices can result in quite a savings. The form in Fig. 7.2 is one that could be used to compare the prices of fresh produce quoted by several vendors.

162 **7 Purchasing Food**

Date _____

Price Quotations on Fresh Produce

Spec. No.	Quantity	Item	Carter's Produce	Henry's Inc.	Ellis Brothers
FP 2		Apples, 138 Delicious			
FP 3		Apples, 100's Winesaps			
FP 5		Bananas, med.			
FP 6		Cantaloupes, No. 45s			
FP 7		Grapefruit, 64s			
FP 9		Grapes, Thompson			
FP 10		Oranges, Navel, 200s			
FP 11		Oranges, Valencia, 200s			
VP 1		Cabbage, Red			
VP 2		Cabbage, Green			
VP 4		Carrots			
VP 5		Celery			
VP 7		Cucumber			
VP 9		Lettuce			
VP 10		Onions			
VP 12		Parsley			
VP 14		Radishes			
VP 16		Peppers, Bell			
VP 17		Potatoes, Idaho Russetts			
VP 18		Potatoes, Red Triumph			
VP 20		Sweet Potatoes			

Received by: _____

FIG. 7.2. Price comparisons can be made easily with a form designed for the purpose.

Informal Bid

The informal bid is used most frequently when limited quantities of an item are needed or when there is not time to receive formal bids. The agreement between buyer and seller often is oral, although a written agreement is preferable. Since an oral agreement is not a legal contract, either the vendor or purchaser can break it without penalty.

Formal Bid

A formal bid is a signed agreement between the vendor and purchaser and is bound by legal contract. In formal-bid situations the purchasing agent should submit an invitation to bid to several vendors. This requires written specifications and estimates of quantitites to be purchased from the foodservice manager or director. The vendor who submits the lowest bid will be awarded the bid. The specifications should convey clearly what the buyer wants. This becomes more and more important with large quantity purchasing and competitive bidding.

Formula-Pricing Bid

Formula pricing is a type of formal bidding where a base price is bid and a special factor price is bid. Together the two prices constitute the net price to be paid the contractor. The base price is usually based on market quotations; in the case of meat, for example, the National Provisioner Daily "Yellow Sheet" is often used. The "Special Factor" is the amount added to the base price as offered by the contractor. This factor remains constant during the duration of the contract. The base price goes up and down as the market quotation for the product goes up and down. Baltimore County (MD) Schools have used this method of setting prices successfully. It usually works best when carloads of a food are being purchased to be delivered to a central location. This method of setting prices can be expected to be used most often when vendors find they are taking too great a risk guessing what prices will be 2 to 6 months later. During an inflationary period, better prices can often be gotten with formula purchasing than with the strict formal bid since the risk involved in estimating future prices is reduced.

The wholesale prices and price indexes for numerous foods are published monthly by the U.S. Dept. of Labor, Bureau of Labor Statistics. The price trends can be followed in these publications.

WRITING AND USING SPECIFICATIONS

As discussed in the previous section, written specifications are often used by foodservices in purchasing. Good specifications are simple but complete written descriptions of the products wanted. All specifications for a given product should contain the following:

1. Official Standard of Identity or common name of the product
2. Quantity required in purchase units, such as cases, cans, or packages (weight, measure, number, etc.)
3. Brand name or quality designated by trade or federal grade
4. Description of the product—class, kind, variety, color, size, texture, cut, style pack, etc.
5. Origin or where the product was produced
6. Unit (size) on which prices shall be quoted (6 No. 10 cans per case; 4 1-gallon jars; per pound)
7. Sanitation standards under which product is to be packed (U.S. inspected)

Foods having a federal specification are listed in the *Federal Supply Catalog,* which is produced by the USDA Food Safety and Quality Service.

Writing specifications can become very involved. A simple guide to writing specifications for a milk bid is shown in Appendix IV. Each foodservice will find from experience certain other clauses and restrictions that need to be written into their specifications. The *School Food Purchasing Guide* (Flanagan 1968) and *Food Purchasing Pointers for School Foodservice* (U.S. Dept. of Agriculture 1977) are excellent guides to writing specifications.

Buying by Brands

Buying by brands has its pros and cons. Brand names may stand for a company's reputation for quality or standards, as a sort of advertisement. Many purchasers buy by brands, including specific brand names in their specifications. Well-known brands, however, can be more expensive than other brands of equivalent quality. Is it necessary to pay the extra price for the assurance of what one will get? It requires time and expertise to save on food cost and at the same time not lower the standard of the foodservice. Through can cuttings, trying limited quantities, experimenting, and keeping informed, it is possible to write specifications that can get the best price, assure the quality wanted, and do not necessarily limit bidding to well-known brands.

Writing specifications usually starts with what you know you want, being as restrictive as necessary to insure the quality desired. It is customary to write specs around a specific product and then add the phrase "or equal." For example:

Apricot, Halves, U.S. Grade B (Choice), Unpeeled, Pitted, in Heavy Syrup, Count 130–145. Packed 6/10, Wt. 70 ounces. Libby Brand or equal.

After experimenting with different brands and qualities and finding that two or three different brands will satisfy the needs, you often can write the specifications more broadly. If the products are so different that one specification cannot be written to cover both, two different specifications can be written with one designated "alternate." This will encourage more than one bid, and the lowest can be accepted. The "or equal" scares some bidders, because they do not want to run a chance of losing the bid. When a bidder bids a product as "equal," he must be prepared to prove it. When large quantities of an item are involved, disputes about what constitutes "equal" may result in a court case.

New Type of Package

The number 10 can is the most familiar of the shelf-stable packaging containers. However, several innovative types of packaging have been tested in recent years. One of these is a flat, half-steamtable-size container; its use reduces processing time and results in a change of taste. Since the sterilization time with this container is about 75% less than with the number 10 can, one wonders why food manufacturers have not adopted it. Change in this industry does not come fast, probably because it necessitates expensive equipment alterations.

The U.S. Army Natick Research and Development Command has been instrumental in developing new, better, and lower cost packaging in recent years. The "retort pouch" is a rectangular, four-seal, flat package. It was first used for military rations. Aseptic techniques have been applied to this flexible package. The product is shelf-stable. Milk packaged in this manner does not have a "canned taste" and was successfully used at the 1982 World's Fair in Knoxville (TN). Packages for food products have taken many shapes and been made of many different materials. Cryovac "Kap-Cold System" is one of the latest U.S. commercial advances. Products aseptically processed in the Cryovac container have a 2- to 6-week shelf-stable life.

In the future, as more types of packaging become available, foodservice purchasers may want to specify particular packaging types that are convenient or fit well in their operation.

General Conditions of Contracts

Specifications should spell out the general conditions of a contract, including the following:

1. When the products are to be delivered
2. Frequency of deliveries
3. Place to be delivered
4. Condition delivered—frozen, refrigerated, etc.

TABLE 7.1. Delivery Schedules and Bid Periods

Commodity	Delivery	Bid Period
Dairy	Daily or every other day	Annual
Bakery products	Daily as required	Annual
Paper supplies	Monthly or bi-monthly	Semi-annually
Cleaning supplies	Monthly	Annual
Canned foods	Monthly or bi-monthly	Annual or quarterly
Staple groceries	Monthly or bi-monthly	Annual or quarterly
Meat, poultry and eggs	Weekly or bi-monthly	Quarterly or monthly
Frozen foods	Weekly or bi-montly	Quarterly or monthly
Fresh produce	Twice weekly or weekly	Annual[1]

[1] Formula bidding works best (see p. 163).

5. How orders are to be placed
6. Billing procedures
7. Payment of bills
8. Length of bid periods

Whether deliveries of an item are expected daily, weekly, or biweekly will be reflected in the bid price; in general, the more frequent deliveries are, the higher the bid price.

Since the market prices of some food items (e.g., fresh produce, meats, eggs) fluctuate more than others, vendors may be unwilling to agree on prices for such products for a whole year. Therefore, bid periods of less than a year should be considered for many items. Also to be considered is whether all bids should expire at the same time or be staggered. Since reviewing bids, testing samples, etc., are time-consuming, it is advisable to stagger the expiration date of the bids. Table 7.1 lists reasonable delivery schedules and bid periods for different commodities.

Ordering Forms

After bids have been received, evaluated, and awarded, the successful bidder and the purchasing agent should work together on the ordering procedure. If the market order form is worked out with both parties, the number of records and the possibility of error can be reduced. The example shown in Fig. 7.3 includes the bid number that correlates with the specifications, the bid price, and the computerized number of each item for the convenience of the wholesale company's warehouse and billing department. If the form has several copies, then one form can act as a purchase order, requisition, invoice, delivery ticket, and bill—saving much time and decreasing the possibilities of errors. Ordering forms, inventory forms, and storage arrangements should be coordinated.

VENDOR NO. 797000

7209

SCHOOL NAME: _____ DATE: _____

ADDRESS: _____ TERMS: _____ CHARGE – NET

LOCATION: _____ Cafeteria
Manager: _____

ALLOW 15 DAYS DELIVERY TIME AFTER RECEIVED BY SCHOOL LUNCH OFFICE

QUANTITY	ITEM NO.	DESCRIPTION	PRODUCT NO.	UNIT PACK	PRICE	TOTAL COST TO BE COMPLETED BY CO.
CASES	22	•332 DISPENSER NAPKIN (TALL)	675100	10 M	7.00 E	
CASES	23	•170 COMPACT NAPKIN (SHORT)	670060	15 M	12.85 E	
CASES	24	WRAPPED STRAWS 6¼"	548360	12,500	9.10 E	
	25	PORTION OR SOUFFLE CUPS				
CASES		•400 · 4 OZ.	122490	5 M	12.80 E	
CASES		•075 · ¾ OZ.	121260	5 M	6.77 E	
CASES	26	•550 LILY DISH	122750	5 M	17.50 E	
CASES	27	4 OZ. SAUCE DISH 008-0006	668390	1 M	6.56 E	
CASES	28	•419 ICE CREAM PLATE 4½ SQ.	668650	2 M	3.96 E	
CASES	29	JUICE CUP, LILY •100 W5G	153660	1200	6.50 E	
CASES	30	•P658 LID FOR JUICE CUP	104040	2500	10.10 E	
BOX	31	WAXED TISSUE (Master Savarap) 1 M Sheet	200531	1 Box	1.79 E	
CASES	32	WAXED TISSUE, PONY · 750 FEET PER ROLL	204370	6 Rolls	15.75 E	
ROLLS	33	•15 ALUMINUM FOIL · 680 FT. ROLL	229981	1 Roll	7.15 E	
ROLLS	34	12 x 12 EM3 ROLL-O-WRAP (1600 Sheets)	395910	1 Roll	4.60 E	
ROLLS	35	PLASTIC WRAP (11 x 2000)	380470	1 Roll	4.40 E	
BOX	36	SANDWICH BAGS 6 x ¾ x 6¼	049861	1M Bags	2.05 E	
BOX	37	BAG–FRENCH FRY	033241	1 M	2.00 E	
TUBE	38	BUTTER CHIPS PAPER	508151	1M Tube	.39 E	
TUBE	39	BAKING CUPS 4½" 500 PER TUBE	161161	1 Tube	.44 E	
BOX	40	SCOTCH BRITE PADS Rubbermaid No. 6297 10 Pads	501331	1 Box	1.89 E	
ONLY	41	•H 1485 A NAPKIN DISPENSER	554871	1	7.25 E	
PKG.	42	PAN LINERS 25 •	339031	1 M	9.50 E	
BOX	43	HAND GUARDS ELL	534491	100	1.65 E	
CASES	44	•983 CHIX WET WIPES	537360	1 M	30.70 E	
ONLY	45	•25 W INSULATED CHEST	357190	1	29.50 E	
CASES	46C	GARBAGE CAN LINERS CP 40LD	062030	250	6.39 E	
					Total Cost	

Contract No. 57-72E-1153

PLEASE PRESS HARD   YOU ARE WRITING SIX COPIES

FIG. 7.3. A well-designed order form, like the one shown, can meet the needs of vendors' and schools' accounting departments. Six copies of the order form are made and used as follows: Two blue copies ("Invoice"); one gold copy ("Delivery and Receipt"); one white copy ("Warehouse Copy"); one pink copy ("Manager's Copy"); and one yellow copy ("Company Bookkeeping Copy").
Courtesy of S. Freeman & Sons.

Evaluation of Products

A purchaser must check the items received to assure that they are as specified and bid. Failure to carry out the specifications of a formal bid contract is a legal matter and can mean the loss of the contract and penalties. This is usually not necessary. In a centralized system a product evaluation sheet or form is recommended for reporting when the quality of the product is unsatisfactory, or for registering a complaint about product, delivery, or service.

GENERAL STEPS IN PURCHASING

In this section, the general steps necessary for efficient, economical purchasing are reviewed. Later in the chapter, specific considerations involved in purchasing different types of commodities are presented in more detail, followed by a quiz to determine what type of buyer you are.

Five important steps to assure quality purchasing should be remembered and followed:

1. Determine the items to be purchased according to menus, recipes, nutritional value, equipment, personnel, and storage.
2. Study the market and know what is available. Compare cost, quality, and yields. Analyze information on product labels.
3. Develop written specifications for the items needed to assure good communication with vendors.
4. Prepare orders according to the specifications in a clearly written form.
5. Check and inspect all foods received to see that what has been ordered and specified has been delivered and that the invoice is correct.

Purchase only those specials that you can use, regardless of how "big a bargain" it is. One hundred cases of canned tuna is not a bargain unless it can be utilized and the storage facilities are adequate. The largest size is not always the best buy.

Purchasing should be done on an objective basis by a designated person who is knowledgeable about purchasing and food. As much as 10 to 15% can be saved on many items if they are purchased through a jobber and large quantities are delivered to one location. "Family style" marketing and small-lot purchasing have no place in a school foodservice.

Determining Quantity to Order

New managers usually have more difficulty in determining how much food to purchase than with any other phase of managing. The quantities purchased should be the quantities needed for the menus to be served. Recipes are very helpful in determining the purchasing list and quantities needed. If a recipe is not used for a particular menu item, such as green beans, then *Food Buying Guide for Child Nutrition Programs* (U.S. Dept. of Agriculture 1984) is an excellent reference to consult, as is *Food for Fifty* (West *et al.* 1978).

Since market orders are usually placed 1 to 2 weeks—sometimes even a month—before the food is to be used, it is necessary to keep in mind what items in current inventory will be used and how much more will be needed to meet the needs of future menus. Dry storage items (canned foods, staples, etc.) usually do not require the close planning that frozen foods and perishables do. Cycle menus can be accompanied by cycle grocery lists from which market orders can be prepared.

The following practical exercise can help you learn to use the *Food Buying Guide for Child Nutrition Programs.*

Practical Exercise No. _____
Determining Quantity of Fruits and Vegetables Needed
Using Food Buying Guide for School Foodservice

The purchase units given for 100 servings in column 5 in the *Food Buying Guide for Child Nutrition Programs* are to be used to determine the amount needed to prepare for 100. To determine the quantity needed for a specific number to be served, move the decimal in column 5 two places to the left and multiply this number by the number of servings needed.

For example: Green Beans, Canned—need 2 cans to serve 100 ¼-cup servings.
To serve 225: $0.02 \times 225 = 4.5$ (or 11) cans

(1) Food as Purchased	(2) Purchase Unit	(3) Serving Size (cup)	(4) Purchase Units for 100 Servings	(5) Number to Be Served	(6) Amount of Food Needed
Green beans, canned	No. 10 can	¼	2	225	4.5 cans
Broccoli, frozen spears	lb	¼	10.4	285	30.6 lb
Cranberries, fresh	lb	¼ cooked	9.00	335	30.15 lb
Grapes, fresh seedless	lb	¼		190	
Lettuce, head fresh	lb	½		480	
Pineapple, crushed	No. 10 can	¼		215	
Potatoes, frozen crinkle french fries	5-lb pkg	½		375	
Orange juice, frozen concentrated	32-fl oz can	½		425	

To complete the rest of the exercise, you will need to refer to the *Food Buying Guide for Child Nutrition Programs* to determine purchase units for 100 servings of each item.

An inventory system with built-in order points and maximum inventory points can result in better control, more assurance of having the needed food when it is needed, and less overstocking. With computers now available in many schools, a cost-effective perpetual inventory is both feasible and desirable. A perpetual inventory coupled with order points provides the data needed to make reliable estimates of needs.

Making Use of Labels

Under the Food, Drug and Cosmetic Act there are minimum requirements that packers and distributors must abide by in labeling. The law requires, for example, that canned fruits be labeled with the following information:

1. The common or usual name of the fruit
2. The form (or style) of fruit, such as whole, slices, or halves
3. For some fruits, the variety or color
4. Syrups, sugars, or liquid in which a fruit is packed (listed near the name of the product)
5. The total contents (net weight) in ounces for containers holding 1 pound or less or in both total ounces and pounds and ounces (or pounds and fractions of a pound), for containers holding 1 to 4 pounds
6. Any special type of treatment
7. Ingredients such as spices, flavoring, coloring, and special sweeteners, if used
8. The packer's or distributor's name and place of business

The labeling laws passed by Congress in 1973 require labeling to be rather complete, concise, and informative. Nutrition labeling can be an aid to school foodservices in determining the nutritional quality of various products. For most foods nutritional labeling is voluntary. If a product is fortified or a nutritional claim is made by the manufacturer, the label must give the nutrients in the product. Labels for foods such as fortified fruit juices and enriched bread or flour generally follow the format for "Nutrition Labeling": (1) serving size, (2) servings per container, (3) caloric content, (4) protein content, (5) carbohydrate content, (6) fat content, and (7) percentage of U.S. recommended daily allowances of protein, vitamins, and minerals.

In addition, labels may give the quality, grade, size, and/or maturity of the product. Cooking directions, recipes, and ideas for serving are sometimes found on labels.

The Food Safety and Inspection Service of USDA enforces the "standards of composition" and "standard of identity." The standards of composition state, for example, the minimum amount of meat and poultry required in a product. The "standard of identity" sets specific requirements for a food's makeup, much like a recipe.

Receiving

Good purchasing practices may be of little value if the food is not checked when received to make sure that what was ordered is the same as what is being delivered. Signing an invoice without checking what has been delivered is a very poor management practice. Managers use the excuse that checking the food is an indication to the deliveryman that he is not trusted. Trustworthy or not, an order should be checked before an invoice or delivery ticket is signed. Much inconvenience and hard feeling can result if later the manager discovers that only four cases of green beans were left when six were ordered and charged for. Checking an order should include the following:

1. *Checking items delivered.* Does each item correspond to what was ordered? Does it meet specifications?
2. *Quantity.* Was the amount indicated on the invoice delivered? Is this the quantity ordered?
3. *Price.* Have the correct quoted or on-bid price been charged? Are the multiplication and addition correct?
4. *Condition of the items delivered.* Are all items in good condition? Are frozen foods frozen, refrigerated items cold, bread today's date, milk fresh according to date, food clean, and are carton, bags, and containers untorn?

The best time to correct errors in deliveries is while the deliveryman is there and a credit memo can be written, unwanted damaged merchandise can be returned, and indications made on the invoice before the manager signs. It should be the policy of the accounts payable department that no invoices are paid that are not signed. In turn, this should be stated in bid contracts. A clear understanding should exist between the purchaser and supplier about delivery procedures if these are not stated in a contract.

The responsibility of receiving deliveries should be assigned to a competent person. In order to make sure that what is received is what is ordered— in the right quantity, in good condition, and at the correct price—the person receiving the food needs some basic information and equipment: (1) set of specifications, (2) weight charts for easy reference, (3) scales and thermometer, and (4) a table located near the service entrance for receiving the food. The receiving area ideally should be near the service entrance and before the area of storage. The larger the foodservice operation, the more elaborate the equipment needed for checking deliveries will be. A set of accurate scales is essential. There are various types of scales from auto-matic-indicating scales to recording scales, which are expensive but easy to use. Beam-type scales are the most commonly used, and are available in floor and table models.

CANNED FRUITS AND VEGETABLES

Specifications

Specifications for canned fruits and vegetables—whether purchased on the open market or by formal bid—should include several types of information: grade, style pack, variety, packing liquid, size, yield, and container size. Each of these factors is described briefly below.

Grade. Canned fruits are graded according to color, uniformity of pieces, and size (Fig. 7.4). The sugar content of the liquid in which they are packed may determine the grade, with the heavier syrup the higher the grade. To reduce sugar content and cost, a fruit can be packed in a lighter syrup or even water. Canned vegetables are graded according to color, uniformity of size and shape, maturity or tenderness, and texture. The grades for canned fruits and vegetables are as follows:

U.S. Fancy or *U.S. Grade A.* The highest quality products that are nearly uniform in size, color, tenderness, and maturity.

U.S. Grade B (Extra Standard for Vegetables; Choice for Fruits). A high-quality product that is not as uniform in color, size, or tenderness as U.S. Grade A.

U.S. Standard or *U.S. Grade C.* A good-quality product less uniform in size and slightly less tender than Grade B products and may not have as good color. However, such items may be used in mixed dishes: for example, Grade B fruits in pies and cobblers and vegetables in soups and stews.

Substandard or *U.S. Grade D.* This product may be broken up and off-color, irregular in shape, and less desirable in color.

Style Pack. The style pack refers to many different things, according to what the food product is. For example:

Green Beans. Cut, such as french style cut, kitchen style, long, whole.
Pineapple. Sliced, tidbits, broken pieces, crushed.
Carrots. Diced, sliced, julienne, whole.
Peaches. Whole, halves, sliced, pieces.
Corn. Whole kernel, creamed style.

Variety. Not only the variety of a fruit or vegetable but also the area of

CANNED PEACHES
Typical samples
U.S. GRADE A

Halves: Good yellow-orange color and texture typical of proper ripeness.

U.S. GRADE B

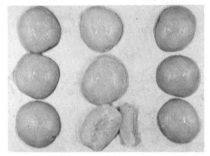

Halves: Some variation in color. Slight defects, such as a partial piece.

U.S. GRADE C

Mixed pieces: Good average quality. Variation in color and ripeness. Some blemished pieces.

FROZEN STRAWBERRIES
Typical samples
U.S. GRADE A

Whole: Color very good—red to pinkish red. Uniform in color and size.

U.S. GRADE B

Whole: Some variation in color and size.

U.S. GRADE C

Sliced: Slight variation in color and some mushiness, characteristic of sliced style.

FIG. 7.4. Examples of different grades of fruit.
Courtesy of U.S. Dept. of Agriculture.

the country in which it was grown may be specified. For example: Blue Lake Green Beans, Concord or Catawba Grapes, Freestone, or Cling Peaches.

Packing Liquid. The packing liquid may mean water, juice, syrup, butter, or vacuum packed. Syrup density for packing fruits is designated by grades. The heavier the syrup, the higher the grade—"Extra Heavy," "Heavy," "Light," "Slightly Sweetened Water," and "Water."

Size. The sieve and count are two ways of determining size. "Tender," "Small," and "Young" are other terms used to designate size. The number or count in the can may be extremely important in institutional foods where cost per serving is a definite consideration. If a No. 10 can of pear halves has only 25 pear halves and the food cost is figured on 30 or 35 halves to the can, the cost per serving will be approximately 20% higher than planned.

Yield or Drained Weight. The drained weight and yield of a canned product is an important consideration in comparing prices.

Size of Container. See Table 7.2 for common can sizes.

TABLE 7.2. Common Can Sizes

Can Size Industry Terms	Approx. Net Weight or Fluid Measure per Can (oz)	Approx. Cups	Cans per Case	Principal Products
8 oz	8	1	48 or 72	Ready-to-serve soups, fruits, vegetables
Picnic	10½–12	1¼	48	Mainly condensed soups, some fruits, vegetables
12 oz (vac.)	12	1½	24	Principally for family-size corn
No. 300	14–16	1¾	24	Family size—pork and beans, cranberry sauce, meat products
No. 303	16–17	2	24 or 36	Family size—fruits and vegetables, some meat products
No. 2	20 oz or 18 fl oz	2½	24	Family size—juices, ready-to-serve soups, some fruits
No. 2½	27–29	3½	24	Family size—fruits, some vegetables
Institutional Sizes				
No. 3 Cyl. or	51	5¾	12	Condensed soups, some vegetables, and some meats
48 fl oz	46	5¾	12	Fruit and vegetable juices
No. 10	6 lb to 7 lb 5 oz	12–13	6	Fruits, vegetables, and some other foods

Source: Adapted from *Food Buying Guide for School Food Service,* U.S. Dept. of Agriculture (1984).

Can Cuttings

One of the best ways of comparing brands and qualities of canned foods is to evaluate the products through a can cutting. Can cuttings may be done by a committee made up of high school students, principals, and foodservice people. Several brands of an item should be evaluated and the *best product* for the purpose with the *most yield* and *best price* selected.

An evaluation form, such as the one shown in Fig. 7.5, can be used in evaluating products. Labels should be removed from the cans and codes used to identify the products. Prices may or may not be given to evaluators before the best quality products are determined.

When evaluating a product, the following factors should be considered: net weight, drained weight, texture, defects, flavor, uniformity of product, color, juice or liquid, cost per case, cost per serving, and number of servings per can. To buy the product best suited for the use at the best price is the objective. Therefore, this should be kept in mind in evaluating products. If

Date _____   Evaluator _____

Instructions: Fill in each column. Circle the product recommended.

Item	Brand or Code	Weight on Can	Drained Weight	Presence of Defects	Condition of Liquid	Uniformity of Pieces	Price
Cut Green Beans							
Cut Green Beans							
Cut Green Beans							
Whole-Grain Corn							
Whole-Grain Corn							
Whole-Grain Corn							

Factors to consider:
  Presence of Defects—strings, tough, husks, bruises, dark spots.
  Condition of Liquid—clear, cloudy, milky.
  Uniformity of Pieces—sieve, broken pieces, size of pieces.
  Maturity of Product—tough, tender, starchy, ends tough, some too mature.
  Color of Product—color is what is expected for product, dark, pale.

FIG. 7.5. An evaluation form, like this sample, should be given to each person taking part in a can cutting.

peaches are to be used in pies and cobblers, the fancy peach halves are unnecessary. Slices or pieces, either U.S. Grade B or U.S. Grade C, should be considered. If the syrup of a canned fruit is not going to be used, a product with a light syrup adds less sugar to the menu and is a good buy at a lower cost than is a higher grade product with heavy syrup.

STAPLES

Writing specifications for staple groceries requires considerable knowledge about a great variety of products. There will be no attempt here to discuss the factors to be considered in writing specifications for these products. Kotschevar (1975) and Peddersen (1977) go into the characteristics of many staple products.

One of the basic staples to specify is flour. The quality and various types of wheats that flours are made from have many different characteristics. All-purpose, general-purpose flour is usually a blend that has a lower protein content than bread flours; it contains enough protein to make good yeast bread but not too much for quick breads. The blends are prepared to conform to the baking demands of different areas of the country.

In order for bread to contribute to meeting the meal pattern requirements under the National School Lunch Program, the bread must be made from enriched or whole-grain flour. Enriched flour is flour to which vitamins and minerals have been added. The milling process takes many of the vitamins and minerals out of the wheat, and enrichment puts them back in. Table 7.3 contains the minimum and maximum amounts of nutrients added per pound of flour.

It is not always a savings to buy a larger size or larger quantity if the product will inconvenience the user or if the product loses its quality before use. This is particularly true of spices—no more than a 3-month supply should be purchased at a time. However, the larger size of some staples may be more economical than the smaller size as illustrated by the price comparisons in Table 7.4.

TABLE 7.3. Nutrients Added
per Pound of Flour

Nutrient	Minimum (mg)	Maximum (mg)
Thiamine	1.1	1.8
Riboflavin	0.7	1.6
Niacin	10.0	15.0
Iron	8.0	12.5

TABLE 7.4. Price Comparison of Different Unit Packs

Item	Size	Price[1] ($)	Price Comparison for Same Quantity ($)	Savings ($)
Flour	25-lb bag	5.35	21.40	6.20
	100-lb bag	15.20	15.20	
Salt	24 26-oz boxes/case	7.92	5.00	2.10
	25-lb bag	2.90	2.90	
Sugar, brown	24 1-lb boxes/case	16.37	17.52	5.57
	25-lb bag	11.95	11.95	
Sugar, granulated	25-lb bag	10.90	43.60	12.83
	100-lb bag	30.77	30.77	
Vanilla flavoring,	1 qt	1.95	7.80	4.05
imitation	1 gal.	3.75	3.75	

[1] Sample prices are used.

MEAT AND POULTRY

The largest percentage of the food dollar is spent for meats; thus, specifications should assure the purchaser of getting what he wants. Meats are graded on three factors: quality, finish, and conformation. The quality is determined by the fineness of texture, deepness of color, and firmness of flesh. The distribution and firmness of the fat and the amount of fat determines the finish. Federal inspection and grading of meat are not compulsory. Meats shipped outside a state are federally inspected for wholesomeness (Fig. 7.6) to assure they were produced from animals free from disease at the time of slaughter and were packed under sanitary conditions.

Writing specifications for meat and being sure one is getting the quality specified can be a battle, depending on the reputation of the meatpacking company. Specifying U.S. Good with 25% fat for ground beef does not guarantee that it is delivered. One way for large-quantity meat buyers to be more assured that what is received is what was specified and paid for is by using the Meat Acceptance Service of the USDA.

Institutional Meat Purchase Specifications

The standards used by the Meat Acceptance Service are based on the USDA-approved Institutional Meat Purchase Specifications, referred to as IMPS. When meat and meat products are inspected by the Meat Acceptance Service, a USDA official must be present at all times while the meat is being ground, processed, and packaged (Fig. 7.7). This service is provided for a fee, which the supplier usually pays but will in turn pass on in the price to the purchaser. This service may increase the price of the meat as much as 6

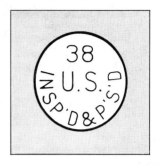

FIG. 7.6.   Inspection stamp for meat. *Courtesy of U.S. Dept. of Agriculture.*

FIG. 7.7.   USDA Acceptance Service stamp. *Courtesy of U.S. Dept. of Agriculture.*

to 10¢ per pound. The question becomes whether it is needed and whether it is worth that much to the buyer.

IMPS are specifications based on extensive testing done by the Livestock Division of USDA's Consumer and Marketing Service. They may be useful in writing meat specifications even without using the inspection of the Meat Acceptance Service. The specifications are available in a series at little cost from the U.S. Govt. Printing Office, Washington, DC (see Table 7.5 for series number for different meat products).

TABLE 7.5. USDA Meat Specifications

Type of Product	Series
Beef, fresh	100
Lamb and mutton, fresh	200
Veal and calf, fresh	300
Pork, fresh	400
Pork products, cured and smoked	500
Beef products, cured	600
Edible by-products, cured	700
Sausage products	800
Canned meat products	900
Portion control products	1000

When the Meat Acceptance Service has been required by a purchaser, the federal grader will need a copy of the purchasers specifications of what is to be delivered. The meat grader is responsible for accepting the product and certifying that it is in compliance with those specifications. The federal grader's stamp ("USDA Accepted as Specified") will appear on each item of meat or on the sealed carton in which it is packed. Information pertaining to the Meat Acceptance Service can be obtained by writing the Meat Grading Branch, Livestock Division, Consumer and Marketing Service, U.S. Dept. of Agriculture, Washington, DC 20250.

Beef

Beef becomes less tender as the animal grows older. The grades of beef are shown in Fig. 7.8 and defined as follows:

U.S. Prime. From steers or heifers no more than 3 years old, it is well marbled with fat, flavorful, and very tender. This grade is used primarily by the best restaurants and hotels.

U.S. Choice. From steers, heifers, and cows no more than 3½ years old, it is very similar to Prime but contains less fat and may not be as tender.

U.S. Standard. From cattle no more than 4 years old, it has little fat and lacks the flavor of the better grades. However, this grade of beef with the addition of fat can be ground to make a very flavorful hamburger patty.

FIG. 7.8. Meat grades are indicated with a shield-shaped grademark with the appropriate grade name.
Courtesy of U.S. Dept. of Agriculture.

U.S. Commercial. From cattle more than 4 years old, this grade requires long, slow, moist cooking in order to become tender enough to eat.

U.S. Utility, Cutter, and Canner. This grade is used in canned meat products primarily or in sausage making.

The grade of beef does not reflect on the wholesomeness of the meat. U.S. Standard beef is as wholesome and sanitary to eat as U.S. Prime. The grade does affect the nutritional value slightly in that Prime is higher in fat content than the other grades. As a matter of fact, the lower grades have less caloric value per pound and more protein, minerals, and vitamins than Prime.

But not all beef is federally graded. Many meat companies have their own grading standards. However, if the terms U.S. Prime, U.S. Choice, etc., are used, the meat must meet the specifications set by the USDA for those grades. *The Meat Handbook* (Levie 1970) has an excellent chapter on meat specifications.

Poultry

Poultry, particularly chicken and turkey, is popular on school menus. Chicken is classified as fryer or broiler, roaster, capon, hen or stewing chicken, and rooster. Turkeys are classified according to age and sex as fryer or roaster, young hen or young tom, and hen or tom.

The Poultry Inspection Act of 1959 assures the purchaser and consumer that all poultry shipped interstate has been federally inspected for wholesomeness. Poultry is graded as U.S. grades A, B, and C. The grades are determined by the general condition, conformation, fat covering, presence of disjointed, broken bones, and absence of missing parts and flesh. Grade A is recommended for frying. Grades B and C may be good buys for stewing or roasting chicken. Chicken and turkey may be purchased whole or cut into pieces—breasts, drumsticks, thighs, wings, and backs. Due to labor cost, lack of equipment, and the waste involved, purchasing chicken pieces of the desired cuts is usually the custom.

Chicken for frying can be purchased in all stages of preparedness—precut, precoated, prebrowned, and fully cooked. The fully cooked chicken requires heating to reconstitute and is a very satisfactory product for schools. Bid chicken for frying or fully cooked "by-the-piece" not "by-the-pound."

Mechanically processed poultry may contain small bone fragments. This may be a problem in certain brands of turkey or chicken hot dogs and other sausage products. The regulations for such products are not as restrictive as those for meat hot dogs, for example. Specifications can be written to limit the amount of mechanically separated poultry used. The use of mechanically separated meat is limited by regulation to 20% of a meat hot dog.

SOY PROTEIN EXTENDERS

Soy protein products—including isolated soy protein, textured vegetable protein, soy flour, and other forms of concentrates—are economical sources of protein. The use of soy protein products in school foodservices increased after USDA approved their use in 1971 for meeting a part of the meat/meat alternate meal pattern requirement. The regulation was updated in 1983 to include isolated soy protein. Though isolates have no economic advantage over concentrates, they may be a better-quality product and result in better acceptability of meats extended with soy products.

FNS Notice 219 (USDA) specifies that a ratio of up to 30 parts hydrated vegetable protein may be used with 70 parts uncooked meat, poultry, or fish on the basis of weight. Hydrated means that moisture has been put back into the product. For example, 12 pounds of dry textured vegetable protein and 18 pounds of water will produce 30 pounds of hydrated product to which 70 pounds of meat, poultry, or fish can be added. The soy product is most frequently and successfully added to ground beef. The maximum ratio works better when soy/meat blend is used in a mixed dish with seasoning, such as tacos, pizza sauce, or spaghetti sauce. Some school foodservice directors prefer using only 15 to 20% hydrated vegetable protein.

EGGS

Eggs can be purchased in many forms—liquid, frozen, dried, and fresh. Care must be taken in storing eggs of any form. Frozen eggs should be kept at 0°F or colder. After eggs are thawed, bacterial growth starts; thus the eggs should be used within two days, to be safe. Frozen eggs come in container sizes up to 30 pounds. The 30-pound size may seem like a bargain but very often this is too large for a school to use within two days.

Dried eggs are appreciated by bakers and cooks who have learned to use them properly. This product can save time and assure more uniformity of product. Dried eggs may be weighed with the dry ingredients, and the water for reconstituting them added with the other liquids. Dried eggs should be stored in the refrigerator after the cans are opened. *Salmonella* bacteria have been found in dried eggs, so it is recommended that dried eggs be used only in foods that are to be cooked thoroughly.

Fresh eggs are graded U.S. Grade AA or Fresh Fancy, Grade A, and Grade B. Grade A is not necessary for all uses. However, Grade A eggs are recommended for fried, scrambled, and hard-cooked eggs and for omelets. Use of Grade B eggs in baking will mean quite a saving. The grades do not reflect the nutritive value or the wholesomeness of the egg, neither does the color of an egg's shell. Eggs that are officially graded under federal or federal-state

**TABLE 7.6.   U.S. Weight Classes
for Consumer Grades of Shell Eggs**

Size or Class	Minimum Weight per Dozen (oz)	Minimum Weight per 30-Dozen Case (lb)
Jumbo	30	56
Extra large	27	50+
Large	24	45
Medium	21	39+
Small	18	34
Peewees	15	28+

Source: Based on information from Home and Garden Bull. 1, U.S. Dept. of Agriculture (1971a).

supervision bear a grademark in the form of a shield, which states the grade (or quality) and the size (based on weight per dozen).

Grading of eggs is voluntary and not required. However, more than 75% of all egg products are processed under the USDA voluntary egg inspection program. It is a service that is available when the processor requests it and pays the fee.

Eggs are also classified according to size. The U.S. weight classes for consumer grades of shell eggs are based on net minimum weights expressed in ounces per dozen (Table 7.6)

FRESH PRODUCE

Fresh produce should be purchased in the quantity needed within the keeping period of the produce. It is frequently purchased on an informal-bid or formula basis. Fresh produce is such a changing market of highly perishable products that it is a huge gamble for a vendor to quote a sealed bid price on the products for 6 to 9 months in advance. Formula bidding works well and allows for the fluctuation of prices; fresh produce also is often purchased on short-term fixed-price bids. The average prices charged at 22 terminals nationwide are published weekly in Market Bulletin No. 16, available through the USDA Marketing Service.

Grades are of little assurance or help in buying fresh produce unless the vendor has a good reputation. The product may be U.S. No. 1 at the time of grading, but at the time of delivery it may not be usable. Although Fancy means top grade for canned foods, this is not always true from one fresh product to another. Grades are just now being standardized.

The cost of fresh produce fluctuates with the seasons, demand, quantity of the crops, and the part of the country the product comes from. Comparative shopping can mean significant savings. Tomatoes may range in price over a year from 49 to 99¢ per pound. Tomatoes differ in quality and the best quality may be available when they sell for 49¢ per pound. That is the season of the year tomatoes should be on menus. Red cabbage, radishes, shredded carrots, or unpeeled cucumber slices can add color and variety to a tossed salad at a fraction of the cost of tomatoes when tomatoes are not in season. Canned frozen, or dehydrated green peppers and onions may be better buys than fresh. Canned celery has been used very satisfactorily in some recipes and at a savings over fresh celery when celery is not in season.

The quantity purchased will also affect the price. Cellophane bags of carrots in 2-pound sizes are much more expensive than 25-, 50-, or 100-pound bags. However, if only a few pounds are needed it would be wiser to pay more per pound and purchase the quantity needed. Buying lettuce by the case is less expensive than buying by the head, but if six heads of lettuce are all that is needed within a week to 8 days, buying the quantity needed would be more economical. Precut lettuce may be the best buy.

When writing specifications for fresh fruits and vegetables the variety, size, degree of maturity, color, and texture are a few of the factors to consider. Recommendations for purchasing specific fruits and vegetables follow.

Fresh Fruits

Apples, Eating (Counter). Specify U.S. Fancy or U.S. No. 1 Grade, a minimum of 2½ inches in diameter. Red Delicious, Golden Delicious, McIntosh, Stayman, Jonathan, Winesap, and Wagoner are all good eating varieties. Order by box or bushel and by count per box or bushel.

Apples, Cooking. Specify U.S. No. 2 or unclassified (depending on use). Tart or slightly acid varieties include Gravenstein, Grimes Golden, Jonathan, and Newtown. Firmer-fleshed varieties are Rome Beauty, Northern Spy, Rhode Island Greening, Wealthy, and Winesap.

Bananas. No federal grade is required. Size of 5 to 6 inches long is suggested for hand eating. Order Bananas by the pound or by count boxes (150). Order "hard ripe" (takes 5 to 6 days to ripen), "turning ripe" (takes 3 days to ripen), or "full ripe" (use within 24 hours) depending on when they will be used. Bananas are available year-round and should be ripened at 60 to 70°F.

Cantaloupes (Muskmelons). Specify U.S. No. 1 Grade in hampers, boxes, or sacks. Size No. 45 is recommended for serving halves or quarters.

Generally cantaloupes are available May through September. They usually are not ripe when delivered; hold 2 to 4 days at room temperature for ripening.

Oranges. Specify U.S. No. 1 Grade, and order by the crate or dozen and by count size. Small-size oranges are approximately 2½ inches in diameter (226 to 324 count per 1⅗ bushel); medium ones are about 3 inches in diameter (144–176 to 200 count per 1⅗ bushel); and large ones are approximately 3½ inches in diameter (96 to 126 count per 1⅗ bushel). The recommended sizes for hand eating are the 150 and 176 counts.

Recommended orange varieties are Navel (winter), Valencia (summer), Temple, and Pineapple (lots of seeds). Strict state regulations require that oranges be well matured before harvest when they are to be shipped out of state. When artificial color has been added, the fruit must be labeled "color added."

Fresh Vegetables

Grading of fresh vegetables is not required, and it is possible to get ungraded vegetables of excellent quality. If vegetables have been graded, the container in which they are packed will bear the official USDA grade shield or the statement "Packed Under Continuous Inspection of the U.S. Dept. of Agriculture," or "USDA Inspected" (Fig. 7.9).

Cabbage. Specify U.S. No. 1 Grade. There are three major types of cabbage: smooth-leaved green cabbage, crinkly-leaved savoy cabbage, and red cabbage. Heads should be firm and the outer leaves green or red depending on type. Cabbage is sold by the pound, 40-pound bushel, and mesh sack of 50 pounds.

Lettuce. Specify U.S. No. 1 Grade. Varieties include iceberg lettuce (heads large, round, solid, medium-green outer leaves), butter-head lettuce

FIG. 7.9. Fresh fruits and vegetables grade shield. *Courtesy of U.S. Dept. of Agriculture.*

(bib or Boston, loose head, flat on top, light to dark green), romaine lettuce (tall, cylindrical with crisp, dark-green leaves), and leaf lettuce (includes many locally grown varieties). Lettuce is sold by the head, crate, or bushel hamper. May through July is the peak season, but lettuce is available year-round. Precut lettuce is available in 10-pound packages.

Potatoes. U.S. No. 1 Grade is the most commonly used grade. There are three types of potato: new, general purpose, and baking. "New" potatoes are dug before fully mature, are waxy, and require moist cooking—not good for mashed or french fried. General-purpose potatoes are round or oval in shape. Baking potatoes are high in starch content. Russet Burbank, White Rose, and Maine Katahdin are the most widely used baking varieties. Potatoes are sold in boxes by count indicating size (50 to 125 per box). New potatoes and all-purpose potatoes are sold in 25-, 50-, and 100-pound mesh bags.

FROZEN FRUITS AND VEGETABLES

The grades of frozen fruits and vegetables are similar to those of canned ones. However, there are usually not as many grades to choose from in a particular food. The grades are U.S. Grade A (Fancy), U.S. Grade B (Choice or Extra Standard), U.S. Grade C (Standard), and Sub-standard. The grades are based on maturity, color, cut, absence of defects, and flavor as they are for canned fruits and vegetables.

Frozen Fruits

Frozen fruits are sold in sizes ranging from 10-ounce packages to 30-pound tins. The grades are A, B, and C, but not all grades are available in each fruit. Factors to be specified are style (sliced, halves, whole, broken pieces, pitted, etc.), type (yellow cling, yellow freestone, light Royal Anne, dark Bing cherries, etc.), sugar-fruit ratio, and package size. For example, specifications for strawberries might read as follows: Strawberries—Sliced, Marshall Variety. Sugar-fruit ratio of 1.4. Medium-size berries. U.S. Grade A. Packaged 30-pound containers.

Frozen Vegetables

The most common package sizes for frozen vegetables for institutional use are 2, 2½, 3, and 3½ pounds; however, some vegetables are packaged in 20- to 30-pound bulk containers. Once vegetables are thawed, they should be used, as their quality deteriorates rapidly. Deliveries should be checked to assure that frozen food is still frozen at the time of delivery.

DAIRY PRODUCTS

The milk used in the federal milk program or as part of the meal may be whole milk, lowfat or skim milk, buttermilk, or chocolate milk. An example of a bid specification for milk is in Appendix IV.

Pasteurized milk has been subjected to temperatures no lower than 145°F for not less than 30 minutes or 161°F for not less than 15 seconds and then promptly cooled to 40°F or lower. *Homogenized* milk is pasteurized milk that has been mechanically treated to reduce the size of the fat globules. This stabilizes the emulsion so the fat does not rise to the top. *Vitamin D* milk is whole or skimmed milk in which the vitamin D content has been increased by addition of at least 400 USP units per quart. *Chocolate milk* is the term used for whole milk to which sugar and chocolate have been added. If cocoa is substituted for chocolate, the milk is designated as *chocolate-flavored.* *Chocolate drink* is made from skim milk or milk that contains less than 3.25% milk fat. If cocoa is used in place of chocolate, it is designated as *chocolate-flavored drink.*

Price changes for fresh fluid milk are published weekly by the Agricultural Marketing Service and can be used in the bid contract as a means to determine justified price increases.

Butter is not required to be graded. However, most of the butter on the market is graded by either a state or federal grader. The grades are U.S. Grade AA, U.S. Grade A, U.S. Grade B, and U.S. Grade C. Butter should be frozen if it is to be stored for more than 2 weeks. Margarine is a good substitute for butter in school lunch programs if it is enriched with at least 15,000 units of vitamin A per pound.

The variety of cheese needed is determined by how it will be used. The flavor desired and the moisture and fat contents are important considerations in selecting cheese for the menus. The most frequently used varieties of cheese in school foodservice are described below.

Cheddar cheese is U.S. graded (AA, A, B, C) and the characteristics differ greatly according to the length of time ripened. It is typically sold by 5- and 10-pound bricks and 30-pound wheels. *Processed cheese* is probably the most popular in the school market. It can be purchased in 5- to 10-pound bricks and even sliced. Processed cheese is frequently used in grilled cheese sandwiches. *Creamed cheese* is a soft cheese which deteriorates rapidly. It is purchased in 1-, 2-, 3-, and 5-pound bricks. *Cottage cheese* is purchased fresh thus the expiration date is very important. It comes in large-soft and small-hard curd varieties, commonly in 5- and 10-pound containers. *Mozzarella cheese* is popular in the making of pizza. Many of the pizza manufacturers, however, use a blend of cheeses for pizza. The fat content of mozzarella cheese varies greatly and has an effect on the melting characteristics.

There are many substitutes for the natural cheese product. They are often made from soy products, but have very similar characteristics to the natural product. The price is usually *lower.* If you choose to use one of the cheese foods or synthetics, be sure the product contributes to the meat/meat alternate of the meal pattern when that is important to the use.

WHAT KIND OF BUYER ARE YOU?

A foodservice manager who neglects to follow businesslike purchasing practices is asking for financial problems. The following self-test will help answer the questions, "Do you buy?" or "Are you sold?"

Test for Buyers

Answer "Yes" or "No" to the questions listed below. Every "Yes" answer equals 10 points.

1. Do you know what you want before the salesman comes or calls? _____

2. Are your menus planned in advance? _____
3. Are purchases made according to specific needs of the menu? _____

4. Do you refuse to accept personal gifts, premiums, stamps, etc.? _____

5. Are specifications written describing the food (quality, grade, etc.) best suited for your needs? _____
6. Are orders checked and inspected at time of delivery to see if they meet specifications? _____
7. Are you up-to-date on foods, packaging, new products? _____
8. Do you try new products in small quantities before buying a large supply? _____
9. Do you refuse to buy "bargains" unless they can be utilized on the menus? _____
10. Do you buy products because they meet your needs rather than by brands? _____

"No" answers indicate that practices need re-evaluating and perhaps changed in order to be a wise buyer.

BIBLIOGRAPHY

ANON. 1975. Almanac of the Canning, Freezing, Preserving Industries. Edward E. Judge & Sons, Westminister, MD.
BEAU, F. N. 1970. Quantity Food Purchasing Guide. Institutions Magazine, Chicago. IL.
FLANAGAN, T. 1968. School Food Purchasing Guide. Am. School Food Service Assoc. and Assoc. of School Business Officials, Chicago.
GOULD, W. A. 1977. Food Quality Assurance. AVI Publishing Co., Westport, CT.
KELLY, H. J. 1970. Food Service Purchasing: Principles and Practices. Chain Store Publishing Corp., New York.
KOTSCHEVAR, L. 1975. Quantity Food Purchasing. 2nd edition. John Wiley & Sons, New York.

LEVIE, A. 1970. The Meat Handbook. 3rd edition. AVI Publishing Co., Westport, CT.

LIVINGSTON, G. E., ed. 1979. Food Service Systems Analysis, Design, and Implementation. Academic Press, New York.

MIESEL, G. E. 1972. What's in the can? School Foodservice J. 26(6):32–35.

MOYER, W. C. 1976. The Buying Guide for Fresh Fruits, Vegetables, Herbs and Nuts. Blue Goose Inc., Fullerton, CA.

NATL. CANNERS ASSOC. 1967. Canned Food Tables. 6th edition. National Canners Assoc., Washington, DC.

NINEMEIER, J. D. 1983. Purchasing, Receiving, and Storage: A Systems Manual for Restaurants, Hotels, and Clubs. CBI Publishing Co., Boston.

PEDDERSEN, R. B. 1977. Specs: The Comprehensive Foodservice Puchasing and Specification Manual. CBI Publishing Co., Boston.

U.S. DEPT. OF AGRICULTURE. 1970. USDA's Acceptance Service for Meat and Meat Products. U.S. Govt. Printing Office, Washington, DC.

U.S. DEPT. OF AGRICULTURE. 1971a. Home and Garden Bulletin: How to Use USDA Grades in Buying Food. U.S. Govt. Printing Office, Washington, DC.

U.S. DEPT. OF AGRICULTURE. 1971b. Institutional Meat Purchase Specifications General Requirements. U.S. Govt. Printing Office, Washington, DC.

U.S. DEPT. OF AGRICULTURE. 1977. Food Purchasing Pointers for School Food Service. U.S. Govt. Printing Office, Washington, DC.

U.S. DEPT. OF AGRICULTURE. 1978a. Food Price Sources for School Food Procurement. U.S. Govt. Printing Office, Washington, DC.

U.S. DEPT. OF AGRICULTURE. 1978b. Study of School Food Procurement Practices. Vols. I and II. U.S. Govt. Printing Office, Washington, DC.

U.S. DEPT. OF AGRICULTURE. 1982. Food—From Farm to Table. 1982 Yearbook of Agriculture. U.S. Govt. Printing Office, Washington, DC.

U.S. DEPT. OF AGRICULTURE. 1984. Food Buying Guide for Child Nutrition Programs. U.S. Govt. Printing Office, Washington, DC.

WEST, B. B., G. S. SHUGART, and M. F. WILSON. 1978. Food for Fifty. 6th edition. John Wiley & Sons, New York.

WEST, B., L. WOOD, V. HARGER, and G. SHUGART. 1977. Food Service in Institutions. 6th edition. John Wiley & Sons, New York.

FOOD PREPARATION

Food preparation has changed greatly in the last 20 years as convenience (pre-prepared) foods have been improved. Food preparation in the original sense was both an art and a science. A knowledge of food preparation as an art and a science is no longer required in school foodservices to meet the objectives of the program and to do it quite satisfactorily.

Creativity and skill are required to make food attractive, appetizing, flavorful, and interesting. A scientific approach is needed to conserve the nutritive value of fruits and vegetables, to understand the principles of cooking, and to understand why certain things happen in food preparation. With pre-prepared items, following the directions precisely is often the secret of success. Even when food is prepared "from scratch," the standardized recipes and controlled equipment of today make it possible—even easy—to turn out good products. The preparation of food in school foodservices as in many other food industries, no longer requires a "chef" per se. It is with this in mind that this chapter is written.

The objectives of food preparation of raw food are (1) to improve the digestibility of the food, (2) to conserve the nutritive value, (3) to improve the flavor and appearance of the food, and (4) to make the food safe for consumption. The degree to which each of these objectives is carried out determines the quality of the food served, as does quality of the purchased food. Only when preparation starts with good-quality food, is it possible to serve a good-quality product.

STANDARDIZED RECIPES

One of the most important tools in preparing food in large quantities is a standardized recipe. A recipe is a written direction for preparing an item. A standardized recipe is a recipe that has been tested for good quality and yield (Table 8.1). School food operations cannot afford to prepare food

TABLE 8.1.   A Standardized Recipe for Barbecue Beef

Ingredients	(lb)	(oz)	Measures	Directions
Ground beef[1]	16	12		1. Brown ground beef and drain thoroughly.
Tomato juice		23 (fl)	2¾ cups	2. Combine tomato juice, tomato
Tomato puree			1 No. 10 can or 3 qt	puree, water, vinegar, catsup, sugar, chili powder, mustard, salt,
Catsup			1¾ cups	and Worcestershire sauce.
Water			2 cups	
Vinegar			1¼ cups	
Brown sugar		13	2½ cups	
Chili powder			2 tsp	
Mustard, dry			2 tsp	
Salt			¼ cup	
Worcestershire sauce			2 Tbsp	
Oil or fat		6	¾ cup	3. Saute onions and celery in oil or
Onions, chopped		7½	1½ cups	fat until transparent.
Celery, chopped		6	1½ cups	
				4. Add tomato mixture and cook 1½ hr. Stir often.
				5. Add sauce to cooked meat. Heat thoroughly.
				6. Serve on heated bun, using No. 12 scoop (approximately ⅓ cup servings).

Column header note: 100 Servings / Weights

[1]Ground pork, canned chicken, roast beef, or pork can be substituted in this recipe.

without standardized recipes because they are part of the blueprint for building a good-quality, sound operation. Using standardized recipes and standard weights and measures in following recipes has many advantages:

1. Insures uniform quality and eliminates "trial and error"
2. Helps to know the yield and prevents waste and running out
3. Saves time and money
4. Enables precosting of menus
5. Simplifies the job of employees
6. Helps in determining what to order and how much
7. Helps assure compliance with meal requirements

When standardized tested recipes are not used, the cost may vary every time a food is prepared. "Trial and error" is too risky for quantity foodservices. Customers who like a certain food want to be able to depend on the food being the same each time; this is especially true of school-age customers. If the spaghetti with meat sauce was good, they want it to taste the same the next time—then the comment, hopefully, will be "I like the spaghetti the way the school makes it."

To most foodservice managers, the two things most feared in their work are food poisoning and running out of food. Food poisoning is discussed in Chapter 10. A standardized recipe will assure the manager of a sufficient yield if the portions are controlled in a standardized method. Running out of food is bad for the reputation of a foodservice, and it cheats the students who must be served a peanut butter and jelly sandwich because the cook did not use a standardized recipe and ran out of spaghetti with meat sauce.

Inexperienced and experienced cooks should use a recipe. There is still room for creativity, of improving on a recipe. Some cooks, who have the ability to prepare good food without recipes, cannot understand why they should use them. If the students are content, costs are not too high, and yields are satisfactory, there may be little reason to urge a cook to change. However, a cook's skill will be of no value to the foodservice if the cook becomes sick or decides to resign. The recipes should be written out and then be standardized.

Numerous published sources of standardized recipes are available. The publication *Quantity Recipes for Type A School Lunches* (U.S. Dept. of Agriculture 1971) is the most familiar source for school foodservices. However, because the yield data for many foods were changed in 1980 and again in 1984, these recipes are obsolete and should be revised soon. These recipes are basic ones that a creative cook or baker can improve, adjust to the taste of the locale, and adjust to the equipment available. The adjustments should be standardized by putting into definite time, weights, and measures. Cooks and bakers should be encouraged to standardize their own recipes. Time required to prepare a recipe is important information that should be added to all recipes. These time requirements help management establish goals and provide gauges for judging the speed of employees. With the current emphasis on reducing the quantity of fat, sugar, and salt in diets, all recipes should be evaluated to determine if these ingredients can be decreased while still producing an acceptable product.

Format for Quantity Recipes

The following format for writing standardized recipes was adapted from *Guides for Writing and Evaluating Quantity Recipes for Type A School Lunches* (U.S. Dept. of Agriculture 1969). It is most convenient to record recipes on 5 × 8 inch cards.

Name of Recipe.   Use chief food in recipe or a name that is readily understood. Simple descriptive terms, such as "Chicken Pot Pies," "Apple Pie," "Chocolate Cake," are examples of good recipe names.

Ingredients.   List ingredients in the order they are used in preparing the recipe. Use a descriptive term *before* an ingredient to indicate the type or style to be purchased or cooking or heating needed before its use (for example, "canned tomatoes," "rolled oats," "cooked rice," "hot milk"). Use a descriptive term *after* the ingredient indicating preparation needed (for example, "cooked turkey, diced"; "onion, chopped"; "apples, pared, sliced").

Weights and Measures.   Give weights and measures when practical, weight alone when the item is not easily measured. Use measure alone for liquids such as water, broth, and milk and for small quantities too small to weigh accurately. The booklet *Average Weight of a Measured Cup of Various Foods* (U.S. Dept. of Agriculture 1977) is useful.

Directions.   Recipe directions should be simply written and easy to understand and follow. The number and size of pans should be indicated. Baking temperature and time required to cook should be given. Many steps can be eliminated or combined to reduce the time required to prepare the recipe. Use as few words as possible in describing procedures.

Yield.   Portion size should be given in common measure or weight units and the total number servings the recipe will yield should be indicated.

Additional Information.   Include other information that is helpful in menu planning. For example:

1. Contribution to the school lunch meal patterns requirements (Fig. 8.1)
2. Cost per portion
3. Variations that can be obtained by changing or replacing an ingredient, by changing the method of cooking, or method of combining ingredients, etc.

Adjusting Yield and Portion Size

When the portions indicated in a recipe are not the size desired, then changes should be made. For example, if a spaghetti with meat sauce recipe yields 100 ⅔-cup portions and the portion size desired for secondary high school students is 1 cup, the recipe will have to be increased by ⅓. Recipes are most frequently written to yield 50 or 100 portions. Ordinarily it will be necessary to adjust recipes to serve different numbers. Adjusting recipes should be done carefully with a second person checking the mathematics. Failures are frequently caused by mathematical errors in adjusting recipes.

(1) SCHOOL NAME _____
(2) Date _____
(3) Day (Circle) M T W T F
(4) Meal (Check) Breakfast
    Snack AM/PM
    Lunch

A SAMPLE FOOD PRODUCTION RECORD

(5) MENU	Recipe Source (6)	Portion Size (7)	Number Portions Planned (8)	(9) FOOD PREPARED			(12) PORTIONS SERVED					
				Foods Used to Meet Requirement* (10)	Quantity Food Used (11)	Students (13)	Adults (14)	A la carte (15)	Other (16)	Left over (17)	Total Portions (18)
(19) MEAT/ ALTERNATES List all menu items in appropriate food category	Give source and number (e.g., USDA: D-14)	Express as weight, measure, scoop or ladle size, or size of piece or portion	Record number of portions prepared	Record name of each food used to meet meal requirement in the appropriate food category (e.g., If beef pie is the *menu item*, beef would be in the meat/ alternate section; potatoes and carrots in pie would be listed in vegetable/fruit section; pie crust in the bread/ alternate section)	Use weight, measures, or numbers	Actual number	Actual number (include staff)	Do not include this column to record portion sold à la carte only	Can use this column to record portion sent out from base kitchen or rec'd by a satellite school	Measure and weigh leftovers and convert to number of portions	Total number of portions served for each menu item
(20) VEGETABLES/ FRUITS											
(21) BREAD/ ALTERNATES											
(22) MILK AS BEVERAGE											
(23) OTHER FOODS											

*Indicate if raw or precooked

(24) Sign to verify correct information

_____
Manager

FIG. 8.1. The production record shows contribution to meal pattern.
Courtesy of Chiquita Brands, Inc., United Brands Company.

Weights and measures should be expressed in the simplest terms (Table 8.2).

It is possible to enlarge a home recipe, but this is not advisable except when testing is possible. When a home recipe for 10 is increased to serve 300, the yield will be slightly more than 300 portions if the original recipe is simply multiplied by 30. The percentage of loss to the pan, in measuring, etc., which is figured into the recipe, decreases when a recipe is enlarged. For example, it has been shown that when a recipe for 50 is adjusted to serve 900 portions the recipe should be increased 18 times, but then decreased by as much as 10%. Also to be considered in adjusting a recipe is the equipment available. If a 30-quart mixer is available, it is useless to increase a cake recipe to 400 portions when the mixer will not hold that quantity.

8 **Food Preparation**

TABLE 8.2. Adjusting a Recipe for Brownies

	100 Portions				400 Portions		
	Weights			For 400	Weights		
Ingredients	(lb)	(oz)	Measures	× Factor =	(lb)	(oz)	Measures
All-purpose flour	1	8		× 4 =	6		
Sugar	3	8		× 4 =	14		
Nonfat dry milk		1		× 4 =		4	
Baking powder		½		× 4 =		2	
Salt			3½ tsp	× 4 =			¼ cup + 2 tsp
Nuts, chopped		12		× 4 =	3		
Bitter chocolate	1			× 4 =	4		
Shortening	1	2		× 4 =	4	8	
Eggs	1	12½		× 4 =	7	2	
Water			1 cup	× 4 =			1 qt
Vanilla			2 tsp	× 4 =			2 Tbsp + 2 tsp

FOLLOWING A RECIPE

The terminology used in recipes must be understood by the person following the recipe. A few common abbreviations, equivalents, and cooking terms are listed here.

Abbreviations
Most Commonly Used

Teaspoon	tsp
Tablespoon	Tbsp
Ounce	oz
Pound	lb
Quart	qt
Gallon	gal.

"Cup" is not abbreviated

Weight and Measure
Equivalents

3 tsp = 1 Tbsp = ½ fluid oz
16 Tbsp = 1 cup = 8 fluid oz
4 cups = 1 qt
4 qt = 1 gal.
16 oz = 1 lb

Oven Temperatures and Descriptive Terms

121 to 135°C–250 to 275°F   very slow oven
149 to 163°C–300 to 325°F   slow oven

177 to 191°C–350 to 375°F   moderate oven
204 to 218°C–400 to 425°F   hot oven
232 to 246°C–450 to 475°F   very hot oven
260 to 274°C–500 to 525°F   extremely hot oven

BASIC TOOLS

The basic tools needed to prepare a standardized recipe are a set of standardized graduated measuring cups and measuring spoons, standard size pans, and table model scales for weighing small and large quantities of ingredients (digitial scales are preferred). Certainly it is most important to have good-quality ingredients as required in the recipe. Sometimes it is necessary or desirable to make substitutions because of an emergency or shortage to save time, to utilize leftovers, to utilize USDA-donated foods, to increase nutritive value, or to reduce cost. Using substitute ingredients requires skill and knowledge. The quality of the finished product may or may not be altered.

When preparing a recipe, one should start by reading the recipe carefully. Then the utensils, tools, and ingredients needed should all be assembled before starting. The ingredients should be weighed or measured carefully. Weighing of ingredients is more accurate and less time-consuming than measuring. It assures a more standardized product. Liquids may be weighed or measured. In baked products, eggs should be weighed. USDA recipes are based on "large" eggs. There are many times during the year when "medium" eggs may be the best buy. However, when the "medium" egg is used in the same number in the recipe, this can affect the outcome of the product, particularly the volume of baked products. Table 8.3 is a guide to substituting eggs of different sizes.

TABLE 8.3. Guide for Using Whole Eggs of Various Sizes
in Recipes

Number of Large Eggs	Extra Large Eggs	Medium Eggs	Small Eggs	Approximate Volume
	In Recipe Use Equivalent to:			
1	1	1	1	3 Tbsp
2	2	2	3	¼ cup + 2 Tbsp
3	3	4	4	½ cup + 2 Tbsp
4	3	5	6	¾ cup
5	4	6	7	1 cup
6	5	7	8	1 cup + 2 Tbsp
8	6	10	11	1½ cups
10	8	12	14	2 cups
12	10	14	17	2½ cups

The directions for combining the ingredients and cooking the product—size and number of pans, temperature, and time—should be followed carefully. The yield of a recipe cannot be depended on unless the correct size and number of pans are used and are uniformly filled. Overcooking will decrease the yield.

CONTROLLING QUALITY

The quality of prepared food is determined in degrees of good or bad according to the standards of the persons judging the food. The quality of food is judged on aroma, appearance, flavor, texture, consistency, and temperature. The objective of a school foodservice manager is to prepare and serve the quality of food considered good by the majority of customers. Rare roast beef may not be considered good by most elementary children, though it will be by many adults. Spaghetti considered good by students in the northeastern United States may be bland to students in Texas. But some basic standards can be applied almost universally in quality judging. What is a good-quality hamburger? The standard definition would be a juicy, tender, flavorful piece of meat served on a fresh warmed bun with the desired condiments. To obtain this standard of quality requires a good-quality ground beef patty that is cooked at the right temperature for the right amount of time, seasoned to accentuate the flavor, and served hot, as soon after cooking as possible, on a fresh warmed bun with the desired condiments.

Both management and employees must be involved in controlling quality in preparation. Management must know the quality desired and how to judge and obtain this quality; must set quality standards; and must check constantly on quality. Employees must be trained to use the basic tools for controlling quality.

Excellence in food preparation requires well-planned menus, standardized recipes, standardized procedures, precise purchasing specifications to obtain the right ingredients and good ingredients, good receiving and storing procedures, and well-trained personnel with good supervision. The basic tools for controlling quality are standardized recipes, thermometers, portion scales, standard measuring utensils, clocks and timers. Timing is one of the crucial factors. Scheduling preparation so that food is ready for serving at its peak has a definite effect on the quality. Holding foods, particularly fresh produce items and protein-rich foods at warming temperatures, decreases their quality rapidly. Those final touches—accentuating and improving flavors according to the likes and dislikes of the customers—can make the difference between food being considered just average or really good. One of the biggest complaints children have about preplated frozen dinners packed by national companies is the lack of flavor, either desired flavor or flavor characteristic to the locale.

Management can judge the quality and acceptability of the food served by evaluating the amount of sales, customer reaction, and plate waste. Plate waste should be checked daily. If food is coming back on the plate, the manager and employees should evaluate the food, get student opinions, and then decide what the problem is—quality, seasonings, temperature, or is it the food itself? Quality, seasoning, and temperature can and should be improved according to customer standards. If a particular food is disliked, management should plan ways of making it acceptable, should provide menu choices when it is served, or should remove it from the menu completely.

An understanding of the basic characteristics of food is needed for controlling the quality of food. If the yeast rolls fail to rise, it is important to know what could have caused this failure. Some of the basic characteristics of different foods and procedures for obtaining high-quality products, which foodservice cooks and bakers should know, are discussed in the remainder of the chapter.

MEAT/MEAT ALTERNATES

Beef and Pork

The tenderness, flavor, and yield of cooked beef and pork is determined to a great extent by the quality and grade of meat purchased. This quality may also determine the method of cooking and the length of time. The reasons for cooking meats are to destroy the pathogenic microorganisms that might be harmful and thus make the meat safe for human consumption, to make the meat tender by softening the white-connective tissue, to develop the flavor and color, and to make it easier to digest. Nutritive value of protein-rich foods is affected very little by ordinary cooking. However, vitamin losses increase with prolonged cooking and high temperatures. Two methods of cooking meat are used most often: (1) dry-heat method—air or fat is used as the medium of heat transfer (examples: baking, roasting, and frying), and (2) moist-heat method—water or other liquids are used as the medium of heat transfer (examples: braising, stewing, simmering, and steaming).

The cut, age, and quality will determine how pieces of meat should be cooked. Meat charts identify the various cuts of beef, pork, veal, and lamb and indicate which method of cooking should be used for each. The time and temperature at which meats are cooked can, if correct, result in maximum flavor, juiciness, nutritive value retention and tenderness, and minimum shrinkage.

School foodservices are using more portion cuts of meats than in the past, as are hospitals and other food industries. Carefully following direc-

TABLE 8.4.   Cost per Pound and per Portion after Roasting 30-Pound Piece
of Roast Beef

			Yield and Cost after Cooking			
Initial Cost @ $2.80/lb	Cooking Temperature	Shrinkage (%)	No. of Pounds	Cost per Pound	No. of 2-oz Portions	Cost per Portion
$84.00	300°F	24	22.8	$3.68	180	$0.47
$84.00	400°F	45	16.5	$5.09	130	$0.65

tions and using timers is very important in cooking portion cuts of meats; overcooking is the biggest problem and damages the quality.

The loss due to shrinkage can be substantial during baking or roasting of large pieces of meat. For this reason precooked meats should be considered. Compare the acceptability and cost of precooked meats with that of baked or roasted meats. Under the best cooking conditions meat can be expected to shrink as little as 24% and as much as 45% (Table 8.4). The cost per pound and per portion is increased considerably because of shrinkage; the post-cooking cost should be used in making comparisons with precooked products. Labor and utility costs also should be considered and generally are higher for preparation of raw meat than precooked meat.

Meat thermometers are an essential tool for the cook. Use of a meat thermometer, which is inserted in a piece of meat, takes the guesswork out of cooking or heating meat.

Poultry

The most important objective in cooking poultry is to cook and handle it in such a way that it is safe for human consumption. Poultry is very perishable and if contaminated with bacteria it affords a favorable environment for bacteria to multiply and possibly cause food poisoning. Points to be remembered in safety of handling poultry are discussed in Chapter 10. However, it should be pointed out here that since poultry is very perishable, defrosting of frozen poultry should be done in a refrigerator at approximately 40°F and *not* at room temperature; defrosting in a refrigerator may require 2 to 3 days. Poultry should be thoroughly cooked and held at hot (150°F or hotter) or cold (50°F or colder) temperatures until served; it should not be held at room temperature.

Poultry has a tendency to dry out and this is a common complaint. This drying-out can be caused by overcooking, allowing air to dry it out, holding at warm temperatures, and cooking too far ahead. Deep-fat frying of chicken is almost out of the question for most school foodservices due to the lack of deep-fat fryers or to the large quantities to be prepared. Oven frying can be done satisfactorily in the schools. However, use of frozen prefried chicken pieces may be the best and most economical way to provide the fried product preferred by school-age customers.

Fish

Fish cookery should enhance flavor, improve appearance, and aid in digestibility. The most common error in cooking fish is overcooking. Fish has a very limited holding time from the fresh state to the cooking point and from the cooking to the serving. Fish should always be thawed under refrigeration. Smell is a good indicator of good fresh fish. Fish requires little cooking since there is no such thing as "tough" fish. Fish is done when it flakes easily and is yet moist. Overcooking results in dry, pulplike flesh.

Eggs

Eggs should be cooked at a low temperature for a short period of time, until just done. Temperatures that are too high will result in toughness and discoloration in hard-cooked eggs. Overcooking will cause a green color around the yolk. For best results in hard-cooking eggs, the following pointers are given:

1. Steam eggs in shell in a perforated pan for 15 minutes at 5 pound pressure; or cover eggs in shell with cold water, heat to boiling point, and turn heat down to *simmer, cook 20 minutes* (possibly longer, depending on the number of eggs in pot).
2. Remove pan from heat and cool eggs quickly under cold running water until cool enough to handle. Putting hard-cooked eggs under cold water immediately will aid in peeling them because the egg will shrink away from the shell slightly.
3. Refrigerate eggs immediately after peeling until time of serving or using.

For ease in peeling hard-cooked eggs use eggs a few days old (very fresh eggs are hard to shell). After cooling, start peeling at the big end of the egg where the air pocket is. When hard-cooking eggs for salads and other mixed dishes, the simplest and most satisfactory method of preparing the eggs is to place shelled eggs (fresh, frozen, or reconstituted dry eggs) in a greased baking pan (12 × 12 × 2 inch steamtable-size pan will hold 25 eggs), cover and bake at 350°F for 20 to 30 minutes or until eggs are firm. This eliminates the peeling of eggs. Reconstituted dry eggs can be used for many purposes, but should be restricted to dishes that are thoroughly cooked, since *Salmonella* bacteria may be present in dry eggs.

Cheese

Because cheese is high in protein, it solidifies when exposed to high temperature. Melt cheese at a temperature no higher than 350°F; at higher temperatures it merely changes shape and becomes touch and stringy. The flavor and texture of cheeses differ greatly; therefore it is important to choose the right cheese for the intended use. Cheese should not be served directly from the refrigerator but should be allowed to sit at room temperature for a short time. Cheese at room temperature is richer in flavor and aroma.

FRUITS AND VEGETABLES

The most important objective in preparing fruits and vegetables is to preserve their nutritive value. Vegetables and fruits are the primary dietary sources of vitamin C and contribute many other vitamins and minerals. Vitamin C and some of the B complex vitamins are very unstable and can be destroyed in preparation. Vegetables and fruits may lose much of their nutritive value if not prepared correctly.

Vegetables should be cooked *quickly* in *small* quantities of water. Water-soluble vitamins could be poured off in cooking water or liquid. Steam cooking retains vitamins and minerals better than any other method of cooking. To retain their nutritive value, cook vegetables in a small amount of liquid, until *just* done, in small batches; stagger the cooking times so the vegetables do not overcook and are not held for long periods of time before serving.

Chopped, shredded, or cut vegetables and fruits, and fruit juices should not be left uncovered and exposed to air for long periods of time. Covering such foods prevents the escape of vitamins into the air. Cooked fruits and vegetables do not hold up well under holding temperatures—green vegetables often turn olive green; their structure breaks down and becomes mush. Since vegetables are the most unpopular food group with school-age children, it is a challenge to make them as appetizing and appealing as possible, with proper seasoning and adequate but not too much cooking.

When canned vegetables are used, some of the packing liquid may need to be drained from the vegetables. For example, when preparing canned green peas, drain and retain 1 cup of the liquid from a No. 10 can; boil and season the liquid. Pour the hot liquid over the peas, which have been put into a steamtable pan from which they will be served. Heat thoroughly. Canned vegetables are already cooked; therefore, heating makes them more flavorful and safe from botulism toxin.

Baking soda should *never* be added to preserve the color of vegetables. Though baking soda makes vegetables look greener, it destroys vitamins.

Vegetables can be made more flavorful and attractive by addition of one or more of the following:

1. Salt, spices
2. Sugar, which brings out the flavor
3. Butter, margarine, or other fat
4. Beef, ham, or chicken base
5. Minced onions, red and/or green peppers, pimiento
6. Mushrooms, tiny onions, water chestnuts, or toasted almonds

Accentuating the flavor of vegetables with good seasoning and serving them thoroughly heated can add much to their taste and acceptability to students.

Facts to remember when cooking fresh and frozen vegetables can be summed up as follows:

1. Cook vegetables for as short a time as possible, until just done.
2. Cook them in a small amount of water.
3. Avoid pouring off liquid in which vegetables were cooked.
4. Do not add baking soda to vegetables.
5. Cook vegetables in small batches as needed and avoid holding them for long periods of time.
6. Do not leave chopped, shredded, or cut vegetables to stand uncovered.
7. Use steam cooker when applicable.

The main objectives in cooking fruits and vegetables are to soften the cellulose, change the texture, make them more digestible by changing the starch, and make them more appetizing. The desired results are good flavor, natural color, tender yet crisp texture, and good nutritive value.

Fresh Fruits and Vegetables

Fresh fruits and vegetables should add texture and crispness to a menu. The freshness of the vegetable will determine its quality. Crispness can be obtained with water and cold temperatures.

Some fruits, such as bananas, apples, pears, and peaches, darken when pared. Preparing these fruits as near serving time as possible and dipping them in citric juices (such as lemon or pineapple juice), ascorbic acid, or a sugar solution quickly after paring will prevent their darkening. Vegetables that discolor can be put into salted water. Antioxidants are not recommended. Cooking or blanching fruits and vegetables will destroy the enzymes that cause discoloration.

When preparing fresh vegetables for a salad bar or for salads, make sure not to bruise them. Using a dull knife to cut fresh produce will cause it to deteriorate faster. Using the proper equipment will assure an attractive product that keeps well (Fig. 8.2).

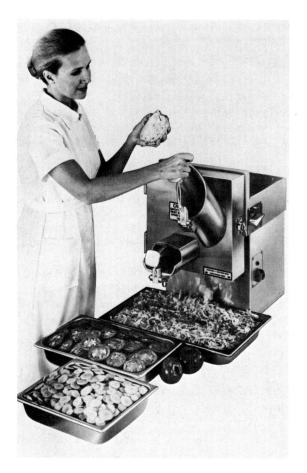

FIG. 8.2. Using the proper equipment produces more uniform pieces and helps fresh produce last longer without deteriorating.
Courtesy of Qualheim, Inc.

CEREALS AND GRAINS

Cereals and breads made from whole-grain, enriched, or fortified products are classified as carbohydrate foods; however, they also contribute minerals, protein, and vitamins. Cooking of cereal products is largely starch cookery, a type of cooking that many cooks have trouble with. Cooking cereals increases palatability, increases digestibility, and improves appearance. Heat and moisture are needed to soften cellulose and start starch granules swelling and gelatinizing. Starches are used for thickening products.

Gravy and Sauces

Many recipes start with a white sauce or end with a gravy or sauce poured over the dish. Foods look larger in quantity and many look more attractive when the juice or liquid is thickened slightly. For example, strawberries for shortcake will go almost twice as far and make a more attractive product if thickened (Table 8.5). Sweet potatoes with orange juice added to the sauce and then thickened will go farther and look more attractive. Yellow corn, white potatoes, and green peas are frequently served in the South in a thickened liquid.

Gravies and sauces give many cooks problems. Common complaints are that the gravy is too thin, thick, or lumpy, or that a crust forms on top.

If gravy is too thin, add additional flour or cornstarch to cold water to make a paste and add this to the gravy or sauce. Cook until the liquid thickened and the starch has cooked.

If gravy is too thick, add more stock, milk, or water slowly until the desired thickness is reached.

If gravy is lumpy, beat it vigorously with a wire whisk or in a mixer, or strain through a colander or cheesecloth. The next time, separate the starch more carefully by adding to fat, mixing with cold liquid, or by mixing with other dry ingredients before adding to hot liquids, and add to hot liquids slowly, stirring briskly.

If a crust forms on gravy, skim it off. Prevent this from happening by

TABLE 8.5. Recipe Using Cornstarch to Thicken Strawberries for Shortcake

Ingredients	100 Portions				Directions
	Weights			For ___	
	(lb)	(oz)	Measures	Portions	
Strawberries, frozen	15				1. Thaw strawberries and drain. Add 2 cups water to liquid. Heat on medium heat.
Water			1 qt		
Cornstarch		8	1¾ cups		2. Mix cornstarch with 2 cups water (cold). Stir until mixture is smooth.
Sugar		8			
Red food coloring			1 Tbsp		3. Add sugar to strawberries liquid; add cornstarch mixture and cook for 10 min (until clear and very thick).
					4. Add food coloring until the desired red color is obtained.
					5. Cool mixture; add strawberries. Use ¼-cup (or No. 16 scoop) portion.

keeping a cover on the gravy or lightly covering the top of the sauce with a thin coat of fat.

Cornstarch is a good thickening agent because it is practically free of flavor and cooks to a clear, almost transparent paste in water or other clear liquid. However, it lumps more readily than flour.

Baked Goods

Breads, cakes, and cookies are ways of adding nutrients and energy foods that have variety and taste appeal. Much skill is required in cooking good baked products. The baker must follow a recipe precisely, accurately measure and weigh ingredients, and correctly mix the ingredients as the recipe directs. Failure to do any of these are most obvious in baking.

Not many schools would be baking "from scratch" today if it were not for the USDA-donated commodities. Flour, shortening, dry milk, and cornmeal are still regularly received commodities. Some school districts are using processing agreements to have such commodities made into cake mixes, cookie doughs, and finished loaves of bread by commercial firms. It is difficult to consistently turn out good baked products at schools with a high turnover of staff. Also, the labor costs per roll, per cookie, or per serving of cake are sometimes very high when these are prepared by foodservice personnel.

Pastry.   Good pastry should be tender, flaky, delicately flavored, crisp, and light golden brown. Plain pastry includes only four ingredients: flour, fat, salt, and water. All-purpose flour is recommended. Hydrogenated shortening and lard make the best pastry. Salt is added for flavor only. Water is added to bind the ingredients together and to furnish steam in the baking, which will result in a flaky crust. To obtain a good pastry follow the basic rules. If pie crust is unsatisfactory, check Table 8.6 for possible causes of the problem.

TABLE 8.6.   Some Reasons for Pie Crust Problems

Problem	Possible Causes
Too tender, falls apart	Too much fat for amount of flour
	Overmixing the shortening into flour
	Flour too low in gluten, soft wheat
	Not enough water added
Tough	Not enough fat
	Overmixing after water has been added
	Undermixing the shortening with flour
	Rolling and handling too much

Many school foodservices bake cobbler-type pies rather than the 9-inch pies due to the lack of oven space, time, and other equipment. The quality of fruit pies (cobbler) is thought to be better by some and to require less time when the crust is baked on a sheet pan completely separate from the filling. In this case, the crust can be cut easily into portions before baking. The fruit filling can be prepared in a steamjacketed kettle or pot on the range by thickening the liquid and adding sugar and spices to the fruit. The pie filling is ready for portioning and is then topped with the golden-brown pastry squares.

Cakes. Successful cake making requires high-quality ingredients that are carefully weighed and mixed. Most recipes for cakes were developed in cities of low altitude; therefore, at higher altitudes the baking powder and sugar generally should be decreased and the liquid increased. Greater volume can be obtained when eggs and other ingredients are at room temperature.

To obtain uniformity in the thickness of cakes, scaling is recommended. Scaling means to portion batter or dough into pans according to weight. For scaling cakes, use the quantities in Table 8.7 as a guide.

Yeast Breads. The basic ingredients in yeast bread are flour, fat, liquid, yeast, and salt; some richer doughs also have eggs, sugar, and spices. The flour used should be either general-purpose or hard-wheat bread flour since the stronger gluten in these is desirable.

Yeast is a live one-cell plant that needs food, moisture, and warmth to grow. The food is obtained from the flour and sugar. Salt retards the development of yeast but adds flavor and aids in strengthening gluten. Sugar increases the growth of yeast, adds flavor, and aids in browning. Temperatures are crucial to the growth of yeast. Temperatures between 78 and 90°F are ideal. Growth slows down at lower temperatures and yeast can be destroyed at temperatures over 140°F. Yeast bread is unlike quick bread in that thorough mixing is desirable and is needed to develop the gluten. The dough will feel springy and elastic when kneaded sufficiently, yet soft. Improper timing, temperature and measuring are the causes for most failures in making yeast breads (Table 8.8).

TABLE 8.7. Cake Scaling

Size of Cake Pan (in.)	Amount of Batter	
	(lb)	(oz)
8 round	1	8
10 round	2	
18 × 26 × 2½	7–8	

TABLE 8.8. Some Reasons for Yeast Bread Problems

Problem	Possible Causes
Lack of volume	Improper mixing Too much salt Insufficient yeast Dough underproofed Oven temperature too high Dough overproofed and fallen Dough chilled Yeast killed
Too much volume	Insufficient salt Too much dough for pan Dough proofed too much Oven temperature too low
Crust color too pale	Insufficient sugar Oven temperature too low Dough proofed too long
Poor texture, crumbly	Dough proofed too long Proofed at too high temperature Oven temperature too low Dough not proofed long enough Dough proofed too long
Gray crumb	Dough not proofed long enough Dough temperatures too hot Proofing temperatures too hot
Coarse grain	Improper mixing Dough proofed too long Dough temperatures too low Dough too old or too young
Poor taste and flavor (soured)	Insufficient salt Dough temperatures too hot Dough too old Dough overproofed

Rice

Light, tender, fluffy rice is often difficult to obtain in large quantities. Ordinarily rice is cooked in too large a batch or quantity, which will most often result in an overcooked, sticky, starchy product. The two most successful methods of cooking rice are in the compartment steamer and in the oven. The oven method is very satisfactory when a compartment steamer is not available.

Rice should be cooked in the correct amount of water, in small batches (approximately 50 servings per pan), and until just done. Since rice continues to cook after being taken from the oven or steamer, particularly when its held on a steamtable, care should be taken not to overcook. Oil added in the ratio of 2 tablespoons per pound of rice helps to separate the grains in cooking and prevents foaming. Rice should be covered when cooked in the oven to allow steam to make the grains tender and fluffy. Since rice is enriched it should not be washed before or after cooking unless the rice is purchased in burlap bags. In that case, the rice should be rinsed quickly before cooking. Washing before cooking may cause a loss of up to 25% of the thiamine. Rinsing after cooking will also cause loss of nutrients.

DEEP-FAT FRIED FOODS

Deep-fat frying is one of the most popular ways to prepare potatoes, chicken, and seafood. When deep-fat frying, one should know some of the controlling factors that affect the quality of fried food. The function of the fat in deep-fat frying is to keep the food being cooked at a uniform and controlled temperature, providing an even browning and imparting flavor to the food.

The kind of fat used is most important, since the flavor and aroma are affected by its temperature breaking point. Fat "breakdown" is to be avoided. When fat smokes, it gives off the "greasy spoon" odor and an unsatisfactory flavor (Table 8.9). Hydrogenated vegetable oils do not break down when heated to 400°F and have other desirable characteristics as well. Other factors, in addition to the temperature being too high, can cause the break down of fats. Detergents remaining in the container after washing, adding salt to the food or to batter in which the food is dipped, and using copper or brass utensils or tools can all cause fat breakdown. The absorption of fat in food is usually considered undesirable and may be caused by frying at too low a temperature.

TABLE 8.9. Smoke Point of Different Fats

Product	Smoke Point (°F)	(°C)
Hydrogenated vegetable oil	440–460	227–238
Standard vegetable shortening	420–440	216–227
Cottonseed oil	410–430	210–221
Chicken fat and corn oil	400–430	204–221
Lard	340–350	171–177
Olive oil	300–315	149–163
Bacon fat	290–300	143–149
Beef suet	235–245	143–149

Source: Thorner (1973).

PRE-PREPARED FOODS

The use of pre-prepared foods in school foodservices has grown tremendously during the last 10 years. The need to provide quicker service and more menu choices, to reduce labor costs and dependence on trained cooks, and other factors have made pre-prepared foods important to the survival of many school foodservices.

A pre-prepared food is one that is ready to be served with little or no preparation. The range of foods available and their degree of readiness are vast: precooked hamburger patties; prefried chicken; precooked prefabricated veal patties; precooked presliced meats; precut salad mixes; prebaked rolls, cakes, and cookies; prefried potatoes; prebaked potatoes; and preportioned frozen milkshakes (ready to spoon out).

The new art of convenience food cookery begins where chefs of early days thought their job ended and where the apprentice took over—that is, garnishing and plating (serving). Overcooking and undercooking are the two greatest problems in preparing convenience foods. Many of these foods come frozen and must be reconstituted in the oven. Because many variables influence how long it will take to reconstitute each frozen product, a good thermometer is a must to determining when the food is ready to serve.

BIBLIOGRAPHY

AM. HOME ECONOMICS ASSOC. 1975. Handbook of Food Preparation. 7th edition. Am. Home Economics Assoc., Washington, DC.
AMENDOLA, J., and J. M. BERRINI. 1971. Practical Cooking and Baking for Schools and Institutions. Ahrens Publishing Co., New York.
ANON. 1963. Conserving the Nutritive Value of Foods. Bull. 90 U.S. Govt. Printing Office, Washington, DC.
ANON. 1979. Nutrient loss in foods. Food Technology 34(2). Institute of Food Technologists, Chicago.
BIRCHFIELD, J. C. 1979. Foodservice Operations Manual: A Guide for Hotels, Restaurants, and Institutions. CBI Publishing Co., Boston.
BORGSTROM, G. 1968. Principles of Food Science, Vol. II. Macmillian, New York.
CASOLA, M. 1969. Successful Mass Cookery and Volume Feeding. Ahrens Publishing Co., New York.
FOLSOM, L. A. 1974. The Professional Chef. 4th edition. Cahners Books, Boston.
GENERAL MILLS. 1975. Baking Handbook for the School Food Service Program. General Mills, Minneapolis.
GREGG, J. B. 1967. Cooking for Food Managers. Wm. C. Brown Co., Dubuque, IA.
KNIGHT, J., and L. H. KOTSCHEVAR. 1979. Quantity Food Production, Planning and Management. CBI, Boston.
KOTSCHEVAR, L. 1974. Standards, Principles, and Techniques in Quantity Food Production. 3rd edition. CBI, Boston.
MARIO, T. 1978. Quantity Cooking. AVI Publishing Co., Westport, CT.
SMITH, E. E., and V. C. CRUSIUS. 1970. A Handbook on Quantity Food Management. 2nd edition. Burgess Publishing Co., Minneapolis.
SULTAN, W. 1976. Practical Baking. 3rd edition. AVI Publishing Co., Westport, CT.
TERRELL, M. E. 1979. Professional Food Preparation. 2nd edition. John Willey & Sons, New York.

THORNER, M. E. 1973. Convenience and Fast Food Handbook. AVI Publishing Co., Westport, CT.

U.S. DEPT. OF AGRICULTURE. 1969. Guides for Writing and Evaluating Quantity Recipes for Type A School Lunches. U.S. Govt. Printing Office, Washington, DC.

U.S. DEPT. OF AGRICULTURE. 1971. Quantity Recipes for Type A School Lunches. U.S. Govt. Printing Office, Washington, DC.

U.S. DEPT. OF AGRICULTURE. 1977. Average Weight of a Measured Cup of Various Foods. U.S. Govt. Printing Office, Washington, DC.

U.S. DEPT. OF AGRICULTURE. 1983. Menu Planning Guide for School Food Service. U.S. Govt. Printing Office, Washington, DC.

WEST, B. B., G. S. SHUGART, and M. F. WILSON. 1978. Food for Fifty. 6th edition. John Wiley & Sons, New York.

PROMOTING
SCHOOL FOODSERVICE

At one time, school foodservice management believed that to achieve success meant to serve good food within the budget. As the food habits of students changed and outside forces like television, advertising, and fast foods became more prevalent and influential, other measures of success came into the picture. It became necessary to create positive images of school foodservice and to stimulate students and adults to want to eat the school lunches.

The age of consumerism started among adults in the early 1970s; it reached the school-age child in the late 1970s. Scholol-age consumers and their parents are better informed and more discriminating consumers today than 10 years ago.

In order to be completely successful today, a school foodservice must satisfy its customers' needs and wants—and that is not limited to just filling the stomach. It is hard for some people to accept this broader definition of success, an approach that may include "selling" school foodservice. Some may argue that it is not necessary. It is argued here, however, that even in school districts where the majority of the students qualify for free or reduced-price meals, their needs and wants, beyond filling the stomach, should be fulfilled.

Perhaps it all can be summed up as providing "good, nutritious food at a price that parents are *willing* to pay and in a form that students will *enjoy* eating." It means food that looks good, served in a fun, happy setting. Eating lunch should be considered a social activity and not just a *necessity.*

BUILDING AN IMAGE

School foodservice has an image in each and every school. What is that image? What does management want that image to be?

The image of a school foodservice is made up of intangible thoughts and impressions that people hold about it. These are influenced by all the senses and can be changed. The first thing to determine is what the current image is. When that has been determined, plans for improving that image or building an entirely different one follow. How much money and other resources are available? What techniques are appropriate to use in establishing a new image? After answering these questions, develop a plan and time schedule for implementing it. Implementation should be followed by evaluation (feedback).

A dull, institutional-type school foodservice can be turned into a fun place to eat. The image of "fun place" to eat may be created by presenting food in a more contemporary way (e.g., fish and chips in a paper cone), by painting the serving and/or dining areas brighter colors, and by having employees smile while serving customers. Adding a "super sack" or "big box" lunch to the menus in the spring when eating outside is possible, or

FIG. 9.1. Portable serving lines (Mobile Merchandiser) makes it possible to serve where the students are.
Courtesy of Cres-Cor.

adding a portable serving line outside (Fig. 9.1), fulfills student needs, creates excitement, and projects a contemporary image.

Images are built positively by using eye-catching posters, clever menu names, and brightly colored labels to identify foods and by promoting the customer's desire for good, tasty, fresh, nutritious and/or value-packed food.

Public Relations

Public relations can be described as the "act of promoting goodwill"; it should result in the public having a positive image of the school foodservice. Dr. R. W. McIntosh, sales promotion and merchandising authority, says that public relations should be "an attitude of management which places first priority on the public interest when making management decisions." Public relations may mean promoting goodwill by giving a straw to the child who brings a drink from home. Though one has to control the "freebies," the public relations of giving or not giving the straw must be considered by management in making the decision. The raising of prices will have a negative impact. If there is no alternative that is more acceptable it will be important to explain the price increases to the public.

To avoid negative public relations within a school system, it is usually best to establish clearly what services and products can and cannot be provided by the foodservice. For example, if a teacher wants free napkins to serve food cooked in the classroom and the manager says "no," the results may be negative public relations. The manager is not wrong, but if the rule has not been established that napkins *cost,* the decision may come across negatively. In this case, it probably would have helped if prices for services and supplies had been established and teachers informed about them. For good public relations, it would be best to announce what can be provided at what price. For some reason people think the food and supplies in the school foodservice kitchen are free. A lot of educating is needed to change that idea without creating bad feelings.

MARKETING

Marketing describes the process of promoting, advertising, merchandising, and selling. It includes defining what the customer wants or needs; providing products or services that meet those wants and needs; informing the customer of the availability of the service or products and the benefits that can be gained by using them; and finally, selling products at at prices the customer considers fair. McDonald's spent more than $311 million in 1983 on marketing their products. Restaurants and fast-food chains led all categories of retail operations in the amount of money spent on advertising in 1984. They certainly must have reasons for believing there are returns realized from this expenditure.

In a school foodservice, marketing involves introducing and getting the product—lunch, a la carte items, breakfast—to new customers and returning customers. It probably should start with determining what image one wants to create in the mind of the customer. Then it becomes very important to understand the customer. Determine the things important to the type and age of student being served. What is the theme to be marketed? Is it "more value for your money"? Is it "very nutritious"? Is it "for your convenience"? Is it "dependability"?

The National Evaluation of School Nutrition Programs found that several factors affected the frequency with which individual students participated in the School Lunch Program. The factors included the following:

1. Price charged students—the single most important variable
2. Value parents place on nutrition, and their perception of how nutritious the meals at school were
3. Age of students—older students participated in school lunch programs less frequently than younger students
4. Sex of students—male students participated more frequently than females
5. Urbanicity—students from rural areas participated more often than students from urban areas

Before selecting a marketing approach, foodservice personnel should examine the factors associated with nonparticipation. To increase participation of females or those concerned with losing weight, for example, a salad bar might be opened and promoted as "make it your way" or "you decide how many calories you eat." To prepare a marketing approach, a school foodservice manager or director also needs to identify the competition. It is usually one or more of the following: fast foods nearby (or a grocery), lunch brought from home, going home for lunch, vending machines, or not eating at all.

The theme and image to be marketed can and should be enhanced by the presentation of the food, type of service offered, appearance of the serving and dining areas, uniforms the employees wear, and the attitudes they display.

MERCHANDISING

Effective merchandising can increase participation in a school lunch program. In narrow terms, merchandising refers to selling a product, in this case, food. In broad terms, it involves offering good food that looks attractive, at a price that the customer considers fair, in a courteous manner, and in a pleasant environment. One of the greatest downfalls of school foodservice has been the lack of merchandising. This may be due to the lack of competition. It has been noted that in school systems where the manager's pay is based on the volume of sales, the manager has shown more interest in merchandising.

Students are more likely to eat food that looks and tastes good than to eat something "because it is good for you." People "eat" with their eyes to a great extent; commercial cafeterias capitalize on this fact. Foods should be attractively displayed on the serving counter. The finishing touches can be a sprig of parsley, dash of paprika, whipped topping, or piece of maraschino cherry. Accentuate colors by adding food coloring; create variety by using interesting shapes. For example, a delicious gingerbread looks unappetizing with white, thick lemon sauce. However, the same lemon sauce becomes appetizing with the addition of yellow food coloring to make it look the expected color. With additional liquid, the lemon sauce can be made the desired consistency.

Before serving lines are opened to customers, take a look at the food as customers see it. How does the food look? How does it smell? Food coloring, parsley, and garnishes will not turn poor-quality food into good food. But there is a definite correlation between the attractiveness of good food and customer satisfaction.

Another way of merchandising is to use catchy names for describing foods on the menu. ARA Food Company has used popular singing groups in the names of their sandwiches. "Mouth watering" descriptions can be used on the menu: hot homemade rolls, tiny green peas, sizzling juicy hamburgers, and fresh green salad.

A variation of this technique is to offer "Combos" and "Specials of the Day" that add variety and attract students' interest. Len Fredrick, former director of the Clark County (NV) School District, made the "combo" famous in the early 1970s. It included a sandwich, with toppings, french fries (or a tossed green salad), plus a milkshake or milk (Fig. 9.2).

The environment in which food is served and eaten can make it seem more desirable or less desirable. A pleasant atmosphere with soft lighting, comfortable seating, fast-moving serving lines, soft music, enough time to eat without rushing, and choices of food can make mealtime a social learning experience. Particularly in high school, round tables or tables seating four to six students will result in fewer discipline problems. The walls of the dining room can be made interesting without great expense by using several shades of paint, art displays, or large posters.

Many factors determine how food is evaluated—from its quality and preparation to the atmosphere in which it is served—and they all center around satisfying the costomer.

Variety in foods eaten is the key to good nutrition. ★ Go easy on the salt—too much is too much! ★ All foods are health foods when properly used in a diet.

(1) Taco Combo ...... 75¢

TWO TACOS with SAUCE
FRENCH FRIES or TOSSED SALAD
MILK SHAKE or MILK

(2) P-T Combo ...... 75¢

1 SLICE PIZZA and 1 TACO
FRENCH FRIES or TOSSED SALAD
MILK SHAKE or MILK

(3) Cheese Pizza Combo ...... 75¢

TWO SLICES OF PIZZA
FRENCH FRIES or TOSSED SALAD
MILK SHAKE or MILK

(15) Fish 'n Chip Combo ...... 75¢

2 PIECES FISH in BATTER
FRENCH FRIES and HOT ROLL
MILK SHAKE or MILK

(16) Chef's Salad Combo ...... 75¢

TOSSED SALAD/TOMATO and DRESSING
HAM and CHEESE, CRACKERS
MILK SHAKE or MILK

Keep the calories consumed in line with those used up to reach your Desirable Weight. ★ Huffing and puffing activities are the only kind that burn up calories.

Don't get in a rut and eat the same thing every day! Eat a variety of foods. Variety is the spice of life and the key to a balanced diet.

The Four Key Factors In Health: A balanced diet, adequate exercise, enough sleep, no smoking!

BUY A COMBO AND SAVE MONEY

★ ALL COMBOS AVAILABLE EVERY DAY ★
"Combo" includes choice of sandwich plus french fries or tossed salad / tomato plus milk shake or milk

Specialty Items

	A LA CARTE	COMBO
(4) ¼lb. TACO BURGER on bun with cheese	.60	Combo .75
(5) JUMBO FRIED BURRITO	.45	Combo .60
(6) MILE LONG CHEESE DOG	.55	Combo .70
(7) DEEP FRIED CHICKEN w/hot roll (2 pcs.)	.55	Combo .70

Deluxe Hamburgers (100% Pure Beef)

On sesame buns with lettuce, pickles, onions and special sauce

| (8) BIG NEVAD'N Super Hamburger | .60 | Combo .75 |
| (9) CHEESE NEVAD'N Super Cheeseburger | .65 | Combo .80 |

Deluxe Hot Sandwiches

On large sesame egg buns

(10) BIG TEX'N (Roast Beef)	.60	Combo .75
(11) BIG WEST'RN (Barbecued Beef)	.60	Combo .75
(12) BIG VIRGINIAN (Ham and Cheese)	.65	Combo .80
(13) HOT TURKEY (Light and Dark Meat)	.55	Combo .70

Cold Sandwich

| (14) CHICK-N-CHEEZ (Triple Decker) | .45 | Combo .60 |

Know and follow the Basic Four Food Guide, something from each of the following four food groups each day: meat, poultry or fish; milk or something made from it; fruits and vegetables; some foods made from cereals.

Hot a la carte Items

FRENCH FRIES with catsup	.30
PIZZA (slice)	.30
TACO with meat and cheese	.30
HOT ROLL with butter	.10
FISH IN BATTER (each piece)	.30

"SUPER CHARGER"

Energy Charged Breakfast
Includes Juice or Fruit and Milk

#1 HOMEMADE CINNAMON ROLL	.25
#2 SCRAMBLED EGG w/bacon bits on roll	.35
#3 HOT HAM & CHEESE on roll	.40

Snack Items

| POTATO CHIPS, CORN CHIPS, etc. | .15 |
| PEANUTS, RAISINS, etc. | .10 |

Salads

| SMALL TOSSED SALAD/Tomato & Dressing | .35 |
| COTTAGE CHEESE Plain .... .40 With Fruit .... | .50 |

Homemade Desserts

COOKIE (large) All Varieties	.15
CINNAMON BREAKFAST ROLL	.20
CAKE (piece) Homemade	.20
RICE PUDDING with Topping	.20

Drinks

| MILK (½ pint) | .15 |

96.75% FAT FREE

SO-O RICH, SO-O THICK
YOU EAT IT WITH A SPOON (FREE with every Combo)
SUPER MILK SHAKE

LARGE SIZE	.20
PURE ORANGE JUICE (medium)	.15
REAL LEMONADE (large)	.20

A Fun Place To Eat

(Health Slogans by Fredrick J. Stare, M.D., Professor of Nutrition, Harvard School of Public Health, Author and Syndicated Columnist.)

FIG. 9.2.   Combo menu offerings are an innovative merchandising approach, which was pioneered in Clark County, Nevada, schools.

Food Presentation

Food may be of excellent quality but be dull and uninteresting. Nutritious foods must be appealing to children if they are to satisfy. The presentation in part determines the images one has of a food. Dr. Robert Buchanan (1979b), professor at Purdue University, has said that the "total image is the sum of the price-quality-portion size-service-atmosphere impressions developed by the consumer in the course of his contact with the establishment."

Factors to be considered in food presentation include the following:

1. *Eye Appeal.* Does the food have that "cafeteria look"? Does it look so good that customers can't resist it? Does it look good enough to make customers want to eat it? Eye appeal is influenced by the color and shape of food, the dishes on which it is served, portion size, the neatness with which it has been served, the expectations the food's appearance arouses in customers, and the colors around/in the setting.

Garnishing is the finishing touch that makes food look better and increases its eye appeal. Garnishes can be as simple as a sprinkle of paprika or as elaborate as a radish rose. The following guidelines to garnishing come from "The Art of Getting Kids to Eat," published by Chiquita Brands, Inc.:

- Choose garnishes that fit the budget.
- Make sure the garnishes can be accomplished by the average worker. (Not everyone is an artist!)
- Make sure garnishes do not require too much time-consuming hand work.
- Use seasonal garnishes and decorations when appropriate.
- Use garnishes that are natural. (Students may be suspicious of colors and garnishes that are highly unusual.)
- Add color to fruit dishes, salads, etc., with red apples. Leave the peel on; it adds texture, color, and freshness.
- Raw carrots have a variety of uses as garnishes; use them chopped, grated, or cut into sticks or circles.
- Small amounts of fresh spinach bring an iceberg lettuce salad to life with color and texture. Spinach also adds nutritional value.
- Onions (green, white, or red) offer color, flavor contrast, and crispness. Chop them, or cut them into rings or strips.
- Though beets are not usually a favorite vegetable, they can be very effective garnishes, particularly when cut in julienne strips.
- Cabbage in all its varieties (red, green, and white) adds color and chewiness when grated or shredded.
- Oranges, lemons, and limes make beautiful garnishes. Cut them into wedges or thin slices, or—if time permits—shape them into a twist.
- Cucumbers—unpeeled or peeled—add snap and interest when sliced

thinly. Run the tines of a fork down the side of an unpeeled cucumber for an interesting fluted effect.

As can be seen from these ideas, garnishes do not have to be costly or exotic, but "good taste" (appropriateness) is important. Whipped topping is much more attractive when dispensed from a pastry bag than when dropped by the spoonful. A twig of parsley or a mint leaf can add the fresh look desired. The line display of fresh fruit (Fig. 9.3) can set the scene. Or, even the way it is stored (Fig. 9.4). The addition of red and green bell peppers to corn will create Mexican corn with all its color. Cutting French bread on an angle not only makes it look like a larger piece, but it looks good. The extra touch is what food presentation and effective merchandising are all about.

2. *Palatability.* It does not matter how pretty food looks if it is not good. The serving temperature should be appropriate to each food. Hot food should be served hot. If served at 140° to 150°F, it will probably cool to 120°F by the time the customer starts eating the food. According to studies done at Iowa State University, 120°F is the most desirable temperature to children in the third grade. Cold food should be served cold. The flavor should be appropriate to the food. Spices should be carefully determined and reflect regional likes and dislikes. For example, chili seasoned heavily with chili powder is acceptable in Texas but not in New England. Elementary students are conservative eaters. They prefer unmixed foods to casseroles. They are not adventurous with new foods, particularly "strange foods."

3. *Service.* Ordinarily, students are not willing to stand in line more than 10 minutes. If the rate of service is 10 meals per minute, then more than 100 students to a line will mean discontent before they are served. The

FIG. 9.3. Displays of fresh fruits and attractive presentations make food interesting and appealing to customers.

FIG. 9.4. Even a refrigeration unit can serve as a merchandiser of food.

attitude of employees makes a lot of difference. Too often when students are questioned about their school foodservice, they complain that servers "are mean," "are always grumpy," "are hollering all the time," etc. Running out of food, not having the advertised menu, and having to make students wait while more food is prepared all make for unhappy customers. They are forgiving the first time (usually), but not after repeated occurrences.

4. *Dishware.* On what, or in what, is the portion of food served? The increased use of "offer versus served" (see Chapter 2) and proliferation of menu choices in school foodservices has led to more individual portioning of food. The disposable ware/paper supplies and/or the dishwashing costs will increase in these cases. However, Shirley Watkins, Director of Memphis (TN) City Schools Food Services, found that "offer versus served" reduced food costs and waste, offsetting the increased costs for other things. Packaging has a great deal of effect on consumers in the grocery store and it does in the school cafeteria, too (Fig. 9.5).

FIG. 9.5. Foil bags help keep food hot, resist moisture transfer, keep food fresh, and act as a merchandiser of the food.
Courtesy of Reynolds Metals Co.

ADVERTISING AND PUBLICITY

The objectives of advertising and publicity are the same, that is to create and reinforce an image. Both are techniques to inform the public; both can be used to call attention to, tell about, or praise someone or something. Advertising generally must be bought, although public service ads are offered free of charge by many local media. Publicity usually is free. Just because publicity is free does not guarantee that it will happen. School foodservice management should be assertive and imaginative in obtaining "free" publicity.

There are several ways to obtain publicity. News releases can be prepared and sent to the local radio station or newspaper. Tantalizing "news tips" and "come-ons" will encourage local news media to develop stories about salad bars at school, taste parties for trying new foods, etc. Good publicity means keeping a school foodservice favorably in the mind of customers or potential customers and the public.

It is best when publicity is positive; however, that is not always possible. Honest responses to a reporter are safer in the long run than attempts to cover up an unfavorable situation. Negative images, caused by bad publicity, can be overcome by a positive, assertive-type campaign.

Paid advertising is rarely used by school foodservices. Yet, Pepsi Cola, for example, has bought an image with its advertising budget, as have thousands of companies and commercial foodservices. The advertisements on television are aimed primarily at promoting an image and finally a desire to have the product. If funds will allow, why not support a school's activities by purchasing an "ad" in the high school newspaper? Perhaps USDA regulations have never dealt with such expenditures, but if such advertising contributes to the success of the school lunch program and its continuance, it would seem to be justifiable.

Advertising of school foodservice activities and offerings usually qualifies for "free time" or "free space." Menus are published in many local newspapers. Even the *Washington Post* carries the local school districts' weekly menus. Radio stations will announce the menus and special events if provided with the information. To get the positive advertisement and publicity desired takes work by foodservice management.

PROMOTIONS

Promotions refer to a wide variety of special marketing techniques. For example, a few years ago, Clorox Company, which makes Hidden Valley Salad Dressings, conducted a promotion in salad bars to increase its sale of dressings. The promotion included "rub-off" cards given to each customer who chose the salad lunch. If the rub-off card had a salad under all three dots, the customer received a free salad lunch. It was fun and created suspense.

The use of promotions in a foodservice can help keep up students' interest in eating at the same place each day throughout the school year. Looking at the commercial industry can provide ideas for many promotional devices. Have a contest to name the dining room and pick a theme for different seasons of the year. Sell a book of lunch tickets for 10 meals at a slight savings. Capitalize on holidays and special school events with decorations and menus that create interest. Send favorite school recipes (adjusted to family size) home at Christmas time or during National School Lunch Week. Celebrate birthdays of the month with specially decorated cupcakes. These efforts will result not only in higher participation, but more satisfied customers.

A promotion can have very positive results. It is an excellent way to encourage students to try something new and buy more than just a lunch (if the customers have money). With the purchase of a milk shake, the customer gets a school cup. Give a decorated cupcake to students on their birthday if they eat the school lunch that day. Promotions come in many forms. They are all around. By being aware of those currently used, it will be possible to plan successful foodservice promotions. Whatever is popular in the grocery

September Grandparents Day Great Cities of the World Series* State Fair Day Good Neighbor Day	*February* History Month (feature Presidents) Valentine's Day Great Cities of the World Series* Potato Lover's Month Friendship Week
October National School Lunch Week National Apple Month Great Cities of the World Series* Columbus Day United Nations Day Halloween	Chinese Festival (New Year or Lantern Festival) *March* Nutrition Month Great Cities of the World Series* St. Patrick's Day Women's History Week
November Thanksgiving Lunch Great Cities of the World Series* Football Season (Homecoming, etc.)	Art Week *April* Spring Fling Spring Sports Day (baseball, golf, tennis)
December Great Cities of the World Series* Winter Holidays	April Showers' Day Picnic Day Great Cities of the World Series* Arbor Day
January Winter Carnival Winter Sports (basketball, skiing, skating, hockey) Citrus Celebration Great Cities of the World Series* Hat Day Pie Eating Contest	World Health Day Secretaries Week *May* Honors Month (honor the graduating class) Great Cities of the World Series* Memorial Day *June* Teacher "Thank You" Week

*This can include great countries, cultures, or regions of the United States. It is tied in with the educational program.

FIG. 9.6.   Sample promotions calendar.

stores or fast-food outlets will probably be the most timely and accepted. A promotions calendar can be planned for the year as shown in Fig. 9.6.

COMMUNICATING WITH CUSTOMERS

Knowing what the students and adults in individual schools think about school foodservice is important. Techniques that can be used in getting to know the students' and adults' likes and dislikes include (1) formal questionnaires and surveys, (2) informal interviewing of students, (3) small-group discussions, (4) suggestion boxes, and (5) taste parties, which are

---

Time of Interview _____ Day of Week _____ Date _____

Hi, I am _____ conducting a survey on the school foodservice. If you have about two minutes to answer a few questions, we would like very much to include your opinion in the survey.

1. How often do you normally eat the school lunch? _____
2. Rate the following *very good, good, fair,* or *poor*:
   a. How would you rate the quality of the meal you had today? _____
   b. What do you think of the variety and choices of food offered? _____
   c. Do you have enough food to satisfy your appetite? What do you think of the size of the servings? _____
   d. How would you rate the food service employees? _____
   e. What rating would you give the atmosphere in the dining area? _____
3. What do you particularly like about your school's foodservice? _____
4. What do you particularly dislike about your school's foodservice? _____
5. How would you rate the value of your meal today in relation to cost? *Very good, good, fair,* or *poor* _____

FIG. 9.7. A short questionnaire can be used to obtain customers' opinions.

described later in this section. Small-group discussions can be very beneficial if suggestions for improving are obtained along with help in carrying out the changes.

Circulating throughout the dining area during lunch time, a manager or designated person(s) can effectively solicit customers' opinions. This should be a regular occurrence. Also, employees on the serving line and at the dishroom window can obtain feedback and identify happy and unhappy customers. This information should be discussed with management.

In 1975, Hardee's, one of the leading fast-food chains, conducted a problem-detection study. It was aimed at identifying consumers' attitudes—especially negative opinions. The study showed that consumers had no definite attitudes about Hardee's. In other words, the company had an image problem—or rather a "lack of image" problem. As Oscar Wilde said, "There's only one thing worse than being talked about, and that's not being talked about."

Monitoring customers' acceptance of new menu items, new brands of products, new recipes, and other changes is needed feedback. It is dangerous to take customers' acceptance for granted; it is also good public relations to let the customers know that management cares. Figure 9.7 is a short questionnaire that can be used to assess customers' opinions about a school foodservice.

Taste Parties

A taste party can be formal or informal, small or large, and involve students, parents, faculty or/and foodservice supervisors or managers. It pro-

FIG. 9.8. Taste parties are an excellent way of involving students in a school foodservice program.

vides an excellent way of obtaining student opinion and of determining an acceptable product for bids in a social atmosphere (Fig. 9.8).

Either a formal or informal taste party must be planned carefully to provide results that can be used in making decisions. No more than 25 to 30 people can participate effectively, unless the taste party is very well organized. The evaluation time can be used to compare similar products to test acceptance of a new recipe, to sample new products, or to determine if a product is acceptable or meets bid specifications. Elementary schools have effectively used the taste-party approach to persuade children to try new foods. The National Dairy Council has provided materials on having taste parties in their kit called "Taste Buddies."

If several foods are to be tested, the party may be scheduled near lunch time and take the place of lunch. In order to have a controlled situation, the party should be held in a room separate from the dining room, with table and chair sit-down arrangements. This is also a good time to explain the lunch program and to get students and adults to complete surveys. Care should be taken that the "party" does not become boring and too lengthy.

Some school districts use taste parties for testing all new products and have involved company representatives in them. As in the procedure for a can cutting, the brands of the products being evaluated are not known by the tasters. This approach has been good public relations with companies as well as students.

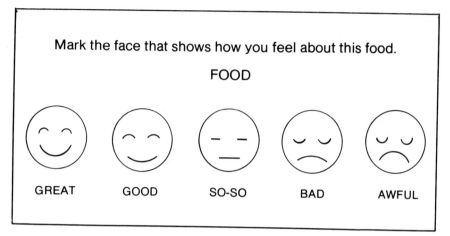

Mark the face that shows how you feel about this food.

FOOD

GREAT   GOOD   SO-SO   BAD   AWFUL

FIG. 9.9. Simple graphical format for expressing opinions is suitable for younger children.

In any taste party, some type of form for expressing opinions should be provided. For younger children, a simple graphical form, as shown in Fig. 9.9, is appropriate. The hedonic scale method also works well in evaluating customers' opinions. A numerical value is given to each possible response ranging from 1 for "like extremely" to 9 for "dislikes extremely." This evaluation method may be particularly useful when different brands of the same type of food item are being evaluated. For example, if brands are to be listed on bid specifications, this is a good method for selecting preferred brands. A hedonic scale might include the following responses: "like extremely," "like very much," "like moderately," "like slightly," "neither like nor dislike," "dislike slightly," "dislike moderately," "dislike very much," and "dislike extremely".

Youth Advisory Council

Involving students in foodservice programs is required under the Child Nutrition Act (see Appendix II). This is an excellent way to get student opinion and help in promoting school foodservice. Often, bad images exist because of misinformation. Communicating the facts to students may relieve potential misunderstandings about foodservice practices.

A Youth Advisory Council (YAC, as it is sometimes called) is an organization made up of students interested in nutrition and school foodservice. It is a national organization sponsored by the American School Food Service Association. The Irving (TX) Independent School District has developed a manual for its Youth Advisory Council that is very useful when establishing a council. The goals of the National Youth Advisory Council are to

1. learn the meaning of school breakfast and lunch, and understand the requirements;
2. strive to make the school foodservice program better meet the needs of the entire student body;
3. offer suggestions to improve the health/nutrition program in a responsible way;
4. develop a better understanding of the need for nutrition and nutrition education;
5. involve youth in planning menus, sampling school food products, and merchandising meals served;
6. become an active part of a statewide YAC program;
7. make the student body more aware of the total school foodservice program; and
8. understand and work with the problems of the school foodservice program at all levels.

The American School Food Service Association has materials available on how to start a Youth Advisory Council. The activities of a YAC, as well as its insight and advice, can be very valuable to a foodservice manager.

BIBLIOGRAPHY

BARKER, L. M. 1982. The Psychology of Human Food Selection. AVI Publishing Co., Westport, CT.
BUCHANAN, R. D. 1979a. Consumer Satisfaction. Cooperative Extension Service, Purdue University, West Lafayette, IN.
BUCHANAN, R. D. 1979b. Food Presentation and Service. Cooperative Extension Service, Purdue University, West Lafayette, IN.
FELTENSTEIN, T. 1983. Restaurant Profits through Advertising and Promotion: The Indispensable Plan. CBI Publishing Co., Boston.
FREDRICK, L. 1977. Fast Food Gets an A in School Lunches. Cahners Books, Boston.
IRVING INDEPENDENT SCHOOL DISTRICT. 1979. Youth Advisory Council Resource Manual. Irving Independent School District, TX.
KRAMER, A. 1980. Food and the Consumer. Revised edition. AVI Publishing Co., Westport, CT.
MARTINEAU, P. 1957. Motivation in Advertising. McGraw-Hill Book Co., New York.
MASLOW, A. H. 1970. Motivation and Personality. Harper & Row, New York.
REDMAN, B. J. 1979. Consumer Behavior: Theory and Applications. AVI Publishing Co., Westport, CT.
REID, R. D. 1983. Foodservice and Restaurant Marketing. CBI Publishing Co., Boston.
SELTZ, D. D. 1977. Food Service Marketing and Promotion. Chain Store Publishing Corp., New York.

SANITATION

Good food is safe food. Safe food is free of microorganisms, chemicals, and foreign substances, such as broken glass. To be safe, food must be purchased clean and kept wholesome and free from spoilage. It must be properly stored under sanitary conditions and be prepared by people who have sanitary habits and who are free from communicable diseases. To keep prepared food safe, it must be held at the proper temperature and be served by people with sanitary habits who are free from communicable diseases.

The primary objective in school foodservices is to serve safe, nutritious food. The responsibility of serving safe food depends on many people— from the grower of the food to the server of the prepared food. Illness from contaminated food is most unpleasant and can even be fatal. There are more than two million reported cases of food poisoning yearly. So many mild cases of foodborne illnesses are not reported each year that it is difficult to know how prevalent they are.

An outbreak of food poisoning is one of the most dreaded events in any food establishment. It is an on-going threat that requires constant vigilance and preventive measures. Foodborne illnesses are caused by careless workers, unsanitary conditions, and lack of caution. The human element is the area where the most emphasis should be placed. Ignorance and negligence are the two greatest problems. At least 25 diseases can enter the human body through improper food handling. Such diseases as typhoid fever, tuberculosis, diphtheria, undulant fever, dysentery, and gastric upsets can be traced back to contaminated foods and water.

For a foodservice to serve food that causes an outbreak of food poisoning is obviously very damaging to its reputation. A commercial foodservice would lose business; a school foodservice would be subject to severe criticism and might lose customers. Even though school foodservices serve a largely captive audience, indeed because they do, they must set and enforce strict standards of sanitation. Also, food poison usually affects the very young and the old the most.

226

Food poisoning can be prevented. Becoming familiar with the problem and wiping out ignorance on the part of all employees who come in contact with the food are the beginning. There are four basic rules for keeping food safe and preventing food-related diseases:

* Buy safe food.
* Keep food safe.
* Keep food cold or keep food hot, not in between.
* When in doubt throw it out.

BACTERIA-CAUSED FOOD POISONING

Bacteria are all around us, but are so small they cannot be seen with the naked eye. Some bacteria are desirable; for example, bacteria are essential to the making of buttermilk, cheese, and apple cider. However, many types of bacteria are dangerous and will cause disease if allowed to multiply and be transmitted to humans. Most bacteria grow very rapidly when conditions are favorable—warm, moist, with food, and enough time. It should be em-

TABLE 10.1. Characteristics of Bacteria-Caused Food Poisoning

Symptoms	Incubation Period	Organism Causing	Ingestion of	
			Toxin	Organisms
Vomiting, nausea, diarrhea	2–4 hr	*Staphylococcus aureus*[1]	Yes	Yes*
Diarrhea, nausea, but little fever or vomiting	9–15 hr	*Clostridium perfringens*[1]	No	Yes
Central nervous system involved, blurred vision, sore throat, vomiting, diarrhea	12–36 hr	*Clostridium botulinum*[2]	Yes	Yes*
Nausea, vomiting, abdominal colic, diarrhea	1–5 hr	*Bacillus cereus*[1]	No	Yes
Watery diarrhea, abdominal cramps, nausea, vomiting, fever	12–24 hr	*Vibrio parahaemolyticus*[1]	No	Yes
Typhoid fever, abdominal pain, diarrhea, fever, vomiting, chills	12–24 hr	*Salmonella*	No	Yes
Scarlet fever, septic sore throat	24–36 hr	*Streptococcus*	No	Yes

Source: Adapted from Guthrie (1980).
[1]Rarely fatal.
[2]Up to 70% fatal.
*Although organisms may be ingested, symptoms are due to ingestion of performed exotoxin.

phasized that food contaminated with bacteria that are capable of making a person sick may have *no off-smell, no off-taste,* and *no difference in appearance.* Therefore, contamination may not be suspected.

Three of the most common types of bacteria causing food poisoning are *Salmonella, Clostridium perfringens,* and *Streptococcus;* however, there are others more dreaded. Some of these bacteria and how they are transmitted, the foods most frequently associated with the infection, symptoms of the food poisoning, and the time that it takes for the bacteria to make a person sick are given below (also see Table 10.1).

Salmonella

Salmonella bacteria may be transmitted by careless food handlers, through animal feeds to a product such as eggs, by contaminated shellfish, and by rodents. The foods in which these bacteria are most frequently found are poultry, eggs, salads, soups, gravies, meats, shellfish, and dairy products. The bacteria cause typhoid fever and salmonellosis, which have a variety of symptoms—abdominal pains, diarrhea, fever, vomiting, and chills. Someone who has been infected by *Salmonella* will usually show symptoms within 12 to 24 hours, except in the case of typhoid fever where it may be 3 weeks before symptoms appear. *Salmonella* outbreaks tend to occur when the weather is very warm.

Streptococcus

Streptococcus bacteria are usually transmitted by careless food handlers with poor personal hygiene. The bacteria are carried in discharges from the nose, throat, ears, and abscesses. When such discharges come into contact with food, it becomes contaminated. Milk is one of the foods most favorable for growth of streptococci. *Streptococcus* causes scarlet fever and septic sore throat. Symptoms of illness usually appear 24 to 36 hours after infection.

Clostridium perfringens

Clostridium perfringens is frequently associated with outbreaks of food poisoning. Since *Clostridium perfringens* is in the human intestinal tract, it is usually transmitted to food by a careless food handler who did not wash his hands after using the toilet or is transmitted by flies. The organisms are difficult to kill even with heat. The foods most favorable to the growth of this bacteria are those made from leftovers, that is, foods that have been reheated after being cooked earlier. The symptoms of *Clostridium* are acute abdominal pains and diarrhea. They usually occur 8 to 22 hours after eating contaiminated food.

Staphylococcus aureus

When *Staphylococcus aureus* bacteria have been transmitted to food and allowed to grow, they produce a toxin that causes illness. These bacteria occur on the skin—particularly in skin infections, cuts, boils, and burns and in the nose. They are transmitted by careless food handlers. The foods most commonly infected are poultry, meat, salads, gravies, potato salad, cream-filled pies, and cooked ham. The toxin produced by *Staphylococcus* is extremely difficult to destroy. The symptoms are nausea, vomiting, abdominal pains, and diarrhea. The illness occurs 1 to 12 hours after food containing *Staphylococcus* toxin has been eaten.

Vibrio parahaemolyticus

An intestinal infection caused by *Vibrio parahaemolyticus* has been on the increase in the United States in recent years. In the past, this had been reported primarily in those countries where raw seafoods are regularly consumed. *Vibrio* organisms may be transmitted when food is inadequately cooked. Symptoms of infection include diarrhea, abdominal cramps, nausea, vomiting, fever, and headache. The infection is noticed 12 to 24 hours after consumption of contaminated food.

Bacillus cereus

Bacillus cereus-induced food poisoning is a bacterial infection causing gastrointestinal disorders. The incubation period ranges from 1 hour to 15 hours. There is usually a sudden onset of nausea and vomiting with abdominal cramps and diarrhea. This type of food poisoning is associated with rice, potatoes, and vegetables. Usually the symptoms last no longer than 24 hours and the disease is rarely fatal.

Clostridium botulinum

Botulism is probably the most widely known type of food poisoning because it is usually fatal. The disease is caused by a toxin produced by *Clostridium botulinum*. These bacteria are most frequently associated with inadequately processed canned and sealed foods low in acid, such as green beans, corn, meats, fish, and spinach. However, they have been found to grow even in pickles. Ironically *Clostridium botulinum* may produce no obvious taste, smell, or visual evidence of its presence. Repugnant food spoilage, which may not even cause food poisoning, will usually produce an acid, causing coagulation of the food, and a sour odor. The smallest bite of food infected with *Clostridium botulinum* can be deadly. However, the toxin is easily destroyed by heat, but has been known to multiply at temperatures below 40°F. Canned foods, particularly home canned foods, should be heated at 212°F for 10 minutes before being served or even tasted. Symptoms of botulism are dizziness, double vision, difficulty in swallowing, speaking and breathing, and muscular weakness. The illness usually starts 12 to 36 hours after food containing the toxin has been consumed.

OTHER FOODBORNE DISEASES

Several other diseases, not usually classified as food poisoning, can be transmitted by contaminated foods. Though not perhaps as prevalent as food poisoning, these diseases should be known to foodservice personnel.

Bacillary Dysentery

Shigella bacteria cause bacillary dysentery. They are transmitted from feces by careless food handlers or by flies and are most frequently associated with moist foods such as egg salad, ham salad, and milk products. The symptoms of bacillary dysentery—diarrhea, cramps, fever, and vomiting—occur 2 to 3 days after eating a contaminated product.

Tuberculosis

Tuberculosis is a foodborne infectious disease that can be transmitted through food to man, particularly from tuberculous cattle through raw milk. However, with pasteurization of milk and better controls and inspection of cattle, it is rarely transmitted in this way today. It is more commonly transmitted from one infectious person to another and readily through food handling or the handling of utensils used by others for eating. Tuberculin tests or X-rays should be required of every foodservice employee and every person who comes in contact with food during its preparation for and serving to others.

Infectious Hepatitis

Infectious hepatitis is caused by a foodborne virus, which may be transmitted through contaminated shellfish, water, or any foods that have been contaminated by a carrier of the disease.

Trichinosis

Trichinosis is a parasitic infection caused by a tiny worm sometimes found in pork. The tiny worm (*Trichina spiralis*) usually infects hogs in the muscles or bones; therefore, government inspection may not catch it. Trichinae are usually transmitted to hogs in the food they eat, particularly food garbage that has not been properly treated before feeding to hogs. Some foodservices sell their food garbage to farmers for hog feed. This is not a safe practice unless the farmer agrees in writing to abide by health department regulations about treatment of garbage. The local health department should be contacted before such a practice is started.

Trichinae are killed by heat. Pork should never be eaten raw or partially cooked, because it may cause an illness that is very difficult to cure. The person may recover but may never be free of this parasite. Heating fresh pork to 137°F destroys trichinae. According to federal standards, any processed cured pork product that might be eaten without further cooking must be subjected to an internal temperature of 160°F.

BACTERIAL GROWTH

For bacteria that cause foodborne illnesses to grow, *food,* favorable *temperature, moisture,* and enough *time* are needed. Since bacteria are all around us, it is of the utmost importance that foodservice employees know the conditions under which bacteria grow so they can control these conditions.

Food

Bacterial growth may occur in any food man eats. *Clostridium botulinum,* the cause of the most serious type of food poisonings, has been found in pickles, though it is usually associated with low-acid canned foods. Protein-rich foods and creamed dishes are most frequently associated with outbreaks of food poisoning. Protein-rich foods, such as poultry and ham, that require a lot of handling and time in their preparation provide perfect conditions for bacterial growth. A creamed dish high in egg content and dairy products has many of the properties needed for bacterial growth—it is moist, it contains protein, and it cools slowly.

The pH (acidity) of a food determines which microorganisms can grow and dominate in it. High-acid foods have a lower pH. Most bacteria grow fastest when the pH is near 7.0. According to the U.S. Food and Drug Administration, *C. botulinum,* for example, can grow, and produce toxin when the pH is 4.8. Few of the bacteria that cause foodborne disease can grow when the pH is below 3.0. Table 10.2 lists the approximate pH of various foods.

232   **10** Sanitation

TABLE 10.2. Approximate pH of Selected Foods

Food	pH Range	Food	pH Range
Egg white	7.6–9.5	Cabbage	5.2–6.3
Shrimp	6.8–8.2	Turnip	5.2–5.6
Crab	6.8–8.0	Spinach	5.1–6.8
Scallops	6.8–7.1	Asparagus	5.0–6.1
Cod, small	6.7–7.1	Cheeses, most	5.0–6.1
Cod, large	6.5–6.9	Camembert	6.1–7.0
Catfish	6.6–7.0	Cottage	4.1–5.4
Soda crackers	6.5–8.5	Gouda	4.7
Maple syrup	6.5–7.0	Bread	5.0–6.0
Milk	6.3–6.8	Carrots	4.9–6.3
Brussels sprouts	6.3–6.6	Beets	4.9–5.8
Whiting	6.2–7.1	Bananas	4.5–5.2
Haddock	6.2–6.7	Dry sausages	4.4–5.6
Cantaloupe	6.2–6.5	Pimientos	4.3–5.2
Dates	6.2–6.4	Tomato juice	3.9–4.7
Herring	6.1–6.6	Mayonnaise	3.8–4.0
Butter	6.1–6.4	Tomatoes	3.7–4.9
Honey	6.0–6.8	Jams	3.5–4.0
Mushrooms	6.0–6.5	Apricots	3.5–4.0
Cauliflower	6.0–6.7	Apple sauce	3.4–3.5
Lettuce	6.0–6.4	Pears	3.4–4.7
Egg yolk	6.0–6.3	Grapes	3.3–4.5
Corn, sweet	5.9–6.5	Cherries	3.2–4.7
Oysters	5.9–6.6	Pineapple	3.2–4.1
Celery	5.7–6.0	Peaches	3.1–4.2
Peas	5.6–6.8	Rhubarb	3.1–3.2
Turkey	5.6–6.0	Strawberries	3.0–4.2
Chicken	5.5–6.4	Grapefruit	2.9–4.0
Halibut	5.5–5.8	Raspberries	2.9–3.7
Beans, lima	5.4–6.5	Apples	2.9–3.5
Potatoes, Irish	5.4–6.3	Plums	2.8–4.6
Walnuts	5.4–5.5	Oranges	2.8–4.0
Pork	5.3–6.4	Cranberries	2.5–2.8
Beef	5.3–6.2	Lemons	2.2–2.4
Onions	5.3–5.8	Limes	1.8–2.0
Sweet potatoes	5.3–5.6		

Source: Banwart (1981).

Foods can be categorized by their pH as follows:

High-acid foods	pH below 3.7
Acid foods	pH 3.7–4.6
Medium-acid foods	pH 4.6–5.3
Low- or non-acid foods	pH over 5.3

Moisture

The moisture content of food needs to be relatively high for bacteria to grow. Dehydrated foods usually do not support bacterial growth until moisture has been added. Much care should be taken when using dried eggs and dried milk—once mixed with liquids they should be treated as fresh. In quantity food preparation a recommended precautionary measure is to use dried eggs and dried milk only in foods that are to be cooked. Heat will destroy any bacteria present and make the food safe to eat.

Temperature

The temperature range at which bacteria grow best is between 60 and 120°F. However, some types of bacteria grow at temperatures as low as 0°F and as high as 140°F. Usually bacterial growth is slowed down at tem-

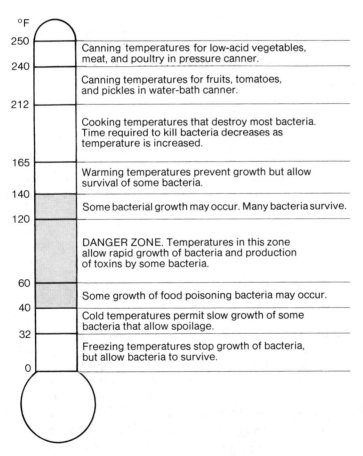

°F
250
240   Canning temperatures for low-acid vegetables, meat, and poultry in pressure canner.

Canning temperatures for fruits, tomatoes, and pickles in water-bath canner.
212

Cooking temperatures that destroy most bacteria. Time required to kill bacteria decreases as temperature is increased.
165
Warming temperatures prevent growth but allow survival of some bacteria.
140
Some bacterial growth may occur. Many bacteria survive.
120

DANGER ZONE. Temperatures in this zone allow rapid growth of bacteria and production of toxins by some bacteria.
60
Some growth of food poisoning bacteria may occur.
40
Cold temperatures permit slow growth of some bacteria that allow spoilage.
32
Freezing temperatures stop growth of bacteria, but allow bacteria to survive.
0

FIG. 10.1. Effects of different temperatures on growth of bacteria. *Courtesy of U.S. Department of Agriculture.*

peratures of 45°F and below. The most ideal temperatures for bacteria to grow are body temperature (98°F) and room temperature (78°F). When temperatures are 120°F or hotter, the growth of bacteria is slowed down, and most bacteria will not survive temperatures over 170°F.

Hot foods should be kept hot, at 150°F or hotter. Cold foods should be kept cold, at 45°F or colder. Freezing does not kill bacteria, but slows down their growth. If frozen food contains bacteria, they will start growing when the food is thawed. For this reason, as well as for quality reasons, it is not a good idea to refreeze thawed foods—particularly those high in protein and moisture.

The temperature at which food is held is crucial. The thermometer in Fig. 10.1 points out the temperatures that are important for foodservice employees to watch.

Time

Time is needed for bacteria to grow. If the discharge (pus) from an infected cuticle were to come in contact with cooked turkey, thousands of tiny *Staphylococcus* bacteria could contaminate the food. At room temperature, the dividing bacteria cells could multiply eightfold within 1 hour. Thus, potentially hazardous foods should not be allowed to sit at room temperature for long periods of time.

In some states, meat salads are almost of the past in institutional food operations. The health departments have enforced a law in some parts of the country that requires these protein salads be kept at 50°F or colder at all times. This means all ingredients and utensils used in the preparation have to be refrigerated in order to keep the salad from going over 50°F during the mixing process.

PREVENTING FOODBORNE ILLNESSES

In looking at the ways bacteria are transmitted, it is evident that in order to be sure one is serving safe, sanitary food, the food must be safe when purchased, kept safe during storage, and be prepared and served in a sanitary manner by employees who are not carriers of communicable diseases and who have good personal hygiene. To be sure food is not contaminated before preparation, it is necessary to buy from reliable companies that meet sanitation standards. Canned foods should not be used if there is a swelling at the top or bottom of the cans, if the cans are dented along the side seams, or if there is an off-odor or foam.

Foods can become contaminated with bacteria from many sources. However, in the school kitchen the most frequent sources of bacterial contamination are humans, equipment, water, and other foods.

The hands are the main culprits in the spread of bacteria that can cause foodborne illness from humans to food, and the digestive tracts of humans and animals are often the source of harmful bacteria. Therefore, it is very important that employees wash their hands well after using the toilet and after handling poultry and meats. Sterilization of equipment will be discussed later. Water from faucets may be contaminated; the potential of sewage backup in faucets is frightening. The importance of using adequate cooking and proper holding temperatures can not be over emphasized. Over 40% of foodborne illnesses are caused because the food was not held at the proper temperature. The handling of food and the food handler also are discussed later in this section.

Meat should be examined for off-odors, slimy surfaces, and broken delivery containers. Only pasteurized milk, commercially processed canned foods, shellfish that has been inspected, and meat and poultry that have been inspected for wholesomeness should be purchased. Much care and precaution should be taken in the handling of high-protein foods, especially those with a high pH (low acid) such as poultry, that require lengthy preparation and much handling. Some useful rules for handling turkeys, which can be applied to other foods, are listed here.

Rules for Keeping Turkeys Sanitary during Handling

1. Store frozen turkeys at 0°F or below.
2. Always defrost frozen turkeys in the wrapper in the *refrigerator* at 45°F or slightly below. Defrosting may take 3 to 4 days.
3. Roast turkey at an internal temperature of 165°F. A 25-lb turkey takes 4 to 6 hours to roast to 165°F. Cutting the turkey into parts can cut the roasting time in half.
4. Do not partially cook a turkey one day and finish cooking it the next day—the internal area may be at a perfect temperature for bacterial growth. Do not roast whole turkeys overnight in a slow oven.
5. After the turkey has cooked, refrigerate at 45°F or below. The broth and turkey should be refrigerated separately within ½ hour after removing from oven. Store turkey in a shallow pan (2½ to 4 inches deep) and pull turkey apart to aid the cooling. Store broth in no larger than 4-gallon quantities.
6. Dressing should be cooked in a separate pan from the turkey and, if desired, the turkey can be stuffed after cooking.
7. A 2-day refrigeration period for cooked turkey parts and broth is the maximum recommended storage time.
8. Employees who have colds, diarrhea, boils, or infected fingers should not work with turkey or any other food.
9. Turkeys should never stand for longer than 3 hours (total) at temperatures between 50 and 120°F; this includes cooling, boning, cutting, etc.

10. Use clean, sanitized equipment in preparing and serving turkey. Wooden cutting boards may harbor *Staphylococcus* and *Salmonella* and should not be used.

Sterilization

Sterilization can eliminate all forms of bacteria. There are several means of sterilization:

1. *Heat* can be used dry or moist. To obtain sterilization with dry heat, the temperature must reach 160 to 180°F for a period of 1–2 hours. Moist-heat sterilization is most often used.
2. *Ultraviolet light* is more effective the closer the light source is to the material being sterilized.
3. *Pasteurization* simply means raising the temperature of food to boiling for a short period of time.
4. *Chemical substances* such as antiseptics, disinfectants, sanitizers, antibiotics, and germicides are effective sterilants.

Storage of Food

Storage of food at the proper temperature within the proper amount of time is extremely important. Refrigerated storage should be at 45°F or below. A thermometer should be placed in each refrigerated unit to monitor the temperature. Food needs air circulation when under refrigeration; therefore, it is recommended that it be packed loosely. Cooked foods high in protein should be refrigerated in shallow pans (no deeper than 4 inches) so they can cool through and through quickly. Food should be covered when refrigerated to prevent foreign matter from getting into the food, to keep moisture in the food, and to prevent off-odors and off-flavors from being absorbed.

Frozen foods should be stored at 0°F or below. Once food is thawed it should be treated as highly perishable fresh food. Some foods can be refrozen safely; however, once foods are thawed, bacterial growth starts. Refreezing should be done with great care. Some foods will keep their quality when frozen for years. The storage times of various frozen foods are listed in Table 10.3; the values are based on storage at 0°F; however, it's better to store frozen foods at −10°F.

Hot foods should be cooled slightly before refrigerating them. However, hot foods placed directly in the refrigerator will not sour as some think. The time required to cool will depend on the quantity. According to West *et al.* (1977) it takes 9 hours to cool a 4-inch deep 50-portion quantity of chicken salad from an internal temperature of 64 to 48°F in a walk-in refrigerator maintained at 35°F. The greatest danger in storing cooked foods is holding

TABLE 10.3. Approximate Storage Life at 0°F for Various Foods

Food Group	Item	No. Months
Fruits	Apples	18
	Apricots and peaches	12
	Strawberries	24
Vegetables	Beans, snap	8–12
	Beans, lima	12–14
	Broccoli	14
	Cauliflower	14
	Corn, cut	24
	Carrots	24
	Peas	14
	Spinach	14
	Potatoes	12
Meats	Bologna	3–6
	Ground beef	3–6
	Cubed beef	6–12
	Veal cutlets, cubes	4–8
	Bacon	1
	Frankfurters	2½
	Ham	6
	Pork chops	4
	Poultry	6–12
	Eggs, whole	9
Baked Goods	Bread, quick	2–4
	Bread, yeast	6
	Rolls	6
	Cake	4–6
	Cookies	4–6
	Combination dishes	4–8
	Fruit pies	4
Miscellaneous	Ice cream	9
	Soups	12
	Sandwiches	2

the foods for any length of time at temperatures above refrigerator temperature but below serving temperature of hot food (140°F).

The food stored in a dry storeroom should be protected from rodents and insects, from high temperature (40 to 70°F is desirable), and from dirty conditions. Storage at 90°F reduces the shelf life of many foods by half or more. Thus, dry-stored food should be used on a first-in, first-out basis.

Handling Leftovers

Leftovers should be handled with much caution. Food that has been held on the serving counter at 150°F (or higher) or at 45° (or lower) may be used again. Leftovers should be refrigerated as soon as possible, and no more than ½ hour after preliminary preparation has been concluded or after their removal from the steamtable. Warm food should be precooled quickly and placed in shallow pans to allow for quick cooling. Cooked foods should not be stored in a refrigerator containing uncooked food items. The uncooked food will contain bacteria that could infect the already sterile products. All food should be covered. Use leftovers the next day or within 36 hours. Do not plan to use leftovers a third time. Throw out leftovers that are over 36 hours old.

The Food Handler

The primary causes of foodborne illnesses are carelessness on the part of food handlers and poor personal hygiene. The health of the food handler is also important. Each employee should have a regular physical examination, and a current health certificate should be required to be on file at the school foodservice. At a minimum this certificate should certify that the employee does not have tuberculosis. Discharges from the human body are the chief sources of contaminating food with unwanted bacteria that can cause illness. Personal hygiene is a way of life—a habit. Many employees need on-the-job training to promote high standards of cleanliness and to build good hygiene habits. Probably the one most important rule for foodservice employees is *wash hands frequently.*

Hands should be thoroughly washed with hot water and soap *before* beginning work; serving food; handling clean dishes and utensils; performing any job where the hands come into direct contact with food—and *after* each visit to the toilet; handling money, tickets, or any soiled items; coughing, sneezing, and fingering face or hair. Utensils, not hands, should be used whenever possible. The mixing of salads should be done with a spoon or other utensil rather than the naked hands. When it is necessary to bring the hands in contact with food, they should be thoroughly washed; when practical, plastic disposable gloves should be worn.

Sick employees should stay home. Cuts, burns, and sores on an employee should be carefully protected so there is no possibility of discharge from the infections getting on utensils or food. Dirty finger nails and broken cuticles can be food hazards. Smoking should be confined to an area where food is not being prepared or served.

Good grooming practices are a must in a foodservice. Not only for sanitation reasons, but for the sake of favorable public relations, employees should be well groomed, clean, and neat. Clean, washable outer garments should be worn when preparing and serving food. Hairnets or caps to confine the hair are required by most health departments. Nobody likes to find hair in his food; furthermore, hair often has bacteria on it that can contaminate the food. School foodservice employees often point to commercial foodservices where the persons preparing food are not wearing hair nets or caps. For the most part, school foodservices are the cleanest, most sanitary of all foodservices and should take pride in this.

Cleaning Equipment

Utensils and equipment can transmit many disease-causing organisms from one person to another. Sterilization of eating utensils is essential to prevent the spread of viruses, particularly those causing the common cold, as well as many more dangerous communicable diseases.

The *Food Service Sanitation Manual* produced by the U.S. Department of Health, Education and Welfare (1976) describes the standards for equipment construction and procedures for cleaning equipment. The *Manual* has served as the basis for the Food Service Equipment Standards developed by the National Sanitation Foundation; these standards are used by manufacturers of foodservice equipment and enforced by local health departments, which often require the NSF seal.

Basically there are three ways of providing clean equipment: manual and mechanical washing of dirty equipment and use of single-service equipment that is discarded after using.

Manual Washing. Washing of dishes, pots, pans, and utensils by hand should be done in a three-compartment sink. In the first compartment, the scraped dishes or utensils should be washed in a detergent solution with water at 110 to 125°F. The second compartment is for rinsing soap off the dishes and utensils. The third compartment is for sterilizing. There are two methods of sanitizing that are accepted: the hot-water method and the chemical method.

In the hot-water method, dishes are immersed in water at 170°F or higher for not less than 30 seconds; in some states the health department specifies 2-minute immersion period. Since the water temperature is so essential, it should be controlled by thermostat and be constant. A booster heater usually is necessary to maintain water at 170°F. Since this temperature is too hot for a person's hands, a dishbasket or rack is necessary for immersing the utensils and dishes.

The chemical method of sanitizing requires immersion for a minimum of 1 minute in water to which has been added a germicide or sanitizer. To be called a germicide or sanitizer, a product must be registered with the USDA as such. A germicide is a chemical that kills or deactivates bacteria on the surface of dishes, utensils, walls, floor, etc. It is very important that the correct amount of the product be used. The directions should be followed carefully. Chlorine may be used at 50 parts per million (ppm) or iodine at 12.5 ppm.

All utensils and dishes, regardless of whether washed by hand or in a mechanical dishwasher, should *air dry;* towels should not be used for drying. Those immersed in the hot water will dry very quickly.

Mechanical Washing. A mechanical dishwasher is a very important piece of equipment. It should be utilized for cleaning and sanitizing any utensil that will fit into the machine and that does not have electrical parts. There are basically two types of dishwashing machines: low temperature and high temperature. When chemicals are used with low temperature, drying is slow and can be a problem in the service end. When hot water is used for sanitizing, then it is essential that the water temperature in a dishwasher be controlled and reach the specified limits. The wash water must be maintained at a temperature of 140 to 160°F. Water higher than 160°F is inclined to cook food on the dishes. The first rinse should be at 170°F and the final rinse must be at 180 to 190°F. A booster heater generally is needed to keep the water from the hot water supply at 180°F. When a sanitizing chemical is used during the rinse cycle, a low-temperature dish machine is satisfactory (Fig. 10.2).

Detergents are needed for cleaning dishes. Manual dispensing of detergent is unsatisfactory, often unreliable, and most frequently more expensive than an automatic dispenser. Detergent requirements vary from one part of the country to another. The representative of a detergent manufacturer can recommend the right detergent and amount.

One of the greatest problems with dishwashing is contamination of cleaned dishes. Frequently the person handling *soiled* dishes will unrack and stack the *clean* dishes without washing his hands. Ideally one person

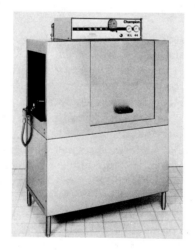

FIG. 10.2. A low-temperature dish machine saves energy and sanitizes with chemicals. *Courtesy of Champion Industries.*

should rack the dirty dishes and another person should unrack the clean dishes.

Disposables. Single-service eating utensils (disposables) are often used where mechanical dishwashing facilities are not available. An emergency supply of disposables should be kept on hand even where dishes are washed by mechanical dishwashers. If the water temperature cannot be maintained at 180°F, disposables should be used until the problem is corrected.

LAWS AND PUBLIC AGENCIES

Federal

There are 10 main federal laws or jurisdictional bodies important in regulating the food market and protecting the public against contaminated foods. A brief description of each follows:

1. The Pure Food, Drug and Cosmetic Act of 1938 prohibits the movement of adulterated and misbranded foods from one state to another.
2. The Meat Inspection Act of 1906 provides for government inspection to assure that all meats sold in interstate commerce are from animals free of disease and that they are slaughtered under sanitary conditions. The stamp "U.S. Government Inspected" will appear on such meat.
3. The Poultry Products Inspection Act provides for inspection of all poultry products sold across state borders.
4. The Agricultural Marketing Act provides for inspection and grading of fresh and processed foods other than meat. There are a number of different inspection agencies under this act. Ordinarily the agencies are located at shipping points or destination markets. Processed foods are checked for quality, identity, and fill.
5. The Perishable Agricultural Commodities Act is administered by the USDA. It regulates the trade of fresh fruit and vegetables in interstate and foreign commerce.
6. The Tea Inspection Act is administered by the Food and Drug Administration and regulates the import of tea.
7. The Bureau of Standards in the Department of Commerce has the responsibility for controlling weights and measures.
8. The Federal Trade Commission Act of 1915 prohibits advertising that misrepresents an item.
9. The Bureau of Public Health in the Department of Health and

Human Services has the greatest responsibility for protecting public health on the local level.

10. The Bureau of Internal Revenue in the Treasury Department has regulatory powers over some foods, either through administrative practices or by law.

Local

Local health department sanitarians have two important responsibilities: promote good standards of sanitation throughout a community and enforce regulations and laws. They should be consulted when in doubt about the wholesomeness of food or other sanitation problem, or if a case of food poisoning exists. They also can be helpful regarding the selection of equipment and planning of a facility. Local sanitarians are responsible for inspecting and grading food establishments, including school foodservices.

OTHER HEALTH AND SAFETY PROBLEMS

Chemical Poisoning

When purchasing food, foodservice managers and directors should check the ingredients carefully. The number of chemicals listed on the label may be staggering; however, the Delaney Law of 1958 does protect the public somewhat from harmful additives. This law states that the government is to stop production of foods containing an additive if the chemical has been demonstrated to cause cancer in animals or humans. Under this law the FDA compiled a list of food additives ranging from salt and pepper to saccharin that are classified legally as "generally regarded as safe" (GRAS). However, some children may be sensitive to some chemicals that are on the GRAS list. Much controversy abounds about food additives and much more research is needed. Several school districts have eliminated certain chemicals from the foods they serve.

Food poisoning from chemicals is usually accidental and is caused most frequently when chemicals are added to food by mistake. Such cases usually occur when an employee mistakes a toxic substance for salt, sugar, dry milk, or flour and puts it into food being prepared. Insecticides, pesticides, and other dangerous chemicals, as well as detergents and cleaning supplies, should be stored in an area completely separate from where food is stored. All products should be distinctly labeled. Washing all fruits and vegetables thoroughly will remove most of the insecticides and chemical residues present on them.

The list of unsafe chemicals grows and some commonly used products have been added to it. For example, in 1983 the safety of sodium bisulfate—a commonly used whitener agent on fresh fruits and vegetables—was questioned. This chemical is thought to cause a severe allergic reaction in certain individuals, particularly asthmatics. As a result, the Food and Drug Administration (FDA) requires retail-level labeling of products containing sulfite. In less than 6 months in 1983, 90 cases of sulfite reactions were reported to FDA, including one death. However, it still remains on FDA's GRAS list.

Monosodium glutamate (MSG), another rather commonly used product, is used to intensify flavors and has been held responsible for the foodborne illness called "Chinese Restaurant Syndrome." Oriental recipes usually list MSG as an ingredient, thus the name of the illness. Some individuals experience headaches, a feeling of weakness, and muscular tingling within ½ hour after eating MSG.

Dr. Ben F. Feingold, reported in 1972 that the synthetic flavorings and food dyes used in many processed foods and beverages may cause behavioral problems, including learning disabilities and hyperkinesis, among children. Hyperkinesis or hyperactivity interfers with some children's attention span, leading to disruptive behavior and in turn learning problems. The disorder occurs primarily in boys. Many parents of such children agree with Feingold's conclusions. They have organized in many cities and forced some school foodservice programs to restrict the use of synthetic flavorings and dyes in foods. It is possible to eliminate these ingredients from menus, but to do so may increase food costs slightly. Also, some foods (for example, gelatins) would have to be removed from menus. The federal government has funded many studies in order to prove or disprove Dr. Feingold's thesis. So far, scientifically designed studies have failed to show any demonstrable effects of the "elimination" diet on the behavior of hyperactive children. This has not satisfied those parents who believe their children are adversely affected by synthetic food flavorings and dyes.

Pests

Rats, mice, flies, roaches, and other unwanted pests may sometimes be found in any foodservice. However, when they are present all the time, it is a sign of poor sanitation standards. These insects and rodents can spread disease organisms and filth. The habits, dangers, life cycle, and ways of controlling three of the most common pests are shown in Table 10.4.

Periodic visits by an exterminator can help control pests in a foodservice, but good housekeeping practices, as described below, are the basic means of controlling pests.

TABLE 10.4.   Three Common Pests: Habits, Life Cycle, and Ways of Controlling

Pest	Habits	Diseases	Life Cycle	Control
Houseflies	Carry disease bacteria on body; live and breed in filth. "Fly specks" are vomited bacteria from fly used to soften foods.	Transmit more than 30 diseases, such as salmonellosis, dysentery, typhoid fever, tuberculosis, cholera, pin worms.	Lay as many as 3,000 eggs in lifetime. Eggs take 10 to 14 days in warm weather to hatch.	Remove breeding places. Screen doors and windows. Use fly-fans. Kill with sprays, etc. Protect food.
Cockroaches	Carry bacteria. Feed on human waste. Odor of roaches caused by oily liquid given off by the scent glands.	Transmit many diseases.	Eggs (25 to 30) hatch in 1 to 2 months; eat much food; grown in one year.	Spray entire area frequently over period of 2 months.
Rats	Eat much food; damage buildings and property with gnawing to keep the teeth worn down. Each rat eats as much as $15 of food a year, and does $120 or more damage a year to property.	Carry many diseases such as salmonellosis, leptospirosis, plaque, and typhus fever.	Born in litters. May have 3 to 5 litters a year—7 to 8 per litter. Average life is 2 to 3 years.	Use traps to kill them.

Control of Roaches, Insects, and Mites

1. Inspect food supplies before storing or using them.
2. Keep stocks of food as fresh as possible. Rotate stock—use older food first.
3. Store foods in containers with tight-fitting lids.
4. Store foods in a dry place.
5. Do not store food or containers directly on floor.
6. Remove and destroy infested food. Clean up all spillage immediately.
7. Clean shelves before adding new stock. Do not use shelf paper.
8. Clean empty bins and containers before refilling.

Control of Flies

1. All windows, doors, and outer openings should be screened.
2. All doors should be self-closing and open outward.
3. Keep all foods covered.

4. Place all garbage promptly into nonabsorbent, easily washed garbage cans with tight-fitting lids.
5. Clean up any spillage of garbage immediately.
6. Have garbage and other wastes removed daily.
7. Scald and air garbage cans daily. Use liners in containers.

Control of Rats and Mice

1. Clean up all piles of rubbish, boxes, rags, etc.
2. Block all possible rodent entrances into the building.
3. Seal all openings around pipes.
4. Prevent access to food.
5. Protect food supplies in safe storage areas.
6. Do a thorough cleanup job at the end of each day.
7. Keep garbage in tightly sealed containers.
8. Use traps when necessary for temporary protection.
9. Use poisons only under direction of the health department.

Choking

Four thousand or more healthy individuals die yearly from choking on food or other objects. Food choking is the sixth leading cause of accidental death in the United States. A choking person can die within 4 minutes if effective measures aren't taken. Over 2000 lives have been saved by someone performing the Heimlich Maneuver®. Many states require that foodservice establishments post a diagram that illustrates this procedure. The Heimlich Maneuver was originated and developed by Dr. Henry Heimlich, a world famous chest surgeon in Cincinnati, Ohio. The technique is simple, and the local Red Cross will often provide someone to demonstrate the technique at a workshop. Posters, kits, and a slide presentation are available.

TRAINING IN SANITATION

To achieve and maintain high sanitary standards requires training of all employees. Training programs should be conducted frequently with refresher courses to create an awareness on the part of the employees of the health aspects of their job, the importance of serving safe food, and the dangers involved. All employees should be aware of the fundamental sanitary practices considered acceptable by the local health authorities. New employees should be given an understanding of sanitation concepts as a part of their orientation. High sanitation standards should be expected in school foodservices and enforced by good on-the-job supervision.

Some states use the National Institute for the Foodservice Industry (1977) course, which consists of 16 hours of training. When foodservice employees successfully complete the training course they are awarded a "sanitation certificate." Fairfax County (VA) requires that a manager with a sanitation certificate be on duty at all times in any food establishment that serves the public.

BIBLIOGRAPHY

ANON. 1966. North Carolina School Food Service Sanitation Manual. N. Carolina State Board of Health and School Food Service.

BANWART, G. J. 1981. Basic Food Microbiology. AVI Publishing Co., Westport, CT.

BLAKER, G., and E. RAMSEY. Holding temperatures and food quality. J. Am. Dietet. Assoc. *38* (5):450–454.

COOPERATIVE EXTENSION SERVICE. 1969. Bacterial Food Poisoning. Univ. of Massachusetts, Amherst.

COOPERATIVE EXTENSION SERVICE. 1970. Frozen foods in food service establishments. Good Management Leaflet 9. Univ. of Massachusetts, Amherst.

FEINBERG, B. F. 1974. Why Your Child Is Hyperactive. Random House, New York.

FOSTER, E.M. 1968. Microbial problems in today's foods. J. Am. Dietet. Assoc. *52:*485.

GRAHAM, H. D. 1980. The Safety of Foods. 2nd edition. AVI Publishing Co., Westport, CT.

GUTHRIE, R. K. 1980. Food Sanitation. 2nd edition. AVI Publishing Co., Westport, CT.

HUNTER, B. T. 1982. Food Additives and Federal Policy: The Mirage of Safety. Stephen Greene Press, Lexington, MA.

LONGREE, K. 1972. Quantity Food Sanitation. 2nd edition. John Wiley & Sons, New York.

LONGREE, K., and G. G. BLAKER. 1971. Sanitary Techniques in Food Service. John Wiley & Sons, New York.

NATIONAL INSTITUTE FOR THE FOODSERVICE INDUSTRY. 1977. Development of a uniform national plan for sanitation training of foodservice managers. Final Report for FDA Contract 233–76–2072. Chicago.

NATIONAL RESTAURANT ASSOCIATION. 1973. A Self Inspection Program for Foodservice Operators. National Restaurant Assoc., Chicago.

RICHARDSON, T. M. 1974. Sanitation for Food Service Workers. 2nd edition. Cahners Books, Boston.

U.S. DEPT. OF AGRICULTURE. 1969a. Food Storage Guide for Schools and Institutions. U.S. Govt. Printing Office, Washington, DC.

U.S. DEPT. OF AGRICULTURE. 1969b. Keeping Food Safe to Eat. U.S. Govt. Printing Office, Washington, DC.

U.S. DEPT. OF HEALTH, EDUCATION AND WELFARE. 1969. Food labeling. Federal Register, (June 9), U.S. Govt. Printing Office, Washington, DC.

U.S. DEPT. OF HEALTH, EDUCATION AND WELFARE. 1976. Food Service Sanitation Manual. Public Health Service, U.S. Govt. Printing Office, Washington, DC.

WEST, B., L. WOOD, V. HARGER and G. SHUGART. 1977. Food Service in Institutions. 6th edition. John Wiley & Sons. New York.

WHITE, J. C. 1966. Bacteriological control in sanitation. The Cornell Hotel and Restaurant Admin. Quart. *7.* Statler Hall, Ithaca, NY.

COST MANAGEMENT AND ACCOUNTABILITY

A school foodservice should operate on a sound financial basis. It should not be a hit-or-miss operation. Accountability is the theme in education today, and this includes foodservice. Federal audits by the Office of the Inspector General and the Government Accounting Office during the 1970s brought the need for stricter accountability to the attention of Congress, as well as private citizens, with headlines in leading newspapers.

In the early 1980s came the first threat of auditing for meal requirement compliance and of sanctions, including loss of funds. This threat sparked much concern among school foodservice directors and companies selling to them. Meeting the meal requirements exactly became the challenge for the eighties. This all resulted in an increased demand for sound business practices and good cost controls. Some school districts believe that school food programs should be self-supporting, and others supplement the income of the feeding program in order to keep the price-to-the-child within the range that the people in the community can afford to pay. In many cases it is not possible to operate the type of program desired on a self-supporting basis. Regardless of the source of the income, expenditures should not be greater than income. The most frequent reason for turning a school's foodservice over to a food management company is a financial deficit in the operation.

Good money management practices are essential in foodservice, whether commercial and profit oriented or public and nonprofit, small or large, centralized or decentralized. Effective controls are necessary to operate under a tight budget and provide good food at a low cost to students. When expenditures are greater than income, too frequently the first impulse of the administration is to increase the cost to the student, decrease portion size, or decrease quality. A good look at management practices might provide other solutions to the problem.

The first step in operating a financially successful operation is for the

247

foodservice management to know the financial objectives and goals of the school board. Is the foodservice to be self-supporting? Who will pay utilities, fringe benefits, telephone bills, etc.? Is it to be operated on a profit-making or break-even basis? Who will pay for equipment replacement? The National School Lunch Act stipulates that schools participating in the federal child nutrition programs shall operate on a nonprofit basis. However, this has been interpreted to permit a cash surplus sufficient to operate for 1 to 3 months, depending on the state's regulations. This cash surplus can be larger for a justifiable reason, such as when planning to purchase large pieces of equipment.

The next step toward operating on a sound financial basis is to know what the possible income and expenses will be. That perhaps sounds very elementary, but the lack of this basic financial information is a common problem in many school districts. Answers to the following questions are needed: How much money is available per meal (income) and how much does each meal cost to produce and serve? It is essential for management to know what the income is and what the expenses are and to compare the two. It may not be possible to operate a foodservice under the standards set for it on the income available. Management should be able to project this— and not be surprised when a deficit occurs. On the other hand, management should also be able to project profits. Management should be in control of the financial situation—profit or loss.

An elaborate accounting system is not necessary to control costs. The system should be simple enough for the manager of a school foodservice to understand and to use effectively. Ultimately, the entire staff should be aware of the objectives and some of the costs of operating.

COST-BASED ACCOUNTING

In 1978 Congress mandated that schools participating in federal child nutrition programs must use a full-cost accounting system, often called cost-based accounting. This requirement was removed in 1981. However, many states have continued to require cost-based accounting of schools within their states. Each state agency determines if cost-based accounting is to be required and what format is to be used. In many cases it is an involved process that does not produce reliable, meaningful figures. However, there is a need for costing out meals and services in a school foodservice. Some state agencies use the cost data to assign variable reimbursement rates to school food authorities. This, in some cases, rewards poor management by giving higher reimbursement rates to foodservices with higher costs; however, this was not the intent of the law.

Allowable costs in a cost-based accounting system may include (1) cost of food used, (2) other supplies and expendable (small) equipment, (3) repairs, equipment rental, and other services, (4) indirect cost or overhead, and (5) labor cost. These costs are distributed over all the various programs and services provided by a school foodservice in an equitable manner.

Use of cost-based accounting also encourages other good management practices, such as keeping records and supporting documents that adequately identify the source and use of all funds, having an effective control system to assure funds are used solely for authorized purposes, and having an effective audit system.

BUDGETS

A school district may or may not require a budget for its foodservice. Many question the value of a budget that includes many estimated quantities. A school foodservice budget is a plan for estimating the income and projecting the expenditures. A budget is important because it requires management to project costs and income, and thus to have a realistic idea of the financial picture. A budget is usually planned on the basis of past records and on future plans. It sets controls and goals for spending, but should be used only as an adjustable guide. Whether the school administration requires a budget or not, budgeting is an important tool for controlling the financial situation and is valuable in planning expenditures.

The financial data in a budget include known fixed costs and projected or estimated income and expenditures. Fixed costs are costs that don't vary greatly with the volume of business, such as much of the administrative cost, telephone service, and management's salary. Variable costs are those that depend on the number of meals served and the volume of business— such as labor cost and food cost.

Projecting Income

Projections or estimates of income are usually based on past operational data, prices to be charged, proposed changes in economic conditions of the community, changes in regulations and objectives, anticipated volume of sales, and student participation. The income for a school foodservice usually includes some combination of the following:

1. Income from sale of food, based on prices to students and adults
2. Federal reimbursement
3. Value of USDA-donated foods
4. State and local funds
5. Donations

A hypothetical example of the projected income for an elementary school foodservice follows:

Elementary School
Projected Daily Income

Cash Income from Students and Adults:

200 paid student lunches @ $0.95.....................	$190.00
25 reduced-price student lunches @ $0.40	10.00
150 milks @ $0.25	37.50
10 adult lunches @ $1.45	14.50

Federal Reimbursement for Student Lunches:

200 paid lunches @ $0.12............................	24.00
25 reduced-price lunches @ $0.82	20.50
50 free lunches @ $1.22	61.00

State and Local Reimbursement for Student Lunches:

275 lunches @ $0.09	24.75
Projected Daily Income................................	$382.25

Projecting the income for a year's budget would be done similarly, as the following example shows.

Elementary School
Projected Annual Income

Cash Income from Students and Adults:

Average of 210 paid student lunches per day × 180 serving days = 37,800 lunches @ $0.95...............	$35,910.00
Average of 30 reduced-price student lunches per day × 180 serving days = 5400 lunches @ $0.40.........	2,160.00
Average of 10 paid adult lunches per day × 180 serving days = 1800 lunches × $1.45...................	2,610.00
Average of $40 of milk (or a la carte items) sold daily × 180 serving days...............................	7,200.00

Federal, State and Local Reimbursement:

Paid student lunches projected × current federal reimbursement rate (37,800 @ $0.12)	$ 4,536.00
Paid student lunches projected × current state and local reimbursement rate, if any (37,800 @ $0.09).......	3,402.00
Reduced-price student lunches projected × current federal reimbursement rate (5,400 @ $0.82)..........	4,428.00
Reduced-price student lunches projected × current state and local reimbursement rate, if any (5,400 @ $0.09)	486.00
Free student lunches projected × current federal reimbursement (50 per day × 180 days × $1.22).......	10,980.00

Free student lunches projected × current state and local
reimbursement rate, if any (9000 @ $0.09) 810.00

Value of federal commodities may be added if food cost
reflects the cost of the commodities.

Projected Annual Income $72,522.00

Estimated Income per Student Lunch ($72,522 ÷ 52,200
lunches)... 1.39
+ Value of Commodities .115

$1.505

Projecting Costs

The menu is the most important factor effecting foodservice costs. It
determines not only the food to be purchased, but the amount of labor
necessary for preparation and serving. In budgeting how the income will be
used, cost estimates should be based on the proposed menus, previous
year's expenses, cost of living increases, and future plans. As a first step, a
percentage of income can be allocated to each major category of costs.
Table 11.1 lists suggested percentages for on-site preparation of lunch or
dinner with some use of convenience foods, such as preportioned hamburger patties, instant potatoes, and some bakery rolls. Based on the income
projected in the previous example, a budget of expenditures might be as
follows:

Elementary School
Projected Annual Expenditures

Projected Income of $72,522.00

Food cost* (55.3% of projected income).............. $40,104.00
Labor cost (32.1% of projected income) 23,280.00
Cleaning and paper supplies cost (6% of projected income) 4,351.00
Equipment replacement cost (1% of projected income).. 725.00
Indirect costs (5% of projected income).............. 3,626.00

Projected Annual Expenditures....................... $72,086.00

Estimated Cost per Student Lunch ($72,086 ÷ 52,200)... $1.38
+ Value of Commodities .115

$1.495

*Not including value of commodities used.

In a survey conducted in the spring of 1980 by the U.S. Department of
Agriculture, the average cost of a school lunch was $1.42 (Table 11.2).
Breakfast entails less preparation than other meals and the percentages of

**TABLE 11.1. Budgeting Cost
for On-Site Preparation of Lunch or Dinner**

Expenditures	As % of Income
Food	50–60
Labor in school	30–38
Cleaning and paper supplies	8
Replacement of equipment	1
Indirect costs	4–5
Total	97–100

income allocated to food and labor would be different in most cases, as suggested below.

	% of Income
Food cost	60–63
Labor cost in school	28–31
Other expenses	9

If the income for breakfast is $0.70 per breakfast, the expenditures budget might look like the following:

Food cost (60% of $0.70)	$0.42
Labor cost (35% of $0.70)	0.245
Other expenses (5% of $0.70)	0.035
	$0.70

A comparison of the budget should be made with the actual income and expenditures (Profit and Loss Statement) at the end of each year. This will help in preparing a more accurate budget the following year. Budgeting should encourage precosting and daily costing and use of other techniques for controlling cost.

**TABLE 11.2. Average Cost
of School Lunch—Spring 1980**

Food cost, including USDA-donated foods	$0.72
Labor cost, including fringe benefits	0.48
Other expenses, including supplies and equipment	0.22
Total	$1.42

Source: U.S. Dept. of Agriculture.

SETTING PRICES

Establishing the prices to be charged in a school foodservice should be done very carefully. The prices charged have a major effect on income and the number of meals served. Many school boards, at the recommendation of the foodservice director, haphazardly raise prices without considering "what the market will bear." A price increase should be based on thorough analysis of costs. Can those costs be reduced? Or, is raising prices the only way to keep the operation financially sound.

If the timing of a price increase is not right and/or if the increase is too much, the result will be a decrease in the number of customers and perhaps even a decrease in income. The federally subsidized pattern lunch and breakfast should be priced at the lowest price possible, based on fixed and variable costs. Often costs decrease as the volume increases.

Studies done by the Department of Agriculture in 1972 showed that there was a 1% decrease in participation in the lunch program for every 1% increase in prices. This phenomenon is not unique to school foodservice: price and sales volume are generally related; when prices are increased, volume decreases.

There are basically four approaches to establishing prices: (1) cost-oriented pricing, (2) competitive pricing, (3) demand-oriented pricing and (4) perceived-value pricing. The objective of a school district may determine which of these approaches is used in setting the price of the pattern school lunch. If the goal is to sell as many students as possible a nutritionally balanced lunch, you may start with cost-oriented pricing. However, if the students do not know the value of a nutritionally balanced lunch, or if the cost is very high, perceived-value pricing may be needed. For example, if the cost of producing and serving a lunch averages $1.42, and the income from federal, state, and local subsidies, including the value of USDA-donated commodities, totals $0.42, the difference is $1.00. If the cost-oriented price of $1.00 is perceived by parents and students as too high, participation in the program may be less than desired. To increase participation, the price may have to be set at a perceived-value price of, perhaps, $0.90, even though this is below cost. The loss would have to be made up through increased sales of other items, or an increased local subsidy.

When pricing a la carte items, use a combination of all four approaches. Know the cost, first of all. Should a la carte items compete with the lunch program? If not, price the a la carte items to make a profit and use the profits to subsidize the lunch program.

Even though most school lunch programs do not have competition in the school building, the presence of competitive food establishments in a community may affect pricing. The "going price" of the same or similar item will become the perceived value. If the school lunch program charges more, it is considered a "rip off." For example, if the local fast-food restaurants charge

65¢ for a 12-ounce milkshake, it is a good strategy to charge 55¢ or 60¢. This gives the customer a feeling that the prices are fair.

Most school foodservices round off prices to the nearest 5¢ for ease in handling change and for banking reasons. Fast-food restaurants are noted for raising prices a penny or two at a time; they are trying to avoid customer awareness of the increase.

School foodservice customers are "captive customers" to some degree, particularly in schools with a closed campus policy. Nonetheless, students do have alternatives to the school lunch: bringing lunch from home, not eating at all, a trip away from campus, and/or purchasing a la carte foods, when available.

When the financial loss of a school foodservice is large because costs have increased drastically or income has decreased substantially, it may be necessary to use several strategies to overcome the deficit. Some suggestions for turning a deficit operation into a solvent operation are given here and discussed in more detail in later sections.

1. Change menu offerings. The emphasis is not on prices totally, but on the menu changes, too. For example, if entree-type hot lunches have been the total offering, change to a sandwich-type lunch with choices.
2. Raise prices over the summer or after a long break to reduce customer awareness and resistance. Remove all posters and reminders of the old price.
3. Raise prices slightly and reduce portions. Package the food differently. Change the type of container in which food is served. For example, six-compartment trays tend to spread portions out too much, whereas, individual portioning in cups, bags, and wraps—just the right size packaging—can make the product look good, even look like more. Also, individual portioning makes carrying out "offer versus served" and offering choices more effective. School districts have reported a reduction in food costs of 10 to 20¢ when they instituted "offer versus served."
4. Maintain the current price and reduce costs by reducing portion sizes, reducing the number of foods on the menu, reducing labor cost, and/or reducing waste.
5. Raise prices and launch an advertising campaign to point up the value received from the lunches.

ESTIMATING COSTS

Projecting income and expenses should be done with the hopes of achieving a balanced outcome. However, if this is not possible, it is far better to know a deficit is likely and make the adjustments needed than to suddenly face a perilous financial crisis. A planned profit or loss is considered better management than an unexpected profit or loss—especially in the views of the finance officer of the school or school district. Since food and labor costs are the largest components in a school foodservice budget, they must be estimated with some accuracy. Procedures for doing so are described here.

Costing Recipes and Menus

Estimating food costs usually starts with precosting of recipes and then precosting of the menus. In order to cost, one must know the price paid per unit of raw food products and other supplies (Table 11.3). This information is not only needed in costing, but also in computing inventories. Costing recipes and menus is a time-consuming process, but it gives essential information for planning expenditures within the budget. To cost a recipe involves totaling the cost of each ingredient to arrive at the total food cost. The food cost is then divided by number of servings the recipe will yield to arrive at the *cost per serving* (Fig. 11.1). Recipe costing is needed to set the a la carte prices to be charged and to cost menus.

TABLE 11.3 Determining Unit Prices of Raw Food Products to Be Used in Costing Recipes

Item	Purchased Amount	Purchase Price ($)	Unit	Unit Price ($)
Flour, all-purpose	100 lb	15.30	lb	0.153
Macaroni	20 lb	7.20	lb	0.36
Sugar	100 lb	30.72	lb	0.31
Applesauce (packed 6/10)[1]	case	15.15	can	2.53
Apricots, halves (packed 6/10)	case	25.60	can	4.27
Peaches				
Halves (packed 6/10)	case	21.75	can	3.63
Slices (packed 6/10)	case	19.50	can	3.25
Beans				
Green (packed 6/10)	case	10.75	can	1.80
Red kidney (packed 6/10)	case	9.70	can	1.62
Corn (packed 6/10)	case	13.80	can	2.30
Peas (packed 6/10)	case	12.00	can	2.00
Cocoa (packed 6/5)	case	65.20	lb	2.17
Coconut	10 lb	8.90	lb	0.89
Cornstarch (packed 24/1)	case	9.90	lb	0.41
Pickle relish (packed 4/gal.)	case	13.90	gal.	3.48
Potatoes, french fried (packed 30 lb)	case	12.60	lb	0.42
Strawberries, frozen (packed 6/6½ lb)	case	33.15	lb	0.85
Beef, ground, 20% soy product	10 lb	9.90	lb	0.99
Cheese, American (packed 6/5)	case	44.10	lb	1.47

[1] Six #10 cans per case.

Recipe Chili Con Carne with Beans D-24   Date June 1984
Source USDA   Size Portion ½ cup
     Yield 100

Ingredients	Weight	Measure	Unit Cost	Total Cost
Ground beef	9 lb		$1.33/lb	$11.97
Onions, chopped	1 lb		0.40/lb	0.40
Tomato puree		1 gal.	3.90/#10 can	5.46
Bean liquid and water		2 qt		
All-purpose flour	4 oz		0.16/lb	0.04
Water		1 cup		
Cooked kidney beans, canned	10 lb 6 oz		1.62/#10 can	3.24
Salt	2 oz		0.22/lb	0.028
Chili powder		⅓ cup	2.45/lb	0.20
				$21.33
			Cost per serving	$0.22

FIG. 11.1. Sample costed recipe.

Once recipes have been costed, it is easier to put together a menu that does not cost more than the amount of money available. For example, if the income per lunch is $1.39 and 55% is allocated to food costs, then 76½¢ is available for food. Table 11.4 is an example of one week of menus that have been costed. If a menu exceeds the budgeted amount, then other menus within the week should cost less so that the average daily food cost is within the budget, as shown in Table 11.4. Purchase prices of foods often change within the school year and recosting recipes and menus may be necessary.

Determining Labor Cost

In 1979 the cost of labor per meal ranged from 23¢ to 44¢ in the Northeast according to a survey of 17 large school districts. To cost labor, it would be most logical to start with the previous year's payroll cost, then add the projected raises for years of service and/or cost of living. Chapter 5 discusses staffing formulas and salary scales. If the income per lunch is $1.39, as in the previous example, and 33% is allocated to labor costs, then approximately 46¢ is available for labor per meal. Once management knows this, it is then important to compute the actual labor cost, based on the current staffing and salary scale. For example:

Staffed: 14 meals per labor-hour
Salary: Average $4.80 per hour + $0.96 fringe benefits (20%)
Labor Cost per Meal: $5.76 ÷ 14 = $0.41

A number of factors will affect the labor cost. In foodservices with many experienced employees high on the salary scale, the labor cost per em-

11.4. Menu Costing for One Week

Item Name	Serving Size	Item Cost/Serving ($)
Barbecued beef	⅓ cup	0.28
Bun	1	0.058
French fries	½ cup	0.082
Catsup	1 Tbsp	0.03
Fruit cup	½ cup	0.16
Milk choice	½ pt	0.12
		0.73
Fishburger	3.6 oz	0.289
Bun	1	0.058
Tartar sauce or catsup	1 Tbsp	0.03
Orange juice	½ cup	0.067
Baby lima beans	½ cup	0.095
Fruit bar	2 × 2½ in.	0.10
Milk choice	½ pt	0.12
		0.759
Choice of cheese pizza or cheese/sausage pizza	5 oz	0.38
Tossed green salad	½ cup	0.11
Banana pudding	½ cup	0.10
Milk choice	½ pt	0.12
		0.71
Grilled ham and cheese sandwich	3 oz	0.35
	2 breads	0.05
Tomato soup	¾ cup	0.10
Crackers	2	0.03
Apple crisp	½ cup	0.15
Milk choice	½ pt	0.12
		0.80
Fried chicken	2 oz	0.34
Buttered green peas	⅓ cup	0.09
Rice and gravy	½ cup	0.08
Hot rolls	2 breads	0.045
Sliced peaches	½ cup	0.13
Milk choice	½ pt	0.12
		0.805
Average daily food cost/menu		$0.761

ployee may be higher than average. However, the number of meals produced per labor-hour should be greater with more experienced employees, so that fewer employees are needed.

CONTROLLING FOOD COSTS

Precosting is an essential step toward estimating expenditures, setting standards and guides, and developing a realistic budget. However, the actual income and expenditures are what is important. In a centralized system with centralized menu planning, bid purchasing, staffing formulas, and salary scales, much is preset, but the variations that can exist among schools within a centralized system (county or city system) are surprising. Precosting may be done by the central administration but the accounting of actual daily costs should be done by individual units in order to keep those in operational control informed and because they are really the only ones who can keep track of actual daily costs. A profit and loss statement of the month's business should be furnished the manager by the 10th or 12th of the following month, showing the actual income and expenditures.

After the menu, purchasing is probably the next most controlling force over costs. Quantity, quality, and price are all interrelated. What quantity is needed is determined by the number to be served, the portion size, and the recipe to be used. High prices and quality are not always synonymous in food. However, poor quality and waste are expensive. The quality needed is the quality appropriate for each recipe and economically feasible for the foodservice to use. The purchase price of foods per pound or whatever unit is used is not the determining factor in most cases; instead, it is how many edible portions are produced and served. The number of portions that a raw food product yields can be surprisingly lower than one might expect, and this in turn increases the food cost. Cooking at high temperatures may reduce the yield considerably, too.

The following practices will aid in controlling food costs:

1. Storing food properly and using storeroom controls
2. Using standardized recipes
3. Using good preparation procedures and techniques
4. Estimating number of portions needed carefully and avoiding excessive leftovers
5. Serving quality food and utilizing leftovers
6. Using standardized portion control
7. Keeping daily records
8. Preparing a monthly profit and loss statement
9. Reducing pilferage

Estimating the number of meals to prepare can be difficult. In many elementary schools, the foodservice manager is given a count of how many students are expected to eat lunch; this makes determining how much to prepare relatively easy. In secondary schools, it is usually not so easy and may be a guessing game. In that case, it takes good planning to use leftovers. There is no excuse for the "habit of running out." It is poor management, particularly if a count is given. However, it is not wise to cook so much that it is not possible to run out, because leftovers are costly and should be avoided as much as possible. If 200 hamburgers are prepared and only 125 sold, the waste would increase the food cost over 50%. Even if the ground beef can be used in spaghetti sauce or chili, the pattie probably costs more than ground beef in bulk, and the labor involved becomes a waste. In addition, leftovers crowd the refrigerator and are sanitation hazards.

Daily Cost of Operation

Precosting may be of little value in itself if relevant controls are not carried out in preparation and serving. Precosting sets a standard by which the actual costs can be evaluated. Costing of the food that was actually used, sold, and leftover should be done daily by each individual food preparation unit. It may be too late to find out at the end of the following month that the foodservice has operated at a deficit. If deficit problems are known on a daily basis, some corrective measures can be taken. Daily accounting of costs can provide a quick, almost instant picture, and it can be done in a simple manner, as illustrated in Fig. 11.2. The total expenditures, which include the labor cost and cost of other items, can be compared with the actual income for the day. This gives the manager and staff a daily summary of the financial situation of the operation.

Neither the accounting office nor management can control costs alone. All the employees must be aware of the financial goals of the foodservice and help in controlling costs. Unless employees are aware of costs, it is easy for them to look at a full storeroom, which is continually replenished, and think the food and supplies are free. If the baker, for example, has no idea that walnuts cost $2.08 per pound, he may be overly generous when using them in brownies. But if the baker is aware of the cost of walnuts, he may be more conservative and, perhaps, decide the brownies could be made without nuts if the financial situation requires some trimming of costs.

Another example of compiling daily costs is given in Table 11.5 for a breakfast menu. The food cost in this example was $13.19, with miscellaneous costs of $4.49 and a labor cost of $12.37, making the total cost for producing 50 breakfasts $30.05. The average cost per meal is ($30.05 ÷ 50) was $0.601. According to a study funded by the Comptroller General of the United States during 1978, the average cost of breakfast was $0.588.

Reasons for High Food Costs
and Ways to Reduce Them

Once the actual cost of food is determined—daily, weekly, monthly—the question becomes, Is it really higher than it should be? What is the norm? If the recipes and menus have been precosted, this should help set the norm. Also, in a centralized school system, the cost of similar operations can be compared. When data processing is available, detailed cost information can be obtained readily and is extremely valuable if used. The actual cost may be slightly more or less and still be in line.

Date: September 20   Menu Cycle No. 222

Item	Quantity Used	Unit Cost ($)	Total Cost ($)
Hamburger patties	500	0.19	95.00
Hamburger buns	42 doz	0.72	30.24
French fries	69 lb	0.41	28.29
Orange juice, frozen (32 oz)	16 cans	2.50	40.00
Brownies (school made)	500	0.0725	36.25
Catsup	4 cans	4.66	18.64
½ pt milk	800	0.15	120.00
Straws and napkins			3.00
Juice cups			5.50
Cleaning supplies			6.32
Administrative cost (indirect cost)			50.00
Other expenses (telephone, utilities, etc.)			31.20
Labor cost			273.00

Total Expenditures for Day $737.44

Income: Total income from receipts (bank deposit) $497.50
(student lunch price, 95¢; adults, $1.50; reduced-price, 40¢)

Federal Reimbursement:

$$\frac{430}{\text{No. Pd. Student Lunches}} \times \frac{\$0.12}{\text{Rate of Reim.}} = \$51.60$$

$$\frac{50}{\text{No. Free Lunches}} \times \frac{1.22}{\text{Rate of Reim.}} = 61.00$$

$$\frac{10}{\text{No. Reduced-Price Lunches}} \times \frac{0.82}{\text{Rate of Reim.}} = 8.20$$

$$\frac{50}{\text{Value of USDA-Donated Foods}} \times \frac{0.12}{} = 6.00$$
$$= 88.00$$

Total Income for Day $712.30
Minus Expenditures . . . . −737.44
Profit (+) *or Loss* (−) . . . . −$25.14

FIG. 11.2. Sample form for daily accounting of costs and income.

TABLE 11.5. Sample Daily Cost Sheet for Breakfast for Week of September 6–10 and Number Served Is 50

Menu	Portion Size	Food Use Cost			Miscellaneous		
		Item	Quantity	Cost	Item	Quantity	Cost
Orange juice	½ cup	Orange juice	1½ can	$1.95	Straws	50	$0.19
Scrambled eggs	1	Eggs	50	3.75	Napkins	50	0.50
Cinnamon toast	1 slice	Bread	2 loaves	1.30	Detergents		0.45
Milk	½ pint	Sugar	1 cup	0.27	Cups	50	0.85
		Cinnamon	2 Tbsp	0.02	Indirect cost		2.50
		Milk	½ pint	5.90	Misc.		$4.49
		Total food		$13.19			

Labor:	1½ hour employee @ $4.75 per hour	$7.12		
	1 hour employee @ 5.25 per hour	5.25		
	Total labor	$12.37	Labor	$12.37
			Food	13.19
			Misc.	4.49
			Total	$30.05

If food costs run much less than estimated costs, one may question if the portions are large enough, if the entire meal was served, or if a different quality of raw materials was used in preparation of the food. If food costs are too high, the reasons frequently are not obvious. It may be a matter of pennies added up to dollars when waste is involved. Following are some reasons for excessive food costs with suggested ways of reducing them.

1. *Failure to follow well-planned menus.* Changing menus or planning menus at the last minute often results in expensive menus. Menus should be planned and precosted before purchasing is done. Menus should be planned within the financial limits.

2. *Failure to purchase on bid or from wholesale vendors.* Food purchased off-bid is usually considerably higher in price. Buying at the local grocery store should be forbidden. "Family-size" packs often cost four to five times more than institutional-size packs. Buying on bid and by written specification can mean lower prices.

3. *Poor purchasing practices.* Purchasing bargains that cannot be used to the best advantage is not a savings. Purchasing food ready-made when it could easily be made by employees will increase cost. Increasing the use of convenience foods without decreasing labor cost can result in an unbalanced budget. Failure to purchase the grade, quality, or type pack of food best suited for the intended use is a poor purchasing practice. For example, fancy peach halves are more expensive than pie peaches. Pie peaches would be the best suited for a cobbler. Purchasing food out of season also can be costly. For example, green peppers at 79¢ each, out of season, are a poor choice.

4. *Low yields of purchased food.*   If precosting has been based on ten frankfurters per pound but eight frankfurters per pound are being delivered, the food cost per serving will be greater than expected and perhaps more than can be afforded. If lettuce is of a poor quality, the yield may be less than planned. Purchased foods should be evaluated regularly—not only for quality but also for quantity yield.

5. *Failure to check deliveries.*   Shortages in deliveries, substitutions in items, and overcharging may occur. Checking deliveries can assure that what was ordered is delivered and in good condition.

6. *Lack of accounting of food purchased and prepared.*   Is food disappearing out of the storeroom? Keep the storeroom locked except for the time needed for filling the needs of the day. Do employees carry leftovers home? This is a practice that should be discontinued. No food should go home with *any employee.* (Leftovers should be utilized the next day, frozen, or destroyed.) Are too many adults being served meals free? Unless a person is a foodservice employee, he should not be receiving a meal free. Are uncollected charges mounting? "Charge it" can become a habit with students. A policy of no charges may have to be enforced.

7. *Failure to follow standardized recipes.*   One of the greatest failures of a manager is not knowing how much food is being prepared and how many servings it will yield. Recipe failures are expensive. What quantity is being prepared? Most recipes are for 50 or 100 portions. When 325 portions are needed, but 400 portions are prepared, this is far too many—wasteful and costly.

8. *Failure to use portion controls.*   Is the correct number of servings obtained from a recipe? The heavy-handed server can cause food cost to mount. Are seconds being given? Can they be afforded? Are correct portion-control tools being used? Standardization of serving size is both economical and fair to customers. Portion control is discussed in more detail later.

9. *Excessive leftovers.*   Failure to utilize leftovers is costly. Careful planning may be necessary to utilize leftovers in a way that students will not object to. In schools where a precount of customers is obtained and/or where the number served is fairly constant from day to day, leftovers should be at a minimum.

10. *Excessive waste in preparation.*   Overcooking and cooking at high temperatures cause shrinkage which is expensive. Broken cookies, burned cakes, and product failures are expensive. Careless trimming of produce—cutting off the outer leaves of lettuce and cabbage and the tops of celery and not utilizing them—is wasteful.

11. *Failure to utilize USDA-donated foods.*   The USDA-donated foods entitlement in 1984 were valued at 11½¢ per meal. If donated foods are not used or utilized in the same way as purchased food, their value will not be realized. It requires careful planning and ingenuity to utilize some donated foods effectively. The attitude toward USDA-donated foods may be an

important factor. If these commodities are thought of as free food, to be used in addition to other food, the value of the commodities is not realized. To the extent possible, donated foods should be used as a substitute for— not a supplement to—purchased foods.

12. *Poor storage practices.* Food thrown out due to spoilage is waste. Is it due to improper storage practices? Foods should be purchased according to shelf life or keeping qualities. A 3-week supply of lettuce and tomatoes will probably not keep under any conditions. The temperatures of storerooms, refrigerators, and freezers should be carefully checked.

13. *Pilferage.* No one wants to believe that employees are stealing money, food, and/or supplies. However, pilferage by employees may be the reason for a financial deficit. School foodservice directors interviewed by *Food Management* said again and again, ". . . I believe people are basically honest." That kind of trust without the assurance that it is true can cost a school foodservice a lot of dollars.

Are safeguards in place to prevent crimes? Are there ways of checking how much the income for the day should have been? Is there a way to determine where the food purchased for the week or month was used? A food production record can provide this information. Employees should never be allowed to take leftover food home. Leftovers should be used or destroyed. Food costs will inch up if taking leftovers home becomes a practice.

There should be an audit trail. At least two people should be involved with reports and bank deposits, each verifying and initialing that a report is accurate. The use of electronic cash registers makes it more difficult for an employee to change reports and take funds.

Economizing is a way of life that some employees are not accustomed to. Putting prices on cases of food in the storeroom will make employees more cost conscious and also will be an aid at inventory time. Substituting a less expensive food that will not reduce the quality of the product substantially can be a step toward cutting costs. For example, when fresh tomatoes are out of season and high in price, red cabbage, radishes, and carrots can add variety and color to a tossed salad at a fraction of the cost. Textured vegetable proteins have been used to reduce the cost of the protein-rich foods in menus (Table 11.6).

Portion Control

The first time you look up from serving and see another 25 students coming through the door and you have only 10 more servings of lasagne, you will know what portion control is not.

Portion control means giving a definite quantity of food for a definite price, and it means getting the number of servings planned from a given

TABLE 11.6. Comparative Cost of Using All Meat
or Meat/Textured Vegetable Protein Mixture

	Formula A			Formula B		
Composition	100 lb ground beef			85 lb ground beef		
	@ $1.60/lb	=	$160.00	@ $1.60/lb	=	$136.00
				6 lb textured		
				vegetable protein		
				@ $0.60	=	3.60
				9 lb water	=	0.00
Total cost			$160.00			$139.60
Cost per lb			1.60			1.40
Cost per serving						
(5.8 per lb)			0.276			0.241
Cost per yr[1]	30,000 × 0.276	=	$8,280.00	30,000 × 0.241	=	$7,230.00
Approximate						
savings per yr						$1,050.00

[1]50 times on the menu × average number served (600) = 30,000 servings.

recipe or product. For example, suppose an employee opens six No. 10 cans of green beans and figures that since each No. 10 can will yield 22 ½-cup servings, six cans will serve 132 ½-cup servings. But after serving only 125 students, he runs out of beans. What happened? The employee correctly figured how many cans he needed to serve 132 ½-cup servings based on how many servings there are in a No. 10 can. However, in order to assure that the calculated number of servings is obtained, the size of the serving must be *exactly* ½ cup, not a *heaping* ½ cup (the difference between these could easily account for coming up seven servings short).

The number of portions to be obtained from a given dish should be predetermined by the manager. Standardized recipes state the total yield in terms of the number of portions of a given size. It is extremely important to control portion sizes in order to control cost, prevent waste, and also create good will—make the customers happy. It is important to a student, as well as a teacher, that his piece of cake is as large as the person's in front of him. If, when preparing roast beef, a manager estimated the cost per portion as 40¢, based on 2-ounce servings, but when the beef is sliced the portions run 3 to 4 ounces, not only will there be a shortage of servings, but the cost per serving will go up to 80¢, or double. Customers who are expecting roast beef for lunch will be unhappy when bologna sandwiches are served them after the roast beef runs out.

The success of many leading fast-food chains is based on keeping the prices reasonable. This is possible primarily because of portion control. Each hamburger pattie is the same size, and so is the quantity of sauce inside the bun.

Portion control starts with the recipe. In order for a recipe to provide the stated yield, the foods used in preparing it must be measured and handled correctly. The product must be cooked in containers of the size called for in the recipe. For example, if a cake recipe reads "two 18× 26 × 2½ inch pans," and instead two 12 × 20 × 2½ inch pans are used, the yield will be different than stated in the recipe. If smaller or larger pans are used, the yield may be different. Suppose a recipe has a stated yield of 25 pie crusts. How can the baker be sure of obtaining 25 pie crusts? By weighing the dough, dividing by 25, and then portioning this amount of dough into each pan. This procedure—weighing the dough for each pan so that the correct amount is used—is called *scaling*. All 25 pie crusts will be equal, no more or no less. These 25 pies should yield 200 servings (8 equal slices per pie). In this case, portioning may be done with a pie marker or, if one is not available, "by eye." The eye can divide by halves more accurately than by thirds or fourths, so more uniform pieces are obtained by cutting in half and then cutting each half in halves, etc., as when cutting a sheet cake (Fig. 11.3).

Portion size is the final factor determining food costs. It is impossible to have effective food-cost control without accurate portion control. Many commercial cafetarias employ line supervisors whose main duty is keeping uniformity in the servings.

Of course, portion sizes will vary according to the type of food being served, its relationship in the meal, and its contribution to meeting the nutritional requirements. The number of items on a menu, size or age of the customers, cost of the food, and the appearance of the portion all affect the

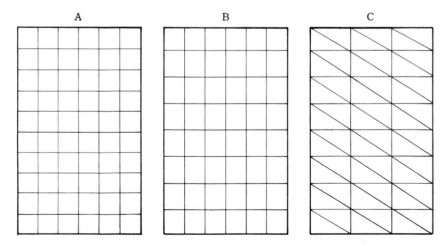

FIG. 11.3.   Cutting a sheet cake to give uniform portions. A—18 × 26 in. sheet pan cut 6 × 10; yield: 60 servings. B—18 × 26 in. sheet pan cut 6 × 8; yield: 48 servings. C—18× 26 in. sheet pan cut 3 × 8 and then diagonally; yield: 48 servings.

decision of the size portion to be given. One-dish meals, such as spaghetti, require larger portions than do meat and potato menus. The richness and lightness of the food may determine the size of the portion. The lunch pattern sets many of the limitations on portion sizes in school foodservices.

There will not be many worse moments for a manager than when he runs out of food. Heavy-handed servers can do the damage, causing food shortages and high food costs. Production records should be kept; these should include the quantity prepared, yield, and leftovers. If the yield is different from the recipe, this indicates that the stated yield is incorrect or that the servings were not controlled. Some suggestions for controlling portions follow:

1. Indicate on menus during planning the size of portion to be given.
2. Be sure servers know the correct portion sizes.
3. Furnish portion-control tools, such as scales for weighing meats, scoops, ladles, portion cups, etc.
4. Set up sample plates with correct portions on them for servers.
5. Check quantity in steamtable pans or number items to know if the quantity prepared will serve the estimated number.

Seconds and Large Portions.   Children may ask for seconds or for larger portions. To handle such situations, a policy should be set about whether seconds other than standard portions can be given. If seconds are allowed, it is wise to decide what food can be given as seconds or in larger portions and prepare extra quantities. Generally, seconds and larger portions should be permitted only for less expensive items. For example, if the menu is Salisbury steak, mashed potatoes and gravy, green beans, roll, butter, milk, and cookies, mashed potatoes would probably be the food to give seconds on. The full meal meets the nutritional requirements; therefore, a filler is what may be needed. In the above menu, more potatoes, if needed, could be prepared quickly by using the instant granules.

Portion Tools.   There are many portion-control tools available. Serving scoops are some of the most familiar. A capacity chart can be very helpful in determining the yield that can be expected from a steamtable pan full of food (Table 11.7). To establish standardized service and avoid running out of food, employees need to know the size and yield of all pans, scoop ladles, and other small equipment used in serving. Charts indicating the size of scoops and yields should be posted at convenient places for easy reference.

It is far more accurate to use a level measure of ½ cup (No. 8 scoop) than to use a heaping ⅓ cup (No. 12 scoop) to obtain a ½-cup portion. Scoop numbers are based on how many of the scoops it takes to equal 1 quart. For example, a No. 8 scoop equals ½ cup; there are 8 ½-cups in a quart.

TABLE 11.7. Pan[1] Capacity and Portion Chart

Size Pan (in.)	Depth (in.)	Capacity		Size Portion		No. Portions Yield[2]
		Quarts	Cups	Cup	Scoop (#)	
Full size, 12 × 20	2¼	7½	30	¼	16	120
				⅓	12	90
				⅜	10	80
				½	8	60
Full size, 12 × 20	4	13	52	¼	16	208
				⅓	12	156
				⅜	10	138
				½	8	104
Full size, 12 × 20	6	19½	78	¼	16	312
				⅓	12	234
				⅜	10	208
				½	8	156
				1	8-oz ladle	78
Half size, 12 × 10	2½	3¾	15	¼	16	60
				⅓	12	45
				⅜	10	40
				½	8	30
Half size, 12 × 10	4	6½	26	¼	16	104
				⅓	12	78
				⅜	10	69
				½	8	52
Half size, 12 × 10	6	9¾	39	¼	16	156
				⅓	12	117
				⅜	10	104
				½	8	78
				1	8-oz ladle	39
Third size, 12 × 6⅞	2½	2⅖	9⅗	⅛	2 Tbsp	76
				¼	16	38
				⅓	12	28
				⅜	10	25
Third size, 12 × 6⅞	4	3⅞	15½	⅛	2 Tbsp	124
				¼	16	62
				⅓	12	46
				⅜	10	41

[1] Foodservice pans are used for cooking and serving.
[2] Rounded off to next lower full portion.

TABLE 11.8. Scoop and Ladle Sizes

Scoop Number	Measure	Equivalent Weight (oz)	Ladles (oz)	Approximate Measure (cup)
6	⅔ cup (10 Tbsp +)	6	2	¼
8	½ cup (8 Tbsp)	4–5	4	½
10	⅜ cup (6 Tbsp)	3–4	6	¾
12	⅓ cup (5 Tbsp +)	2½–3	8	1
16	¼ cup (4 Tbsp)	2–2¼		
20	3⅕ Tbsp	1¾–2		
24	2⅔ Tbsp	1½–1¾		
30	2⅕ Tbsp	1–1½		
40	1⅗ Tbsp	¾–1		

Likewise, a No. 16 scoop equals ¼ cup; there are 16 ¼-cups in a quart. Table 11.8 lists common scoop and ladle sizes and their equivalent measures.

REDUCING LABOR COSTS

Reducing labor costs may be harder than reducing food costs. The first question should be "Is the operation overstaffed?" The staffing guidelines in Chapter 5 may be used to determine if overstaffing exists. If the majority of employees are high on the pay scale due to years of service, this can cause a high labor cost. Are substitutes being used frequently? Why? Is employee time being used efficiently? Can business volume be increased rather than reducing the labor force?

Small operations serving less than 300 to 350 lunches will find it difficult to keep productivity high and the labor cost within the desired bounds. It may be impossible for an operation this size or smaller to be self-supporting. Systems other than on-site preparation may have to be considered for smaller operations, as discussed in Chapter 14.

The cost of labor is taking increasingly more of the school foodservice dollar, thus increasing the need for effective personnel management. A foodservice that had a starting salary of $1.80 an hour in 1972 may be paying 2 to 3 times that today. Excessive labor costs may be due to several factors. The following are ways of increasing productivity and reducing labor costs:

1. Training employees well and motivating them to work more efficiently.
2. Using work simplification principles.
3. Rearranging kitchen and service areas to save steps and motions.
4. Using work schedules and efficiently distributing labor-hours over the day. If an employee is not really needed until 10 A.M., do not have her come in at 9 A. M.

5. Planning menus that require less preparation.
6. Rescheduling serving periods.
7. Using vending machines for dispensing some items.
8. Finding more efficient ways of performing time-consuming jobs.
9. Comparing the cost of using more prepared foods and reducing labor needs.
10. Comparing the cost of using disposables instead of dishwashing.
11. Using more labor-saving equipment.

Motivating employees to be more efficient is a challenge. Recognition is one of the most effective ways to motivate an individual. This recognition can be in the form of an award and/or bonus or publicity. A team spirit approach is used successfully by some managers.

TABLE 11.9. Cost Comparison of Dishwashing versus Disposables for 300 Meals

Item	Cost Calculation		Cost per Day
Using Dishes and Silver			
Straws	$17.00/12,500	for 325	$0.42
Napkins	29.90/10,000	for 325	0.98
Plates[1]	14.90/doz × 25[3]	÷ 360 days	1.04
Trays[1]	30.50/doz × 25	÷ 360 days	2.12
Salad/Vegetable dishes[1]	17.52/doz × 25	÷ 360 days	1.22
Forks[2]	2.05/doz × 25	÷ 180 days	0.29
Spoons[2]	1.42/doz × 25	÷ 180 days	0.20
Dish detergent	31.61/cs of 28, $1.13 each	for 3 pkgs	3.39
Drying agent	36.12/cs of 4 gal., $9.03 gal.	for ½ gal.	4.52
Utilities (estimated)			13.89
Labor cost (including fringe benefits)	7.00/hr × 3.5 hr		24.50
Depreciation on machine			15.56
		Total cost per day	$68.13
Using Disposables			
A. 5-compartment tray	$0.032 × 300		$9.60
Fork & spoon kit (including napkins and straws)	0.028 × 300		8.40
Insert (salad/veg/fruit)	0.01 × 300		3.00
		Total cost per day	$31.00
B. Sandwich wrap	$0.018 × 300		$5.40
Paper tray	0.028 × 300		8.40
Fork kit (including napkins and straws)	0.026 × 300		7.80
Insert (salad/veg/fruit)	0.01 × 300		3.00
French fry bag	0.005 × 300		1.50
		Total cost per day	$26.10

[1]Used for 2 school years (360 days).
[2]Used for 1 school year (180 days).
[3]25 dozen equals 300.

To keep labor costs as low as possible, it is necessary to periodically compare the cost of alternative practices. What is cost effective one year may not be cost effective another year. It is wise to do "mini studies" of different ways of doing the job. Cooking a particular food item "from scratch" may be cost effective now; however, as the cost of labor goes up this may not continue to be true. Five years ago, dishwashing cost less per student in many parts of the country than did using disposables. A similar cost comparison today might well favor disposables, as illustrated in Table 11.9.

RECORDS

Preparing costed recipes and menus and a daily accounting of expenses and income is only part of the record keeping needed in a school foodservice. Each state requires individual operations to keep records of the number served in each category. Much of the accounting is required by the state to furnish the information needed for federal reimbursement claim forms. Since initiation of the pilot breakfast program, the records required for federal reimbursement for the severely needy have been detailed. Many school systems using data processing have found themselves back to a hand process. However, the records required for severely needy breakfasts are records that any well-managed operation would normally do in one form or another in order to know its daily income and expenditures. The records required for the regular breakfast program, as in the lunch program, account for numbers served in every category, for example:

Daily Number Students Served Free Breakfast
Daily Number Students Served Reduced-Price Breakfast
Daily Number Students Served Paid Breakfast
Daily Number Adults Served Paid Breakfast
Daily Number Adults Served Free Breakfast

Income

Income from Student Payments
Income from Adult Payments
Income from Other Sales
Income from Federal, State, and Local Reimbursements

Expenditures

Amount and Cost of Purchased Food Used
Amount and Value of USDA-Donated Foods Used
Cost of Procuring USDA-Donated Food (transporting, storing, etc.)
Labor Cost
Other Directly Related Costs

Menu Served

Menu Items and Serving Size

Profit and Loss Statements

Some basic understanding of accounting terms is needed to interpret the data in a financial statement or profit and loss statement (as is shown in Fig. 11.4). A profit and loss statement compares income and expenditures to determine if a profit or loss resulted for the specific period of time. Since

Profit and Loss Statement

Month of February

Income:		% of Income
Student Lunches	$38,070.00	52
A la Carte Sales	7,200.00	10
Other Sales (including adults)	2,610.00	4
Federal Reimbursement	19,944.00	28
State Reimbursement	4,698.00	6
Interest Income	—0—	
Total Income	$72,522.0	100

Expenditure/Cost of Operating:

Beginning Purchased Food Inventory	$ 750.00	
Purchases	40,179.00	
Ending Inventory	825.00	
Cost of Food	$40,104.00	55
Beginning Supplies Inventory	$ 185.00	
Purchases	4,366.00	
Ending Inventory	200.00	
Cost of Supplies	4,351.00	6
Salaries	$20,000.00	
Fringe Benefits	3,280.00	
Labor Costs	23,280.00	32
Equipment Purchases	725.00	1
Other Costs	3,626.00	5
Total Expenditures	$72,086.00	
Profit (or loss)	$ 432.00	1

FIG. 11.4. A typical profit and loss statement.

federal and state reporting is generally required on a monthly basis, it is logical to prepare a monthly profit and loss statement.

It is essential that a physical inventory of food and surplus on hand be taken at the beginning of the period and again at the end of the period. This provides the data needed to determine true cost of operating. The value of the beginning inventory plus the purchases during the specific period of time less the ending inventory provides true cost of food and supplies.

Receivables (e.g., outstanding federal reimbursements) and payables (e.g., outstanding payroll, invoices, and other costs) should be accounted for in order to get a true financial picture for the specific period of time.

In a centralized system, a profit and loss statement should be done on each school foodservice operation in each operating facility. The manager of each operation should be made aware of the profit and loss statement and accountable for the profit or loss. When there are several similar size/type operations, comparisons can be made to help determine what is the "norm" or what can be expected. These comparisons can help a supervisor identify problem areas.

Inventory

The inventory value is an important factor in arriving at the total cost for a month (or other accounting period) and should be shown on the profit and loss statement. The quantity of food and supplies on hand at any time is the *physical inventory*, which is obtained by actually counting all goods. The *opening inventory* value is the value of food and supplies on hand at the beginning of the accounting period (usually a month). The value of the food on hand at the end of the month is the *closing inventory*. A profit and loss statement will show the opening inventory value plus purchases less the closing inventory value as the cost of the food and supplies used for the month. For example:

Opening inventory (beginning of month)	$2,800.00
Total purchases	4,800.00
Less closing inventory (end of month)	1,805.00
Month's total food and supplies	$5,795.00

Two people can take inventory very efficiently, with one counting and the other tabulating. It is helpful to have prices marked on the cases of goods. The storeroom and inventory sheet should be organized in the same sequence. If the storeroom is organized in categories and alphabetically arranged and the inventory sheet is set up in the same order, the inventory will not only be easier to do but probably more accurate (Table 11.10).

In a small single-unit operation, workers may each take what is needed from the storeroom without anyone to check what is being taken. This may

TABLE 11.10. Sample Monthly Physical Inventory Form

ITEM	PACK	No. on Hand	Cost per Pack	TOTAL VALUE	ITEM	PACK	No. on Hand	Cost per Pack	TOTAL VALUE
ED FRUIT:					Pears, diced	6/10		$21.75	
sliced	6/10		$17.75			Can		3.63	
	Can		2.96		Pears, halves	6/10		21.75	
auce	6/10		12.10			Can		3.63	
	Can		2.02		Pineapple, cubes	6/10		20.30	
s	6/10		24.60			Can		3.38	
	Can		4.10		Plums	6/10		15.10	
es, Maraschino	Gal.		8.60			Can		2.52	
ocktail	6/10		20.50		Raisins	30 lb		42.95	
	Can		3.42			lb		1.43	
es, diced	6/10		19.70						
	Can		3.28						
es, halves	6/10		20.40						
	Can		3.40						

Total this page $_____

Source: Fairfax County (VA) Schools, Food Services Office.

work satisfactorily in a small operation, but the larger the operation, the more important it is that one or more persons be responsible for controlling and recording what is taken from the storeroom. For this purpose, storeroom requisition forms will be necessary. A *requisition* is a request for something, and in this case it will show the items and quantities wanted, and perhaps the prices. The requisition can become a part of a *perpetual inventory* system, which is a running record, up-to-date, of each item on hand in the storeroom. It provides ready information to a manager for placing orders. In small operations, it may not be feasible to keep a perpetual inventory. However, if a form such as that shown in Table 11.11 is placed on the door of the walk-in refrigerator or just inside the storeroom, a perpetual inventory could be kept rather easily. This also gives a double check on the physical inventory.

Evaluating Records

Evaluating the records of an operation month-to-month can provide valuable insight into the operation. Participation records show the trend of sales. Are sales up or down? Why? Is the staffing adequate for the number

TABLE 11.11.   Sample Weekly Record of Foods on Hand and Used

Item (a)	Quantity on Hand (Date) (b)	Quantity Used					Total Quantity Used (h)	Quantity Left (i)	Quantity Received (j)	Qu on (C
		Mon. (c)	Tues. (d)	Wed. (e)	Thurs. (f)	Fri. (g)				

being served? Does overstaffing exist? What percentage of the income is spent on food, labor, and miscellaneous? If a deficit (minus balance) exists, an analysis of the profit and loss statement should tell why.

In a centralized system, norms can be arrived at through comparison of individual units. For example, the percentage of the total food cost attributed to meats, produce, canned foods, frozen foods, etc., can be calculated; comparison of these figures with those for several other operations of similar size will indicate where the cost is higher than normal. Once the specific source of a higher-than-normal cost is identified, it can be traced to, perhaps, overusage or waste, and be corrected.

Data Processing

Use of data processing equipment can relieve personnel from many time-consuming, clerical type duties and is more efficient than manual calculations. Such equipment is being used in calculating nutritional values, planning menus, ordering, and taking inventory. The Memphis (TN) City Schools are using computers for handling many transactions, preparing reports, and doing analyses: invoices, commodity inventories, biweekly time reports, free lunch application approvals, school lunch program analysis, state statistical and financial reports, profit and loss statements, monthly and year-to-date balance sheets, small equipment inventory, allocation of commodities, analysis of expenses by item by school, reports of equipment repairs, and accounts payable. Because of the speed and accuracy of data processing, there are unlimited possibilities to obtain very detailed money management controls and information. If a problem can be pinpointed, correcting it is usually a relatively simple matter. In order to obtain this information, however, norms must be set and controls built into the programmed data processing. The various uses of computers in school foodservice is discussed in detail in the next chapter.

BIBLIOGRAPHY

ANON. 1972. State directors cost out school meals. School Foodservice J. *26*(7):20–23.
AMERICAN SCHOOL FOOD SERVICE ASSOC. and ASSOC. OF SCHOOL BUSINESS OFFICIALS. 1970. A Guide for Financing School Food and Nutrition Services. Research Corporation of ASBO and ASFSA, Denver.
COLTMAN, M. M. 1977. Food and Beverage Cost Control. Prentice-Hall, Englewood Cliffs, NJ.
FELTENSTEIN, T. 1983. Restaurant Profits Through Advertising and Promotion: The Indispensable Plan. CBI Publishing Co., Boston.
KAHRL, W. L. 1974. Foodservice on a Budget for Schools, Senior Citizens, Nursing Homes, Hospitals, Industrial and Correctional Institutions. Cahners Publishing Co., Boston.
KEISER, J., and E. KALLIO. 1974. Controlling and Analyzing Costs in Food Service Operations. John Wiley & Sons, New York.
KOTSCHEVAR, L. 1966. Standards, Principles, and Techniques in Quantity Food Production. McCutchan, Berkeley, CA.
MILLER, E. 1966. Profitable Cafeteria Operation. Ahrens and Co., New York.
REID, R. D. 1983. Foodservice and Restaurant Marketing. CBI Publishing Co., Boston.
STOKES, J. W. 1973. How to Manage a Restaurant or Institutional Food Service. W. C. Brown Co., Dubuque, IA.
U.S. COMPTROLLER GENERAL. 1978. Major Factors Inhibit Expansion of the School Breakfast Program. U.S. Govt. Printing Office, Washington, DC.
U.S. DEPT. OF AGRICULTURE. 1973. School Food Service Financial Management Handbook for Uniform Accounting. U.S. Govt. Printing Office, Washington, DC.
U.S. DEPT. OF AGRICULTURE. 1975. Financial Management—Cost-Based Accountability. U.S. Govt. Printing Office, Washington, DC.
U.S. DEPT. OF AGRICULTURE. 1979. A Guide for Precosting Food for School Food Service. U.S. Govt. Printing Office, Washington, DC.
WEST, B., L. WOOD, V. HARGER, and G. SHUGART. 1977. Food Service in Institutions. 6th edition. John Wiley & Sons, New York.

COMPUTERIZATION

As early as 1964 a few school districts had entered the computer age. Caddo Parish (LA) School Food Service and St. Louis (MO) City School Food Service were among those that began computerizing their school foodservice operations in the mid-sixties. Their computer systems produced not only payroll checks but also management reports. The Caddo Parish computer system even assisted in analyzing bid proposals and preparing meat orders.

Despite these early forays into the world of computers, automation and high technology had barely touched school foodservice by the early 1980s. There was little progress during the 1970s toward computerization, and what there was occurred mainly among large school districts, which could afford large (*mainframe*) computers. Applications included handling of payrolls, student records and attendance records, and, in some cases, accounts receivable and payable. But little else was computerized.

The onset of microcomputers in the early 1980s changed the situation dramatically. Computer hardware was now within the price range that even the smallest school system could afford. Dembowski (1983) predicted that there would be a microcomputer in every school business office within 5 years. Although the advent of microcomputers solved the hardware problem, *software* (programs) relevant to school foodservice was not widely available until the mid 1980s.

Commercial companies were too busy developing software for the home computer to see the market in school foodservice. However, with USDA funds, several software systems have been developed and made available at little cost to local school districts. A system involving a mainframe was developed in the Irving (TX) School District. Gaston County (NC) developed software for the Apple microcomputer and TRS 80 microcomputer in BASIC language. The latter software system, which has been reproduced and distributed widely, can be used for the following applications: (1) participation and revenue record keeping, (2) precosting and postcosting,

(3) inventory control, and (4) processing free and reduced-price meal applications. In cooperation with Fairfax County (VA), USDA programmers developed software for an on-line microcomputer arrangement using COBOL language.

In this chapter, no attempt is made to go into all the technical details of computer hardware or software. Instead, the potential uses and the advantages of computers in school foodservice operations are stressed. In addition, general considerations involved in selecting a computer system and introducing employees to computers are discussed. Figure 12.1 provides definitions of many computers terms that will be useful to those readers who wish or need to become more knowledgeable about computers.

COMPUTER APPLICATIONS

There is probably no department in a school district with as much need for computerization as the school foodservice, which must meet strict standards of accountability, requires various types of analyses for efficient management, and must keep many basic records just to operate reliably from day to day. The information needed to run a school foodservice is extensive and varied. And that is where computers can help; their virtue and glory is the ability to handle large amounts of information quickly, reliably, and logically. For example, a computer could help in each of the steps in the flow of information diagrammed in Fig. 12.2. Some of those areas to computerize are described below.

Inventory Control

A system is needed to maintain inventory cost data and a perpetual inventory of food and of small and large equipment. A food inventory computer program could be set up for a central warehouse, as well as for individual schools. The ultimate objective is to maintain a perpetual inventory at each school, ascertaining its accuracy with a physical inventory once a month. This is possible if the amounts of food used, food received, and food lost are entered (*input*) into the computer system daily, preferably at the school level. In a computerized foodservice, many other programs would be connected with the inventory program, since this is where purchase sizes and cost data are determined and stored.

In some school districts, the inventory program might be used only to calculate the value of weekly physical inventories. This may save considerable time. It should be kept current since there are many other uses to be made of inventory information, for example, in preparing food orders and costing of recipes and menus.

Acoustic coupler is a modem that allows the transmission of data via a telephone attached to a terminal.

ASCII is the acronym for American Standard Code for Information Interchange.

BASIC language is the Beginner's All-purpose Symbolic Instruction Code. It is a widely used interactive programming language, developed by Dartmouth College, that is especially well suited to personal computers and beginning users.

Batch processing is accumulating data over a period of time and then processing it all at the same time in the same run.

Baud is a unit of measuring speed at which data travels between a computer and a peripheral or between two computers.

Benchmark problem is a problem used to evaluate the performance of hardware or software or both.

Bit is short for binary digit, which can have only two possible values, 0 and 1. It is the smallest unit of information recognized by the computer. All data (letters, numbers, symbols) handled by a computer are digitized and expressed in bits—0s and 1s.

Bugs are programming errors, defects, or problems.

Byte is a series of eight bits that represent a number or character.

Central processing unit (CPU) is the electronic component of a computer that controls the transfer of data and performs arithmetic and logic calculations.

Clear display key is a key that causes the data on the screen to be erased.

COBOL is the Common Business Oriented Language. About 80% of business application programs are written in COBOL.

Computer network is a complex consisting of two or more interconnected computers.

Configuration is the particular set of CPU-type, memory-type, and area devices, and other parameters that make up a microcomputer system.

CP/M is an acronym for Control Program for Microprocessors. It is an operating system that is found in many small computers.

CRT terminal is an acronym for Cathode Ray Tube, which is a television-like terminal with a keyboard. It is used to display and to enter information.

Cursor is a movable, usually blinking spot of light, showing the position in which information is to be entered or erased.

Daisywheel is a print head that forms full characters rather than characters formed of dots. The print method used is similar to that of a regular typewriter. This is the type of print head that produces letter-quality characters.

Data is any information that can be acted on or produced by a computer.

Digital is a way of representing data in the form of two-state binary numbers.

Disk is a round piece of magnetic-coated material, much like a phonograph record, on which data is stored.

Disk drive is a piece of hardward on which a floppy or hard disk pack is mounted for electronically storing data.

Dot-matrix printer is a printer that forms characters from an array of dots. The more dots in a given space, the more legible is the character. Used primarily for reports.

Down time is the time when a computer will not function due to machine failure.

Edit is to make additions, deletions, or changes to an existing document or program.

Electronic mail is a feature that allows short memos or messages to be sent to another computer terminal.

File is a set of similarly constructed records.

Floppy disk is a flat circular magnetic storage medium which continuously rotates when in use.

Flow chart is a blueprint to writing a program.

FORTRAN is an acronym for Formula Translation and is a high-level programming language well suited to algebraic type problems and often used in scientific applications.

Function keys are the special keys on many computer keyboards that initiate certain predefined functions.

Garbage is meaningless information.

Hard copy is a printout on paper by a printer of information generated by the computer.

Hardware refers to computer equipment including the CRT, CPU, memory, printer, etc.

Host computer is the main computer in a network on which the data base resides. In a network, data is passed to and from the host computer over telecommunication lines.

Input is any data entered into a computer for processing.

Interactive refers to a computer system that allows communication between the user and the computer.

Interface is an electronic assembly that connects an external device, such as a printer, to the computer.

K is used to describe the memory capacity of a computer. It means approximately 1000 information units. An 8K computer memory can store over 8000 pieces of information (8192 to be exact).

Load is to move data or programs from auxiliary storage into internal storage for use.

Magnetic tape is a tape with a magnetic surface, used to store data.

Mainframe is a large computer that is capable of performing applications that require large amounts of data.

Memory is the portion of the computer that stores programs and/or data.

Menu is a list of programs, procedures, or other information displayed for selection by the operator to get into a program.

Menu-driven is a computer system that primarily uses menus for its user interface rather than a command language.

Microcomputer system is a digital system generally consisting of a controller, CRT, keyboard, and a limited storage and usually costing less than $10,000.

Minicomputer is a type of computer that is usually smaller in size than a mainframe. They are larger and usually can perform more than a microcomputer.

Modem is an acronym for MOdulation/DEModulation. A device that allows computers to communicate with one another.

Numeric pad is a keyboard or a section of the keyboard that allows input of the numeric digits, 0 through 9.

Off-line is a piece of equipment that is not under the control of the CPU of the computer.

On-line refers to a piece of equipment under the control of the CPU of the computer.

Operating system is the software that controls the execution of the computer programs.

Output is the information produced by the computer as a result of processing input.

Parity setting is used to check for errors in computer circuitry.

Peripherals are the input and output devices connected to a computer, such as printer and modem.

Printer is an output device that prints a hard copy.

RAM (Random Access Memory) is the memory that can both be read and written into during normal operation. RAM is the type of memory used in most computers to store the instructions of programs currently being run.

Realtime pertains to the actual time during which a physical process transpires.

Remote mode is when the terminal is interacting with a computer at a different location.

ROM (Read Only Memory) is the memory containing fixed data or instructions that are permanently loaded during the manufacturing process. A computer can use the data in the ROM, but cannot change it.

Scroll is to move the lines displayed on a screen up or down.

Software is programming systems or programs used to operate a computer.

Sort is the rearranging of records in a file so that the order is convenient to the user. For example, putting something into alphabetical order.

Terminal is an input or output peripheral that allows communication with the computer; a piece of equipment that allows input via a keyboard and output via a CRT or printer.

Winchester-disk drive is a hard disk drive. It is an 8¼ inch, two-sided, lubricant-coated aluminum disk in a sealed housing.

Word processing system is a system that processes text, performing such functions as paragraphing, paging, left and right justification, rearrangement of lines, and printing the text.

FIG. 12.1.   Definitions of selected computer terms.

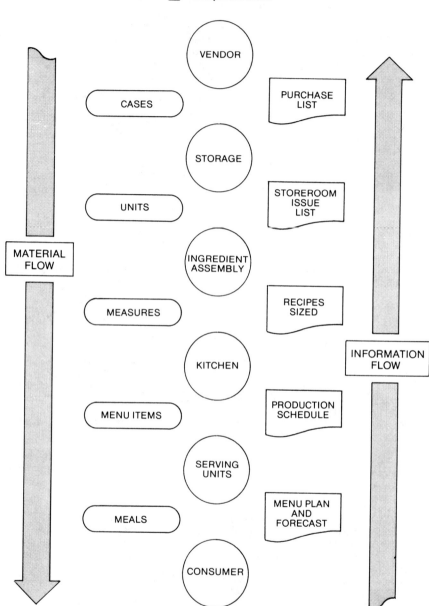

FIG. 12.2. Flow of materials and information in a foodservice operation. *Courtesy of TransTech, Inc.*

Costing of Recipes and Menus

Precosting and postcosting of recipes and menus are management tools that are useful if there are strict standardization and control procedures in place. A computer can calculate the projected cost of a recipe, a serving, and/or a menu, based on the total cost of the ingredients divided by the number of projected servings.

The precosting of recipes and menus is tied to the inventory system, where data on the cost of food is located. Many foodservice directors or managers precost a menu to determine if they can afford to serve the item. The test is what it really cost to serve it. The differences can be surprisingly great. A computer program could routinely compare the precost with the actual cost (postcost), which is determined best by how much food was actually removed from inventory.

The first step to getting ready for computerization to this detail is to standardize recipes with exact weights, measures, and yields. Once this information is entered into a computer system, it can be used not only for costing but also for recipe adjustment and nutritional analyses.

Purchasing and Market Orders

A computer program to handle purchasing and market orders should be closely tied to the inventory program. This can be an automated "forced" ordering system such that when the "reorder" point is reached, the program will calculate the quantities and items to be purchased. The inventory on hand and projected food needs can be taken into consideration so that a "grocery list" for each vendor is produced on a timely basis. Computer-assisted purchasing often makes it possible to reduce inventory volume and keep the food coming as needed. The University of Wisconsin foodservice, for example, was able to reduce its inventory by almost 75% as a result of computerization; its annual food costs were reduced by about $92,000 in one year. With such an automated system, the manager or someone else has to determine the "reorder" point, as well as the maximum stock level, for each item in inventory.

Adjusting Recipes

A side benefit of having standardized recipes computerized is the capability of easily adjusting recipes for larger or smaller yields. For example, it is a simple arithmetic process for a computer to increase a recipe yielding 100 servings to one serving 375, 550, or 724. All quantities in the adjusted recipe would be given in the largest applicable measure (e.g., 16 cups would be expressed as 1 gallon). A listing of recipe ingredients with re-

282 Computerization

quired quantities can also be used to prepare food orders and storeroom requisitions. Recipes that have been adjusted can be printed out for the cook or baker to use and later thrown away if not needed again.

Scheduling Employees

A computerized recipe *file* can be helpful in scheduling employees. However, to do this, the file must include the time required to prepare each item. The sequence of jobs, the time required for each job, and the time meals are to be served are all factors to be considered in scheduling employees.

Nutritional Analysis

Preparing a nutritional analysis manually is a time-consuming process that a computer can do in moments and far more accurately. A nutritional analysis starts with the ingredients in recipes (and thus is linked to the program for storing standardized recipes) and with data on the nutritional content of various food items. Once recipes have been analyzed, then the nutritional content of entire menus can be determined easily. Nutritional analysis also can be used in planning menus and/or to provide information that some parents want.

CANS (Computer Assisted Nutritional System) was developed by USDA during the 1970s as an alternative to planning menus using the Type A lunch pattern. CANS was tested by several school districts and was well received by some. However, because it was written in FORTRAN, it had limited appeal. A new approach (Nutrient Standard Menu Planning) that is designed for use with microcomputers was introduced in 1983. See Chapter 2 for further information on nutrient standards.

Menu Planning

Computer programs based either on nutritional analyses or nutrient standards could be used to assist in menu planning. However, as indicated in Chapter 2, there are many criteria besides nutritional requirements that should be considered in menu planning. Many of these criteria could be included in a menu-planning program.

Free and Reduced-Price Meal Applications

A computer program has been designed to record the information on a free and reduced-price meal application necessary to take action. In Fairfax

County (VA), one application is used per family and the program accepts all children in that family. However, one application per student could be used. The data could be entered at either the school level or at a central location and dispersed to each school. After a determination has been made (free, reduced, or denied), a notification letter is written to the parent or guardian. A list of students by school and category can be produced.

The notification letter can be personalized with name and address since information on the parent is entered. However, if one application per student is used, the parent's name could be dropped to save time. In this case, the notification letter could be addressed to The Parents of (student's name). If notification letters are not going to be mailed, the address is unnecessary.

A system with one application per family works well when applications are processed at a central location for many schools. However, if processing is done by individual schools, then a system with one application per student is best because children in the same family may attend different schools. Retrieval of applications for individual school audits must be considered. If one application per family is used, a file numbering system in the computer program could be used so that an application could be retrieved for each student in a school.

Distribution of Meal Tickets

Information from a free and reduced-price meal application computer program can be used to produce personalized meal tickets. The ticket would designate the appropriate meals, the appropriate price, and the precise period of time that it is valid. This not only saves time but controls the issuance of tickets.

Payroll and Time Records

Computerization in a school district often begins with the payroll. There are many commercial software packages available that can be adapted to fit the needs of most school districts. This type of program also can produce many analyses that can be valuable to a foodservice manager or director.

Bank Statement Reconciliation

Reconciling bank statements is a tedious job that can be computerized. As the cash register calculates the revenue for the day, the daily bank deposit is recorded. A matching of the data from the bank statement with that from the daily revenue reports is necessary. As banks become more computerized, computer tapes of the bank's data can make the job much simpler.

Profit and Loss Statements

With the use of a computer, profit and loss statements can be prepared easily on a timely basis. Much of the required information for a profit and loss statement would already be stored in a computer system that included the various programs described so far. Regular profit and loss statements, prepared daily, weekly, or monthly, will quickly reveal if a foodservice is getting into financial difficulty, thus permitting corrective measures to prevent the situation from deteriorating.

Travel Reimbursement

Computerization of the processing of travel vouchers and reimbursement of employees can reduce paperwork and permit easy checking of the distances claimed against standard distances from one location to another.

Word Processing

Any office that handles many written documents will welcome a word processor, which uses computer *memory* to edit memos, reports, and other text. There are numerous software packages available, such as Easywriter and Wordstar. With a word processor, one can personalize large numbers of correspondence in the matter of a few minutes or extensively edit text and produce revised finished copies quickly, without retyping.

Electronic Mail

If a school district has more than 20 schools, communication may be one of its greatest challenges. The more standardized a school district tries to be, the more paper is transmitted, and the more time required to communicate. Microcomputers in each school make it possible for all parts of the system to communicate almost immediately with each other (director with schools, schools with director, and schools with schools).

In effect, the computer system is used as an electronic bulletin board to exchange information. For example, a foodservice manager in one school might enter a message at her computer *terminal* for the district director; the next time the director logs into the computer, the message would be immediately available. If an electronic mail system is to be used frequently, a schedule should be established so that each school logs into the system on a regular basis; this is necessary to assure timely communication.

Management Information

Computerization of a school foodservice can eliminate much paperwork and make the preparation of required reports easier. However, as important as these is the capability of a system to provide all kinds of information useful to management in making decisions. The possibilities in this area are vast, limited mostly by the ingenuity of users to ask pertinent questions. Why is one high school running a profit of $2000 while another high school has a deficit of $3000? On what food items is there a loss? What is the labor cost per meal? Has increasing the use of convenience foods decreased the labor cost per meal? Comparisons among individual schools and from year to year can reveal much useful information needed to run a cost-effective system.

SOFTWARE

Software is the programs needed to make a computer do a particular job. The costly part of computerization these days is the software. The programs described in the previous section are mostly customized programs, developed for individual school systems. Developing customized programs requires the services of skilled computer programmers who work with users to fashion programs that fit the needs of individual foodservices.

Many commercial programs are available, and generally these are less expensive than customized programs. Unfortunately, they may not have the capabilities required by a foodservice. However, if 70% of a commercial software program is relevant and useful for a foodservice, it would probably be cheaper to modify the commercial program than to have a customized program developed.

Several commercial software packages can perform graphic comparisons that managers and directors like. VisiCalc and Lotus 1-2-3 are examples of popular software programs on the market. VisiCalc is an electronic spreadsheet of financial data. Computer graphics make it possible to display information in various formats (e.g., line and bar graphs or pie charts) that allow an analysis of a situation to be seen and understood in seconds.

During the late 1980s numerous computer software packages will be available on the market to chose from. The most useful ones to management will be those that analyze data and provide sound information on which to make decisions. CBORD was one of the first commercial software companies to enter the school foodservices field with their "menu management"package. The CBORD software operates on IBM XTs.

The programs that a particular microcomputer will run depend upon the type of *operating system* built into the computer. CP/M (Control Program for Microcomputers) and MS DOS allow more commercial software to be used than do some other operating systems. It has become the standard operating system for many smaller microcomputers. However, Apple and Radio Shack computers have their own operating systems. Programs for one operating system will not work on a different operating system without some hardware adaptation.

SELECTING A MICROCOMPUTER AND PERIPHERALS

This discussion is limited to microcomputers since this is the type of system that a school foodservice is likely to purchase. The growth of microcomputers has been overwhelming since they first became commercially available in 1975. In the early 1980s, more than 150 models of microcomputers were on the market.

The first step in selecting a microcomputer is to identify the functional requirements, that is, what is to be done with the computer now and over the next 3 to 5 years. It is necessary to know what a computer will be used for in order to intelligently select the make, model, amount of *memory*, and *peripherals* needed. The second step is to evaluate the characteristics of different microcomputers to determine which one will do the job most economically. The following characteristics should be considered:

- Type of microprocessor
- Memory capacity
- Disk capacity
- Peripheral capacity
- Size and quality of the video display unit
- Software availability
- Price

The main component of a computer is the central processing unit (CPU), called a microprocessor in microcomputers. The most common microprocessors come with 8, 16, or 32 *bits*. A 16-bit unit can perform more functions and is more desirable than an 8-bit microprocessor.

Memory capacity is measured in *bytes*, which represent characters. Some microcomputers store up to one million bytes of data. The most common, however, have 64K (64,000+ bytes) or 128K. Ask how much memory capacity a model has in *RAM* (Random Access Memory) and *ROM* (Read Only Memory) in evaluating its potential.

Different computer models utilize different mechanisms for storing data. The most common and convenient in microcomputers is *disk* storage. The storage capacity and other characteristics of disks vary and should be evaluated in terms of the intended uses of the computer system.

There are several things to consider in evaluating a video display unit, or screen. How many characters per line and how many lines are displayed? If a screen is to be used for word processing, an 80-character display is desirable. The resolution, or quality, of the characters is also important. The greater the resolution, the easier it is to view and to read the display. Video displays with green phosphor characters are best for extended periods of use, particularly if the unit is located near a window. Nonglare coated surfaces reduce reflections, enchance character contrast, and improve readability. Full and split screen (where more than one screen can be viewed at the same time) as well as horizontal and vertical *scrolling* are desirable. Special features that may be desirable in a display unit are highlighting with bold letters, blinking, or reverse video features. Color can be useful with graphs and is available on many models.

A keyboard should have as a minimum a standard typewriter layout with upper and lower case letters. Since so much of school foodservice use of the computer involves numbers, a numeric keypad like that on a calculator is desirable. Movable keyboards, called "lap" boards, provide flexibility in positioning.

There are more than 100 models of printers on the market, priced from $300 to $3000+, with speeds of 15 characters per second to more than 300 characters per second. The two basic types of printer are dot matrix and daisy wheel. Daisy wheel printers produce letter-quality printing. Most printers use 80-column paper.

The model of computer chosen should be flexible enough to perform mathematical computations, text editing, information retrieval, communications, and a variety of business applications. Preferably, the memory and disk capacity should be expandable. The reputation and stability of the manufacturer and the company selling a computer are important. As indicated in the previous section, the type of software to be used should be considered in selecting a computer. Is it to be customized software or commercial software? The latter is far more economical, but not all commercial software programs fit all computers. Discuss the commercial software available for each model being considered with sales personnel. Also, find out about maintenance services and warranties. A 90-day warranty period is standard, but when does the 90-day period begin? Annual maintenance contracts are advisable and are available from many computer service companies.

This is only an overview of what to consider when purchasing a computer. Several sources of information—books, magazines, product information brochures, and sales personnel—are available and should be consulted for details about different models. Because computer technology is changing rapidly, it is important to obtain up-to-date information and advice before selecting a computer and peripherals.

TRAINING

The first step in introducing most adults to computers is overcoming their fear of the unknown. Computer literacy is the ability to communicate with and understand the basics of computers—a working knowledge of computers. Using a computer does not require the ability to program or to understand the internal workings of a computer. It does involve being comfortable with computer keyboards and knowing how to enter data into a terminal, and how to get information out.

Hands-on experience and the opportunity to practice the kinds of operations that will be performed in the working situation are essential to training

---

I. Maintains daily inventory balances at the central warehouse and at each of the schools.

    A. Allows adjustment for physical inventory, spoilage, theft, or damage.
    B. Prints physical inventory recording sheets for schools and warehouse.
    C. Prints physical vs. perpetual inventory report for schools and warehouse, with dollar values.
    D. Provides on line access (CRT) to on-hand inventory balance in warehouse or schools.

II. Maintains a file of recipes up-to-date at least 2 weeks before scheduled preparation.

    A. Prints recipes, displays recipes (CRT).
    B. Prints (or displays CRT) a list of all recipes that use a particular ingredient.
    C. Prints an ingredient list.

III. Schedules meals at each school with an estimate of number of meals to be prepared.

    A. Each school provides estimates (count) for meal preparation. The computer program generates the quantity of all ingredients required (orders).
    B. Prints school meal scheduling worksheets: prints list of scheduled meals with the number of servings planned previously to allow for recording new or revised estimates of servings to be prepared.
    C. Prints school meal preparation worksheets: allows for recording of actual servings prepared and ingredient usage.

IV. Plans school transfers.

    A. Maintains file of school transfer orders: allows for canceling order, adding items to order, updating quantity ordered, and processing pickup orders (from warehouse).
    B. Prints transfer order delivery list (items and quantity to be delivered) for review by each school before delivery (because ordering is done by computer).
    C. Updates school inventory: multiplies number of servings of recipe × ingredients to get amount used for each ingredient.

V. Provides an item shortage list for each school where scheduled requirements will not be satisfied by existing inventory and incoming transfer orders.

VI. Provides an item shortage list for the warehouse where scheduled requirements will not be satisfied by existing inventory and purchase orders.

VII. Calculates and provides food and supply cost of the following:

    A. Meals for each school
    B. Transfer orders (deliveries) for each school
    C. End of month inventory for each school and warehouse

FIG 12.3. Summary of jobs performed by computer in San Jose (CA) School Foodservice.

in computerization. High school teachers make excellent trainers of school foodservice managers. Also, there are videotaped training programs that can be used with groups or by individuals very effectively.

Employees may be ambivalent about computerization because of fear that computers will take their place. In practice, this rarely occurs. Instead, computers provide managers and directors with more information than is available without them and provide more time to manage. Computerization of a school foodservice is likely to make many jobs easier and less tedious. Once employees realize just how many repetitive, often boring, tasks computers can do for them, they are likely to welcome the computer revolution, not resist it. Figure 12.3 is a summary of the jobs performed with the computer system in the San Jose (CA) School Foodservice.

The full benefits of computerization—decreased work loads, decreased errors, more timely information, and analytical tools to help make management decisions—can be realized only if employees are comfortable with the computer system and well trained in using it. Indeed, it is not unusual for 30% of the cost of computerization to go for staff training. Without this investment in human resources, the investment in computer hardware and software will not pay off to the fullest extent possible.

OTHER ADVANCED TECHNOLOGY

Not only computers but other forms of advanced technology are beginning to make an appearance in the school foodservice industry. These innovations are likely to come slowly, but eventually many of them will find widespread use in school foodservices.

Many of the companies that serve the foodservice industry already are using high technology to reduce their costs and improve their services. Cini-Grissom Association, for example, is using Computer Assisted Drafting (CAD) to produce kitchen layouts. Many food distribution operations are highly computerized. In many cases, this means a distributor can meet the needs of its customers better.

Many food and supply companies are using scanners and laser beams in taking inventory. The Universal Product Code (UPC), which is a national system of product identification, consists of small blocks of parallel lines and numbers unique to each product. The UPC symbol is printed on many food packages. These symbols can be scanned with a bar code scanner by moving it over the code. With a laser beam device the code can be read at a greater distance. The use of a scanning device and portable handheld computer can reduce inventory taking to a few minutes.

Deep-fat fryers and ovens are using electronic "chips" to automate their procedures. Refrigeration equipment is becoming more energy efficient with the use of computer memory.

An automated or electronic cash register (ECR) is a cash-control device with electronic, rather than manual or mechanical, parts. Almost all ECRs function as microcomputers. They can work at high speeds to store data and information. They generate information by doing computations with the input data and then print out the results. ECRs can communicate with microcomputers making it possible for a manager to do a reading of all ECRs without leaving the manager's office.

Robots are still too expensive to be used in school foodservice production and service. However, as their prices come down, they may well turn up in school kitchens or cafeterias. A delicatessen in Pasadena, California, has had much success with two robot waiters, which have voice synthesizers and optical sensors. The fast-food drive-ins will probably be among the first to use robotic technology on a large scale.

BIBLIOGRAPHY

ANON. 1978. Consumer guide to home computers. Consumer Guide Magazine, Skokie, IL.

BENDER, F. E., A. KRAMER, and G. KAHAN. 1976. Systems Analysis for the Food Industry. AVI Publishing Co., Westport, CT.

DEMBOWSKI, F. (ed.) 1983a. Administrative Uses for Microcomputers: Software. Association of School Business Officials, Park Ridge, IL.

DEMBOWSKI, F. (ed.) 1983b. Administrative Uses for Microcomputers: Hardware. Association of School Business Officials, Park Ridge, IL.

DEMBOWSKI, F. (ed.) 1983c. Office Management/Word Processing. Association of School Business Officials, Park Ridge, IL.

FEINGOLD, C. 1980. Introduction to Data Processing. 3rd edition. Wm. C. Brown Company, Dubuque, IA.

GULEY, H., and J. STINSON. 1980. Computer simulation for production scheduling in a ready foods system. J. Am. Dietet. Assoc. 76(5):482.

JOHNSON, M. 1983. The Hidden Cost of Buying a Computer. School Business Affairs. Association of School Business Officials, Park Ridge, IL.

MOULTON, P., and R. COLFIN. 1983. Personal Computers Answering User Needs. American Management Associations, New York.

NEILL, C. 1982. Computers on line. School Foodservice J. 36(10):37, 41.

OSBORNE, A. 1978. An Introduction to Microcomputers. Vols. 0, I, and II. Adam Osborne & Associates, San Francisco.

U.S. DEPT. OF AGRICULTURE. 1982. Food and Nutrition Newsletter. Vol. 12, No. 2. U.S. Govt. Printing Office, Washington, DC.

13

THE FOODSERVICE
MANAGEMENT COMPANY

When foodservice management companies first entered school foodservice operations more than 28 years ago, they did not have the benefit of federal support in the form of cash reimbursements or USDA-donated foods. For many years management companies were not very interested in entering the school foodservice market, partly because of the federal regulations and low profits. However, in 1970 the Child Nutrition Act was amended (Appendix II) to allow any school food authority to employ ". . . a food service management company in the conduct of its feeding operations, in one or more schools." Under the law, the school food authority retains responsibility ". . . for seeing that the feeding operation is in conformance with its agreement with the State Agency or the FNS Regional Office." By the early 1980s, partly as a result of the changes in the law, about 8% of all school foodservice programs were operated by food management companies.

In 1979 some guidelines on contracting with foodservice management companies were released by USDA. Section 210.8 of the regulations authorized a school food authority to employ a foodservice management company to provide and operate its foodservice program. However, the responsibility for assuring that all the provisions of the regulations are followed is still that of the school authority. The state agency does not have the power of prohibiting a school from contracting with any reputable company that agrees to provide nutritious meals which will meet the program's requirements. Contracts, however, must be reviewed by the state agency.

With these rulings, foodservice management companies can enter into a contract with a school or a school district and, though profit oriented, may still receive federal funds and USDA-donated foods. Many school foodservice leaders have feared that the relaxed laws would put an end to school lunch as it has been known. The American School Food Service Association's house of delegates voted in 1978 to disallow management company employees membership in the Association. A few members expressed the following concerns:

1. Industry will take over, and there will be no place left for school foodservice people.
2. The nutritional aspect will be ignored and profit will be the chief motive for having a foodservice.
3. The prices will be higher than the students can afford to pay; therefore, the diet at school will be junk foods.

Management companies have said that these fears are unfounded. They point out the advantages of having a food management company with its business experience and management ability, especially during a period of rising labor costs. The advantages and possible disadvantages of food management companies should become clearer as a result of an experimental program in the Chicago City Schools. In 1983, ARA Company, a leading management firm, was employed on a pilot basis in 35 Chicago schools. The cost effectiveness and service delivered by ARA in this pilot study will be assessed carefully by school administrators across the country. For many schools, high labor costs—especially the high cost of fringe benefits—make it difficult to operate a self-supporting foodservice. As with the airlines in the mid 1980s, school systems may find that contracting out certain services—like food and transportation—is a way to escape high labor costs.

WHEN IS A FOOD MANAGEMENT COMPANY NEEDED?

There is a place and a need for food management companies in school feeding. The leading food management companies have trained their people and are business oriented. Indeed, a shortage of qualified school foodservice people for supervisory positions exists in some parts of the country. A food management company may be needed in the following situations:

1. When a trained school foodservice supervisor is not available
2. When the current management has failed
3. When the district or school is too small to afford the salary of a trained school foodservice supervisor
4. When student demands require changes that cannot be brought about by the present operation

When can a foodservice be considered a failure? To a business manager or a board of education, the standards for judging may be threefold: that the foodservice is financially sound, that students are satisfied with the food and service, and that it is a smooth operation in accord with the administration.

When faced with an unsatisfactory foodservice, school administrators should ask several questions:

1. What are the objectives or standards for the school foodservice from the viewpoint of the administration? Students? Community?
2. Can the school's own foodservice meet these objectives? If not, why? What is needed?
3. What can a food management company offer? At what cost? Can the administration afford it? Students?

Foodservice management companies have used as their main selling points their professionalism, efficiency, and expertise, pointing out that educational institutions should not have to worry with running a "restaurant," but should leave that to the experts. The competition that school foodservice management has had as a result of the entrance of business-oriented companies into the field has generally been beneficial to school food programs.

TYPES OF MANAGEMENT SERVICES

Management companies are involved in school foodservice in three main ways: consulting; providing food; and providing and serving food. The needs and financial situation of a particular school district will determine which type of management company service is most appropriate.

Consulting

If a school foodservice has good leadership but has financial problems and/or suffers from low productivity, inability to supply quantity of food needed, low participation, low sanitation standards, or labor problems, the expertise of a foodservice management company or a successful foodservice director as a consultant may be extremely beneficial. Most frequently what the school foodservice needs is the business advice and direction that a consultant may be able to furnish. This seems to be an area where the foodservice management companies could work most effectively.

Furnishing Food

Where facilities are not available or inadequate for on-site preparation, a management company may be equipped to furnish good food at a price per lunch that can be afforded. Many large city systems have turned large kitchens into central kitchens preparing thousands of lunches to go out to many different schools daily. Other districts do not feel they want to make the large capital outlay necessary for such an operation, nor do they want to enter the food industry. Food management companies may be the answer in such cases.

Furnishing and Serving Food

In the third type of arrangement, food is prepared by management company employees, either in a commissary or on-site, and is served by them. Some administrators want this complete service rather than getting involved in feeding children; or facilities and staff may be lacking and a complete management service seems to be the best solution.

CONTRACTING WITH A MANAGEMENT COMPANY

Contracting must adhere to procurement standards and the invitation to bid must be advertised. Checking with the state agency is advisable. When a school or school district enters into a contract with a foodservice management company, both should be fair to each other and have a clear understanding of what the profits or management fee will be. A school administration should not fool itself that a management company will provide its services without receiving enough money to cover the cost of labor and food and to provide a profit for the company. In some cases a school or school district will come out with a more efficient foodservice with better food at no greater cost to the student when it employs a management company, regardless of the profits figured into the contract. In other cases, higher prices for students may be justified if a management company offers more menu variety and provides services that the school management can not.

A very clear understanding and a detailed written contract between a school administration and management company are essential for both parties to avoid problems that could arise later. Among other provisions, a contract should specify the following:

1. That the management company will provide records to support reimbursement claims on a timely basis and that such records will be kept for 3 years.
2. That current health certification will be maintained for facilities outside the school where food is prepared.
3. That no payment will be made for meals spoiled or unwholesome at the time of delivery or for meals that do not meet specifications.
4. That the management company will direct those who serve food to provide sufficient quantities to meet federal meal requirements.

Competitive Bids

Many school administrations have experienced difficulties in handling competitive bids for the services of management companies. It is difficult to write "quality" into bid specifications. To assure its profits, a company that has bid "too close" may cut the quality of food and service, perhaps by using lower grade food, using less labor, serving smaller portions, or offering less variety.

The cycle menu should be included in the bid specifications or, with state approval, it can be requested that the proposal from a bidding company contain menus. The company winning the contract should be required to adhere to that cycle for the length of the cycle; thereafter, it may make changes with the school system's approval. Additionally, an advisory board composed of parents, teachers, and students is required; its purpose is to aid in planning menus and evaluating the services of the management company.

Some of the questions asked by administrators are, "What happens to my present employees if a management company comes in? Are they given jobs? Will the large boys get enough food to fill them up within a cost they can afford? How is the value of USDA-donated foods figured into the income or cost? What happens if the USDA-donated foods are not furnished in the quantity expected or planned on?" These and other questions should be considered and taken into account in bid specifications.

Each state department of education has its own requirements governing contracts between schools and management companies. These requirements include the minimum regulations released by USDA in 1979. The experiences of another school district can be very helpful to someone about to put out a "request for proposal" for a foodservice management company.

According to Zaccarelli and Ninemeier (1982), a "request for proposal" (RFP) should include the following:

1. General introductory information about the facility
2. Specific information about dietary services
3. Invitation to bid/purpose of RFP
4. General conditions/specific requirements and instructions
5. Dietary specifications
6. Personnel requirements
7. Responsibilities of food management company
8. Responsibilities of the school food authority
9. Accountability standards for handling records, payments, and fees

Do not simply accept the lowest bid in a competitive-bid situation. Carefully evaluate every part of a company's proposal—menu cycles, nutritional goals, quality of food, meal counts, record keeping procedures, etc. However, in order to be able legally to take other than the lowest bid, a school administration must carefully word the RFP.

Responsibilities of Management Company and School

As long as the school administration furnishes the customers (with closed campus, a captive customer), the equipment, and housing for a foodservice, it is involved in the operation. A food management company cannot relieve the school administration of all involvement. Moreover, the school district retains the ultimate legal responsibility for assuring that its foodservice program meets applicable regulations and standards.

The school administration and foodservice management company should have a written agreement about the following aspects of the operation:

1. Is the foodservice to be operated under federal regulations and receive federal reimbursement and USDA-donated foods?
   a. If so, who does the claim forms for the state agency?
   b. Who takes care of transportation and storage of USDA-donated foods?
2. What quality and quantity of food will be served? Will textured protein be used? Enriched products?
3. What menus will be served? Are they acceptable menus with variety? Will a la carte be sold? Will choices be given in the menu?
4. What type of service will be used? Will speed lines, vending machines, and/or made-to-order service be offered?
5. Where will the food be prepared? Will it be prepared at a commissary, on-site, and when?
6. What are the nutritious standards of the food to be served? Will they be presented in a way to encourage acceptance?
7. What costs are to be borne by each party?
   a. Labor cost, payroll, personnel records, fringe benefits
   b. Trash and garbage collection and disposal
   c. Free and reduced-price lunches
   d. Accounting system for federal and state claim forms
   e. Payment of bills and payroll
   f. Insurance—liability, workmen's compensation, fire insurance, and theft
   g. Maintenance and replacement of equipment
   h. Utilities—electricity, water, gas, etc.
   i. Extermination service
   j. Cleaning of the dining room, kitchen, tables and chairs in dining area, floors, walls, and waxing of floors
   k. Sales tax
   l. Telephone
   m. Leftovers, overordering, school dismissal due to emergency and students not eating at school that day.
8. Who is responsible for the following:
   a. Setting lunch hours
   b. Purchasing food
   c. Ordering quantities, counts, etc.
   d. Cashiering, bank deposits, records, and reports
   e. Sanitation standards, outbreak of food poisoning
   f. Labor negotiations

g. Setting price charged to students
h. Hearing student, parent, faculty, and community complaints
i. Sale of lunch tickets and maintaining anonymity of students receiving free lunch
j. Training new employees

School administrators and foodservice management company administrators need to assess the financial advantages of participating in the federal school lunch program versus the greater flexibility possible by not participating. The cost to students can be reduced under the federal program because of the cash subsidy and USDA-donated foods. Furthermore, the regulations set by Congress and enforced by USDA can help protect students and the school administration.

Nutrition and Meal Requirements

A major concern of any school district contracting with a foodservice management company is that nutritional standards and meal requirements be met, especially in programs operating under the federal lunch program. Federal audits in 1978–1979 pointed out the need to assure that the food

FIG. 13.1. The Rainbow Lunch teaches nutrition by guiding students to choose a nutritionally balanced meal.
Courtesy of ARA Services, Philadelphia, PA.

being served by management companies meet meal requirements. The responsibility for meeting federal requirements rests with the school food authority; however, penalties for failing to meet certain requirements can be written into the contract with the management company.

The marketing approach that a management company uses may be innovative and unfamiliar to school personnel. But if the nutritional requirements are met, new approaches may be beneficial and encourage student participation. For example, the ARA Company has developed the Rainbow System a la carte or choice menu type lunches (Fig. 13.1). This approach to selecting nutritious foods uses four colors to stand for the requirements of the lunch pattern: red for protein, bread and butter; green for fruits and vegetables rich in vitamin A; yellow for fruits and vegetables rich in vitamin C; and blue for milk. With choices of foods in the first three groups, the students are guided to choose one food from each color group, thus fulfilling the lunch requirements.

Nonperformance and Discharge of Contracts

A 60-day cancellation clause should be written into any contract between a school district and foodservice management company. This clause can be exercised at the discretion of either party without the need for demonstrating nonperformance.

In addition, a management company and school should each have a way out of their contractual obligations at any time during the term of the contract when one or more of the following can be shown to exist: failure of the other party to perform a stipulated condition; fraud and misrepresentation; lack of ability to perform; failure to perform because of actions of the other party; waiver of performance by the other party.

There are three situations in which the parties to a contract between a school district and management company are released from the duty to perform (Zaccarelli and Ninemeier 1982):

1. When performance becomes illegal because of enactment of a new law
2. When property or material that is required to complete the contract is destroyed
3. When an essential element that the contracting parties assumed to exist is lacking (e.g., when a school is closed)

MANAGEMENT FEES OR PROFITS

Federal regulations prohibit contracts that permit management company fees to be based on "cost-plus-a-percentage-of-cost" or "cost-plus-a-percentage-of-income." Management fees established on a per meal basis serve as an incentive to the contractor to serve more meals and have worked best for most school districts. A fixed fee does not motivate the company to provide the best meal or to increases student participation in the lunch program. Most school administrations agree that basing fees, and thus company profits, on performance is the most satisfactory procedure.

Foodservice management companies are realizing that in order to make a reasonable profit in serving nutritious food to students, they must attract many customers because the markup, or profit per meal, is low. To be successful in the school foodservice market, a management company must keep food quality high, prices low, sanitation standards high, customers happy, and service good. A good working relationship between the company, students, and administration of the school can be very valuable to the success of the program. A committee made up of teachers, students, parents, school administration, and the company management working together on menus, grievances, and plans can be effective.

A major concern for a management company when in school foodservice may be cash flow. Federal reimbursements may take 60 to 90 days after the month's claim report has been submitted by the school food authority. This should be considered by the management company and school food authority when establishing the contract. If the contract requires the school food authority to pay the management company within 30 days or less, the school food authority must consider the source of funds. If payment is dependent upon receipt of federal reimbursement, the management company may have a cash flow problem. This may be a particular problem for school districts where the source of income is primarily from federal funds.

VENDING MACHINES IN SCHOOLS

Prior to 1984, the competitive food regulations prohibited the sale of some foods frequently found in vending machines, e.g., carbonated beverages. With the changes in those regulations (Chapter 1) the vending business will pick up.

Vending machines are most frequently associated with commercially operated, profit-making machines dispensing candy, carbonated beverages, gum, and cigarettes. However, there are some vending machines operated by profit-making foodservices dispensing milk, ice cream, apples, cans of soup, sandwiches, and even full lunches (Fig. 13.2).

Before September 1972, it was illegal to operate commercial vending machines in schools that were participating in the National School Lunch Program or Special Milk Program, and for sometime after that their legality was questionable. Vending machines have been used in schools where no foodservice facilities are available, where there is an overcrowded situation,

FIG. 13.2. Food vending machines in convenient locations allow students to easily select desired items.
Courtesy of The Macke Company, Washington, DC.

where time is a huge factor, and where there are split shifts. The vending machine has been one solution for offering "something" in the way of a snack to students.

Effect on Nutrition

Despite their association with "junk foods," vending machines can be used in a truly beneficial way and have a definite place in school feeding. Dispensing good, nutritious food can be a means of teaching nutrition education and making nutritious foods appealing. If children regularly see good, nutritious foods with eye appeal in a vending machine and have a choice of nutritious foods such as an apple or orange, a ham or a peanut-butter and jelly sandwich, real or enriched orange and grape juice over ice or in a zip top can, they may start expecting that quality of good food all the time.

Many nutritionists and school foodservice-oriented people are concerned and rightfully so, about commercial vending companies having free range in schools, with student government organizations seeing the rebates dangling before their eyes. However, local school officials have the authority to determine what competitive foods, if any, can be sold in their schools, even if the federal regulations are relaxed. According to the USDA, the American diet has increased considerably in the proportion of sugar and other sweeteners consumed in the last two generations. The White House Conference on Food, Nutrition, and Health (1970) expressed concern over the eating habits of the American people and their lack of nutrition knowledge. It was pointed out in the report of this conference that

> Significant changes in our eating patterns are taking place, including the consumption of more snack foods between meals, more eating away from home, and greater use of convenience foods. . . .
> Every child has a right to the nutritional resources he needs to achieve optimal health. The school is unequaled as the institution by which this right can be fulfilled, and with enormous impact on the nutritional status of the people as a whole.

Outstanding nutritionists at this conference expressed their concerns about snacks, fads, empty calories, and foods high in carbohydrates becoming the most serious nutritional problem facing this country. The competitive food regulations issued by USDA in 1980 restrict slightly what can be sold in schools (see Chapter 1).

Labor-Saving Advantages

Vending machines dispensing nutritious food can speed up service, reduce labor needs, save space, and make it possible to offer food at any time during the day and in several locations. The problems sometimes experienced are with mechanical breakdowns, the use of slugs, and impersonal atmosphere.

Revenue

Vending companies may or may not share the receipts with schools. The percentage of profit received by schools ranges from none to 20% when vending companies operate the service. As with any other type of contracted food company, keeping food quality high and prices down are the greatest problems. The freshness of the food being sold should be checked carefully, as well as the sanitary conditions in and around machines. Sometimes students, particularly boys, find they spend almost twice as much money to "get full" when there are only vended foods. The reputation of the company for fresh, high-quality food and for good sanitary practices is what one has to rely on. Sometimes the prices are low to begin with and slowly rise. Many school systems find they have to go out on bid for a vending service, with the lowest bidder receiving the business. Specifications are difficult to write in order to keep quality and sanitation high.

As discussed previously, a school administrator should know what he is getting and how much it is costing him before signing any foodservice contract. Microwave ovens placed near vending machines can use a considerable amount of electricity. Payments for utilities and cleanup are usually the school's responsibility. Also, attendants are needed to continually load the machines and make change. Who will furnish the attendant—the school or the vending company? Maintenance of machines may prove to be quite a problem if trained mechanics are not readily available.

BIBLIOGRAPHY

ANON. 1970a. Federal Register *35*(41):3900.
ANON. 1970b. School food service: new laws can help you provide it. Nation's Schools *86*(5):61–63.
ANON. 1972a. Contract foodservice—pros and cons. School Foodservice J. *26*(9):45–46.
ANON. 1972b. Teaching nutrition with rainbows. Food Management 7(1):72–75.
ANON. 1972c. Wait and see is watchword on section 7. School Foodservice J. *26*(10):29–30.
BARD, B. 1968. The School Lunchroom: Time of Trial. John Wiley & Sons, New York.
CRIMMINS, M. B. 1978. We belong in school foodservice. Food Management *13*(1):31–32.
ELLER, J. 1972. FTU: Before and after fee-management. School Foodservice J. *26*(4):19–20.
EYSTER, J. 1980. The Negotiation and Administration of Hotel Management Contracts. 2nd edition. Cornell University Press, Ithaca, NY.
FARLEY, T. J. 1970. Expanding the conventional school food service program. pp. 86–104. *In* Proc. Northeast School Food Service Seminar, Univ. of Massachusetts.
GARDNER, J. G. 1973. Contract Foodservice/Vending. Cahner's Publishing Co., Boston.
HOLGATE, M. 1970. Utilizing outside contractors to expand school food service operations. pp. 179–189. *In* Proc. Northeast School Food Service Seminar, Univ. of Massachusetts.
LICHTENFELT, R. J. 1971. Let's tell it like it is. School Lunch J. *26*(2):47–48.
PAGE, D. 1970. Food management in school foodservice. pp. 105–122. *In* Proc. Southwestern Regional Seminar for School Food Service Administrators, Oklahoma State University, Stillwater.
PAYNE, N. E., A. L. DUNGAN, and D. L. CALL. 1973. The Economics of Alternative School Feeding Systems. College of Agriculture and Life Sciences, Cornell University, Ithaca, NY.
PERRYMAN, J. 1968. Food management companies threaten. School Lunch J. *21*(10):70–72.
U.S. DEPT. OF AGRICULTURE. 1977. Evaluation of the Child Nutrition Programs. U.S. Govt. Printing Office, Washington, DC.
U.S. PUBLIC LAW 91–248. 1970. 84 Stat. 207 (May 14).
WHITE HOUSE CONFERENCE ON FOOD, NUTRITION AND HEALTH. 1970. Final Report. U.S. Govt. Printing Office, Washington, DC.
ZACCARELLI, BROTHER H. E., and J. D. NINEMEIER. 1982. Cost Effective Contract Food Service: An Institutional Guide. Aspen Systems Corporation, Rockville, MD.

SATELLITE FOOD SYSTEM

This book has been geared primarily to traditional school foodservice in which food is prepared and served at the same location; this on-site system is still the most common system used in feeding children at school. However, in the last 18–20 years, new preparation and delivery systems have flourished and now produce 20 to 25% of the meals served in schools. This has happened due to many reasons; the main ones have been (1) decreasing enrollments, (2) increasing labor and operating costs, (3) increasing numbers to be served because of federal subsidies for free and reduced-price meals, and (4) lack of facilities. Under the Federal Food Service Assistance Program, funds were available for several years during the 1970s for establishing, maintaining, and expanding foodservices. These funds covered up to 75% of the costs for expanding and upgrading foodservice facilities in schools in which 33% of the children qualified for free or reduced-price meals. This program was particularly helpful to inner-city schools, in cities such as Philadelphia, Baltimore, St. Louis, and Los Angeles, that were built without kitchen facilities. Funds for this program were discontinued in 1981.

New food systems were developed out of necessity by those charged with the responsibility for feeding school children, and by manufacturers who had products to sell. Most agree that on-site preparation is preferred in most situations, but impossible or impractical in others. Central kitchens and commissary-type preparation that resemble a factory have come from the need to prepare food in one location for transporting to another for serving. *Central kitchen* is defined as any kitchen where preparation of food is done for serving in several other locations. The central kitchen may be referred to as the *feeder school.* The school receiving the food prepared at the central kitchen is referred to as a *satellite, receiving, or finishing school.*

Commercial frozen food companies have entered school foodservice by preparing frozen entrees, resembling a TV dinner or modified in-flight meal for reheating in the school before serving. Also available are multiportion frozen foods in throw away steamtable inserts.

Some school districts have manufacturing kitchens that prepare parts or all of the lunch, particularly baked products, for the entire district or city. Los Angeles and Corpus Christi are preparing food in manufacturing kitchens for serving in many of their schools. Most school districts, however, are not large enough or do not have the capital outlay to get into the manufacturing business and will use one school kitchen to serve another smaller school or use food purchased already prepared.

Some major food systems are classified here as follows:

On-site preparation system. Self-contained unit prepares and serves the food for customers housed on-site.

Satellite food system in bulk. In a satellite system the food is prepared

FIG. 14.1. Preplated hot portion of the lunch is being prepared by the school foodservice.
Courtesy of Keyes Fibre Company.

at one place for serving at another location. The satellite or receiving school is dependent on another location for its food. The source of the food and the form in which it is transported varies. The food may be prepared at another school, at a central kitchen operated by the school system, or purchased already prepared. The food is transported in bulk for portioning at the receiving kitchen at serving time.

Satellite food system—preplated meals. In this satellite system food is prepared and portioned into individual meals ready for service or for heating and then serving. The food may be prepared at another school, at a central kitchen operated by the school system, or purchased already prepared (Fig. 14.1). An automated assembly line is necessary for any volume.

PROS AND CONS OF CENTRAL KITCHENS

School administrators sometimes go into one of the satellite-type food systems with false hopes of making a foodservice into a profitable or self-supporting program. A central kitchen does not solve the problem of a poorly functioning foodservice. As a matter of fact, especially good management is required in centralized kitchens where large quantities of food are prepared and large numbers of employees must be supervised. For a central kitchen to be productive and efficient, well-trained employees are required. Time and motion economy are of utmost importance. Layout faults are more noticeable and become more of a problem. Work scheduling and time scheduling are absolutes for high productivity. The production-line type of work that is required may cause morale problems for employees. Other disadvantages of central kitchens, compared with on-site preparation, include the following:

1. High transportation cost
2. Cost of delivery equipment
3. Less menu variety
4. Potential loss in nutritional value
5. Lower quality
6. Lack of personal service to students at satellite schools
7. Greater waste from leftovers
8. Large expense involved in equipping central kitchen

On the other hand, central kitchens have several advantages over the on-site preparation system with a kitchen in each school. For example:

1. Fewer supervisory and trained personnel required
2. Greater productivity and lower labor cost
3. Capital outlay savings—two kitchens would cost one-third more than one kitchen large enough to serve the two. Savings increase with the number of satellites
4. Standardization of quality and quality control

5. Centralized purchasing results in better prices
6. Uniformity of portions and portion control

How many central kitchens and where should they be located are questions asked by administrators. In a metropolitan area such as Washington, DC, with traffic problems, a number of central kitchens would be recommended over a single huge one. New York City has seen the problems of serving over 600 locations from one kitchen. Points to be considered in locating a central kitchen are (1) length of haul to receiving schools, (2) breakdown problems, (3) expansion, and (4) ethnic groups and menu modifications. A central kitchen should be located where it is accessible to the primary traffic routes into the area where receiving schools are located. Noise and traffic from delivery trucks may be distracting unless the central kitchen is located separately from the school proper.

Some central kitchens take the form of a junior or senior high school kitchen that has been enlarged or built for the purpose of preparing food for surrounding schools. Actually, many kitchens can prepare another 200 to 400 lunches without additional equipment. Using the large kitchen of a junior or senior high has worked particularly well when the satellite schools, usually elementary schools, are within a short distance. Columbia City (MD) built its schools with this plan in mind, and realized significant capital outlay savings. As another example, the kitchen in Yorktown (Arlington, VA) Senior High was turned into a preparation kitchen for 11 elementary schools.

The rising cost and lack of skilled labor, teamed with low productivity, particularly in small elementary schools serving less than 200 to 250, have been the main reasons for satelliting food in many areas. Several subsystems of the satellite system are discussed in detail below.

A study by Colorado State University (Anon. 1976) of sixteen school districts showed that the management of the program rather than system type had the greatest impact on the nutritive value and microbiological safety of the meal. The delivery systems tested were (1) on-site, (2) base or central bulk transport, (3) base or central hot-and-cold pack transport, and (4) commercially purchased preportioned frozen. Meals served in bulk form were more acceptable to students than those served in preportioned form. However, within each delivery system, some schools had higher acceptability than did others.

SATELLITE FOOD SYSTEM—IN BULK

Bulk Transporting System

Transporting food in bulk is one of the oldest and most widely used methods for moving prepared food from the point of preparation to the point of serving. The oldest means is by insulated containers—heated food carriers and cold food carriers—to the receiving school where the food is portioned and served. In recent years the chill-pack method of transporting food in bulk has been used very successfully. Both methods allow for service resembling on-site preparation. Many school districts are using the bulk method of satelliting very effectively. Frequently, the students and parents are not aware that the food was not prepared in their own school's kitchen.

The reasons that this system of satelliting might be chosen for a particular school include the following:

1. Kitchen facilities are available but participation is too low to afford the labor to prepare the food. The school has a deficit. (Schools serving less than 250 lunches have difficulty operating a self-supporing on-site preparation foodservice.)
2. Kitchen facilities are inadequate for the number to be served. Space and/or money for enlarging the facilities are not available.
3. Facilities and staff at a large kitchen nearby are capable of greater productivity.
4. Trained management and labor are not available.
5. Food quality is poor.
6. Satelliting is planned to save money in the building and equipping of new schools.

Transporting in Hot and Cold Carriers

The cooked, ready-to-serve food is transported at the temperature it is to be served. Usually this is within 2 to 3 hours following preparation. Timing is very important to maintaining a good quality product at the proper temperature.

Equipment. Well-insulated and electrically heated food carriers are necessary for bulk transporting of hot foods. These usually must be preheated for 45 to 60 minutes to the required temperature and then will stay warm for up to 3 hours. Carriers are available that will hold five 12 × 20 × 2½ inch pans and three 12 × 20 × 4 inch pans. Utility carriers, used with eutectic plates for keeping food cold, are available that hold 12 × 20 inch or 18 × 26 inch pans. In addition to eutectic plates, insulated containers and dry ice are used to keep food cold. The carriers can be obtained with wheels or fitted with dollies for ease in handling (Fig. 14.2). Food is prepared and transported in steamtable pans or sheet pans from which the food can be served. The advantages of the module design of equipment are exemplified in this method of satelliting food. The carriers are designed to accommodate 12 × 20 inch pans which also fit into compartment steamers, ovens, and steamtable, or serving counter openings. This eliminates unnecessary handling of the food and means less pot and pan washing.

FIG. 14.2. Bulk food transporter is insulated to keep food hot or cold.
Courtesy of Polyfoam Packers Corp.

Bulk satelliting requires more equipment at the receiving school than the prepacked methods. It is desirable that the receiving school have (1) serving counter (perhaps portable), (2) refrigerator, (3) milk cooler, (4) three-compartment sink, and (5) work table; optional equipment includes (6) dishwashing facilities and (7) oven.

Serving. Students may be served from a serving line, cafeteria-style, picking up their tray, milk, silverware, and napkin. The receiving school may need from one to three employees at serving time, depending on the size of operation, the menu, and whether disposables are used.

An emergency backup supply of food is recommended for the receiving (satellite) school in case of truck breakdown, spillage, or an unexpected high lunch count. An emergency shelf might contain such items as canned beef or pork, canned tuna, canned spaghetti and meatballs, peanut butter, canned fruits and vegetables, canned juices, canned soups, and crackers.

There must be good communication between the feeder school and the satellite schools. The feeder (central) kitchen may need projected figures as much as 2 weeks ahead for ordering and preparing food. An accurate meal count is needed by the central kitchen each day for the meals to be prepared that day. This is needed to avoid excessive leftover wastes resulting from preparing too much food and food shortages caused by preparing too little. The waste that results from "guessing" meal counts can be too costly for this system to work economically. The quantities of food sent from the central kitchen must be measured carefully and the portioning of the food at serving time must be exact to prevent overage and shortage. Refer to Table 11.7 for the capacity of steamtable pans and the size portions to be used for a specific number of servings. Good communication is necessary between the employee preparing the quantities to go to the satellite school and the employee serving the food at the satellite school. Each food container should be labeled with the number of servings and portion size. If this system is conscientiously used and an accurate meal count is obtained from the satellite school, a smooth operation can result without costly leftovers.

Advantages. The greatest advantage to the bulk transporting system is that it maintains the personal atmosphere in the serving of food characteristic of on-site preparation and serving. Also, portions can be adjusted to the student's size, appetites, and personal likes and dislikes. The quality and nutritive value of the food is not reduced greatly in comparison with on-site preparation if extreme care is taken in limiting holding time and temperatures. There are few limitations to the menu necessary with the bulk transporting system. Disposables may be used in the serving of the food, or reusable dishes and silverware when dishwashing facilities are available.

To maintain the quality, nutritive value, and safety of the food, it should be held at temperatures of 150°F or hotter and 45°F or colder. Food should not be held at the hot temperature more than 3 hours. Extreme care should be taken to keep food from being held at temperatures of 60° to 120°F, since bacterial growth is most rapid in this temperature range. Local and state health departments have regulations concerning the handling and serving of transported foods. Their recommendations and regulations should be followed.

Disadvantages. The most frequent problem with the bulk transporting system is running out of food at the satellite school. This problem can be eliminated with more careful planning and better communication. Transporting of the food may present problems. The food containers may be heavy and require lifting. A loading dock at the feeder kitchen and the satellite school needs to be level with the transporting vehicle. A truck, bus, or large station wagon is needed. The serving time at the satellite school may require more labor hours than is economically practical.

Procedures. To explain the operation of the bulk transporting system, a hypothetical example is used. Rogers Senior High School serves 700 lunches and a la carte items to its student body and prepares 300 lunches for bulk satelliting to two nearby elementary schools. Rogers' kitchen is staffed with a manager and nine employees for a total of 60 hours. Each of the elementary schools has a cashier, server, and two 3-hour employees, who arrive 45 minutes before serving time.

One person is in charge at each of the elementary schools. The duties of the central kitchen manager and the person-in-charge at the satellite school are well defined. (An explanation of these duties is given later in this section.)

DAILY TALLY OF REQUESTED MEALS AND SALADS FOR RECEIVING SCHOOL

SCHOOL _____   DATE _____

TEACHER A LA CARTE   FOOD ITEM
Name

_____ _____   MEAL COUNT TELEPHONED IN BY
_____ _____   RECEIVING SCHOOL:
_____ _____
_____ _____   Student Lunch
_____ _____   Hot Lunches: _____
_____ _____   Salad Lunches: _____
_____ _____   Super Sack Lunches: _____
_____ _____   Adult Lunch
_____ _____   Hot Lunches: _____
_____ _____   Salad Lunches: _____
_____ _____   Super Sack Lunches: _____
_____ _____   A la Carte _____

                                     TOTAL: _____

Components of Meal	Serving Size	PRODUCTION KITCHEN Completes Columns 1 and 2		RECEIVING KITCHEN Completes Columns 3, 4, and 5		
		Column 1 No. of Servings Transported	Column 2 Departing Temp	Column 3 Receiving Temp.	Column 4 No. Served	Column 5 No. of Servings Left Over
Entree:						
Vegetables/ fruit						
Bread or Rolls:						
Dessert:						
Other:						
		Initial _____		Initial _____		

Complete 2 copies: Return 1 copy to the production kitchen at the end of the day and retain 1 copy in the receiving kitchen.

FIG. 14.3. Sample Satellite School Record for use with bulk transporting system.

Preparation is always begun at Rogers the day before, in order to assure that the food will be ready the next morning. The food for the satellite school is prepared in much the same way as it is for serving the students at Rogers, in some instances as a part of the same mixing and preparation. The food must be ready and in the carriers for transporting to the elementary schools by 10:30 A.M.; lunch is served at 11:15 at one of the satellite schools, and 11:30 at the other.

Before food is sent to the satellite schools, the temperature and quantity of each item is recorded (Fig. 14.3), and a final check is made by the manager to assure that all parts of the menu, in the correct amounts, are loaded in the carriers for transporting. The carriers and clean pans are returned to Rogers' kitchen later in the day. The employees at each of the satellite schools have their duties detailed on work schedules prepared by the manager of the central kitchen. Milk is delivered directly to the satellite schools daily. When the food leaves Rogers' central kitchen for the satellite schools, the employees start setting up for the 700 lunches to be served and the a la carte at their own school.

Duties of Central Kitchen Manager. The duties of the central kitchen manager in relation to a satellite kitchen may be as follows:

1. General supervision for preparation of food
2. Verification of the quantity of food being transported
3. Checking to see that temperatures of all hot foods are 150°F or hotter, and of cold foods are 45°F or colder
4. Labeling food carriers as to contents, quantity, and size of portions (scoop or ladle number, etc.) to be given
5. Completing central kitchen's part of Satellite Record (Fig. 14.3)
6. Responsible for accurate records being kept of what is sent to satellite
7. Responsible for records required for reimbursement being kept at satellite
8. Responsible for daily bank deposit being made
9. Making work schedules for each employee at satellite school
10. Training new employees
11. Visiting and evaluating the program at the satellite school. Keeping in contact with the principal for comments, complaints, and suggestions
12. Responsible for time sheet and payroll reports at satellite school
13. Responsible for obtaining substitute workers when needed
14. Planning salad menus for teachers and sending copy to satellite school for posting

Duties of Person-in-Charge at Satellite School. The duties of the satellite kitchen person-in-charge may be as follows:

1. Follow work schedules and see that other employees understand and carry out their jobs.
2. Check quantity of food on arrival at school to see that all parts of the menu have been delivered.
3. Check labels on carriers for portion size and utensils to use.
4. Check information on Satellite Record (Fig. 14.3) and record temperature of food upon arrival at school.
5. Refrigerate all cold foods upon arrival. Use proper procedures for maintaining the hot temperatures.
6. Order milk and ice cream for the following day. Order napkins, straws, etc., from central kitchen.
7. Check milk and ice cream deliveries and sign invoices.
8. Inform central kitchen immediately if additional meals are needed.
9. Complete all necessary reports and keep information needed by central kitchen.
10. Collect money for meals and deposit in bank daily.
11. Check and record temperature of last pan of food served.
12. Complete satellite's portion of the Satellite Record.
13. Inform central kitchen manager of any problems, complaints, and suggestions.
14. Work with principal and teachers in making the foodservice a part of the education program.

Chill-Pack System. Another way of transporting food in bulk is in the chilled state. This method has not been in use very long. The Groen Company has developed a chill-pack system using Cryovac™ bags and Groen equipment. The system involves bringing the temperature of hot food (170–180°F) to below 40°F quickly. This provides a sterile product if kept airtight and completely free of contamination. The products can be kept for several days at refrigerator temperatures (32–40°) or can be frozen for later use. The Groen Company provides for an efficient operation and the equipment is necessary for large volume production. Cryovac Food Service System has developed a heavy plastic "freezer" bag that was especially constructed to withstand temperatures from 0 to 200°. They also developed a ring stand or holder which holds the heavy bags open while being filled with steaming hot food.

The Groen Company System includes a mechanized pump for removing the hot food from the Groen stock pots. The closing of the cryovac containers can be done by a machine. It includes an ice bath that provides for chilling the product quickly.

This system is particularly desirable for soups, sauces, and mixed items. The chill-pack products are ready for serving with heating in hot water, in the compartment steamer, in the microwave oven, or in a regular oven, if surrounded by water. The quality and nutritional value are maintained quite well. The sanitation risk is less than when transporting and holding hot food in bulk.

For a small-scale operation this system can be modified using existing equipment and work well with a minimum outlay of funds. In the modified system the Cryovac ring stand is needed along with the Cryovac bags. A vegetable sink can be converted into an ice bath for chilling the prepared food. A source of crushed ice is essential to the chill-pack system.

Following the quick chilling of the products they should be stored in a refrigerator or freezer with good air circulation. To assure the process is sterile and completely safe, bacteria counts can be run. Most health departments can have such tests run.

The chill-pack system provides a way of "storing labor" and allows for greater variety. Soups and sauces can be made in large quantities at on-site production kitchens for use today and enough stored for serving at a later date.

Advantages.   Some of the advantages of the chill-pack method of transporting food in bulk are as follows:

1. *Timing of preparation.*   More flexibility, can plan preparation for down time periods.
2. *Scheduling the transporting of food.*   More flexibility, can transport the day before or when ever is best for the schools involved.
3. *Equipment needed.*   The heated carriers are not needed. However, equipment for heating the product at the receiving school may be necessary. More refrigeration may be needed.
4. *Volume transported.*   The weight of the product transported is usually much less when the hot carriers have been replaced with cold carriers.
5. *Quality of food.*   The quality of the food can be maintained for a longer period of time when the product is at a chilled state.
6. *Nutritional value.*   The nutritional value of the food can be maintained for a longer period of time for some nutrients when the product is at a chilled state.

SATELLITE FOOD SYSTEM—PREPLATED MEALS

Preplated Hot and/or Cold Meals

Preplated meals may be ready-to-eat or need reconstituting. There are several versions of the preplated hot and/or cold meals. Several of the methods used by school districts are described below.

Preplated Ready-to-Eat. In the preplated ready-to-eat system, hot and cold food is delivered ready to serve, without reheating or further preparation. The simplest system of this type uses covered styrofoam trays to hold the hot portion of the meal. Food will stay hot for up to 3 hours in these trays, when kept in insulated tote boxes; however, it is recommended that food be served within 2 hours.

The food is fully cooked, ready for eating when portioned into the styrofoam trays and other dishes. Casseroles and foods in liquid hold hot temperature best, whereas hamburgers, fishburgers, and similar items may not hold as well. The fully-cooked food is portioned in a central kitchen for delivery to another school. This system may be used when hot lunches are desired and the distance between the feeder school and the satellite school is short. This system is most frequently used when less than 100 are to be served; it would seldom be recommended for more than 200 lunches. The most important factor to be considered in this system is time—how long from the time the food is portioned until it is served.

Assembly. The trays should be filled in an assembly-line fashion with hot foods. The food can be portioned into the trays from the regular serving line. The filled trays are covered with a styrofoam lid and placed into an insulated tote box, which holds approximately 26 to 36 trays (Fig. 14.4). There should be as little delay as possible before filled trays are transported to their destination. The cold portion of the lunch may be put into a tray or into lidded bowls. Bread can usually be put with the hot portion. Students in the satellite school will pick up a tray, milk, and napkin-straw-silverware pack. Juice and soups are usually best transported in bulk in thermos jugs and portioned at the satellite school. However, cups with tight-fitting lids are available for preportioning juice and soup at the control kitchen before transporting them.

Advantages. The preplated ready-to-eat system using hinged styrofoam trays provides rapid serving with little or no labor at the satellite school. Often, existing labor at a production school can be used for food preparation. In addition, this system requires little or no additional equipment at either the production or receiving school. Other advantages are that the food containers and tote boxes are lightweight and relatively inexpensive. Children can be served directly from the tote box where desired, thus providing great flexibility in serving.

Disadvantages. This method is limited by the time factor. When used for more than 200 lunches, it is usually a temporary solution. Some foods transport better than others, and menus may be slightly affected and limited. Caution must be taken with sanitation in preparing, portioning, transporting, and serving food. The food must be *very hot* or *very cold* when portioned in order to hold the temperature below 45°F or above 150°F until

FIG. 14.4. *Left:* Styrofoam trays containing the hot or cold portion of the meal are packed into an insulated tote box to maintain the temperature until serving time. *Right:* Tote boxes are light in weight.
Courtesy of Polyfoam Packers Corp.

the food is served. Leftovers should be destroyed and not reheated, which may lead to considerable waste.

Common problems with the use of preplated trays are that food is sometimes cold when served and that disposal of styrofoam products may be messy. In addition, it is difficult to adjust portions or to provide the "offer versus served" option with this system.

Cold-Pack Lunch System

Cold-pack lunch systems go by various names in different school systems: bag lunch, Super Sack, Vit-A-Lunch, Vita Pak, Astro-Pak, and others (Fig. 14.5). The brown bag lunch is the most common example of the cold-pack method; however, bag lunches are more often brought from home than served by a foodservice. When the cold-pack method is used by institutional foodservices to provide lunches for students, the sanitation aspects will limit what can go into the lunch, how long it can be held, and at what temperature it must be held. When these lunches are prepared under the federal program for reimbursement, then they must provide the meal pattern nutritional requirements.

FIG. 14.5. This box lunch, an example of the cold-pack method, is designed for schools without heating equipment, for field trips, and for summer prpgrams at playgrounds. *Courtesy of ITT Continental Baking Company.*

Bag or Box Lunch. A bag or box lunch program can be initiated at less cost and more quickly than any other type of school food program. The District of Columbia at one time had the largest bag lunch program in the country, producing thousands daily to be distributed to schools without facilities.

Good communications between the preparation kitchen and the receiving school are always essential in satelliting food to avoid waste. In large production, the projected counts are needed as far as a week ahead, with adjustments to the count made on the morning of distribution.

A typical menu for a bag or box lunch is sliced ham sandwich, cole slaw, mustard (individual pack), apple, and ½ pint of milk. Preparation for this menu may be scheduled as follows:

Afternoon Before

1. Slice meat.
2. Wash and break up lettuce.
3. Wash and clean cabbage and other vegetables for slaw.

4. Wash apples.
5. Whip butter to go on sandwiches.

Morning

1. Prepare cole slaw. Portion into 4-ounce cups with tight-fitting lids.
2. Prepare sandwiches in assembly line. Cut and wrap.
3. Fill the paper bags or boxes in an assembly-line fashion—fruit, salad, sandwich, unit pack (napkin, straw, fork), and mustard pack.
4. Place bags or boxes in tote boxes—same number in each box or as otherwise indicated.
5. Refrigerate until time of pickup.

Careful coordination is necessary to get bag or box lunches to children without the lunches reaching temperatures above 50°F. Trucks or other vehicles can deliver lunches to the satellite school and pick up the tote boxes from the day before at the same time. Having two sets of tote boxes will save a trip to the school to pick them up after lunch is served. The receiving school will need someone to serve the lunches and collect money. It is desirable to have refrigeration at the receiving school for storing milk and keeping the bags cold until serving time.

Prince George's County (MD) took the bag lunch concept a step further by making it available as a choice for the convenience of those in a hurry and for those who think of lunch as a sandwich-type meal. Fairfax County (VA) merchandised the bag lunch by putting it in a decorative bag and calling it "Super Sack." The popularity of the bag lunch in these counties proves the importance of clever merchandising.

Vit-A-Lunch.   The Vit-A-Lunch, or Vita Pak, is a cold-packed lunch, packed on a disposable tray covered with clear cellophane. St. Louis (MO) Public School Food Service developed the Vit-A-Lunch in 1967, though the lunches were at first packed in a paper bag. The program was developed when their foodservice expanded suddenly from feeding 55 elementary schools to feeding 158 elementary schools. The name Vit-A-Lunch is a descriptive name that combines "Vit" for nutritionally sound, "A" for Type A, and "Lunch."

Menus.   The most satisfactory menus for use in a cold-pack Vit-A-Lunch consist of a meat, cheese, or peanut butter and jelly sandwich, or sliced bread and fried chicken, a salad or raw vegetable, fruit and cookies or dessert, and milk (Table 14.1). More variety can be obtained in the Vit-A-Lunch or any covered-tray lunch than in the bag lunch. Baltimore City Public Schools (MD) found that cold vegetables and salads were often not eaten by children. They then tried using two fruits to meet the fruit and/or vegetable meal requirement. This was better accepted. Salad-type sandwiches do not hold up well because the bread becomes soaked; such sand-

TABLE 14.1.   Vit-A-Lunch Menus[1]

Tuesday, Feb. 24	Wednesday, Feb. 25	Thursday, Feb. 26	Friday, Feb. 27
Bologna sandwich (2 oz)	Salami sandwich (2 oz)	Braunschweiger sandwich (2 oz)	Turkey sandwich (2 oz)
Pickled green beans (½ cup)	Potato salad (½ cup)	Cole slaw (½ cup)	Carrot sticks (½ cup)
Blue plums (½ cup)	Orange	Banana	Raisins (½ cup)
Mustard cup	Mustard cup	Mustard cup	Mustard cup
Crackers, jelly, and butter	Crackers, butter, and peanut butter	Crackers and butter	½ pt milk
½ pt milk	½ pt milk	½ pt milk	Ice cream novelties
Ice cream novelties	Ice cream novelties	Ice cream novelties	

Tuesday, March 3	Wednesday, March 4	Thursday, March 5	Friday, March 6
Cheese sandwich w/dill pickle slices (2 oz)	Salami and bologna sandwich (1 oz each)	Minced ham sandwich (2 oz)	Meat loaf sandwich (2
Salad dressing cup	Catsup cup	Mustard cup	Celery sticks (½ cup)
Tossed salad (½ cup)	Baked beans (½ cup)	Cole slaw (½ cup)	Pineapple chunks (½ c
Apple	Molded fruit cocktail (½ cup)	Banana	Crackers, butter, and j
Crackers and butter	Crackers, butter, and peanut butter	Crackers and butter	½ pt milk
½ pt milk	½ pt milk	½ pt milk	Ice cream novelties
Ice cream novelties	Ice cream novelties	Ice cream novelties	

[1] Served in St. Louis City (MO) Public Schools (1973).

wiches also require much care in refrigeration to avoid bacterial growth, which might result in food poisoning.

Assembly. Covered-tray packaged lunches are more suitable for assembly on a conveyor belt than paper bag lunches. In most cases, the entire lunch—with the exception of canned fruits or combination salads and gelatin—can be put together in an assembly line of 8–10 people using a conveyor belt to promote speed. Portioning of canned fruits, salads, and gelatin is usually done as a separate operation, sometimes with use of a conveyor belt. School employees in Philadelphia average 21 Vita-Pak lunches a minute in a centralized operation with a conveyor line.

Disposable trays (approximately 6 × 10 inch) similar to the meat trays used in grocery stores but generally with higher sides are used for the Vit-A-Lunch. On the assembly line the unit pack containing a straw, napkin and "spork" or spoon is placed on the bottom of the tray. The sandwich can be assembled on the tray as the conveyor belt moves: One person puts on each part of the sandwich—bottom slice of bread, then meat or cheese, lettuce, and then top slice of bread. The relish, mayonnaise, and mustard in individual packages can be made available at the receiving school or put in the packaged lunch. The amount of preparation, length of the conveyor belt, number of people on the assembly, and speed of the belt will affect the number of meals per labor-hour produced; however, 20 to 25 meals per labor-hour is average.

The assembled trays are covered with a cellophane or polyethylene shrink film; this can be put on by hand or by machine. Use of a shrink tunnel machine will increase productivity. Shrink tunnel machines, which are made by several companies, seal the film over the tray in an air-tight fashion (Fig. 14.6).

Covered-tray cold-pack lunches are often assembled and wrapped the

FIG. 14.6.   This sealing machine automatically seals, cuts film, and discharges tray from the machine.
Courtesy of Servpak Packaging Machinery Systems and Service.

day before they are to be served, refrigerated overnight, and then transported the next day by refrigerated truck to the receiving school. Cold-pack lunches can be transported in corrugated cartons (30 to 36 per carton) or in wire baskets made for the purpose that accommodate from 9 to 15 covered-tray-lunches (Fig. 14.7). The wire baskets are stackable and fit onto a dolly that facilitates ease in loading and unloading. The space between each basket is sufficient for good air circulation and prevents the lunches from getting mashed.

Transporting.   The method of transporting the lunches differs according to weather conditions, temperatures, health regulations and what is in the lunches, and what type transportation is available. Refrigerated vehicles designed for transporting food are most convenient for loading and unloading and also allow for more variety in the menu. However, school buses, station wagons, and trucks have and are being used.

Advantages.   A cold-pack lunch system—whether it involves bag lunches or covered-tray lunches—is an interim solution. It is a way of

FIG. 14.7.   Wire baskets are used for transporting cold- and hot-pack meals.
Courtesy of Keyes Fibre Company.

getting a nutritious lunch to children where there are no facilities. With this system it is possible to serve the lunch in the classroom or at any other location without any equipment. It is desirable to have a milk cooler in the satellite school, otherwise the delivery of milk will have to be carefully timed or milk will have to be sent with the lunches on the refrigerated truck.

The "kitchen" where the assembly of the lunch is done may not resemble a kitchen at all. Actually the essentials are assembly space (preferably with a conveyor belt), refrigeration, and dry storage. No cooking is necessary, but it does add some variety. Sandwich meats and cheese can be purchased presliced and delivered frequently to assure freshness; therefore, a slicer and freezer are unnecessary. Bakery bread and cookies, butter or margarine, canned fruits, fresh fruits and vegetables or juices, with ½ pint of milk can complete the menu.

Ten people on one assembly line with a shrink tunnel machine can back from 6000 to 9000 covered-tray cold lunches daily on a 6-hour work shift. The containers holding the cold-pack lunches can be delivered directly to classrooms with the milk, or the children can come to a dispensing area to pick up their lunch. When the costs of different systems are compared, the cold-pack system is the least expensive to produce.

Disadvantages. There are some obvious disadvantages to the cold-pack lunch system. These include limited variety in menus, lack of hot food, a factory approach that reduces the social aspects of eating, difficulty in finding drivers for transport vehicles, cost of transportation, and, in the case of covered-tray lunches, breakdowns of the conveyor belt or shrink tunnel machine, requiring trained mechanics immediately. Timing is a huge factor and speed is essential. The food cost may run higher than for on-site preparation of a hot lunch, but the labor cost will be considerably less. USDA commodities are difficult to use in this system. Contracting with a bakery to use donated commodities such as flour, nonfat dry milk, shortening, butter, and peanut butter can reduce the cost of bakery breads and increase utilization of USDA commodities without reducing the convenience aspect of this system of feeding children.

Few problems have arisen in school districts using the cold-pack system that influence the quality, safety, and nutritive value of the food. Acceptability varies from one part of the country to another.

School Preplated Hot- and Cold-Pack System

Hot- and cold-preplated school meals can be prepared in a central kitchen or commissary or in one school's kitchen for another, or they may be purchased commercially already preplated. The hot portion resembles a "TV Dinner" entree. Whether prepared by the schools or commercially, the meal can meet the federal regulations and qualify for federal cash subsidy and commodities. This system uses disposables that eliminate the need for dishwashing equipment and labor. It is being used widely throughout the country and has the following advantages in comparison with on-site preparation:

1. Enables schools with limited kitchen facilities to serve hot lunches.
2. Saves space and reduces equipment capital investment in the building of new schools.
3. Cuts the operating cost, increases productivity, and uses less labor.
4. Permits better quality control and portion control.
5. Provides faster service.

In contrast to the hot- and cold-pack transport system described already, in which food is delivered to a satellite school ready to serve, the hot entree in this system generally needs to be reconstituted (reheated) before serving; sometimes the cold portion also must be reconstituted in some way.

Some school districts started preplating their own lunches before federal regulations were changed to allow commercially preplated meals to qualify for federal reimbursement. Some districts still prefer to preplate their own meals, both the hot and cold portions. They feel they can provide better-quality food and meet the likes and dislikes of the children better than can a commercial firm. Other school districts choose not to preplate food themselves, believing that it requires far more expertise than they have or that they cannot produce lunches as economically as a commercial operation. Some school districts preplate only the cold portion (the easier of the two) and purchase the hot portion from a commercial company. Other school districts purchase both the hot and cold portions and reconstitute them before serving. This type of system may be referred to by the name of the manufacturer of the equipment or disposables, or the frozen food company packaging the food used, such as Ecko, Lincoln, and Mighty Mort systems.

The hot portion of the lunch is usually a main dish and one vegetable or a combination dish that includes a vegetable; the cold portion usually contains bread and butter, one other fruit or vegetable, dessert, and a unit pack containing the napkin-straw-silverware. The hot portion is packaged in disposable aluminum foil or ovenware container (approximately 4 × 6 inch) and capped with an ovenware cover. The cold portion is packaged on a plastic, paper, or styrofoam tray and covered with a plastic film. The food may or may not be fully cooked. It may or may not be frozen. It may or may not require reheating (Fig. 14.8).

School Preplated Meals. A school foodservice may choose to preplate the hot and/or cold portion of the lunch, with the hot portion to be reheated at the receiving school before serving. One or more central kitchens or a commissary may prepare and portion the food, and distribute the preplated lunches in a refrigerated or frozen state. Bremerton (WA) was one of the first school systems to use this system. Hundreds of school districts have used this method totally or partially to get food to children.

The hot portion of the lunch may be flash-frozen or refrigerated and reheated for use later. If food is refrigerated (not frozen), it should be used within 36 hours. The regulations governing the handling of food for transporting differ from one state to another. The local health department should be contacted for regulations. The freezing of food for reconstitution at a later time requires strict controls, temperatures at −40°F or below, and technical knowledge for maintaining the quality and low bacterial count of the food. The characteristics of foods under freezing conditions differ. School districts without the equipment and/or technical knowledge to

FIG. 14.8.   Preplated meals contain a hot pack which is reheated before serving and a cold pack which is to be kept cold until serving time.
Courtesy of ITT Continental Baking Company.

freeze food must refrigerate and reheat preplated meals within the designated time.

Assembly.   For efficiency, the food is portioned into the hot and cold trays on a conveyor belt. An aluminum or oven film cover is placed on the hot portion by hand or with an automatic hooding machine. The same conveyor can be used for the cold pack, with a plastic film applied either by hand or automatically and sealed by a shrink tunnel where heat is applied. The sealed trays are placed into wire baskets that allow for good air circulation (Figs. 14.9A–F).

Equipment is available that is made for this system and can make for greater efficiency. Wire baskets are made that are stackable that fit on a dolly for easy movement (Figure 14.7). The loaded wire baskets fit into the ovens and refrigerators. Insulated blankets may be used to cover the loaded wire racks during transporting to maintain the temperatures.

A complete lunch consists of a hot package, a cold package, and ½ pint of milk. The menus in Table 14.2 are typical hot and cold packaged lunches. The hot pack usually contains one or two items placed on a flat or compart-

FIG. 14.9A. Trays are deposited onto a traveling conveyor belt.

14.9B. Entree items are put on the trays as they move on the conveyor belt.

14.9C. Each person on the assembly line adds a part of the meal.

14.9D. Speed has to be kept up as the trays move toward the sealing machine

14.9E. Sealing machine cuts and seals a heat-resistant film over the food containers.

14.9F. Meals are packed into wire baskets that are stacked on a dolly for moving to refrigeration unit until being transported to satellite school for reheating.

TABLE 14.2.   Elementary Menus for Preplated Hot and Cold Packed Meals

Monday, Feb. 1	Tuesday, Feb. 2	Wednesday, Feb. 3	Thursday, Feb. 4	Friday, Feb. 5
Hot: Hot dog—roll Baked beans Cold: Jellied salad Peaches Milk	Hot: Spaghetti w/meat sauce Cold: Shredded lettuce French bread Fruit crisp Milk	Hot: Hamburger—roll Buttered corn Cold: Tossed salad Ice cream Milk	Hot: Turkey Mashed potatoes Cold: Jellied fruit salad Roll—Butter Baked dessert Milk	Hot: Fishwich—roll Tater tots Cold: Pepper cole sla Ice cream Milk
Monday, Feb. 8	Tuesday, Feb. 9	Wednesday, Feb. 10	Thursday, Feb. 11	Friday, Feb. 12
Hot: Cheeseburger—roll Tator tots Bu. mixed vegetables Cold: Lincoln logs Milk	Hot: Meat loaf—gravy Mashed potatoes Green beans Cold: Roll—Butter Fruit Milk	Hot: Chicken Green peas Cold: Sweetheart salad Roll—Butter Valentine cake Milk	Hot: Pizza Cold: Green salad Potato chips Fruit jello Milk	Hot: Salisbury steak Mashed potato Bu. broccoli Cold: Roll—Butter Pineapple tidbit Milk
Monday, Feb. 15	Tuesday, Feb. 16	Wednesday, Feb. 17	Thursday, Feb. 18	Friday, Feb. 19
Hot: Hot dog—roll Baked beans Cold: Jellied salad Peaches Milk	Hot: Spaghetti w/meat sauce Cold: Shredded lettuce French bread Fruit crisp Milk	Hot: Meat loaf—gravy Mashed potatoes Green beans Cold: Roll—Butter Baked dessert Milk	Hot: Chili con carne Cold: Tossed salad French bread Fruit Milk	Hot: Fishwich—roll Tator tots Cold: Pepper cole sla Ice cream Milk

Source: Arlington Public Schools (VA), Food Services, used during the 1970s.

ment tray. The food is often prepared the day before it is to be served, then cooled and packaged into portions, and refrigerated at below 40°F until time for reheating. The food is transported at 40°F to the receiving school where the food is refrigerated until just before serving. The hot portion is heated for 15 to 30 minutes or until the internal temperature is 155 to 160°F.

Equipment.   To prepare preplated meals, the central kitchen needs equipment adequate for the preparation of the food and adequate refrigeration. Large amounts of refrigeration—at both freezing and refrigerating temperatures—are required. Greatest efficiency can be achieved with a conveyor belt, packaging-closure equipment, wire baskets made for the packing material, and mobile dollies on which the baskets are stacked for greater mobility. Use of ovens and refrigeration made to accommodate the wire baskets reduces the handling necessary. It is possible for a small operation to package 24 to 50 meals per minute. The speed of the conveyor belt can be regulated according to the number of employees on the assembly line and their speed. Additional equipment recommended for packaging up to 1000 hot- and cold-pack lunches are a 10-foot long conveyor, automatic sealing machine, and shrink tunnel.

The satellite or receiving school will need, as a minimum, an oven for heating the hot portion and a milk cooler. Optional items are a refrigerator and freezer, three-compartment sink, and worktable.

If refrigeration is available at the receiving school, the scheduling of food deliveries is more flexible and desirable. A double set of baskets is suggested so the driver of the truck can deliver the number of meals needed for the day's lunch and pick up the baskets from the previous day at the same time.

Commercially Preplated Frozen Meals

Commercial frozen food companies did not enter the school foodservice market with much enthusiasm until after 1970, when changes in the federal laws made more money available for free and reduced-price lunches. These changes resulted in a significant increase in the number of students participating in school lunch programs in areas where equipment and facilities often were inadequate. This market opportunity attracted frozen food companies, and many companies have developed hot and cold packs that, when combined with ½ pint of milk, meet the nutritional requirements set by the meal pattern and qualify for federal subsidy. There is limited use of USDA-donated foods in the preparation of the meals. The companies have been more successful in elementary school feeding than in secondary school feeding. Some of the companies offer their products and accessory equipment on a purchased or leased plan.

Many school districts have chosen to prepare their own cold packs, using donated commodities in this portion of the lunch, and to purchase commercially prepared hot packs. The hot portion and cold portion of the meal are delivered in the frozen state ready for reconstituting. The preplated packs must be stored at freezer temperatures until day before use. Storage and distribution of the dinners are possibly the greatest problems facing school districts. Central warehouses are usually necessary to obtain the meals at quantity prices. Some school districts have found it more economical or feasible to purchase through a local distributor who will schedule deliveries once or twice a week.

Purchasing on a competitive-bid basis can mean better prices, but very detailed, explicit specifications are needed to assure the quality and quantity desired. Controlling the quality and quantity (portion control) is a problem that even some of the commercial companies have.

A receiving school will need from one to three employees for heating and serving the food and collecting the money or tickets. The labor recommended for a school serving 300 to 500 is one 4-hour worker and one 3-hour cashier.

A school district that plans to use this type of feeding system in a school that is to be constructed should consult with commercial firms. Many of the companies serving the foodservice market can offer recommendations as to equipment and space needed for an efficient operation.

Procedures. A typical day in a school where frozen dinners are used might go as follows:

TABLE 14.3. Week of Menus Using Commercially Prepared Hot and Cold Packs

Monday	Hot: Sicilian meat loaf Golden corn niblets	Cold:	Georgia peaches in jel Golden twin roll
Tuesday	Hot: Slice roast turkey with savory dressing and gravy Sweet taters	Cold:	California strawberries in jel Golden twin roll
Wednesday	Hot: Milano pizza topped w/beef'n cheese	Cold:	Creamy cole slaw Fruit medley in jel
Thursday	Hot: Southern deep fried chicken Sweet and tender corn	Cold:	Potomac cherries in jel Golden twin roll
Friday	Hot: Fish'n cheese burger Mixed-up vegetables	Cold:	Puerto Rican pineapple in jel Burger bun

Source: ITT Continental Baking Company.

1. One hour before serving time, the frozen entrees are placed on wire racks to be reconstituted.
2. Thirty-five minutes before serving time the entrees are put into a preheated oven for up to 25 minutes.
3. Cold portion of the lunch, put into the refrigerator the day before, is taken out to serve just before serving time.
4. At serving time the students move through the line picking up the cold pack, then the hot pack, unit pack (containing the napkin-straw- and plasticware), and ½ pint of milk.

The coverings of both the hot and cold pack are removed by the students. The variety available in entrees and cold packs vary from one company to another. An example of a week's menus using commercially prepared hot and cold packs is shown in Table 14.3.

Advantages and Disadvantages. Compared with traditional on-site preparation, the use of commercial preplated meals requires less labor, both in preparation and in serving. Commercial firms that sell preplated meals insist that one employee can serve 800 lunches using preplated hot and cold packs. The timing would have to be perfect with much cooperation and organization of the students to accomplish that, but certainly two people could serve this number, which is considerably less labor than would be required for serving on the conventional line. Since there is little food preparation with this system, employees need less training and experience; for the same reason, less equipment and space are needed. In addition, when food is prepared in a standard, assembly line operation, it is easier to control food quality, portion size, and sanitation standards.

On the other hand, employees in a foodservice that uses commercial preplated meals may take little pride in their work because of the feeling that anybody could do the relatively simple tasks involved with this feeding system. Other disadvantages when compared with on-site preparation include limited menu variety, increased possibility of plate waste because portions cannot be adjusted for students of different sizes and ages, inability to carry out "offer versus served," and inability to tailor seasonings to regional or local preferences.

INTRODUCING NEW SYSTEMS

Any time a new system for providing food is started in a school—particularly when it is replacing on-site preparation—the school administration, parents, and students have to be receptive to the system in order for it to work well. Not all of the systems described in this chapter will work for all situations. Each fits a different need. If no foodservice at all has been available, parents and students are more receptive to any system that will make food available. Making parents aware of the plans through parent–teacher meetings and involving the students in menu planning and other activities will help with acceptability.

System of Tomorrow

Little is known about the aseptic system in school foodservice in this country, although it may well be the best of all the systems for holding cooked foods for serving later. Military feeding operations and the space program were pioneers in this means of preserving foods. The aseptic system uses hot-air sterilization and packaging in retort-type pouches or containers. The advantage of the aseptic process—which flash heats, sterilizes, and then rapidly cools the product—is that the products do not require refrigeration until they are opened. The products can be kept on the pantry shelf for 6 months or more, depending on the food, without losing flavor, nutrients, or color.

The aseptic system has been slow to catch on, perhaps because industry is not ready to give up traditional methods and because of the significant investment required in new machinery. The high price of aseptic products has discouraged foodservice directors from taking a serious look at this system. However, as sales volume increases, the prices of aseptic products will decrease and in time they may become competitive with regular canned foods. It is conceivable that a production kitchen could have its own packaging machines, whereby spaghetti sauce could be prepared and packaged for serving several weeks later, and stored on the storeroom shelf until time for reheating for serving. With our concern for energy and increasing needs for freezer space, the idea is exciting.

Ocean Spray Cranberries, Inc., is one of the first companies to use aseptic packaging in this country. The Food and Drug Administration put its stamp of approval on the procedure in January 1983. Dairymen Inc., located in the southeastern states, has spent $16 million to equip its plant for packaging milk and several milk-flavored drinks aseptically. The process was begun in Sweden and is used extensively by Del Monte in its European plants.

BIBLIOGRAPHY

ANON. 1966. Which system suits your needs? School Lunch J. 20(7):13–32.

ANON. 1972. The cup-can approach. School Foodservice J. 26(10):41, 43.

ANON. 1976. Contract Feeders Survey. American School Food Service Association, Denver.

ANON. 1976. Pilot Study to Assess, Audit and Evaluate Food Delivery Systems Used in School Food Service. Colorado State University, Fort Collins.

AVERY, A. C. 1967. Work design and food service systems. J. Am. Dietet. Assoc. 51(8):148.

BLAKER, G., and E. RAMSEY. 1961. Holding temperatures and food quality. J. Am. Dietet. Assoc. 38(5):450–454.

EMERSON, R. L. 1979. Fast Food: The Endless Shakeout. Chain Store Publishing Corp., New York.

FAIRFAX COUNTY (VA) OFFICE OF FOOD SERVICE. 1982. Food Service Manual. Fairfax County Schools, Fairfax, VA.

KOTSCHEVAR, L. H., and M. E. TERRELL. 1977. Foodservice Planning: Layout and Equipment. 2nd edition. John Wiley & Sons, New York.

LIVINGSTON, G. E., and C. M. CHANG. 1979. Food Service Systems: Analysis, Design, and Implementation. Academic Press, New York.

POLEDOR, A. P. 1977. Determining the Feasibility of a Total Convenience Food System. CBI Publishing Company, Boston.

U.S. DEPT. OF AGRICULTURE. 1965. Establishing central school lunch kitchens in urban areas: problems and costs. Econ. Report 72 U.S. Govt. Printing Office, Washington, DC.

U.S. DEPT. OF AGRICULTURE. 1977. Evaluation of the Child Nutrition Programs. U.S. Govt. Printing Office, Washington, DC.

PLANNING FOODSERVICE FACILITIES

A question frequently asked by boards of education is "Should we continue to build kitchens and equip them for the preparation of food?" It was predicted by some in 1980 that by 1990 each school would have its own machines for packing shelf-stable foods using the aseptic process described at the end of Chapter 14. Although there has been a steady trend toward central kitchens, commissaries, and satellite feeding for many years, the number of self-contained units engaged in on-site preparation also increased during the 1970s when school foodservice doubled its operation. Self-contained units are still the rule, accounting for 75 to 80% of the meals served to school children. But in some situations and locations, the food factory is the solution, and for others the use of frozen preplated dinners may be the solution. The challenge is to plan flexible foodservice facilities that can be adapted to the needs of the future, which may see more feeding programs during the summer and for the elderly and more breakfast programs. A few communities have been able to effectively plan a secondary school surrounded by elementary schools. This presents the ideal situation in which the secondary school can serve as a feeder school supplying food to nearby elementary schools. However, there is no set pattern for planning foodservice facilities that will meet the needs of all.

GENERAL CONSIDERATIONS

Good planning is necessary for high productivity and the greatest efficiency. When working in an old building with construction faults and poor layout, the waste of time and motion is costly, but often unavoidable. However, when a new facility is being planned and constructed, it would be expected that these faults could be avoided. Too frequently the same mistakes are made or new ones are planned. With the virtues and faults of so many school plants to use as guides, it would seem that a perfect plan could be developed.

When construction funds run low, often the kitchen becomes smaller and results in a facility too small for the number to be served. However, too large a kitchen may be almost as bad since it results in wasted time walking between work areas and low productivity. Plans should be made on the basis of what is needed now and with consideration for future needs.

Foodservice management must insist on being a part of a proposed school's planning team. It is hard to explain why so many poorly planned and poorly arranged kitchens are still being built. One of the reasons, it seems, is that foodservice people are not involved in the planning. The planning team should consist of representatives of the school board, architects, construction specialists, and those who will use the facilities. The local and state health departments should be consulted during the planning stages. Since such facilities are a long-range project and a great cost, the planning should be done carefully.

The factors to be considered in planning a school foodservice include the following:

1. Capacity of the school
2. Future expansion plans
3. How many meals will be served—breakfast, lunch, dinner
4. Menus and type service to be offered—single menu, choice menus, a la carte, vending machines, etc.
5. Age of children
6. Location of building
7. Type of facility—feeder kitchen, satellite kitchen, self-contained unit
8. Type of equipment needed
9. Utilities to be used
10. The uses of the school building and foodservice by the community

Kitchen

The kitchen should be located on the ground floor with a service driveway accessible for deliveries to be made. The delivery entrance should be located away from the playground and students' traffic lane. The kitchen should have an outside entrance that opens onto a loading dock. If the foodservice facilities are in a separate building, a covered walkway to the main school building is desirable. The noise of the kitchen should be considered in locating the facility.

Since a kitchen is not easy to enlarge, it should be built to accommodate future needs. The space required in square feet depends on what equipment

TABLE 15.1. Guide to Space (in Square Feet) Required for School Foodservice On-Site Preparation

Area	Up to 350	351–500	501–700	701–1000
		Meals		
Receiving area				
Loading platform	60	80	100	100
Receiving area inside building	48	48	60	80
Storage				
Dry storage, ⅓–½ sq ft per meal	175	250	325	450
Nonfood storage	30	50	70	90
Office space	40–48	48	60	80
Lockers and toilet for employees	45	60	75	85
Kitchen and serving preparation including refrigeration,				
1.1–1.5 sq ft per meal	500	650	800	980
Serving	200	300	400	600
Dishwashing	150	150	180	210
Maintenance area				
Mop area	25	25	30	30
Garbage area	30	48	60	75
Total kitchen and serving area	1303	1709	2135	2780
Dining area (based on two seatings)				
Elementary—10 sq ft/meal	1750	1750–2500	2500–3500	3500–5000
Secondary—12 sq ft/meal	2100	2100–3000	3000–4200	4200–6000
Total dining, kitchen and serving area				
Elementary	3053	3459–4209	4635–5635	6280–7780
Secondary	4303	3809–4709	5135–6335	6980–8780

is needed to do the preparation and serving. Ideally the equipment should be selected and arranged to permit the best flow of work with adequate aisle space around the equipment. Some guides are needed in the early stages of planning to assure that sufficient space will be available. Table 15.1 gives the space requirements for different areas of a foodservice operation based on standard equipment.

Dining Area

The dining area should be attached to the kitchen and convenient to the students from all parts of the school building. It should be constructed as attractively as possible. The cost of construction is such that it is hard to justify using a room the size of a dining room for only 2 hours a day. Therefore, many elementary schools use the dining room as a multi-purpose room. In secondary schools, the dining room often is used as a lounge, activity room with music and games, or as a study hall. With breakfast and dinner being added to some foodservices, the dining room may be used as a place for eating 4 or 6 hours a day. If at all possible, the furnishings should accommodate small groups in senior high schools, middle-size groups in junior high schools, and perhaps larger groups in elementary schools. Even in elementary schools, when students eat together in small groups rather than at long institution-type tables, discipline problems have been far fewer. The increased enjoyment of students during lunch hour is also noticeable.

The dining room should be attractive, bright colored, cheerful, non-institutional in atmosphere, and interesting. The tables and chairs should be varied in size and shape and color. Since elementary schools often use the dining room as a multi-purpose room, the tables may need to have attached chairs that fold and be on rollers to make moving them easier. The different size and shape tables that seat 4 to 12 people *can create* an entirely different atmosphere. The atmosphere should be carefully planned.

The size of dining area needed will depend on how many are to be seated at one time and the seating arrangement (small groups, long tables, etc.). The space required for a standard chair or seat is 24 inches, and the standard lunch tray is 12 × 16 inches. Round tables that seat four or six students require less space per seat than any other of the shapes, as shown in Table 15.2.

Ordinarily the seating should accommodate 30 to 40% of the projected enrollment at one time. On the average, 10 square feet are needed per student to be seated in elementary schools, and 12 square feet per student in secondary schools. For example, if the projected enrollment for an elementary school is 800, then

$$800 \times 0.40 = 320 \text{ students per seating}$$
$$320 \times 10 = 3200 \text{ sq ft}$$

TABLE 15.2. Net Square Feet Required per Seat

Table Shape	Dimensions (in.)	Number of Seats	Floor Dim. per Table[1] (in.)	Floor Space per Table (sq ft)	Net Floor Space per Seat (sq ft)
Round	42 diam	4	66 × 72[2]	33.00	8.25
Round	54 diam	6	90 × 90	56.25	9.38
Rectangular	30 × 72	6	78 × 108	58.50	9.75
Rectangular	30 × 96	8	78 × 144	78.00	9.75
Rectangular	30 × 48	4	78 × 78[2]	42.25	10.56
Round	66 diam	8	114 × 114	90.25	11.28
Square	80 × 80	8	126 × 126	110.25	13.78
Square	42 × 42	4	90 × 90	56.25	14.06

Source: McGuffey and Harrison (1970).
[1]Floor dimensions per table include circulation space required between tables.
[2]Average figure; one foot added to every second row for interior circulation.

This example assumes that students will be served in three seatings. If only two seatings are planned, then space must be available to seat 50% of the students at one time. The space requirement can be cut considerably by using continuous service.

With long rectangular tables, it is possible to cut the space requirement from 10 square feet for elementary students to 7 to 8 square feet per student and from 12 square feet per person for secondary students to 8 to 10 square feet per student. When seating capacity needs to be more that 350, two similar dining rooms should be considered.

The serving area, trash area, and dishwashing area should be closed off from the dining area. The walls lend themselves to art exhibits and other attractive displays. Draperies and carpets will help absorb the sounds. For elementary students, the tables should be 26 inches high with chairs or stools 15 inches high. A table 29 inches high is satisfactory for secondary-age children and can be used by all age groups; the chair should have a standard 17-inch seat height.

Serving Area

The serving area should be separate from the dining area and be separated by some type of partition from the preparation area. Cafeteria-type service is most commonly used in school feeding. The arrangement of the serving lines should be such as to accommodate all the foods and encourage fast service. How many serving lines are needed? In elementary schools one serving line can serve 10 to 12 children per minute. In secondary schools, one serving line should be able to serve 12 to 14 per minute. The number of serving lines needed will depend on the speed of service, number to be served, and length of lunch period. One serving line can serve approximately 150 students in 13 minutes. Students do not like to stand in line, and discipline problems may result when they have to wait too long to be served.

In estimating the space needed per serving line, allow for the following:

Student lane space	30 inches
Tray slide	1 foot
Serving counter width	2 to 3 feet
Worker's space	4 feet
Counter in back of worker	2½ feet

The menu, number of choices, and other offerings will determine the length of the serving counter. Ordinarily 20 feet is the minimum length, with a height that fits the students. The area must be equipped to keep the temperatures of perishable foods either hot or cold as required. Heated units are needed to hold hot food at 150°F or hotter, and refrigerated units are needed to hold cold foods at 45°F or colder. With the usual cafeteria-type service, the student picks up the tray, napkin, flatware, and milk. Self-service can be increased to include desserts, salads, bread, and other foods. The sequence of these items should be studied to avoid a bottleneck at any one point in the line. Mobile tray and silver carts, which can be taken quickly to the dishroom for refilling, are recommended, as are mobile dish storage carts. Sneeze guards should protect all foods on display on the serving line. A left-to-right serving line results in greater speed in serving than the opposite pattern.

Straight-line serving counters are the most common. However, some secondary schools have tried rotary counters or shopping-center-type lines, called the "island type," "scramble," "hollow square," and other names. When multiple-choice menus and/or a la carte items are available, rotary counters and the shopping-center approach make for much flexibility. With shopping-center service, the serving line is broken up into sections, so that, for example, a student who wants just a bowl of soup can go directly to that section and not have to wait in line behind someone who wants the whole lunch. A cashier station located at the exit handles customers from all the lines. Broken-up serving lines have been used satisfactorily in commercial, college, in-plant, and school cafeterias. Avoiding bottlenecks in a shopping-center serving line is difficult and requires careful planning. Popular items like hamburgers and french fries may need to be offered at several stations. Rotary mechanized serving counters have successfully worked for schools, eliminating long lines and speeding up service. The popularity of salad bars and self-service is opening up a new concept in feeding people both institutionally and commercially.

KITCHEN

The overall features to consider when planning the layout of foodservice production areas are the total space needed and the arrangement of equipment in that space. The design should encourage a smooth flow of work, provide adequate facilities and space for accomplishing the work in an efficient manner, aid in fast service with a pleasant atmosphere, and contribute to high sanitation standards.

The flow of work in preparation areas should be smooth and in a logical sequence. The principles of time and motion are applicable in planning the arrangement of equipment. Determining the desired flow of work is a good first step in planning the arrangement or layout. To check the flow, trace the steps of several foods from receiving through preparation to serving. With the use of colored pencils and arrows one can easily trace the flow and spot any problem (Fig. 15.1). The flow should be direct in sequence with a minimum of crossing and back-tracking.

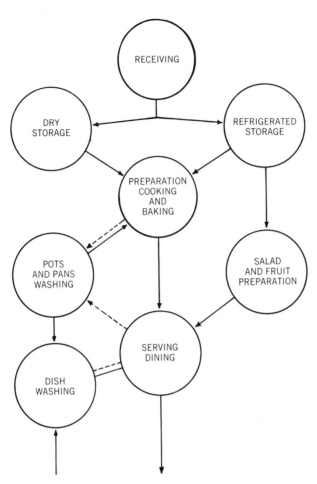

FIG. 15.1. Chart of work flow in foodservice facility.

The layout can be divided into work centers. The larger the operation the more specialized the work centers will be. A *work center* is the area within which one person works with perhaps an assistant. Each work center should have in it basically all the equipment needed to perform the job. Occasionally a piece of equipment is used by more than one work center. When possible this piece of equipment should be put on wheels and stationed in the work center that uses it most. Any equipment that is used *frequently* in two or more work centers should, if at all possible, be purchased in duplicate. If the equipment within the work centers is placed in sequence, then little working time is wasted because of poor layout. The work centers should be located only as far away from each others as is necessary for an adequate traffic lane. The layout should aim at maximum utilization of space and equipment. Most foodservice managers would select a kitchen slightly smaller than desired over one too large.

The kitchen should be planned with main traffic aisles adequate to accommodate the movement of mobile equipment. These aisles should be approximately 5 feet wide. Work centers should have 3 to 4 feet of aisle space for employees to move freely. When doors open into an aisle, 4 feet is recommended. The centers should be planned to discourage traffic through the center. Common arrangements are straightline, parallel arrangement; U-arrangement; and L-arrangement. The U-arrangement works best to discourage through traffic.

The kitchen is often planned around the cooking area, and perhaps this is where one might start planning, then work outward toward associated areas. The cooking and baking equipment is often grouped back-to-back. This grouping is convenient for the installation and repair of power lines and requires only one ventilated hood.

The kitchen should be planned with good lighting and soft colors which reduce glare. Light intensities of 35 to 100 foot candles are recommended: 70 for general preparation and serving areas and 50 to 80 for the sink and cooking areas. Shadows should be avoided. Sound-absorbing materials that meet local health codes can be used in construction to reduce the sound of the equipment. Good circulation of air is necessary; air conditioning may be needed in the warmer areas of the country. The comfort of employees is directly connected to their productivity.

When arranging and planning a layout, the most helpful tools are templets. *Equipment templets* are plastic or cardboard scale models of equipment. The scale most commonly used is ¼ inch equals 1 foot. If the templets are on the same scale as the plans drawn, one can fasten the templets into place with pins and get a miniature picture of the arrangements. Many of the larger equipment companies can supply these scale models.

RECEIVING AND STORAGE AREAS

The receiving and storage areas should be planned in conjunction with each other and in relation to the typical quantities and types of food used by a foodservice.

Receiving Area

The receiving area should be located near an outside entrance but be connected to the kitchen and convenient to the storage area. The doors leading in and out of this area should be wide and tall enough to accommodate the kitchen equipment that may need to pass through the area (minimum of 2 doors, each 36 inches wide; and 6 feet 8 inches tall). Clear vinyl strip curtains on the doors can be a protection in cold areas of the country. The receiving area should be well lighted and be equipped with scales for weighing foods as they are received and a table or counter on which invoices may be signed and small items put. A covered ramp at the loading and unloading area at a height that will fit the bed of delivery trucks, from 36 to 44 inches high is desirable. The depth of this loading dock should be 8 feet, and the width planned according to the number of trucks expected at one time. If the school will satellite other schools, this area should be planned carefully for ease in loading and unloading the transporting equipmnt, with space for two or three vehicles. "Fly Chasing Fans" should be located in the receiving area.

Storage Area

The dry storeroom should be located near the receiving area and also be convenient to the kitchen. The area should be so situated that people entering or leaving the storeroom can be seen from the kitchen. The storeroom should be dry, well ventilated with a turnover of air six times per hour, and cool with a temperature of 40 to 70°F. The humidity should be kept between 50 and 60%. In warm and cold climates, the temperature and/or humidity may have to be controlled for proper storage of canned and dry foods. The area should be free of direct sunlight and unwanted heat, such as the heat from a self-contained refrigerator or freezer. The lighting should not be as bright as in other parts of the kitchen; automatic lighting that goes off when the door is closed is energy efficient.

Storage shelves should be of the steel wire type, washable, rust proof, and raised off the floor enough to permit cleaning underneath (Fig. 15.2). Mobile shelving is growing in popularity. Most state and local health departments have definite regulations as to the height these shelves should be off the floor and the distance away from the wall. In order to get maximum storage space from the area, the shelves should save space (Fig. 15.3). The dimensions of shelves should be planned to accommodate the items to be stored there. For example, two of the most common institutional can sizes would require the following space:

Pack Size	Diam	Height	No. per Case	Size of Case
No. 3 can (cylinder)	4¼ inch	7½ inch	12	17½ × 13½ × 7¾ inch
No. 10 can	6¼ inch	7½ inch	6	19 × 12¾ × 7¼ inch

Many shelving units are adjustable; these provide flexibility in storing products of different sizes and are a good investment (Fig. 15.4).

Good planning can triple the storage capacity of an area. The height of

FIG. 15.2.   Wire shelving is easy to clean.
Courtesy of Metropolitan Wire Goods Corp.

the shelves from the floor to the top shelf should not exceed 7½ feet. One of the best and most efficient systems is the hi-density shelving system, which can increase storage capacity by 40% or more depending upon the number of units used. The shelving units are mobile, rolling on a track like an accordian, allowing space between two units when needed and closing the other units together. The units are available in many different sizes and with different weight capacities.

A school serving 1000 customers, with a food cost of 75¢ per customer in 1984, will use the equivalent of 38 cases of food products per day or 760 cases every 4 weeks, approximately. A rule of thumb for allocating total storage space is 30% for dry storage, 40% for frozen, and 30% for chilled. Thus, in the example with 1000 customers, 135 square feet of dry storage, 180 square feet of frozen, and 135 square feet of chilled would be needed (see Table 15.1). However, this method of allocating storage space is based on averages and may not apply to all foodservice operations. The proportion of dry, frozen, and chilled storage space needed depends largely on the usual type of menus and foods served in a particular school. A school that

FIG. 15.3. Space-saving racks can be built in the wall between the storage area and kitchen for first-in, first-out use.
Courtesy of Storage Unlimited, Inc.

uses mostly canned fruits, vegetables, and meats will have different storage needs from one that uses mostly frozen foods. The trend today is toward greater use of frozen foods, and two of the favorites—pizza and french fries—are quite bulky. The frequency of deliveries also influences storage needs. The trend is toward carrying less than a 4-week inventory. However, rural schools generally require larger storage areas than urban schools; often adequate storage in a rural school will pay for itself because of reduced delivery costs.

Walk-in refrigeration units can handle bulk reserve storage better and more efficiently than reach-ins. Most people prefer to use reach-in units for finished, ready-to-serve food. In estimating the size of walk-in needed, you can assume that 30 pounds of food can be stored in each cubic food of space and that approximately 2 pounds of food are needed for each meal. Thus,

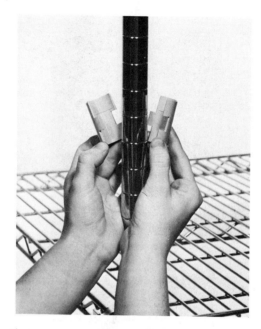

FIG. 15.4. Shelves that can be adjusted to different heights are recommended. *Courtesy of Metropolitan Wire Goods Corp.*

the number of lunches per day × 2 pounds of food per meal × number of days between deliveries ÷ 30 pounds of food per cubic foot = amount of walk-in space needed. The usable space in a walk-in averages 40% of the total capacity. Three-feet aisles are needed. Each shelf measures about 12 cubic feet, so a four-shelf unit that is 6 feet high provides 48 cubic feet of storage space. A walk-in unit 7 feet high by 9 feet deep will provide space for four shelving units, or 192 cubic feet of usable space.

The door to a walk-in refrigeration unit should open outward. The floor should be level with the floor in the kitchen so that carts can be rolled in. A reach-in unit to supplement the walk-in for storage of frequently used or ready-to-serve items can reduce energy usage and cost.

In summary, the following all affect the quantity of dry, frozen, and chilled storage needed:

1. Menu
2. Frequency of deliveries
3. Number of meals per day
4. Space available
5. Amounts of frozen, canned, and chilled foods to be used

It is extremely important that the foodservice manager or director be involved in assessing these factors and in deciding the type and quantity of storage needed. In addition, the probable growth of the operation in the next 5 or 10 years should be considered in the planning of storage areas.

WORK CENTERS

As discussed in the section on kitchen design, dividing the available space into work centers provides an organized, efficient layout. The number and type of centers that are appropriate depend on the size of the operation and type of foods routinely prepared. Common types of work centers are described in this section.

Salad and Fruit Preparation Center

The work center for preparing salads and fruits should contain a two-compartment sink for cleaning fruits and vegetables. A work table and cutting machines also are needed. The center should be located near a refrigerator where finished salads and fruits can be held until serving time. A reach-through refrigerator that opens onto the serving line can be a labor-saving arrangement. Additional equipment that may be included in the center are disposals and a vertical cutter-mixer. This area lends itself to a U-shape or L-shape design that discourages traffic.

This center may also be used for pre-preparation of raw foods for the cooking center. However, with the increased use of convenience foods less and less pre-preparation is being done in the kitchen.

Cooking Center

The cooking area is usually the hub of the kitchen. Its size will depend on the amount of equipment needed for a particular operation. The basic equipment needed are an oven, work table, scales for weighing ingredients, and steam kettle. A sink and refrigerator should be convenient to this area. In large operations the cooking center should have a one-compartment sink. A water supply is needed for the kettle, usually in the form of a swivel faucet. Other equipment may include compartment steamers, slicing machine, hot-food storage boxes, refrigeration, mixer, and range. Whether the cooking center needs its own mixer or vertical cutter-mixer for mixing meat loaves, potatoes, etc., depends on how frequently this piece of equipment is used and whether it can be shared with the baker without interfering with the baking schedule. The flow of food should be from the kitchen area to the serving line, and therefore the equipment should be arranged in a logical sequence to that point.

Storage space for pots, pans, and utensils for measuring and mixing will be needed as well as for spices frequently used. The cook's table often is equipped with a pot rack for holding the most frequently used pots. Portable racks that can be moved from the washing area to point of use are most convenient and are recommended. In designing the work space for the cooking area, plan for a "landing" space for hot food from each piece of cooking equipment.

Baking Center

Although many schools today are using mixes for their cakes and purchasing commercially prepared breads, the baking center is still equipped very much as it was 15 years ago. This center needs a convection oven, mixer or vertical cutter-mixer, work table, portable bins, scales for weighing ingredients, and cooling rack. Other equipment that may be included are sink, refrigeration, small kettle or range top, and proofing box. Equipment should be arranged in a sequence that will encourage a flow of the work to the oven and to the serving line. This area should be convenient to refrigeration, a sink, and the serving line.

The baker's table has changed from a wood-top table with bins underneath to a stainless steel-top table with portable bins. Some wood-top tables are in use, but for the most part they have been replaced by more durable and sanitary stainless steel ones. Storage areas for items frequently used are needed and will reduce the number of trips to the storage area.

Sandwich Center

In secondary schools with sandwich lines or a la carte service, a sandwich-making center may be essential. This area needs access to refrigeration, sink, slicing machine, chopping machines, and a work table with cutting boards.

Cleaning Center

The dishwashing area has an important part in the sanitation of any foodservice operation. This area should be located near the serving line for returning the clean dishes and attached to the dining room for students to return the soiled dishes. A frequent mistake in planning is to locate the serving line near the traffic of the dishroom, resulting in criss-crossing.

The facilities needed in this area are soiled dish tables (100 feet minimum length), prerinse sink and disposal, dishwasher adequate for the size of operation, booster heater, and clean dish table (minimum length 100 feet).

The prerinse sink should be approximately 24 inches square with rails that guide the dish racks over the sink. A disposal located in the prerinse sink works very satisfactorily. If the hot-water method of sanitizing dishes is to be used, the water temperature in the dishwasher must be 140–160°F for the wash cycle and 180–200°F for the final rinse. The cleaning area should have adequate ventilation to remove the steam that accumulates.

A three-compartment sink for pot washing may be located in cleaning center, near to the cooking area. If the pot sink is located near the dish machine, the pots and pans can be washed and sterilized in the dish machine. If the dish machine is not used for washing and sterilizing, the pot-washing area will need rinse water at 180°F (or chemicals could be used for sterilizing). Drainboards are needed on the sink for air drying. A portable rack for the pots and pans is convenient.

In order to maintain water at 180°F a booster heater near the sink will be needed. Assure when specifying the sink that the sink is large enough to accommodate 18 × 26 inch pans. Also, avoid galvanized metals and insist on stainless steel.

MANAGER'S OFFICE AND EMPLOYEE FACILITIES

Even the smallest operation needs an office for the manager. The space should be adequate for at least a desk, two chairs, and file cabinet. Larger operations will need larger offices to afford room for the counting of money and for conferences. The manager's office should be so located that the manager can sit at the desk and have a view of the kitchen and outside entrances. Enclosures with glass above 4 feet are most satisfactory.

Locker rooms where employees can hang their coats and store personal belongings safely are recommended. These areas are usually near the toilet area. Many states have regulations forbidding the opening of a toilet directly into any food storage, serving, or preparation area. Hand-washing sinks with towels and soap should be located conveniently throughout the kitchen, especially near the locker room and in toilet areas. Foot controls or automatic turn-off faucets are recommended for the hand sink.

SUMMARY

This chapter has not gone into all the details of designing and planning foodservice facilities. Rather, the purpose has been to give an overall understanding of how an efficient layout is developed based on the flow of work, the relationship of work centers, and careful planning around actual needs. The size and amount of equipment to be included in the facility and its arrangement should be determined through the foodservice management working closely with an architect. A knowledgeable consultant can save not only headaches but money.

BIBLIOGRAPHY

BARNES, R. M. 1968. Motion and Time Study: Design and Measurement of Work. 6th edition. John Wiley & Sons, New York.

BUCHANAN, R. D., and JULE WILKINSON. 1975. The Anatomy of Foodservice. Design 1. Cahners Books, Boston.

KAZARIAN, E. A. 1975. Food Service Facilities Planning. AVI Publishing Co., Westport, CT.

KAZARIAN, E. A. 1979. Work Analysis & Design for Hotels, Restaurants, and Institutions. 2nd edition. AVI Publishing Co., Westport, CT.

KOTSCHEVAR L. H., and M. E. TERRELL. 1977. Foodservice Planning Layout and Equipment. 2nd edition. John Wiley & Sons, New York.

McGUFFEY, C. W., and D. J. HARRISON. 1970. What is the best seating for lunchrooms? School Lunch J. 25(9):59–68.

MILLER, E. 1966. Profitable Cafeteria Operation. Ahrens Book Co., New York.

MYERS, J. R. 1979. Commercial Kitchens. 6th edition. American Gas Association, Arlington, VA.

SCRIVEN, C., and J. STEVENS. 1980. Food Equipment Facts—A Handbook of the Food Service Industry. Conceptual Design, New York.

UNKLESBAY, N., and K. UNKLESBAY. 1982. Energy Management in Foodservice. AVI Publishing Co., Westport, CT.

U.S. DEPT. of Agriculture. 1974. Equipment Guide for On-Site School Kitchens. U.S. Govt. Printing Office, Washington, DC.

U.S. DEPT. of Agriculture. 1975. Food Storage Guide for Schools and Institutions. PA. 403. U.S. Govt. Printing Office, Washington, DC.

U.S. DEPT. of Agriculture. 1980. Food Service Equipment Guide for Child Care Institutions. U.S. Govt. Printing Office, Washington, DC.

WEST, B., L. WOOD, V. HARGER, and G. SHUGART. 1977. Food Service in Institutions. 6th edition. John Wiley & Sons, New York.

EQUIPMENT

Today there are so many equipment companies in business that the challenge is greater than ever before to specify and purchase a good piece of equipment that will do the job. The range in quality for foodservice equipment is almost as great as that for home equipment, but harder for the buyer to judge without the aid of consumer studies. The answers to the following questions will help determine what specific equipment should be purchased for a particular school foodservice:

1. How much money is available?
2. How large an operation is the equipment for?
3. What is the expected growth in the next 10 years?
4. What is the cost of labor? Is labor available? Is equipment needed that will take the place of labor?
5. What is the menu, the variety, to be prepared? What will the equipment be used for? How frequently?
6. What form will the food be purchased in—fresh, frozen, prepared, etc.?
7. What is the floor plan? How much space is available?

Not only the initial price of equipment but also the cost of installation, repairs, and operating should be considered. Also important are the years of service that can be expected from a piece of equipment and its value to the operation. Individual pieces of equipment should be judged on their design, durability, cleanability, construction, safety, and the materials used in relation to the job to be performed.

Thirty years ago, equipment for institutional foods was made to last a lifetime, and it was expensive in those years. Some of that equipment is still in use today; however, for the most part foodservices have outgrown such equipment, have found a need for more efficient equipment, or cannot obtain parts for repairing older equipment. With today's rapid advances in technology, foodservice administrators should not necessarily be buying equipment to last a lifetime or even 30 years.

347

Equipment should be purchased for one or more of the following reasons: to improve sanitation, to reduce labor cost, to improve the nutritional value of food at serving, to lower food cost, to add appeal and variety to the menu, or to make the work easier. Equipment should be purchased to meet the particular need of the foodservice purchasing it. A 60-quart mixer may be a white elephant in the kitchen of one school but a practical necessity in another.

The amount of equipment needed for a foodservice should not be determined by a chart in a book, but rather by the operation's needs. Will a piece

TABLE 16.1.   **Equipment Recommendations for On-Site Preparation Kitchens**

	Number of Lunches Prepared per Day				
Equipment	Up to 250	251–400	401–600	601–800	801–1000
Oven					
Convection oven	1	1	2	2	3
Range					
Range with oven to hold 2 pans	1 section	1	2	2	2
Steam					
Compartment steamer (optional)	—	1	2	2	3
Jacketed kettle	20 gal.[1]	30 gal.	40 gal.	40 gal. and 30 gal.	(2) 40 gal.
Mixer					
Mixer with attachments and	30 qt	60 qt	60 qt and 20 qt	60 qt and 30 qt	60 qt and 30 qt
Food cutter (optional) or	—	—	—	1 large	1 large
Vertical cutter-mixer	—	—	40 qt	40 qt	60 qt
Slicer	1 electric	1 electric	1 automatic (angle feed)	1 automatic (angle feed)	1 automatic (angle fe
Deep-fat fryer (optional)	15-lb capacity	26-lb capacity	35-lb capacity	45-lb capacity	(2) 35-lb capacity
Refrigeration					
Reach-in refrigerator	71 cu ft	71 cu ft	71 cu ft	47 cu ft	71 cu ft
Pass-through refrigerator		25 cu ft	(2) 25 cu ft	(2) 25 cu ft	(3) 25 cu ft
Walk-in refrigerator				9 × 16 ft	9 × 18 ft
Reach-in freezer	47 cu ft	47 cu ft			
Walk-in freezer			7 × 10 ft	9 × 11 ft	9 × 11 ft
Milk cooler	10 cu ft	10 cu ft	(2) 10 cu ft	(3) 10 cu ft	(3) 10 cu ft
Work tables					
Cook's table with pan rack	6 ft × 30 in. × 34 in. high	6 ft × 30 in. × 34 in. high	8 ft × 30 in. × 34 in. high	(2) 6 ft × 30 in. × 34 in. high	(2) 8 ft × 42 in. × 34 in. high
Baker's table with portable storage bins	6 ft × 30 in. × 34 in. high	6 ft × 30 in. × 34 in. high	8 ft × 30 in. × 34 in. high	8 ft × 30 in. × 34 in. high	8 ft × 30 in. × 34 in. high
Preparation table		6 ft × 30 in. × 34 in. high	6 ft × 30 in. × 34 in. high	8 ft × 42 in. × 34 in. high	(2) 8 ft × 42 in. × 34 in. high
Portable table		5 ft × 30 in. × 34 in. high	5 ft × 30 in. × 34 in. high	5 ft × 30 in. × 34 in. high	5 ft × 30 in. × 34 in. high
Dish machine					
Single tank (door)	1	—	—	—	—
Single tank (conveyor)	—	1	1		
Double tank (conveyor)	—	—	—	1	1
Soiled-dish table with disposal	9 ft	9 ft	10 ft	11 ft	12 ft
Clean-dish table	8 ft	9 ft	10 ft	11 ft	12 ft
Dishwashing racks (plastic)	3 (plate) and 1 (flat)	5 (plate) and 2 (flat)	6 (plate) and 2 (flat)	8 (plate) and 3 (flat)	8 (plate) and 4 (flat)
Disposal unit (optional)	¾ hp	1 hp	1 hp	1 hp	(2) 1 hp (2 dish windows)
Sinks					
Pot sink (3 compartment)	1	1	1	1	1
Vegetable sink (2 compartment)	1	1	1	1	1
Cook sink (1 compartment)	—	—	—	1	1
Utility carts	1	2	3	3	3–4
Cooling racks	1	1	2	3	3
Scales					
Portion, 5 lb × ⅛ oz	1	1	1	2	2
Baker's with scoop and weight	1	1	1	1	1
Platform with beam, 500-lb capacity, ¼ in. graduations	1	1	1	1	1
Serving Counter	1 line	1 line	1–2 lines	2 lines	3 lines

[1] Unless indicated otherwise by a number in parentheses one of each item in the size specified is recommended.

of equipment be used daily? Weekly? Monthly? Can the job this equipment does be obtained in any other way? For example, potato peelers have continued to go into some new foodservice facilities with the argument that they are needed for parsley potatoes. How often are parsley potatoes on the menu? Weekly at the most. Frozen and canned whole potatoes are available. Would these products work satisfactorily in place of fresh potatoes, considering the cost and flavor? The decision is for the individual foodservice to make. Buy only equipment that is needed and that will be used. Tables in the kitchen can be catch-alls. So often when there is a space, a table is put there. Is it needed? Does a foodservice need more work tables than workers?

Overequipping and overdesigning a kitchen is a waste of materials and will hamper efficiency. Although anticipated needs for a reasonable period into the future should be considered when selecting equipment, it is unwise to buy oversized equipment in anticipation of future growth many years away. Oversized equipment can cause as much wasted effort as equipment that is too small for the job. Recommendations for the equipment needed in operations of different sizes are given in Table 16.1.

CONSTRUCTION MATERIALS AND STANDARDS

The materials from which equipment is being manufactured are constantly changing. Many man-made materials have proved very satisfactory and in some cases do the job better and less expensively than stainless steel or cast iron.

Stainless steel is the most accepted metal for table tops, sinks, dish tables, dishwasher bodies, etc. The commonly used 18–8, Type 302 contains 18% chrome and 8% nickel. Stainless steel has been the ultimate in quality for many years but has also been quite expensive. An all stainless-steel kitchen was the pride of the designer, but a nightmare for those who had to remove the smudges and streaks. Today plastics, fiberglass, other man-made fabrics, and new processed enamels on aluminum are being considered cautiously. There is a place for using these new materials if they lower the cost of equipment, make for easier cleaning, are lighter in weight, or add color, as long as they still maintain durability and do the job. Tests have shown that plastics and fiberglass can be made to be as strong as the strongest metals.

Gage (or gauge) refers to the thickness of sheet metal or the weight of the metal. Gages are designated by numbers; 10 to 22 gage are most common in foodservice equipment. The larger the number, the thinner and lighter in weight the metal is (Table 16.2).

The *finish* of metals may be polished or dull. The more polished the metal, the more easily it is scratched.

TABLE 16.2. Thickness of Stainless Steel[1]

Gage Number	Approximate Decimal Parts of an Inch	Approximate Equivalents (mm)
10	0.140625	3.57
11	0.125	3.18
12	0.109375	2.77
13	0.09375	2.38
14	0.078125	1.98
15	0.0703125	1.78
16	0.0625	1.59
17	0.05625	1.43
18	0.050	1.27
19	0.04375	1.11
20	0.0375	0.95
22	0.031	0.81

[1] The use of gage to designate approximate thickness dates back to the years when sheet metal was cut on hand mills and broad tolerances were necessary. The decimal part of an inch is used to designate exact thickness and is slowly being converted to metric equivalents.

Equipment should be constructed to do the job in a sanitary and safe way. The National Sanitation Foundation (NSF) has done much to establish construction standards. The NSF was started in 1948 by public health authorities, industrialists, and businessmen who saw a need for research in the field of environmental safety and health, for uniform equipment standards, for laboratory testing of equipment and materials by an independent testing laboratory, for some means of identifying equipment that did meet the standards (Seal of Approval), and for relating the research and test results to industry, public health people, and the public. The NSF is an authoritative liaison among business, industry, and health authorities. The headquarters are at the University of Michigan. It is a noncommercial, nonprofit organization. As stated by the National Sanitation Foundation, it is "dedicated to the prevention of illness, the promotion of health, and the enrichment of the quality of American living through preplanning of preventive programs for the improvement of the environment."

The NSF booklets of standards for different pieces of equipment may be helpful in writing specifications. The insigne, NSF, on a piece of equipment indicates that it meets the requirements set in the standards booklet, that NSF periodically checks the manufacturer's methods in the factory, and that sample pieces of the same design and model have been tested for performance in the laboratory and in the field. The seal of approval is no guarantee that a specific piece of equipment will be free of defect, but it does indicate the item meets the minimum standards set forth by the National Sanitation Foundation.

WRITING SPECIFICATIONS

Specifications for equipment must be in writing. For the best price, bid buying should be carried out. However, federal regulations do not require advertising procurements of $10,000 or less unless required by states. Written specifications will prevent hard feelings and misunderstandings. They should define exactly what is desired and the conditions under which the equipment is to be purchased in a precise, clear manner. Other school foodservice's specifications can be helpful in writing specifications, but the needs of one foodservice will differ from those of another. There are a few guides that can be turned to in writing specifications. The best aids are experience with the equipment, printed literature, equipment manufacturers' representatives or salesmen, the United States Government bid specifications, and the National Sanitation Foundation standards. Specifications can be broad and descriptive or may be short and specify manufacturers and model. Usually when brands and models are specified, "approved equal" is indicated as being acceptable.

Specifications should include any features desired, such as metal exterior and interior finishes, attachments, or other available options. The purchaser should not take for granted that a piece of equipment comes with certain "necessities"; these may be considered extras by the company. For example, do not take for granted that four racks come with the dishwasher or six shelves come in the refrigerator. Instead, specify how many racks are wanted. Additional racks or shelves and other extras can often be obtained at a better price if purchased with the equipment rather than separately at a later time.

A mandatory demonstration of the equipment following its installation should be specified. Also specify that two operational manuals are to be furnished—one for the equipment maintenance file and the other for use in the kitchen. Indicate in the specifications if the equipment is to be installed by the seller or buyer, date and time of delivery, method of delivery, type of warranty or guarantee expected, and method of payment the vendor can expect. Also, it is important that parts and service be available in the area. Ordinarily equipment is drop-shipped to the loading dock of the kitchen in a crate if not otherwise specified.

If equipment is bought on competitive bid, a better price can be obtained. Grouping of similar equipment to be purchased into an aggregate

352   🔞 Equipment

can mean an even better price. The larger the order, the better the prices may be. Vendors often cut their profits close when bidding, therefore the buyer should have specified every detail of what he wants and must not start adding after the bid has been awarded.

Specifications should indicate the seals of approval, such as NSF, ASA, UL, and others, when applicable. These seals protect the customer to some degree; some health departments require the NSF seal on equipment.

DESIGN CONCEPTS AND PRACTICES

Several equipment design concepts are discussed in this section. These can be helpful in selecting appropriate equipment and writing specifications.

Modular Equipment

The modular design concept involves the use of uniform sizing, so that different items of equipment can be used together. Common module sizes for foodservice equipment are 14 × 18 inches, 18 × 26 inches, and 12 × 20 inches.

Coordinating equipment is a rather new idea. Until the early 1960s, oven manufacturers made their ovens with chambers all different sizes. They seemed to change the size as models and designs changed. The companies manufacturing pans went their separate way making pans in whatever size they liked. This was also true with refrigerators and dishwashers. As a result, a school might well have an oven with 28 × 34-inch chambers, a range oven with 18 × 20-inch chambers, baking pans that were 22 × 22 inches, and a pot-washing sink that was 20 × 20 inches. Nothing fit exactly, resulting in wasted space, wasted money, and exasperation. Often a school's menu was governed by which pans fit in which oven. Then manufacturers started working together, and today the standard module sizes are the rule with other sizes being the exception.

Modules make for adaptability and better utilization of space. Every piece of equipment works together. Cooling racks, ovens, refrigerators, steamers, carts, pot sinks, and pans can all be purchased in sizes that are interchangeable and coordinated. The three sizes of pans that fit standard modular equipment are as follows:

18 × 26 inches—bun pans, baking sheet pans, roasting pans
14 × 20 inches—cafeteria trays
12 × 20 inches—steamtable pans (20-inch measure from outer rim; these pans will fit 18-inch modules)

Standard or Custom-Made Equipment

Standard stock equipment is produced in quantity based on a standard design. It is far less expensive than is custom-made equipment, which is made according to the customer's specifications. Yet, most foodservice buyers find that designing a custom piece of equipment is a difficult, time-consuming job. Standard stock equipment has been tested and many problems corrected. For most foodservice needs, standard equipment is the best buy.

Self-Contained or Remote Control

Self-contained equipment is less expensive than remote-controlled units. This is particularly true with refrigerators. In self-contained units the motor and controls are built in during construction. Remote control means the motor and/or controls are located separately from the piece of equipment. In some cases it is advisable and desirable to pay more to have remote control (e.g., with walk-in refrigeration).

Mobile Units

"Put it on wheels" has been the motto of those urging work simplification. Mobile or portable units are now available in most types of equipment. Mobile units, particularly tables and carts, can reduce the amount of equipment needed. When a piece of equipment is used by more than one work center, and it is possible to schedule use of the equipment by the different centers, putting that piece of equipment on wheels makes it more accessible. Mobile units can be easily moved to where the work is done, saving steps, lessening fatigue, and reducing labor. The principles of time and motion are exemplified in this concept.

Labor-Saving Equipment

In certain respects, all the equipment in a foodservice could be considered labor-saving equipment. However, the chief advantage of certain types of equipment is not that they do a better job than other equipment or alternative procedures but that they save employee time. Such labor-saving equipment has become more important to the food industry as labor costs have increased. With the aid of labor-saving equipment, the number of employees can be reduced because each employee can do more work in less time. Common examples of labor-saving equipment in school foodservice include the following:

1. Automatic slicer instead of manual slicer
2. Conveyor dishwasher instead of door-type dishwasher
3. Convection oven instead of conventional deck oven
4. Automatic timer shut-offs on equipment instead of employee watching the clock
5. Automatic counters on a slicer instead of employee counting the slices
6. Vertical cutter-mixer instead of the worker cutting and mixing by hand
7. Automatic defrost and condensator instead of employee taking food out and defrosting
8. Prerinse on dishwasher instead of employee scraping and prerinsing
9. Conveyor belts on assembly line instead of manual movements
10. Utility carts, portable tables, and wheels on equipment instead of stationary equipment

Energy-Efficient Equipment and Practices

The concern for conserving energy has brought about tremendous changes in the equipment purchased by school foodservices and stimulated development of new types of equipment or new features. Recovering and reusing heat energy from exhaust air and from condenser water from refrigerators presents many challenges and opportunities for saving energy. Soon to come are computers in ovens and use of more aseptic processing.

Making employees aware of how they are wasting energy can help con-

TABLE 16.3. Form for Recording Energy Usage and Cost by Energy Type

		Electricity				Fuel Oil [ ] #2 [ ] #4 [ ] #5 [ ] #6				Natural Gas				Coal [ ] Wood [ ]	Purchased Steam [ ] Other ____ [ ]			
Month	Year	Est. Meals Served	Quantity kWh	Cost ($) Total $	$/kWh	$/MMBtu	Quantity Gallons	$/Gal.	Costs $ Total $	$/MMBtu	Quantity CCF	Costs ($) Total	$/CCF	$/MMBtu	Quantity Unit	Costs ($) Total $	$/Unit	$/MMBtu	Ener Cos ($)
1	2	3	4	5	6	7	8	9	10	11	12	13	14	15	16	17	18	19	20
January February March																			
April May June																			
July August September																			
October November December																			
Annual Totals																			
Annual Averages																			

Source: U.S. Dept. of Agriculture.

Design Concepts and Practices 355

TABLE 16.4. Effect of Energy-Conservation Measures

Measure	Reduction in Energy Usage (%)
Reduced number of hours equipment is used	55
Added control devices	36
Added insulation	23
Switched energy sources	8
Turned lights off	3

Source: U.S. Dept. of Agriculture (1974).

siderably. Knowing what the usage of energy is and charting it month-by-month from year-to-year can motivate employees to help reduce usage (Table 16.3). Dividing the previous total energy bills by the number of meals or customers served gives the total energy cost per meal.

The rates charged for electricity are based on the peak demand—the highest average usage during the billing period. If the use of electricity is more evenly distributed throughout the day so that the peak demand is lowered (e.g., by baking cookies during nonpeak time), the rate reduction can be considerable. To help reduce "peak demand," install a "demand limiter" which can be set to sound a warning bell when energy usage reaches a predetermined level. Simple conservation measures can reduce energy use by 10 to 20%. These include using computer-controlled timers and more energy-efficient equipment, turning on equipment only when needed, and installing timers on all types of equipment (Table 16.4).

Reusing Energy. Energy recovery is defined as the utilization of heat energy that is usually lost. Heat energy could be recovered and reused from such sources as hood exhaust fans, laundry dryer exhaust, condensers on freezers and coolers, hot waste water and steam condensate.

The Wolf Snorkler convection oven recirculates heated air that in other ovens is exhausted out the hood. Recovered heat energy also can be used to preheat incoming cold water to a hot water heater, thus reducing the energy needed to heat water to the required temperature. Another possibility would be to use recovered heat in steamtables or other warming devices.

Reducing Energy Use. There are any number of ways that a foodservice can become more energy efficient and thus reduce energy costs. Replacing existing equipment with more energy-efficient types may be cost effective in the long run. Selection of equipment for new facilities should take energy considerations into account. For example, cooking time in forced-air convection ovens is at least 25% less than that in conventional

FIG. 16.1. In this forced-air convection oven, heat exchangers along each side, behind the perforated side panels, pull air through and recirculate it back into the oven. This design reduces energy use by 40% compared with other types of convection ovens.
Courtesy of Vulcan-Hart Corp.

deck-type ovens (Fig. 16.1). Microcomputers will soon be placed in many of ovens to aid in adjusting temperatures and to eliminate over- and underheating.

Fluorescent lights are more energy efficient than incandescent ones. In an effort to reduce energy costs, however, do not reduce lighting in the kitchen area. The kitchen area should have a minimum lighting of 70 foot-candles; where quick service is to be encouraged increase that to 100 foot-candles.

Use chemicals to sanitize dishes and utensils, thus eliminating the need to heat water to 180°F. Lower the hot water heater to 140°F for washing pots and pans. Use a wetting agent in rinse water to help speed drying. Other recommendations for saving energy are summarized below:

1. Preheat cooking equipment only as long as necessary at the temperature desired.
2. Adjust heat of stove-top cooking units to size of pan.
3. Cook at the lowest temperature needed.
4. Load an oven to capacity, schedule food products to use receding heat.
5. Reduce frequency of opening oven and refrigeration doors.
6. Turn off equipment (including lights) when not in use.
7. Use timers.
8. Repair leaky faucets.
9. Load and unload refrigeration in the shortest time possible and open units as seldom as possible.
10. Install entry drapes on walk-in refrigeration.
11. Establish a preventive maintenance program.

Energy conservation principles must be adapted and integrated throughout a foodservice operation. Since the oil embargo of 1973, conserving energy has been an important national objective. The foodservice industry may be using 35 to 50% more energy than is necessary.

Automation

The late 1980s will bring a new world in equipment automation with the use of "chips" (computerization) and solar energy. Much of what can be expected can be previewed at the U.S. Naval Academy in Annapolis where an advanced food preparation system called "Rapid Automatic Food Preparation Techniques" (RAFT), was installed in the mid-1980s. This system uses equipment such as continuous infrared broilers, fryers, blanchers steam kettle elevators, and pumps. The goal is to provide 4000 meals in 30 minutes. Preparation time has been reduced from 2 hours to 30 minutes. Labor-hours were reduced by 25–30%, for an estimated savings the first year of $137,000. Additionally, the floor space requirements were reduced by 2000 square feet.

By 1990, microcomputers will be commonplace in all types of equipment, doing everything from detecting doneness in deep-fat fryers to automatically turning on equipment for preheating based on preprogrammed cycle menus.

PREPARATION EQUIPMENT

The preparation of food for cooking and serving is time-consuming without power equipment. The amount and type of preparation equipment needed for a foodservice is directly related to the amount of preparation to be done. When presliced meats and cheese are purchased, the need for a slicing machine may be questioned. Some of the most commonly used preparation equipment are discussed in this section.

Mixing Machines

Mixers come in many different sizes and are manufactured by many different companies. They are usually trouble-free if properly operated. The sizes most frequently used in school preparation are 20 quart, 30 quart, and 60 quart. Using a mixer of the correct size is very important. A mixer that is too large can be as much a problem for the operator as one too small. The correct-sized mixer can reduce the time spent in preparation by one-half. If a baker is mixing a cake for 400 servings in a 30-quart mixer, two mixings will be required. This means that ingredients have to be weighed and combined twice, and the possibility of error in weighing is triple, since the average baker becomes less cautious on the second weighing. Yet, if a 60-quart mixer is available, mixing takes half the baker's time. Some companies have bowl adapters for their mixers. Thus, a 30-quart bowl will fit a 60-quart mixer, and a 20-quart bowl can be used on the 30-quart mixer. Again, determining the size mixer needed depends on what is to be mixed, and how much. To compute this accurately, the menus and recipes should be consulted. The capacity of mixers given in Table 16.5 will be helpful.

Bench model mixers usually hold 5 to 20 quarts. Mixers with a greater capacity are attached to the floor. Recommended features are sealed-in motor, stainless steel bowls, timer, adequate horsepower ($\frac{1}{2}$ hp for 20 quart, $\frac{3}{4}$ hp for 30 quart (and 1$\frac{1}{2}$ hp for a 60 quart), and attachment hub. The larger mixers—60 quart and up—need bowl dollies; an electric bowl raiser is also available. Additional extras for mixers are dough arms (particularly good for mixing yeast bread), pastry-blending beater (used for cutting in fat), bowl rim extenders, and bowl splash covers (Figs. 16.2A and B). It's helpful if service and replacement parts are available in the local area.

An attachment hub allows the motor of the mixer to be used for operating attachments that slice, dice, grate, and chop. The standard equipment that comes with most mixers are a flat beater, a wire whip, and a tinned steel bowl. The attachments for slicing, dicing, grating, and chopping are pur-

TABLE 16.5. Mixer Capacities

Capacity	20-Qt Mixer	30-Qt Mixer	60-Qt Mixer
Cookies	420 (32 doz)	600 (50 doz)	1200 (100 doz)
Sheet cakes	20 lb	30 lb	60 lb
Pie dough	18 lb	27 lb	50 lb
Yeast rolls	27 lb	45 lb	80 lb

FIG. 16.2A. Mixer with batter-beater attachment.
Courtesy of Hobart Company.

FIG. 16.2B. Mixer with pastry-blending-beater attachment.
Courtesy of Hobart Company.

chased separately. The tinned steel bowl has a short life, thus stainless steel bowls are recommended.

Cutting Machines

Food cutters are available in two very different pieces of equipment. One is referred to as a food cutter and the other as a vertical cutter-mixer. The food cutter has a rotating bowl with two power-driven knives (Figs. 16.3A and B) ranging in size and power. Some cutters have an attachment hub with which the motor can be used for attachments that slice, dice, grate, and chop. If the mixer and the cutter are made by the same manufacturing company, the attachments are interchangeable. Safety features are of utmost importance on this piece of equipment. It should be easy to clean and be heavy duty with sufficient horsepower. Cutters are available in bench or pedestal models. The cutter can be utilized more efficiently in most kitchens when it's placed on a mobile table.

The vertical cutter-mixer (VCM), when first introduced to this country about 20 to 25 years ago, was called a *schnellcutter,* German for "fast cutting." The vertical cutter operates at very high speeds, and will cut, mix, and blend in seconds (Table 16.6). It has replaced both the mixer and

Top opening for strips 7/16 in. square. Great for french fries, salad lettuce, and soup stocks.

Top opening for strips 3/16 in. square. Ideal for julienne strips, carrot and beet sticks; fine chopping of celery for chicken and tuna salads and soup stocks.

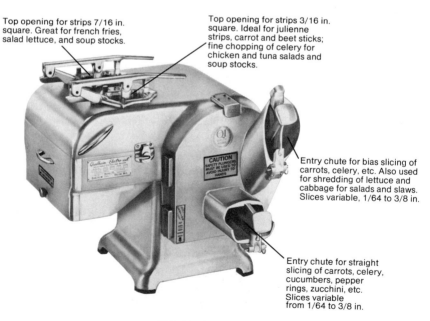

Entry chute for bias slicing of carrots, celery, etc. Also used for shredding of lettuce and cabbage for salads and slaws. Slices variable, 1/64 to 3/8 in.

Entry chute for straight slicing of carrots, celery, cucumbers, pepper rings, zucchini, etc. Slices variable from 1/64 to 3/8 in.

FIG. 16.3A. Food cutter.
Courtesy of Qualheim, Inc.

FIG. 16.3B. Food cutter (front) and slicer (rear).
Courtesy of Hobart Company.

cutter in some foodservices at a reduced cost and with increased efficiency (Fig. 16.4). The VCM will not incorporate air, therefore will not whip meringues or cream. Standard VCMs come in 25-, 40-, and 60-quart sizes; larger sizes up to 120 quarts are available on special order. Since a VCM is much faster than a regular cutter or mixer, sometimes a smaller size of VCM is selected; however, to obtain the maximum speed and labor saving that this piece of equipment can provide, a large foodservice should purchase

**TABLE 16.6. Preparation Time
with Vertical Cutter-Mixer**

Product	Quantities	Processing Time
Chopped cheese	10–20 lb	30–45 sec
Tossed salad	4–6 heads	4 sec
Coleslaw	10–20 lb	30 sec
Salad dressing	10–20 qt	2–3 min
Vegetable chunks	5–10 lb	15–30 sec

Source: Hidden Valley Ranch Secret Salad System.

362 Equipment

FIG. 16.4. Vertical cutter-mixer has many uses and operates at very high speeds. *Courtesy of Hobart Company.*

the size most near the mixer size appropriate for the operation. Recipes may need slight adjustments in order for cakes, breads, cookies, pastries, and dressings previously mixed in a mixer to be mixed in a VCM. The staff must be properly trained to get the full benefit from a VCM. Training is imperative—and it takes more than one demonstration.

For efficient use and ease of cleaning a source of water with wash-down hose must be available at the VCM. Three-phase electrical outlets are required. A 40-quart VCM operates with 9 hp at 1750 rpm and with 12 hp at 3500 rpm. A recessed floor drain enclosure is desirable; however, other types of drains can be hooked up. The bowl tilts forward for easy pouring. A mobile cart is available that holds pans at the right height for the lip of the bowl when it is tilted for easy pouring.

Slicing machines come in a variety of sizes. The diameter of the blades determines the size of foods that can be sliced. The thickness of slices is easily set on all models and the range in thickness is broad. Gravity feed, which is at an angle, is recommended over vertical feed, which requires

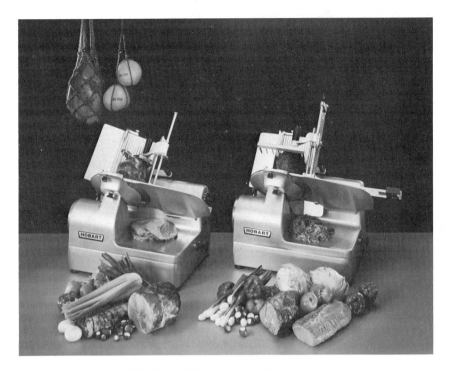

FIG. 16.5. Slicing machine with gravity feed.
Courtesy of Hobart Company.

more physical manpower to operate (Fig. 16.5). An automatic gravity feed is also available and is a labor-saving feature to be considered in larger foodservices.

Much of the exterior of slicing machines should be stainless steel with anodized aluminum used for economy. The knives should be made from high-quality stainless steel, which will take and hold a keen edge. Sharpening devices are needed. The knives should be well guarded with all safety features possible. A slicing machine should be easy to take apart for cleaning with no crevices where food will get caught. Self-contained scales to weigh portions as they are sliced and counters to count the portions as sliced are added features available on some brands.

COOKING EQUIPMENT

The type and quantities of food to be prepared in a foodservice are prime considerations in selecting cooking equipment.

Ovens

Ovens have changed a great deal in the last 20 years with a greater variety now available and with the standardization of chambers. Convection ovens are rapidly replacing deck ovens.

Deck Ovens. The traditional (standard) deck oven has been reduced in size and bulkiness but increased in capacity. Heavy-duty ovens are now standardized to fit the 18-inch modular. For school foodservice a standard heavy-duty oven is recommended over restaurant range-type ovens.

Ovens are available in two main deck heights, known as bake ovens and roast ovens. Bake oven decks are 4 to 8 inches high. Roast oven decks are between 11 and 15 inches high. Frequently a roast oven and a bake oven are stacked. The height of the ovens when stacked should be considered. When more than two ovens are stacked, the top deck door may be too high for the operator to remove pans without using a stool, which is a safety hazard. The bottom deck, if too close to the floor, is inconvenient to use.

An oven should be easy to clean and safe to use. It should have good insulation, handles that are cool to the touch, doors that will hold up under weight, thermostatic controls of 150 to 550°F on each deck, signal lights to indicate when the oven is on, vented chambers, dampered with baffling, controls in front, easy-to-get-to heights that can be reached by the operator, and construction of 16 to 18 gage metal. The oven should preheat to 450°F in 20 minutes and after the door has been opened have good recovery to the set temperature. The insulation is very important to the efficient, economical operation of the oven. If it is gas operated, the decks give best results when separately fired. When decks are stacked, the heat sometimes is uneven and affected by the heat from the decks above or below. Insulation and proper venting are important, particularly when ovens are stacked.

Convection Ovens. Savings in time, space, and fuel are possible with convection ovens. These ovens can produce more in 30% less space than conventional ovens. They have high-speed blowers that constantly circulate heated air around the food in the oven. The forced air motion increases the absorption of heat and decreases the time needed for cooking most foods by at least 25%. The temperature at which most foods are cooked is on the average 25 degrees lower in convection ovens than in conventional ovens. The decreased time and lower temperatures needed for cooking mean an economy of fuel in operation. A convection oven bakes, roasts/browns, reconstitutes, defrosts, and reheats food (Fig. 16.6).

The outside dimensions differ from one manufacturer to another, but most standard single-stack ovens hold pans up to 11 × 18 × 26 inches. Double stacks can be used if there is limited space in the kitchen. The

FIG. 16.6. Convection oven such as this with forced-circulated air will brown, bake, reconstitute, defrost, and reheat food in less time, and with less energy, than a standard deck oven.
Courtesy of Garland Commercial Industries, Inc.

thermostat controls are more reliable on single stacks. Some manufacturers have had problems with thermostats when units are stacked.

The oven front should be of stainless steel with either a stainless steel or porcelainized interior. A minimum of a ⅓-hp driven motor is needed on the fan. The exterior sides and back may be of enamel or stainless steel finishes. Different types of doors are available, but the French doors have proved very accessible. Heavy-duty, chrome-plated racks are recommended. Other desirable features include controls located on front with timer; overload protection; easy-to-read dials that will keep the printed numbers after wear; and lights on the inside with see-through windows.

The capacity of one convection oven has been estimated by Wilkinson (1975) as follows:

366　　　　　　　🔟 Equipment

Reheats 88 frozen meals to hot in 20 minutes.
Cooks 150 pounds of beef at one time.
Cooks 120 pounds of poultry at one time.
Cooks 480 orders of 2 eggs each.
Bakes six 18- by 26-inch pans of pastries.
Bakes 24 1¼-pound loaves of bread.
Bakes 36 8- to 10-inch pies.
Bakes 75 casserole dishes.
Bakes 3 bushels of 80-count Idaho potatoes.

The roll-in rack convection oven has been designed for reconstituting frozen dinners (Fig. 16.7). The dinners can be placed in the rack to store overnight in the freezer or refrigerator, then rolled into the oven for reconstitution. The same racks are rolled from the oven to the serving area to be served from. This reduces handling and saves time. The manufacturers have designed efficiency into these pieces of equipment. Temperature of the oven is very important and should be checked frequently for accuracy.

FIG. 16.7. Roll-in rack convection oven with a high-cart docking device is very convenient for reconstituting frozen dinners.
Courtesy of Vulcan-Hart Corp.

Microwave Ovens. Microwave ovens are being used very successfully in connection with vending machines in some operations and occasionally are used as a backup to the serving counter. Their capacity varies from just large enough to cook or heat individual entrees up to large enough to cook or heat food in bulk. Microwave ovens are used for thawing, heating, and reheating.

Commercial microwave ovens are available with output rates of 600 to 2000 watts. The higher the wattage, the greater the cooking speed. An oven with 1200 watts of power will heat food twice as fast as one with 600 watts. The following points should be remembered when using a microwave oven:

1. The higher the initial temperature of the product, the faster it will reach the desired temperature.
2. The heavier the weight of the product, the longer it will take to cook.
3. Even-shaped foods heat faster and more uniformly than irregular-shaped foods.
4. Denser foods take longer to heat than porous ones.
5. Most foods heat better and faster if covered; however covered sandwiches may become soggy.
6. Large pieces should be placed on the outside edge of the dish or tray.

The advantage of the microwave oven is its speed. It cooks small quantities in seconds and can be operated by students. One potato, requiring 60 minutes in a conventional oven and 50 minutes in a convection oven, will bake in 2¼ minutes in a microwave oven. However, it takes 3½ minutes to bake two potatoes and 5½ minutes to bake four potatoes. The microwave oven is not efficient enough in quantity cooking but is excellent as a support to quantity cooking.

Ranges

Ranges (top-of-stove cooking) are not used much today, but are being replaced by grills, tilting skillets, and steam-cooking facilities. Some kitchens are completely without top-of-stove cooking facilities. Development of ranges with a magnetic field, which is energized by a coil under the cooking surface, have brought new interest to top-of-stove cooking. With this equipment, the range top does not heat up the room and utilizes energy quite efficiently, as the heat goes directly into the pan and stops when the pan is removed.

The heavy-duty or hotel range is designed for large-volume cooking and the wear resulting from use of heavy utensils. The tops are of three main kinds: open top (conventional), hot top (closed top), and fry top (griddle top). An open-top range has grates directly over the burners. The heat is instant and may be shut off instantly. It has less capacity than a hot top. Hot tops (closed tops) have continuous heat under the top and their efficiency depends on the types and location of the burners. A hot-top range may have an oven underneath or a cabinet for storage.

Grills and Griddles

Grills have top and bottom heat, whereas griddles have bottom heat only (Fig. 16.8). Cast-metal plates are not recommended for either because their porous surfaces cause foods to stick. The best heat transfer is obtained with chrome-finished plates, which are available grooved and flat. These plates are easy to clean and require no seasoning. Cold-rolled steel plates also have good heat transfer and are easy to clean. The 0.006 finish is desirable. The adherence quality of this finish reduces shrinkage.

Season the grid plate of a grill or griddle by preheating to 400°F. Apply a light coat of unsalted cooking oil and let stand 2 to 3 minutes, then wipe off. Repeat this procedure once more and it is ready to use.

Avoid rear grease drains on grills because they are very difficult to clean. Be sure the recovery of the unit will provide the volume product you need. Zone control of heat is more energy efficient and provides better temperature control when cooking different items. Splash guards on the back and sides are recommended. Timers are a must. The size grill needed by a school foodservice is probably best determined by how many hamburger patties will be cooked at one time. For example, an 18- by 24-inch electric grill can cook 32 patties per load and produce 480 per hour; an 18- by 48-inch grill can handle 86 per load or 1300 per hour.

Griddles are being used by some schools to prepare breakfast foods, such as pancakes and bacon. They are particularly good for cooking steaks. The Btu input is very important; for example, a modern gas-fired griddle would need about 30,000 Btu per burner. It is important that specifications state the Btu input per square inch and call for evenly spaced "snap-action" thermostats. Griddles range in width from 18 to 72 inches. The surface

FIG. 16.8.   This gas countertop griddle can cook 1392 hamburgers per hour.
Courtesy of Wells Manufacturing Co.

should be smooth so that fat does not accumulate but runs off providing an ungreased surface.

Steamers and Pressure Cookers

Steam cooking is efficient and fast. Four different types of equipment are used to cook by steam: the compartment steamer, steam-jacketed kettle, convection steamer, and countertop pressure cooker. Some steamers use live steam under pressure, whereas others are pressureless. To utilize steam cooking to the fullest, the physical layout must provide the following:

1. *Adequate steam pressure.* For pressurized steamers, a minimum steam pressure of 15 pounds per square inch is needed the year round. Live steam from a boiler may produce uneven pressure in different seasons of the year. Self-contained steam-operated equipment is available. An independent boiler for just the foodservice is usually more economical and performs more satisfactorily than self-contained units.

2. *Water supply.* A supply of hot and cold water is needed at the point of use. A swing or swivel faucet is recommended, particularly with the steam-jacketed kettle.

3. *Adequate drainage.* Drainage at the point of use is essential for ease in cleaning. A recessed floor with drain pipes at least 4 inches in diameter are needed. For more than two pieces of steam equipment, 6-inch pipes or two 4-inch pipes are recommended.

4. *Ventilation.* Good ventilation is necessary. The area needs to be hooded with exhaust fans to remove the steam.

5. *Adequate power source.* Adequate voltage and phase are required for electric steamers. If the unit is gas powered, the supply of gas must be sufficient for efficient use of the equipment.

Pressurized Steamers. Low-pressure steamers provide 3–5 pounds per square inch pressure on the food; high-pressure steamers, 13–15 pounds per square inch. These steamers use live steam in direct contact with the food. Pressure steam cooking is the preferred method for cooking vegetables largely because it retains the nutritional value of food better than most other cooking methods. Pressure steamers are fast and efficient, eliminate the need for heavy pots and pans, and encourage batch (as you need it) preparation, which helps eliminate leftovers. The color and texture of food are preserved. There is a reduction in shrinkage of meats when cooked by steam. The food is cooked and served in the same pans, thus eliminating some pot and pan washing. Many foods, in addition to vegetables, can be cooked efficiently by steam; these include pasta, rice, eggs, and moist-heat cooked meats.

Further arguments in favor of the steamer are that it requires little floor space, reduces the loss of heat in the kitchen while cooking, and permits cooking of different foods in the same chamber without transfer of flavor.

Pressure steamers should have stainless steel interior finish and automatic safety devices that will prevent the door from being opened when the unit is on. Baked-on enamel is a satisfactory exterior finish; however, stainless steel is available. Employees are often afraid to use pressurized steam equipment, so thorough demonstration and follow-up is recommended to be certain the equipment is utilized. New employees should be trained in how to operate steam equipment.

The convection steamer combines convection cooking and steam (Figs. 16.9 and 16.10). The steam circulates through convection generators around the food, providing a cooking speed comparable to 15 pounds pressure. Since there is no pressure in the compartment you can open the door at any point to add more food without interrupting the cooking. Each compartment has the capacity for three 12 × 20 × 2½ inch steamtable pans.

Pressureless Steamers. With pressureless steamers, the cooking starts the instant the compartment door is closed and stops the instant the door is opened. They pose none of the safety problems that live-steam pressure cookers do. Cooking is done at atmospheric pressure with a constant circular flow of steam around the food. The pressureless steamer does an excellent job of defrosting foods.

The energy used by a pressureless steamer is comparable to a pressurized steamer when the unit is filled to capacity. It is more efficient to have two smaller units than one large unit, unless the full capacity of a large unit will be needed frequently.

FIG. 16.9. This countertop natural convection steamer has a self-contained steam generator. It is perfect for batch cooking right behind a serving line and makes offering choices relatively simple.
Courtesy of Cleveland Range Co.

FIG. 16.10. This revolutionary steamer is a pressureless forced convection steamer with fully automatic operation that provides fast cooking. The steamer can be opened safely with the touch-on panel.
Courtesy of Cleveland Range Co.

Steam-Jacketed Kettle. The steam-jacketed kettle is described by Wilkinson (1975) as "two stainless steel hemispheres, or bowls, one sealed inside the other with about 2 inches space in between for the steam" (Fig. 16.11). Steam-jacketed kettles come full jacketed, with steam all the way to the top, and two-thirds jacketed. The diameters vary as well as the capacity. Kettles range in size from 1 quart to 200 gallons. The most common table models are 10- to 20-quart tilting kettles, sometimes referred to as *trunnion* kettles. These units afford the ability to provide choices to students and to cook in batches, as needed. The floor or wall models come in many sizes but the most commonly used sizes in school feeding are 20, 30, 40, and 60 gallons. Kettles larger than 60 gallons are actually too large for people to

FIG. 16.11.   Steam kettles are often used for sauces, soups, and gravies.
Courtesy of U.S. Dept. of Agriculture.

operate—too high and really unmanageable. Two 30-gallon kettles, or a 40 and a 20, would be a better choice, perhaps, than a 60-gallon kettle. A stationary large kettle is safer, less trouble, and more satisfactory for a school foodservice than a large tilting kettle.

In selecting the size kettle needed, consider the number of portions, size of portions, and types of food to be prepared. Table 16.7 is a good guide for determining size. For example, if spaghetti sauce and soup are on the menu frequently and 1-cup portions will be used, the kettle chosen should be large enough to prepare in one batch the total amount of soup or sauce needed for serving the required number of 1-cup portions. The kettle lends itself to the cooking of soups, sauces, gravies, chili con carne, stews, puddings, pie fillings, gelatins, and other foods that can be prepared in bulk and not in small batches.

A trunnion or tilting kettle—table mounted, with a 10- to 20-quart capacity—along with a larger steam-jacketed kettle can eliminate the need for top-of-stove cooking. The small kettles that tilt can be used for everything ordinarily done on the top of the stove.

The interior of the steam-jacketed kettle is 18-8 gage stainless steel, and the exterior is stainless steel or aluminum with the former recommended. The rim should be rounded for safety. A draw-off value is very convenient. There should be safety features, such as a safety valve and pressure gauge

TABLE 16.7. Total Usable Capacities of Steam-Jacketed Kettles[1]

Kettle Size (gal.)	Gal.	Total Usable Capacity			
		Number of Individual Servings			
		Full Cup	¾ Cup	½ Cup	¼ Cup
20	16	256	341	512	1024
30	24	384	512	768	1536
40	32	512	683	1024	2048
60	48	768	1024	1536	3072

Source: *Planning School Food Service Facilities*, U.S. Dept. of Agriculture (1974).
[1]Table is based on usable capacity. Manufacturers generally express kettle size as total kettle capacity (level full) and the usable capacity is approximately 20% less than what is stated.

that is easy to read located in a convenient place. The stationary kettles can be mounted on legs, on a wall, or on a pedestal.

Counter Top Pressure Cookers. The counter or table top pressure cookers usually hold only one to two pans. They are designed for batch cooking (cooking as needed) and should be located as near to the serving line as possible.

Braising Pan. A tilting braising pan is an oversized skillet. It can braise, boil, sauté, pan-fry, simmer, kettle-cook, steam, proof, and even hold food like a steamtable. In fact one might consider purchasing one instead of a griddle because of its versatility. Again, a trough in the front of unit makes it easier to clean. This type of equipment can be mobile or permanently installed. A floor drain is desirable. The pans have thermostatically controlled temperatures and are made of stainless steel or cast iron.

Fryers

Deep-fat fryers are more and more prevalent in school feeding today with deep-fried foods being very popular. Features to look for in a deep-fat fryer are temperature control; fast recovery time; self-draining devices with continual or cycle filtering of food; sturdy, heavy-duty features; ease of cleaning; and all the safety features possible. The number and capacity of fryers needed depend on the quantity of food to be fried during the meal.

Pressure fryers cook with fat as the medium in a tightly covered "pot." Moisture is held in and the cooking temperature can be lower than with regular fryers. Since water is an enemy to fat, it is essential that the condensate be removed. Air fryers cook and brown the product without the use of fat. It is questionable how popular air fryers will become since the taste of fried foods most desired comes from the cooking of foods in fat.

Fryers are now available with built-in or remote computers that automate the basket lifts with timers that cook product to the perfect color. Computerized fryers with remote computers have probes to monitor crispness and doneness of product. Tests show that these fryers give a 10% better yield than do fryers without computer technology. Overcooking and undercooking are eliminated and fat life is extended.

Fire Protection Equipment

When fryers, ovens, and grills are added to a facility, the fire protection system must be evaluated. Older hoods over cooking equipment will probably have to be equipped with fire-extinguishing equipment, particularly if fryers or grills are added. Bulletin 96 from the National Fire Protection Association is useful in determining the system needed to meet fire department regulations and to make a kitchen safe.

Before going too far with the purchase of new cooking equipment, it is wise to check out the physical limitations and additional ventilation and fire protection requirements. The costs involved can exceed the cost of new cooking equipment.

REFRIGERATION

Self-contained refrigerator and freezer units have far more capacity today than a few years back. The compressors are more compact and are frequently housed at the top, which means the unit can be taller, utilizing all the space and increasing capacity. Self-defrosting refrigeration is equipped with a cycle-timed clock so that the unit automatically defrosts at specific times of the day with continuous condensate evaporation. This has eliminated the need for a plumbing connection and for manual defrosting. A one-piece interior of stainless steel is recommended. The exterior may be of porcelain enamel finish, aluminum, or stainless steel. The porcelain enamel finishes have added colors to the kitchen. A mounted exterior thermometer should be visible on the front of the unit with colors indicating temperature zones: for example, red markings indicating danger zone, with green indicating safe temperatures. A visual alarm system that will indicate when the temperature is above the recommended safe zone is helpful.

The doors of refrigerators and freezers come full or half, hinged, and self-closing or sliding. The quality of the hinges and tightness of the gasket fit should be closely checked. The standard number of shelves supplied with the units is usually not sufficient for most foodservices. The shelves should be of heavy-duty material and have adjustable brackets to space the shelves as wanted. If over 60 cubic feet of refrigeration is needed, a walk-in unit is recommended. The shelves should be adjustable and the size to accommodate modulars of 14 × 18 inches and 18 × 26 inches. Self-contained units are not built to take rough treatment, and the storage of heavy meats and crates will show on a unit quickly. Refrigeration units seem to be the least durable of kitchen equipment today and need considerable improvement.

There are various types of refrigerated units: reach-ins, pass-throughs, roll-ins, counter-type, display, portable or mobile, and dispensing (Fig. 16.12). The size refrigerator or freezer needed depends on whether a walk-in unit is available and what is going to be stored in the unit and how much. With an increase in frozen foods used, many foodservices need more freezer space than previously allocated. In determining the number of cubic feet of space needed, it is helpful to know that one cubic foot will hold approximately 30 pounds of food. Approximately 2.1 pounds of food (as pur-

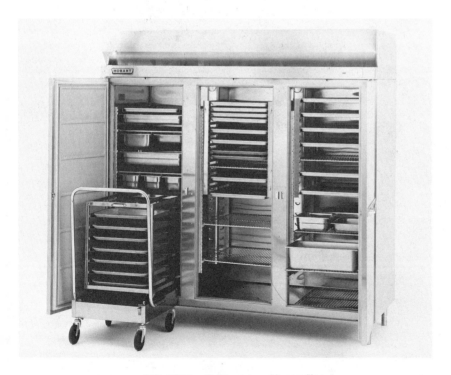

FIG. 16.12. Refrigerator with pan files.
Courtesy of Hobart Company.

chased) are used in preparing one meal. Schools serving 125 to 200 meals per day will need 17 to 20 cubic feet of refrigeration. Plan for 10 cubic feet more per each 100 meals.

MOBILE EQUIPMENT

Mobile equipment is flexible and convenient, saving space and labor-hours (Fig. 16.13). Mobile equipment makes work easier and reduces the handling of foods and supplies. A lightweight cart will not hold up under heavy-duty jobs. Mobile equipment is subject to heavy impact loads and heavy stress, and the design, materials, and construction have to be adequate to take this. Mobile equipment should contain few bolts and screws and be welded where possible. The wheels should be easy to roll and built to maneuver quietly and easily. The capacity of mobile units and the wheel

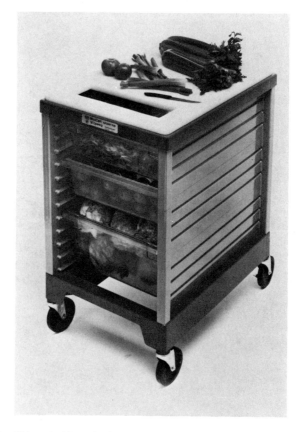

FIG. 16.13.   This cart with cutting board and storage space provides work space where it is needed.
Courtesy of Rubbermaid Commercial Products, Inc.

size should be coordinated. The 3-inch wheels will hold loads up to 200 pounds; 5-inch wheels will hold loads up to 400 pounds; 8-inch wheels will hold up to 600 pounds; and 10-inch wheels will carry loads exceeding 600 pounds. Therefore, utility carts and wheel size needed will be determined by the load to be carried and the space for maneuvering the carts in.

Wheels are easier to guide when rigid casters are at the guiding end and swivel casters are at the front end. All-swivel casters on a piece of equipment ensure easy movement from side to side, and these are recommended for dolly equipment that is to be moved short distances. However, equipment with all-swivel casters is hard to guide in straight travel. Wheel locks that will hold when the cart is stopped are recommended. Bumpers on mobile equipment will protect the walls and other equipment. Rubber tread wheels with ball bearings are recommended.

SERVING EQUIPMENT

Although cafeteria-style service is still the most common in school food-services, self-service is growing in popularity. Portable serving units can be used to supplement regular serving lines (Fig. 16.14).

How many students are served per minute? This will be determined by the speed of employees, number of menu items, complexity of the menu, and general arrangement of the serving area. Average serving speeds are 10 meals per minute for lunch without choice, 7–9 meals per minute for lunch with choice, and 5–7 meals per minute for lunch plus a la carte.

To determine how many serving areas should be set up, divide the seating capacity of the dining room (or number of students in a lunch period)

FIG. 16.14. Portable four-well serving unit.
Courtesy of Seco Products.

by the speed of service. For example, if seating capacity is 350 and choice is offered, it will take approximately 44 minutes to serve everyone on one serving line (350 ÷ 8). Since students will not stand in line that long in high schools, it would be desirable to have at least two serving areas and a snack bar to relieve the serving line of milk and a la carte sales.

Avoid the sterile look in serving areas by chosing colorful equipment and using lively wall decor. Serving equipment should have 14-gage stainless steel tops; the sides and ends may be 20-gage stainless steel, colorful fiberglass, or formed plastic. Avoid custom-designed equipment if possible, as it is expensive. Modular units that are portable and that can be taken apart and rearranged have many advantages. If population shifts occur, centralized school districts can move modular equipment where needed. Also, changes in menu offerings that change the equipment needs may be accommodated with modular units.

The "shopping-center" arrangement is popular with universities and colleges. The concept is good for high school students, too. Food is set up in stations, such as a deli or grill for sandwiches, "greenery" for salads, dessert bar, beverage area, special of the day (hot entree), etc.

An interesting concept is the carousel or moving circular unit. It is a complete circle, approximately 86 inches in diameter, up to 75 inches high. The carousel rotates at the rate of one revolution per minute. If built into the wall between the dining area and the kitchen, the food can be replenished as the carousel makes its revolutions. The advantage is that six to eight people can be served at the same time. The manufacturers claim it occupies 35% to 50% less space than a traditional serving line accommodating the same numbers.

Serving equipment needs will be determined by the menu offerings. How large does the hot table need to be? The most common hot tables range in size from those with four wells to those with eight wells. The wells each hold a 12- by 20-inch steamtable pan. On the servers' side there is usually a shelf or cutting board, made of Richlite maple or stainless steel; the latter is preferred.

If self-service is going to be used, a tray rail may be located on both sides of the serving unit with a double sneeze guard. Cold sections come in 3-foot to 8-foot units. They are available with built-in refrigeration or with wells to accommodate the use of ice for keeping food cold.

Be aware of the height of the tray rail. For elementary children, 30 to 32 inches high is recommended; secondary-age students can use 34 to 36 inches high.

Ice Cream Cabinets

Ice cream cabinet sizes are expressed in the number of gallons of ice cream units hold. A unit 3 feet 6 inches long holds 25 gallons and usually has

FIG. 16.15. This floor model milkshake machine dispenses two flavors. *Courtesy of Taylor Freezer Co.*

a ¼-hp motor. A 6-foot 6-inch unit holds 55 gallons and has a ½-hp motor. The interior should be of stainless steel to avoid rust problems. The lining also comes in galvanized steel, anodized aluminum, and plastic. The hinged top should lift completely out easily. Also to be considered are milkshake machines (Fig. 16.15).

Milk Cooler

Since milk is generally self-service, the height of the milk cooler opening is very important, especially in elementary school. Dispensing-type milk coolers are convenient for customers, but are time-consuming to fill. Also, if these units stand open for long periods, they sometimes frost up and prevent the dispensing mechanism from functioning correctly.

Drop-front milk coolers are very popular. The units are mobile and are available with interiors and exteriors of stainless steel, fiberglass, formed plastic, etc. Make sure the interior materials do not rust. Determine the size of cooler needed by the number of milk containers the unit holds. For example:

Size Cooler	Flat-Top Cartons	Gable-Top Cartons
36 inches wide	864	680
48 inches wide	1368	1020
63 inches wide	1800	1360

CLEANING EQUIPMENT

Dishwashing machines are an intricate part of sanitation, and they are a large investment. The price difference among models often encourages unwise decisions. The size of the operation, the number of dishes, the amount of labor, and the time available to wash dishes should be considered in making a selection. Will a door-type, a single- or double-tank conveyor, or a flight-type dishwasher be needed?

Dish Table

The dish table setup is as important to the efficient operation as the dishwasher. A minimum 100-inch clean dish table is needed for a conveyor machine. And if only one dishroom operator is available, 120 inches should be considered minimum. The 100 inches is sufficient space for four racks to dry. The soiled dish table also should be a minimum of 100 inches. The tables should be constructed of 14-gage polished stainless steel. The arrangement of the disposal and prerinse sink can make for an efficiently flowing operation or become a bottleneck. The length and arrangement of the layout can yield maximum efficiency or, if incorrect, can cut output to 25% or less of the maximum.

General Features of Dishwashers

The interior of a dishwasher should be constructed of 16-gage stainless steel or of a material that has been proved to hold up under heat and detergents. Galvanized metals have a life of 7 to 10 years, whereas stainless steel can be expected to last 14 to 20 years, depending on care and use. A 14- to 16-gage stainless steel is recommended for the interior and exterior of the machine. Automatic thermostats and automatic cycles are essential for the best operation. The legs should be seated with adjustable bullet-type or sanitary-type feet. A front inspection door is recommended. Ease in cleaning the machine should be considered. The NSF and UL approval seals should be on the machine.

The 20 × 20 inch racks are standard. All plastic racks are light in weight and hold up well. Adequate supply of water is essential. The wash water temperature must be 140 to 160°F with the rinse water 180 to 200°F. A booster heater or electric tank heater is used to raise the temperature of the fill water from 140 to 180°F. Three dial-type hydraulic thermometers at the top of the machine should indicate the temperatures of the water in each cycle. Adequate ventilation is necessary for removing the steam and heat. Electronic or hydraulic detergent dispensers and rinse injectors are available and recommended.

With increased concerns for energy costs have come many advancements and changes in equipment. Low-temperature dishwashers reduce energy usage, have a lower initial cost, but have a lower capacity. For example, a single-rack low-temperature machine will wash only 28 racks of dishes per hour compared to 53 racks per hour for a hot-temperature machine. The level of sanitation with chemicals in low-temperature dishwashers is higher than with hot-temperature machines.

The base price of a dishwasher may be deceiving. The options considered essential by the purchaser will increase the price considerably. The standard number of racks furnished with each machine is usually not adequate. The efficiency of the machine would be hampered by lack of racks.

The capacity of a machine can be misleading. Company, advertisements may be based on 100% capacity, which is impossible to accomplish in a normal operation. Seventy percent of the actual capacity of the machine is a more realistic figure.

The use of a dishwasher only as a sterilizer is a complete waste of detergent and water. The machine should be used for cleaning as well as sterilizing. Dishwashers can and should be used to wash utensils and equipment other than dishes. Any piece of equipment that can be immersed into 180°F water and that will fit into or on a rack with sufficient top of machine clearance—and this should be checked carefully—can be washed quickly, sterilized, and started on its way to drying by the dishwasher, especially pots and pans. Low-temperature dishwashing, using chemicals for sanitizing, slows the drying process.

Door-Type Machine. A door-type single-tank machine is suitable for up to 250, possibly 300 lunches. It requires opening and closing of the doors. The machine fits into a small area for a straight-through operation or a corner operation. Manually or electrically timed wash and rinse cycles are available. An electrically timed model is recommended.

Single-Tank Conveyor A single-tank conveyor is adequate for 600 to 800 lunches. A conveyor machine has curtains at either end and the racks

382

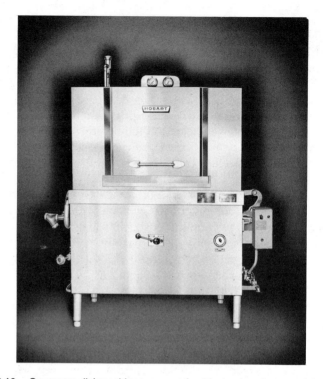

FIG. 16.16. Conveyor dishmachines are preferable to door-type models for larger operations.
Courtesy of Hobart Company.

are carried by a conveyor through the machine, from the wash to the rinse, and to the drying, and out the machine (Fig. 16.16). The clearance (height) inside the tank should be noted. The water is usually recycled, and this helps economize on water used. The speed of the conveyor is preset under regulations of the National Sanitation Foundation.

Two-Tank Machine Two-tank machines feature power-wash and power-rinse that result in a faster operation. This size machine can accommodate dishes for 2000 satisfactorily. The quantity of water used by a particular machine should be considered. The addition of a belt conveyor leading into the machine can increase the efficiency of the operation twofold. The belt tends to cause employees to work rhythmically and to keep their minds on the assembling and speed of the operation.

Three-Tank Machine. A three-tank machine has a prewash tank that saves considerable time. Many of the one-, two-, and three-tank machines with forced water have been able to virtually eliminate the need for prerinse, which can slow down an operation. The only objection to this is the food accumulation and the water being recycled. A high-pressured, hand-operated spray over a sink with a disposal unit is efficient for prerinsing racked dishes if employees are trained in using it.

Flight-Type Machine. The flight-type machine is a rackless operation that is available with one, two, or three tanks. It has continuous action and therefore uses a lot of water and detergents. Two to four people are required for loading and unloading this type of machine to obtain the efficiency intended. It does accommodate all sizes and shapes of dishes and small equipment, and requires no lifting of trays. The speed of the conveyor can be regulated according to the number of workers and number of soiled dishes. This is a piece of equipment that may be considered when serving over 1000 lunches. Considerable space is required.

Sinks

Sinks are ordinarily a part of the initial layout, and sinks made of stainless steel will usually last the life of the building. However, if it is necessary to purchase a sink, only stainless steel should be considered. Galvanized is most unsatisfactory. The sinks should be constructed of stainless steel, welded seamless, with coved corners, drain boards that slope toward the center for draining, a bottom that slopes toward the drain, and a mixing faucet with swing spout.

Local and state health department codes specify the minimum number of hand sinks and compartment sinks needed in a foodservice. The basic design and construction of a pot sink, vegetable sink, or cook's sink should include rounded corners, made of 14-gage 18-8 stainless steel with one-piece or seamless construction and knee-action drain stoppers. The legs should be 14-gage tubular stainless steel with adjusting bullet feet. The height of the sink bottom from the floor should be considered, as well as the dimensions of the compartments. A vegetable sink has two compartments, and the recommended size for each compartment is 20 inches square by 14 inches deep, inside measurement. Two drainboards each 24 inches long are suggested; both should drain into the sink. The pot and pan sink is a three-compartment sink with drainboards at either end. The cook's sink may have only one compartment, as small as 15 inches square and 8 or 12 inches deep.

SMALL EQUIPMENT

When purchasing small equipment, check for durable, heavy-duty construction and for materials that will withstand sterilizing temperatures and strong detergents. Institutional small equipment should be of a better, heavier quality than would normally be used at home. One of the most common problems with metal equipment is rusting. Stainless steel and heavy aluminum are recommended. Construction materials should be smooth, nontoxic, nonabsorbent, sanitary, and corrosion resistant.

Aluminum has the advantage of being lighter in weight than some other metals and is a good conductor of heat. However, aluminum utensils may become discolored by alkali and acid foods.

Stainless steel wears indefinitely. It has the advantage of being easy to clean, resistant to ordinary stains and corrosion, and sanitary. Stainless steel withstands temperatures and holds up well to sudden changes in temperatures.

Plastics are most frequently used for tableware in schools. The choices are limitless, and checking quality and durability is the job of the foodservice. Small equipment includes numerous items, which are available in many grades and designs. Therefore, they will not be discussed in detail here. Trade catalogs and current publications offer the most help in writing specifications and making selections. Testing small quantities before purchasing in large quantities is recommended.

RECORDS

Records should be kept on each piece of large or mechanical equipment purchased. These records should contain information as to when purchased, from whom, model, serial number, electrical information, etc. (Fig. 16.17). For guaranteed equipment, the warranty card has to be completed and returned to the manufacturer. The guarantee period should be recorded. Repairs to and problems with each piece of equipment should be recorded. This information will be very useful in the future for determining if a brand of equipment should be purchased again. This record may be kept by the individual foodservice or by the main office if a centralized system is to be used.

Depreciation of Equipment

Depreciation of nonexpendable equipment may be calculated in connection with cost accounting and the depreciation treated as an expense. It is usually to the advantage of the school foodservice program to set aside funds for replacing the equipment. Nonexpendable equipment includes all foodservice equipment with a useful life of more than one year and a purchase price of $300 or more. Depreciation is based on the concept of "using up" the equipment. For example, if a piece of equipment is expected to last

Item_____ Trade Name_____

Manufacturer_____ Model No._____

Serial No._____ Description_____

Capacity_____ Attachments_____

Operation: ____Gas ____Steam ____Hand ____Elect ____Voltage____

Cycle____ Phase____

Dealer or Vendor_____ Address_____

_____ Person to Contact_____ Phone No.____

Date Purchased_____ Warranty Period_____

Purchased Price_____ Life of Equipment_____

Remarks:

SERVICE AND REPAIRS

Date	Nature of Service	Parts, etc.	Service Co.	Cost

FIG. 16.17. Sample foodservice equipment record.

12 years, one-twelfth of the equipment's usefulness is "used up" each year of service. After 12 years, it is considered fully depreciated.

A depreciation record is needed on each piece of nonexpendable equipment that includes (1) net acquisition cost, (2) date purchased, (3) federal equipment funds used, if any, and (4) depreciable life. All nonexpendable equipment is considered to have a useful life of 12 years, whereas transporting equipment, used in transporting food from one location to another, has a shorter life. These records can be useful in determining the life of different pieces and brands of equipment.

TRAINING AND DEMONSTRATIONS

On-the-job training is important for employees to operate each piece of equipment correctly and to get full value of the equipment. If steps are to be followed in sequence during operation, they may be numbered and written on or posted near the equipment. Giving workers a manual to read is not as effective as on-the-job training with a demonstration of the correct ways to use, care for, and clean. Vendors should be requested to give demonstrations and instruction on the use and care of each new piece of equipment. This should be written into the bid specifications. Films are available that show step-by-step how to use and clean various pieces of equipment. Manufacturers can furnish these films.

CARE AND MAINTENANCE

High-quality equipment, though more expensive initially, may be the most economical in the long run. Handling and care of equipment by employees will determine the life of equipment. An untrained employee operating a mixer can do considerable damage to the motor.

Preventive maintenance requires periodic checking of equipment for loose bolts, worn parts, greasing if needed, and general repairs before the equipment has broken down. The advantages are longer equipment life and reduced maintenance costs. Breakdowns of equipment during operation are inconvenient to the operator and are more costly than preventive maintenance in time and money. A maintenance checklist is shown in Fig. 16.18.

A franchised factory service agency should be used when repairs are needed. Manufacturers will stand behind their own service work and usually have well-trained servicemen for each type of equipment. Specifications for purchasing equipment may include that a local service company carries parts for the equipment purchased. Many larger school systems have their own maintenance department with servicemen trained to repair the equipment in the schools.

Obsolete Equipment

Equipment of the past, such as vegetable peelers, meat saws, huge mixers, and meat grinders, should be removed from a kitchen if they are not being used. Such equipment has been displaced by convenience foods—preportioned and dehydrated and frozen prepared foods—in many schools. Sometimes the equipment put into new schools is obsolete by the time the school opens. This may happen when plans are designed years earlier and by the time the school opens the philosophy of the foodservice and its

SCHOOL LUNCH
PREVENTIVE MAINTENANCE
CHECKLIST

School   School No.   Address

Dishwasher
- [ ] Lubricate all points
- [ ] Change oil in transmission (once a year)
- [ ] Check pump assembly for leaks
- [ ] Check pump impeller
- [ ] Check pump pressure
- [ ] Check manifolds for play
- [ ] Check spray tubes
- [ ] Check and clean rinse nozzles
- [ ] Check final rinse lever
- [ ] Check drain and overflow
- [ ] Check fill valve washers for leaks
- [ ] Check rinse rapid action valve
- [ ] Check conveyor for tension and adjustment
- [ ] Check curtains (2 complete sets)
- [ ] Check door cables and pulley
- [ ] Check thermometers
- [ ] Check scrap trays
- [ ] Clean pump intake screen

Convection Oven
- [ ] Lubricate all points
- [ ] Check chamber seal
- [ ] Check timer
- [ ] Replace defective bulbs
- [ ] Check and adjust door tension

Slicers
- [ ] Sharpen blade
- [ ] Lubricate all points

Food Chopper
- [ ] Hone blades
- [ ] Tighten and adjust knives
- [ ] Lubricate all points
- [ ] Check hydraulic system
- [ ] Check for play in shaft
- [ ] Check brushes
- [ ] Check bowl rotation
- [ ] Clean and lubricate under bowl and top of plate

Steamers
- [ ] Drain, clean, flush and refill boiler
- [ ] Check safety valves
- [ ] Check door gaskets
- [ ] Lubricate handwheel shaft
- [ ] Check thermostatic vent
- [ ] Replace hand hole gasket
- [ ] Check muffler

Knives
- [ ] Sharpen and hone all knives
  Except Wearever Serrated

Dippers
- [ ] Replace springs
- [ ] Leave (2) extra springs*

Note: Dipper springs (2) and extra can opener blade will be left on school's copy of checklist—on table in kitchen.

T & S Pre-Rinse
- [ ] Check base
- [ ] Check squeeze valve
- [ ] Check check valves
- [ ] Check rubber bumper
- [ ] Clean spray head
- [ ] Check bracket
- [ ] Check hose

Can Opener
- [ ] Check blades
- [ ] Check gears
- [ ] Lubricate
- [ ] Leave (1) extra blade*

Stock Kettle
- [ ] Drain, flush and refill with rush inhibitor
- [ ] Check safety valves

Refrigeration Units
- [ ] Clean condensers and unit
- [ ] Lubricate all points
- [ ] Check belts, condition, tension and alignment
- [ ] Check head and back pressure
- [ ] Check sight glass for proper charge
- [ ] Check gaskets on water cooled condensers
- [ ] Check oil in compressor body
- [ ] Check tubing brackets
- [ ] Check and eliminate tubing rub
- [ ] Check door gaskets for condition and seal
- [ ] Check door hinges and latches
- [ ] Check door locks
- [ ] Clean all fixture drains
- [ ] Oil condenser fan motor
- [ ] Check fan blades for alignment
- [ ] Note if suction line insulation is needed

  Note: Pump down all open units on the spring check; electrically disconnect all others

Mixer or VCM
- [ ] Lubricate
- [ ] Check for oil leaks
- [ ] Remove broken whip wires
- [ ] Check switch
- [ ] Check blades
- [ ] Check lid gasket

Disposal
- [ ] Lubricate all points
- [ ] Check for sharpness
- [ ] Check seals for leaks
- [ ] Check flow switch and rapid action valve

Equipment Maintenance _____ Date _____
Signature of Service Man   Signature of School Representative
Refrigeration Maintenance _____ Date _____
Signature of Service Man   Signature of School Representative

FIG. 16.18. Sample preventive maintenance checklist.
Courtesy of Baltimore County (MD) Board of Education, School Lunch Office.

needs have changed. An example of this was an eastern university where the foodservice in one of the dormitories was equipped with more than $85,000 of preparation equipment, from a rotary oven to a combination steamer and numerous kettles. This plan was against the recommendations of the food director. Eight years later the equipment had still not been used, and was in the way of the unit that reconstituted frozen foods. Though that food director has since left, the university's foodservice philosophy now is—due to labor cost and supply—basically that the use of commercial baked goods, preportioned meats, and frozen prepared entrees is more economical than on-site preparation. The equipment required for a foodservice with this philosophy is different from that for one where on-site preparation is done. The equipment for an existing kitchen or for a new facility should be what the foodservice needs. Thus, those in foodservice should be a part of the planning committee that determines the equipment to be purchased.

BIBLIOGRAPHY

AVERY, A. C. 1980. A Modern Guide to Foodservice Equipment. CBI Publishing Co., Boston.

BURNHAM, L. J. 1979. The Delphi technique—National fast food executives to project industrial trends. M.S. Thesis, Univ. of Missouri, Columbia.

GREENWAY, D., T. SMALL, and R. HAGGUIST. 1979. The Food Service Operator's Guide to Energy Cost Savings. Texas Restaurant Association, Austin.

JERNIGAN, A. K., and L. N. ROSS. 1974. Food Service Equipment: Selection, Arrangement, and Use. Iowa State Univ. Press, Ames.

KAZARIAN, E. A. 1975. Food Service Facilities Planning. AVI Publishing Co., Westport, CT.

KOTSCHEVAR, L. H., and M. E. TERRELL. 1977. Foodservice Planning Layout and Equipment. 2nd edition. John Wiley & Sons, New York.

KRIMMEL, G. 1977. Energy and the kitchen. Food Management *12*(6):43–46+.

MYERS, M. R. 1979. Commercial Kitchens. 6th edition. American Gas Association, Arlington, VA.

SCRIVEN, C., and J. STEVENS. 1980. Food Equipment Facts: A Handbook for the Food Service Industry. Conceptual Design, New York.

THORNER, M. E. 1973. Convenience and Fast Food Handbook. AVI Publishing Co., Westport, CT.

TINSLEY, E. 1979. Energy for the Future: Can Kitchens Operate with Limited Power? Institutions/Volume Feeding *82*(5):43.

UNKLESBAY, N., and K. UNKLESBAY. 1982. Energy Management in Foodservice. AVI Publishing Co., Westport, CT.

U.S. DEPT. OF AGRICULTURE. 1974. Equipment Guide for On-Site School Kitchens. U.S. Govt. Printing Office, Washington, DC.

U.S. DEPT. OF AGRICULTURE. 1980. Equipment Guide for Child Care Centers. U.S. Govt. Printing Office, Washington, DC.

U.S. DEPT. OF LABOR. 1970. All about OSHA. U.S. Govt. Printing Office, Washington, DC.

WEST, B. B., L. WOOD, V. HARGER, and G. SHUGART. 1977. Food Service in Institutions. 6th edition. John Wiley & Sons, New York.

WILKINSON, J. 1975. The Complete Book of Cooking Equipment. Revised edition. Cahners Publishing Co., Boston.

Appendix I

NATIONAL SCHOOL LUNCH ACT OF 1946

ORIGINAL BILL—JUNE 4, 1946—AN ACT

To provide assistance to the States in the establishment, maintenance, operation, and expansion of school-lunch programs, and for other purposes.

Be it enacted by the Senate and House of Representatives of the United States of America in Congress assembled, That this Act may be cited as the "National School Lunch Act."

DECLARATION OF POLICY

SEC. 2. It is hereby declared to be the policy of Congress, as a measure of national security, to safeguard the health and well-being of the Nation's children and to encourage the domestic consumption of nutritious agricultural commodities and other food, by assisting the States, through grants-in-aid and other means, in providing an adequate supply of foods and other facilities for the establishment, maintenance, operation, and expansion of nonprofit school-lunch programs.

APPROPRIATIONS AUTHORIZED

SEC. 3. For each fiscal year, beginning with the fiscal year ending June 30, 1947, there is hereby authorized to be appropriated, out of money in the Treasury not otherwise appropriated, such sums as may be necessary to enable the Secretary of Agriculture (hereinafter referred to as "the Secretary") to carry out the provisions of this Act.

APPORTIONMENTS TO STATES

SEC. 4. The sums appropriated for any fiscal year pursuant to the authorization contained in section 3 of this Act, excluding the sum specified in section 5, shall be available to the Secretary for supplying, during such fiscal year, agricultural commodities and other foods for the school-lunch program in accordance with the provisions of this Act. The Secretary shall apportion among the States during each fiscal year not less than 75 per centum of the aforesaid funds made available for such year for supplying agricultural commodities and other foods under the provisions of this Act, except that the total of such apportionment of funds for use in Alaska, Territory of Hawaii, Puerto Rico, and the Virgin Islands shall not exceed 3 per centum of the funds appropriated for agricultural commodities and other food for the school-lunch program. Apportionment among the States shall be made on the basis of two factors: (1) The number of school children in the State and (2) the need for assistance in the State as indicated by the relation of the per capita income in the United States to the per capita income in the State. The amount of the initial apportionment to any State shall be determined by the following method: First, determine an index for the State by multiplying factors (1) and (2); second, divide this index by the sum of the indices for all the States; and, finally, apply the figure thus obtained to the total funds to be apportioned. For the purpose of this section, the number of school children in the State shall be the number of children therein between the ages of five and seventeen, inclusive; such figures and per capita income figures shall be the latest figures certified by the Department of Commerce. For the purposes of this Act, "school" means any public or nonprofit private school of high-school grade or under and, with respect to Puerto Rico, shall also include nonprofit child-care centers certified as such by the Governor of Puerto Rico. If any State cannot utilize all funds so apportioned to it, or if additional funds are available under this Act for apportionment among the States, the Secretary shall make further apportionments to the remaining States in the same manner.

SEC. 5. Of the sums appropriated for any fiscal year pursuant to the authorization contained in section 3 of this Act, $10,000,000 shall be available to the Secretary for the purpose of providing, during such fiscal year, nonfood assistance for the school-lunch program pursuant to the provisions of this Act. The Secretary shall apportion among the States during each fiscal year the aforesaid sum of $10,000,000, and such apportionment among the States shall be on the basis of the factors, and in accordance with the standards, set forth in section 4 with respect to the apportionment for agricultural commodities and other foods. The total of such funds apportioned for nonfood assistance for use in Alaska, Territory of Hawaii, Puerto Rico, and the Virgin Islands shall not exceed 3 per centum of the funds appropriated for nonfood assistance in accordance with the provisions of this Act.

DIRECT FEDERAL EXPENDITURES

SEC. 6. The funds appropriated for any fiscal year for carrying out the provisions of this Act, less not to exceed 3½ per centum thereof hereby made available to the Secretary for his administrative expenses and less the amount apportioned by him pursuant to sections 4, 5, and 10, shall be available to the Secretary during such year for direct expenditure by him for agricultural commodities and other foods to be distributed among the States and schools participating in the school-lunch program under this Act in accordance with the needs as determined by the local school authorities. The provisions of law contained in the proviso of the Act of June 28, 1937 (50 Stat. 323), facilitating operations with respect to the purchase and disposition of surplus agricultural commodities under section 32 of the Act approved August 24, 1935 (49 Stat. 774), as amended, shall, to the extent not inconsistent with the provisions of this Act, also be applicable to expenditures of funds by the Secretary under this Act.

PAYMENTS TO STATES

SEC. 7. Funds apportioned to any State pursuant to section 4 or 5 during any fiscal year shall be available for payment to such State for disbursement by the State educational agency, in accordance with such agreements not inconsistent with the provisions of this Act, as may be entered into by the Secretary and such State educational agency, for the purpose of assisting schools of that State during such fiscal year, in supplying (1) agricultural commodities and other foods for consumption by children and (2) nonfood assistance in furtherance of the school-lunch program authorized under this Act. Such payments to any State in any fiscal year during the period 1947 to 1950, inclusive, shall be made upon condition that each dollar thereof will be matched during such year by $1 from sources within the State determined by the Secretary to have been expended in connection with the school-lunch program under this Act. Such payments in any fiscal year during the period 1951 to 1955, inclusive, shall be made upon condition that each dollar thereof will be so matched by one and one-half dollars; and for any fiscal year thereafter, such payments shall be made upon condition that each dollar will be so matched by $3. In the case of any State whose per capita income is less than the per capita income of the United States, the matching required for any fiscal year shall be decreased by the percentage which the State per capita income is below the per capita income of the United States. For the purpose of determining whether the matching requirements of this section and section 10, respectively, have been met, the reasonable value of donated services, suppliers, facilities, and equipment as certified, respectively, by the State educational agency and in case of schools receiving funds pursuant to section 10, by such schools (but not the cost or value of land, of the acquisition, construction, or alteration of buildings of commodities donated by the Secretary, or of Federal contributions), may be regarded as funds from sources within the State expended in connection with the school-lunch program. The Secretary shall certify to the Secretary of the Treasury from time to time the amounts to be paid to any State under this section and the time or times such amounts are to be paid; and the Secretary of the Treasury shall pay to the State at the time or times fixed by the Secretary the amounts so certified.

STATE DISBURSEMENT TO SCHOOLS

SEC. 8. Funds paid to any State during any fiscal year pursuant to section 4 or 5 shall be disbursed by the State educational agency, in accordance with such agreements approved by the Secretary as may be entered into by such State agency and the schools in the State, to those schools in the State which the State educational agency, taking into account need and attendance, determines are eligible to participate in the school-lunch program. Such disbursement to any school shall be made only for the purpose of reimbursing it for the cost of obtaining agricultural commodities and other foods for consumption by children in the school-lunch program and nonfood assistance in connection with such program. Such food costs may include, in addition to the purchase price of agricultural commodities and other foods, the cost of processing, distributing, transporting, storing, or handling thereof. In no event shall such disbursement for food to any school for any fiscal year exceed an amount determined by multiplying the number of lunches served in the school in the school-lunch program under this Act during such year by the maximum Federal food-cost contribution rate for the State, for the type of lunch served, as prescribed by the Secretary.

NUTRITIONAL AND OTHER PROGRAM REQUIREMENTS

SEC. 9. Lunches served by schools participating in the school-lunch program under this Act shall meet minimum nutritional requirements prescribed by the Secretary on the basis of tested nutritional research. Such meals shall be served without cost or at a reduced cost to children who are determined by local school authorities to be unable to pay the full cost of the lunch. No physical segregation of or other discrimination against any child shall be made by the school because of his inability to pay. School-lunch programs under this Act shall be operated on a nonprofit basis. Each school shall, insofar as practicable, utilize in its lunch program commodities designated from time to time by the Secretary as being in abundance, either nationally or in the school area, or commodities donated by the Secretary. Commodities purchased under the authority of section 32 of the Act of August 24, 1935 (49 Stat. 774), as amended, may be donated by the Secretary to schools, in accordance with the needs as determined by local school authorities, for utilization in the school-lunch program under this Act as well as to other schools carrying out nonprofit school-lunch programs and institutions authorized to receive such commodities.

SEC. 10. If, in any State, the State educational agency is not permitted by law to disburse the funds paid to it under this Act to nonprofit private schools in the State, or is not permitted by law to match Federal funds made available for use by such nonprofit private schools, the Secretary shall withhold from the funds apportioned to any such State under sections 4 and 5 of this Act the same proportion of the funds as the number of children between the ages of five and seventeen, inclusive, attending nonprofit private schools within the State is of the total number of persons of those ages within the State attending school. The Secretary shall disburse the funds so withheld directly to the nonprofit private schools within said State for the same purposes and subject to the same conditions as are authorized or required with respect to the disbursements to schools within the State by the State educational agency, including the requirement that any such payment or payments shall be matched, in the proportion specified in section 7 for such State, by funds from sources within the State expended by nonprofit private schools within the State participating in the school-lunch program under this Act. Such funds shall not be considered a part of the funds constituting the matching funds under the terms of section 7.

MISCELLANEOUS PROVISIONS AND DEFINITIONS

Sec. 11 (a) States, State educational agencies, and schools participating in the school-lunch program under this Act shall keep such accounts and records as may be necessary to enable the Secretary to determine whether the provisions of this Act are being complied with. Such accounts and records shall at all times be available for inspection and audit by representatives of the Secretary and shall be preserved for such period of time, not in excess of five years, as the Secretary determines is necessary.

(b) The Secretary shall incorporate, in his agreements with the State educational agencies, the express requirements under this Act with respect to the operation of the school-lunch program under this Act insofar as they may be applicable and such other provisions as in his opinion are reasonably necessary or appropriate to effectuate the purposes of this Act.

(c) In carrying out the provisions of this Act, neither the Secretary nor the State shall impose any requirement with respect to teaching, personnel, curriculum, instruction, methods of instruction, and materials of instruction in any school. If a State maintains separate schools for minority and for majority races, no funds made available pursuant to this Act shall be paid or disbursed to it unless a just and equitable distribution is made within the State, for the benefit of such minority races, of funds paid to it under this Act.

(d) For the purposes of this Act—

(1) "State" includes any of the forty-eight States and the District of Columbia, Territory of Hawaii, Puerto Rico, Alaska, and the Virgin Islands.

(2) "State educational agency" means, as the State legislature may determine, (a) the chief State school officer (such as the State superintendent of public instruction, commissioner of education, or similar officer), or (b) a board of education controlling the State department of education; except that in the District of Columbia it shall mean the Board of Education, and except that for the period ending June 30, 1948, "State educational agency" may mean any agency or agencies within the State designated by the Governor to carry out the functions herein required of a State educational agency.

(3) "Nonprofit private school" means any private school exempt from income tax under section 101 (6) of the Internal Revenue Code, as amended.

(4) "Nonfood assistance" means equipment used on school premises in storing, preparing, or serving food for school children.

Approved June 4, 1946.

Appendix II

CHILD NUTRITION ACT OF 1966, AS AMENDED

AN ACT

To strengthen and expand food service programs for children. *Be it enacted by the Senate and House of Representatives of the United States of America in Congress assembled,* That this Act may be cited as the "Child Nutrition Act of 1966." (42 U.S.C. 1771, note.)

DECLARATION OF PURPOSE

SEC. 2. In recognition of the demonstrated relationship between food and good nutrition and the capacity of children to develop and learn, based on the years of cumulative successful experience under the national school lunch program with its significant contributions in the field of applied nutrition research, it is hereby declared to be the policy of Congress that these efforts shall be extended, expanded, and strengthened under the authority of the Secretary of Agriculture as a measure to safeguard the health and well-being of the Nation's children, and to encourage the domestic consumption of agricultural and other foods, by assisting States, through grants-in-aid and other means, to meet more effectively the nutritional needs of our children. (42 U.S.C. 1771.)

SPECIAL MILK PROGRAM AUTHORIZATION

SEC. 3.[2] (a)[3] There is hereby authorized to be appropriated for the fiscal year ending June 30, 1970, and for each succeeding fiscal year such sums as may be necessary to enable the Secretary of Agriculture, under such rules and regulations as he may deem in the public interest, to encourage consumption of fluid milk by children in the United States in (1) nonprofit schools of high school grade and under, which do not participate in a meal service program authorized under this Act or the National School Lunch Act,[4] and (2) nonprofit nursery schools, child-care centers, settlement houses, summer camps, and similar nonprofit institutions devoted to the care and training of children, which do not participate in a meal service program authorized under this Act or the National School Lunch Act.[4] For the purposes of this section "United States" means the fifty States, Guam, the Commonwealth of Puerto Rico, the Virgin Islands, American Samoa, the Trust Territory of the Pacific Islands, and the District of Columbia.[5] The Secretary shall administer the special milk program provided for by this section to the maximum extent practicable in the same manner as he administered the special milk program provided for by Public Law 89–642, as amended, during the fiscal year ending June 30, 1969. Any school or nonprofit child care institution which does not participate in a meal service program authorized under this Act or the National School Lunch Act[4] shall receive the special milk program upon their request. Children who qualify for free lunches under guidelines established by the Secretary shall, at the option of the school involved (or of the local educational agency involved in the case of a public school) be eligible for free milk upon their request.[6] For the fiscal year ending June 30, 1975, and for subsequent school years, the minimum rate of reimbursement for a half-pint of milk served in schools and other eligible institutions shall not be less then 5 cents per half-pint served to eligible children, and such minimum rate of reimbursement shall be adjusted on an annual basis each school year to reflect changes in the Producer Price Index for Fresh Processed Milk[7] published by the Bureau of Labor Statistics of the Department of Labor. Such adjustment shall be computed to the nearest one-fourth cent.[8] [8a]

(b)[10] Commodity only schools shall not be eligible to participate in the special milk program under this section. For the purposes of the preceding sentence, the term "commodity only schools" means schools that do not participate in the school lunch program under the National School Lunch Act, but which receive commodities made available by the Secretary for use by such schools in nonprofit lunch programs.

SCHOOL BREAKFAST PROGRAM AUTHORIZATION

SEC. 4. (a)[11] There is hereby authorized to be appropriated such sums as are necessary to enable the Secretary to carry out a program to assist the States and the Department of Defense through grants-in-aid and other means to initiate, maintain, or expand nonprofit breakfast programs in all schools which make application for assistance and agree to carry out a non-profit breakfast program in accordance with this Act. Appropriations and expenditures for this Act shall be considered Health, Education, and Welfare* functions for budget purposes rather than functions of Agriculture.

APPORTIONMENT TO STATES

(b)(1)(A)[12] The Secretary shall make breakfast assistance payments to each State educational agency each fiscal year, at such times as the Secretary may determine, from the sums appropriated for such purpose, in an amount equal to the product obtained by multiplying—

(i) the number of breakfasts served during such fiscal year to children in schools in such States which participate in the school breakfast program under agreements with such State educational agency; by

(ii) the national average breakfast payment for free breakfasts, for reduced-price breakfasts, or for breakfasts served to children not eligible for free or reduced-price meals, as appropriate, as prescribed in clause (B) of this paragraph.

(B) The national average payment for each free breakfast shall be 57 cents (as adjusted pursuant to section 11(a) of the National School Lunch Act). The national average payment for each reduced-price breakfast shall be one-half of the national average payment for each free breakfast, adjusted to the nearest one-fourth cent, except than in no case shall the difference between the amount of the national average payment for a free breakfast and the national average payment for a reduced-price breakfast, adjusted to the nearest one-fourth cent, except than in no case shall the difference between the amount of the national average payment for a free breakfast and the national average payment for a reduced-price breakfast exceed 30 cents. The national average payment for each breakfast served to a child not eligible for free or reduced-price meals shall be 8.25 cents (as adjusted pursuant to section 11(a) of the National School Lunch Act).

(C) No school which receives breakfast assistance payments under this section may charge a price of more than 30 cents for a reduced-price breakfast.

(D) No breakfast assistance payment may be made under this subsection for any breakfast served by a school unless such breakfast consists of a combination of foods which meet the minimum nutritional requirements prescribed by the Secretary under subsection (e) of this section.

(2) (A) The Secretary shall make additional payments for breakfasts served to children qualifying for a free or reduced-price meal at schools that are in severe need.

(B) The maximum payment for each such free breakfast shall be the higher of—

(i) the national average payment established by the Secretary for free breakfast plus 10 cents, or

(ii) 45 cents, which shall be adjusted on an annual basis each July 1 [13] to the nearest one-fourth cent in accordance with changes in the series for food away from home of the Consumer Price Index published by the Bureau of Labor Statistics of the Department of Labor for the most recent twelve-month [14] period for which such data are available, except that the initial such adjustment shall be made on January 1, 1978, and shall reflect the change in the series of food away from home during the period November 1, 1976, to October 31, 1977.

(C) The maximum payment for each such reduced-price breakfast shall be thirty [15] cents less than the maximum payment for each free breakfast as determined under clause (B) of the paragraph.

STATE DISBURSEMENT TO SCHOOLS

(c) Funds apportioned and paid to any State for the purpose of this section shall be disbursed by the State educational agency to schools selected by the State educational agency to assist such schools in [16] operating a breakfast program and for the purpose of subsection (d). [17] Disbursement to schools shall be made at such rates per meal or on such other basis as the Secretary shall prescribe. In selecting schools for participation, the State educational agency shall, to the extent practicable, give first consideration to those schools drawing attendance from areas in which poor economic conditions exist, to those schools in which a substantial proportion of the children enrolled must travel long distances daily, and to those schools in which there is a special need for improving the nutrition and dietary practices of children of working mothers and children from low-income families. [18] Breakfast assistance disbursements to schools under this section may be made in advance or by way of reimbursement in accordance with procedures prescribed by the Secretary. [19]

(d)(1) [20] Each State educational agency shall provide additional assistance to schools in severe need, which shall include only—

(A) those schools in which the service of breakfasts is required pursuant to State law; and

(B) those schools (having a breakfast program or desiring to initiate a breakfast program) in which, during the most recent second preceding school year for which lunches were served, 40 percent or more of the lunches served to students at the school were served free or at a reduced-price, and in which the rate per meal established by the Secretary is insufficient to cover the costs of the breakfast program. The provision of eligibility specified in clause (A) of this paragraph shall terminate effective July 1, 1983, for schools in States where the State legislatures meet annually and shall terminate effective July 1, 1984, for schools in States where the State legislatures meet biennially.

(2) A school, upon the submission of appropriate documentation about the need circumstances in that school and the school's eligibility for additional assistance, shall be entitled to receive 100 percent of the operating costs of the breakfast program, including the costs of obtaining, preparing, and serving food, or the meal reimbursement rate specified in paragraph (2) of section 4(b) of this Act, whichever is less.

NUTRITIONAL AND OTHER PROGRAM REQUIREMENTS

(e) [21] Breakfasts served by schools participating in the school breakfast program under this section shall consist of a combination of foods and shall meet minimum nutritional requirements prescribed by the Secretary on the basis of tested nutritional research. Such breakfasts shall be served free or at a reduced price to children in school under the same terms and conditions as are set forth with respect to the service of lunches free or at a reduced price in section 9 of the National School Lunch Act.

NONPROFIT PRIVATE SCHOOLS

(f)[22] As a national nutrition and health policy, it is the purpose and intent of the Congress that the school breakfast program be made available in all schools where it is needed to provide adequate nutrition for children in attendance. The Secretary is hereby directed, in cooperation with State educational agencies, to carry out a program of information in furtherance of this policy. Within 4 months after the enactment of this subsection, the Secretary shall report to the committees of jurisdiction in the Congress his plans and those of the cooperating State agencies to bring about the needed expansion in the school breakfast program (42 U.S.C. 1773.)

DISBURSEMENT TO SCHOOLS BY THE SECRETARY[23]

SEC. 5.(a) The Secretary shall withhold funds payable to a State under this Act and disburse the funds directly to schools or institutions within the State for the purposes authorized by this Act to the extent that the Secretary has so withheld and disbursed such funds continuously since October 1, 1980, but only to such extent (except as otherwise required by subsection (b)). Any funds so withheld and disbursed by the Secretary shall be used for the same purposes, and shall be subject to the same conditions, as applicable to a State disbursing funds made available under this Act. If the Secretary is administering (in whole or in part) any program authorized under this Act, the State in which the Secretary is administering the program may, upon request to the Secretary, assume administration of that program.

(b) If a State educational agency is not permitted by law to disburse the funds paid to it under this Act to any of the nonpublic schools in the State, the Secretary shall disburse the funds directly to such schools within the State for the same purposes and subject to the same conditions as are authorized or required with respect to the disbursements to public schools within the State by the State educational agency.

PAYMENTS TO STATES

SEC. 6. The Secretary shall certify to the Secretary of the Treasury from time to time the amounts to be paid to any State under sections 3 through 7 of this Act and the time or times such amounts are to be paid; and the Secretary of the Treasury shall pay to the State at the time or times fixed by the Secretary the amounts so certified. (42 U.S.C. 1775.)

STATE ADMINISTRATIVE EXPENSES

SEC. 7.[24] (a)[25] (1) Each fiscal year, the Secretary shall make available to the States for their administrative costs an amount equal to not less than 1½ percent of the Federal funds expended under sections 4, 11 and 17 of the National School Lunch Act and 3 and 4[26] of this Act during the second preceding fiscal year. The Secretary shall allocate the funds so provided in accordance with paragraphs (2), (3), and (4) of this subsection. There are hereby authorized to be appropriated such sums as may be necessary to carry out the purposes of this section.

(2) The Secretary shall allocate to each State for administrative costs incurred in any fiscal year in connection with the programs authorized under the National School Lunch Act or under this Act, except for the programs authorized under section 13 or 17 of the National School Lunch Act or under section 17 of this Act, an amount equal to not less than 1 percent and not more than 1½ percent of the funds expended by each State under sections 4 and 11 of the National School Lunch Act and sections 3 and 4[27] of this Act during the second preceding fiscal year. In no case shall the grant available to any State under this subsection be less than the amount such State was allocated in the fiscal year ending September 30, 1981,[28] or $100,000, whichever is larger.

(3) The Secretary shall allocate to each State for its administrative costs incurred under the

program authorized by section 17 of the National School Lunch Act in any fiscal year an amount, based upon funds expended under that program in the second preceding fiscal year, equal to (A) 20 percent of the first $50,000, (B) 10 percent of the next $100,000, (C) 5 percent of the next $250,000, and (D) 2½ percent of any remaining funds. The Secretary may adjust any State's allocation to reflect changes in the size of its program.

(4) The remaining funds appropriated under this section shall be allocated among the States by the Secretary in amounts the Secretary determines necessary for the improvement in the States of the administration of the programs authorized under the National School Lunch Act and this Act, except for section 17 of this Act, including, but not limited to, improved program integrity and the quality of meals served to children.

(5) Funds available to States under this subsection and under section 13(k)(1) of the National School Lunch Act shall be used for the costs of administration of the programs for which the allocations are made, except that States may transfer up to 10 percent of any of the amounts allocated among such programs.

(6) Where the Secretary is responsible for the administration of programs under this Act or the National School Lunch Act, the amount of funds that would be allocated to the State agency under this section and under section 13(k)(1) of the National School Lunch Act shall be retained by the Secretary for the Secretary's use in the administration of such programs.

(b) The Secretary, in cooperation with the several States, shall develop State staffing standards for the administration by each State of sections 4, 11, and 17 of the National School Lunch Act and sections 3 and 4[29] of this Act, that will ensure sufficient staff for the planning and administration of programs covered by State administrative expenses.

(c) Funds paid to a State under subsection (a) of this section may be used to pay salaries, including employee benefits and travel expenses, for administrative and supervisory personnel; for support services; for office equipment; and for staff development.

(d) If any State agency agrees to assume responsibility for the administration of food service programs in nonprofit private schools or child care institutions that were previously administered by the Secretary, an appropriate adjustment shall be made in the administrative funds paid under this section to the State not later than the succeeding fiscal year.

(e)[30] Notwithstanding any other provision of law, funds made available to each State under this section shall remain available for obligation and expenditure by that State during the fiscal year immediately following the fiscal year for which such funds were made available. For each fiscal year the Secretary shall establish a date by which each State shall submit to the Secretary a plan for the disbursement of funds provided under this section for each such year, and the Secretary shall reallocate any unused funds, as evidenced by such plans, to other States as the Secretary considers appropriate.

(f) The State may use a portion of the funds available under this section to assist in the administration of the commodity distribution program.

(g) Each State shall submit to the Secretary for approval by October 1 of each year an annual plan for the use of State administrative expense funds, including a staff formula for State personnel, system level supervisory and operating personnel, and school level personnel.

(h) Payments of funds under this section shall be made only to States that agree to maintain a level of funding out of State revenues, for administrative costs in connection with programs under this Act (except section 17 of this Act) and the National School Lunch Act (except section 13 of that Act), not less than the amount expended or obligated in fiscal year 1977.

(i) For the fiscal years beginning October 1, 1977, and ending September 30, 1984,[31] there are hereby authorized to be appropriated such sums as may be necessary for purposes of this section. (42 U.S.C. 1776.)

UTILIZATION OF FOODS

SEC. 8. Each school participating under section 4 of this Act shall, insofar as practicable, utilize in its program foods designated from time to time by the Secretary as being in abundance, either nationally or in the school area, or foods donated by the Secretary. Foods available under section 416 of the Agricultural Act of 1949 (63 Stat. 1058), as amended, or purchased under section 32 of the Act of August 24, 1935 (49 Stat. 744), as amended, or section 709 of the Food and Agriculture Act of 1965 (79 Stat. 1212), may be donated by the Secretary to schools, in accordance with the needs as determined by local school authorities, for utilization in their feeding programs under this Act. (42 U.S.C. 1777).

NONPROFIT PROGRAMS

SEC. 9. The food and milk service programs in schools and nonprofit institutions receiving assistance under this Act shall be conducted on a nonprofit basis. (42 U.S.C. 1778.)

REGULATIONS

SEC. 10.[32] The Secretary shall prescribe such regulations as he may deem necessary to carry out this Act and the National School Lunch Act, including regulations relating to the service of food in participating schools and service institutions in competition with the programs authorized under this Act and the National School Lunch Act. Such regulations shall not prohibit the sale of competitive foods approved by the Secretary in food service facilities or areas during the time of service of food under this Act or the National School Lunch Act if the proceeds from the sales of such foods will inure to the benefit of the schools or of organizations of students approved by the schools.[33] In such regulations the Secretary may provide for the transfer of funds by any State between the programs authorized under this Act and the National School Lunch Act on the basis of an approved State plan of operation for the use of the funds and may provide for the reserve of up to 1 per centum of the funds available for apportionment to any State to carry out special developmental projects. (42 U.S.C. 1779.)

PROHIBITIONS

SEC. 11.(a) In carrying out the provisions of sections 3 and 4 [34] of this Act, neither the Secretary nor the State shall impose any requirements with respect to teaching personnel, curriculum, instruction, methods of instruction, and materials of instruction.

(b) The value of assistance to children under this Act shall not be considered to be income or resources for any purpose under any Federal or State laws including, but not limited to, laws relating to taxation, welfare, and public assistance programs. Expenditures of funds from State and local sources for the maintenance of food programs for children shall not be diminished as a result of funds received under this Act. (42 U.S.C. 1780.)

PRESCHOOL PROGRAMS

SEC. 12. The Secretary may extend the benefits of all school feeding programs conducted and supervised by the Department of Agriculture to include preschool programs operated as part of the school system. (42 U.S.C. 1781.)

CENTRALIZATION OF ADMINISTRATION

SEC. 13. Authority for the conduct and supervision of Federal programs to assist schools in providing food service programs for children is assigned to the Department of Agriculture. To the extent practicable, other Federal agencies administering programs under which funds are to be provided to schools for such assistance shall transfer such funds to the Department of Agriculture for distribution through the administrative channels and in accordance with the standards established under this Act and the National School Lunch Act. (42 U.S.C. 1782.)

APPROPRIATIONS FOR ADMINISTRATIVE EXPENSE

SEC. 14. There is hereby authorized to be appropriated for any fiscal year such sums as may be necessary to the Secretary for his administrative expense under this Act. (42 U.S.C. 1783.)

SEC. 15.[35] For the purpose of this Act—

(a) "State" means any of the fifty States, the District of Columbia, the Commonwealth of Puerto Rico, the Virgin Islands, Guam, American Samoa, or the Trust Territory of the Pacific Islands.[36]

(b) "State educational agency" means, as the State legislature may determine, (1) the chief State school officer (such as the State superintendent of public instruction, commissioner of education, or similar officer), or (2) a board of education controlling the State department of education.

(c) "School" means (A) any public or nonprofit private school of high school grade or under, including kindergarten and preschool programs operated by such school, except private schools whose average yearly tuition exceeds $1,500 per child,[37] (B) any public or licensed nonprofit private residential child care institution (including, but not limited to, orphanages and homes for the mentally retarded, but excluding Job Corps Centers funded by the Department of Labor),[38] and (C) with respect to the Commonwealth of Puerto Rico, nonprofit child care centers certified as such by the governor of Puerto Rico. For purposes of clauses (A) and (B) of this subsection, the term "nonprofit," when applied to any such private school or institution, means any such school or institution which is exempt from tax under section 501(c)(3) of the Internal Revenue Code of 1954.

(d) "Secretary" means the Secretary of Agriculture.

(e) "School year" means the annual period from July 1 through June 30.[39]

(f)[39] Except as used in section 17 of this Act, the terms "child" and "children" as used in this Act, shall be deemed to include persons regardless of age who are determined by the State educational agency, in accordance with regulations prescribed by the Secretary, to be mentally or physically handicapped and who are attending any nonresidential public or nonprofit private school of high school grade or under for the purpose of participating in a school program established for mentally or physically handicapped. (42 U.S.C. 1784.)

ACCOUNTS AND RECORDS

SEC. 16. (a)[40] States, State educational agencies, schools, and nonprofit institutions participating in programs under this Act shall keep such accounts and records as may be necessary to enable the Secretary to determine whether there has been compliance with this Act and the regulations hereunder. Such accounts and records shall at all times be available for inspection and audit by representatives of the Secretary and shall be preserved for such period of time, not in excess of three years, as the Secretary determines is necessary.

(b)[41] With regard to any claim arising under this Act or under the National School Lunch Act, the Secretary shall have the authority to determine the amount of, to settle and to adjust any such claim, and to compromise or deny such claim or any part thereof. The Secretary shall also have the authority to waive such claims if the Secretary determines that to do so would serve the purposes of either such Act. Nothing contained in this subsection shall be construed to diminish the authority of the Attorney General of the United States under section 516 of title 28, United States Code, to conduct litigation on behalf of the United States. (42 U.S.C. 1785.)

SPECIAL SUPPLEMENTAL FOOD PROGRAM

[Section 17 is omitted as this book deals only with school foodservice.]

CASH GRANTS FOR NUTRITION EDUCATION

SEC. 18.[46] (a) The Secretary is hereby authorized and directed to make cash grants to state educational agencies for the purpose of conducting experimental or demonstration projects to teach schoolchildren the nutritional value of foods and the relationship of nutrition to human health.

(b) In order to carry out the program, provided for in subsection (a) of this section, there is hereby authorized to be appropriated not to exceed $1,000,000 annually. The Secretary shall withhold not less than 1 per centum of any funds appropriated under this section and shall expend these funds to carry out research and development projects relevant to the purpose of this section, particularly to develop materials and techniques for the innovative presentation of nutritional information. (42 U.S.C. 1787.)

NUTRITION EDUCATION AND TRAINING

SEC. 19.[47] (a) Congress finds that—
(1) the proper nutrition of the Nation's children is a matter of highest priority;
(2) the lack of understanding of the principles of good nutrition and their relationship to health can contribute to a child's rejection of highly nutritious foods and consequent plate waste in school food service operations;
(3) many school food service personnel have not had adequate training in food service management skills and principles, and many teachers and school food service operators have not had adequate training in the fundamentals of nutrition or how to convey this information so as to motivate children to practice sound eating habits;
(4) parents exert a significant influence on children in the development of nutritional habits and lack of nutritional knowledge on the part of parents can have detrimental effects on children's nutritional development; and
(5) there is a need to create opportunities for children to learn about the importance of the principles of good nutrition in their daily lives and how these principles are applied in the school cafeteria.

PURPOSE

(b) It is the purpose of this section to encourage effective dissemination of scientifically valid information to children participating or eligible to participate in the school lunch and related child nutrition programs by establishing a system of grants to State educational agencies for the development of comprehensive nutrition information and education programs. Such nutrition education programs shall fully use as a learning laboratory the school lunch and child nutrition programs.

DEFINITIONS

(c) For purposes of this section, the term "nutrition information and education program" means a multidisciplinary program by which scientifically valid information about foods and nutrients is imparted in a manner that individuals receiving such information will understand the principles of nutrition and seek to maximize their well-being through food consumption practices. Nutrition education programs shall include, but not be limited to, (A) instructing students with regard to the nutritional value of foods and the relationship between food and human health; (B) training school food service personnel in the principles and practices of food service management; (C) instructing teachers in sound principles of nutrition education; and (D) developing and using classroom materials and curricula.

NUTRITION INFORMATION AND TRAINING

(d)(1) The Secretary is authorized to formulate and carry out a nutrition information and education program, through a system of grants to State educational agencies, to provide for (A) the nutritional training of educational and food service personnel, (B) the food service management training of school food service personnel, and (C) the conduct of nutrition education activities in schools and child care institutions.
(2) The program is to be coordinated at the State level with other nutrition activities conducted by education, health, and State Cooperative Extension Service agencies. In formulat-

ing the program, the Secretary and the State may solicit the advice and recommendations of the National Advisory Council on Child Nutrition; State educational agencies; the Department of Health, Education, and Welfare; and other interested groups and individuals concerned with improvement of child nutrition.

(3) If a State educational agency is conducting or applying to conduct a health education program which includes a school-related nutrition education component as defined by the Secretary, and that health education program is eligible for funds under programs administered by the Department of Health, Education, and Welfare, the Secretary may make funds authorized in this section available to the Department of Health, Education, and Welfare* to fund the nutrition education component of the State program without requiring an additional grant application.

(4) The Secretary, in carrying out the provisions of this subsection, shall make grants to State educational agencies who, in turn, may contract with land-grant colleges eligible to receive funds under the Act of July 2, 1862 (12 Stat. 503, as amended; 7 U.S.C. 301–305, 307, and 308), or the Act of August 30, 1890 (26 Stat. 417, as amended; 7 U.S.C. 321–326 and 328), including the Tuskegee Institute, other institutions of higher education, and nonprofit organizations and agencies, for the training of educational and school food service personnel with respect to providing nutrition education programs in schools and the training of school food service personnel in school food service management. Such grants may be used to develop and conduct training programs for early childhood, elementary, and secondary educational personnel and food service personnel with respect to the relationship between food, nutrition, and health; educational methods and techniques, and issues relating to nutrition education; and principles and skills of food service management for cafeteria personnel.

(5) The State, in carrying out the provisions of this subsection, may contract with State and local educational agencies, land-grant colleges eligible to receive funds under the Act of July 2, 1862 (12 Stat. 503, as amended; 7 U.S.C. 301–305, 307, and 308), or the Act of August 30, 1890 (26 Stat. 417, as amended; 7 U.S.C. 321–326 and 328), including the Tuskegee Institute, other institutions of higher education, and other public or private nonprofit educational or research agencies, institutions, or organizations to pay the cost of pilot demonstration projects in elementary and secondary schools with respect to nutrition education. Such projects may include, but are not limited to, projects for the development, demonstration, testing, and evaluation of curricula for use in early childhood, elementary, and secondary education programs.[48]

AGREEMENTS WITH STATE AGENCIES

(e) The Secretary is authorized to enter into agreements with State educational agencies incorporating the provisions of this section, and issue such regulations as are necessary to implement this section.

USE OF FUNDS

(f)(1) The funds made available under this section may, under guidelines established by the Secretary, be used by State education agencies for (A) employing a nutrition education specialist to coordinate the program, including travel and related personnel costs; (B) undertaking an assessment of the nutrition education needs of the State; (C) developing a State plan of operation and management for nutrition education; (D) applying for and carrying out planning and assessment grants; (E) pilot projects and related purposes; (F) the planning, development, and conduct of nutrition education programs and workshops for food service and educational personnel; (G) coordinating and promoting nutrition information and education activities in local school districts (incorporating, to the maximum extent practicable, as a learning laboratory, the child nutrition programs); (H) contracting with public and private nonprofit educational institutions for the conduct of nutrition education instruction and programs relating to the purposes of this section; and (I) related nutrition education purposes, including the preparation, testing, distribution, and evaluation of visual aids and other informational and educational materials.

(2) Any State desiring to receive grants authorized by this section may, from the funds appropriated to carry out this section, receive a planning and assessment grant for the purposes of carrying out the responsibilities described in clauses (A), (B), (C), and (D) of paragraph (1) of this subsection. Any State receiving a planning and assessment grant, may, during the first year of participation, be advanced a portion of the funds necessary to carry out such responsibilities: *Provided,* That in order o receive additional funding, the State must carry out such responsibilities.

(3) An amount not to exceed 15 percent of each State's grant may be used for up to 50 percent of the expenditures for overall administrative and supervisory purposes in connection with the program authorized under this section.

(4) Nothing in this section shall prohibit State or local educational agencies from making available or distributing to adults nutrition education materials, resources, activities, or programs authorized under this section.

ACCOUNTS, RECORDS, AND REPORTS

(g)(1) State educational agencies participating in programs under this section shall keep such accounts and records as may be necessary to enable the Secretary to determine whether there has been compliance with this section and the regulations issued hereunder. Such accounts and records shall at all times be available for inspection and audit by representatives of the Secretary and shall be preserved for such period of time, not in excess of five years, as the Secretary determines to be necessary.

(2) State educational agencies shall provide reports on expenditures of Federal funds, program participation, program costs, and related matters, in such form and at such times as the Secretary may prescribe.

STATE COORDINATORS FOR NUTRITION; STATE PLAN

(h)(1) In order to be eligible for assistance under this section, a State shall appoint a nutrition education specialist to serve as a State coordinator for school nutrition education. It shall be the responsibility of the State coordinator to make an assessment of the nutrition education needs in the State as provided in paragraph (2) of this subsection, prepare a State plan as provided in paragraph (3) of this subsection, and coordinate programs under this Act with all other nutrition education programs provided by the State with Federal or State funds.

(2) Upon receipt of funds authorized by this section, the State coordinator shall prepare an itemized budget and assess the nutrition education needs of the State. Such assessment shall include, but not be limited to, the identification and location of all students in need of nutrition education. The assessment shall also identify State and local individual, group, and institutional resources within the State for materials, facilities, staffs, and methods related to nutrition education.

(3) Within nine months after the award of the planning and assessment grant, the State coordinator shall develop, prepare, and furnish the Secretary, for approval, a comprehensive plan for nutrition education within such State. The Secretary shall act on such plan not later than sixty days after it is received. Each such plan shall describe (A) the findings of the nutrition education needs assessment within the State; (B) provisions for coordinating the nutrition education program carried out with funds made available under this section with any related publicly supported programs being carried out within the State; (C) plans for soliciting the advice and recommendations of the National Advisory Council on Child Nutrition, the State educational agency, interested teachers, food nutrition professionals and paraprofessionals, school food service personnel, administrators, representatives from consumer groups, parents, and other individuals concerned with the improvement of child nutrition; (D) plans for reach-

ing all students in the State with instruction in the nutritional value of food and the relationships among food, nutrition, and health, for training food service personnel in the principles and skills of food service management, and for instructing teachers in sound principles of nutrition education; and (E) plans for using, on a priority basis, the resources of the land-grant colleges eligible to receive funds under the Act of July 2, 1862 (12 Stat. 503; 7 U.S.C. 301–305, 307, and 308), or the Act of August 30, 1890 (26 Stat. 417, as amended; 7 U.S.C. 321–326 and 328), including the Tuskegee Institute. To the maximum extent practicable, the State's performance under such plan shall be reviewed and evaluated by the Secretary on a regular basis, including the use of public hearings.

APPROPRIATIONS AUTHORIZED

(j)[sic](1) For the fiscal years beginning October 1, 1977, and October 1, 1978, grants to the States for the conduct of nutrition education and information programs shall be based on a rate of 50 cents for each child enrolled in schools or in institutions within the State, except that no State shall receive an amount less than $75,000 per year.

(2) For the fiscal year ending September 30, 1980, and for each succeeding fiscal year ending on or before September 30, 1984,[49] there is hereby authorized to be appropriated for grants to each State for the conduct of nutrition education and information programs, an amount equal to the higher of (A) 50 cents for each child enrolled in schools or in institutions within each State, or (B) $75,000 for each State. There is authorized to be appropriated for the grants referred to in the preceding sentence not more than $15,000,000 for fiscal year 1981, and not more than $5,000,000 for each subsequent fiscal year.[50]Grants to each State from such appropriations shall be based on a rate of 50 cents for each child enrolled in schools or in institutions within such State, except that no State shall receive an amount less than $75,000 for that year. If funds appropriated for such year are insufficient to pay the amount to which each State is entitled under the second preceding sentence, the amount of such grant shall be ratably reduced to the extent necessary so that the total of such amounts paid does not exceed the amount of the appropriated funds. If additional funds become available for making such payments, such amounts shall be increased on the same basis as they were reduced.

(3) Enrollment data used for purposes of this subsection shall be the latest available as certified by the Office of Education of the Department of Health, Education, and Welfare. (42 U.S.C. 1788.)

DEPARTMENT OF DEFENSE OVERSEAS DEPENDENTS' SCHOOLS[51]

SEC. 20. (a) For the purpose of obtaining Federal payments and commodities in conjunction with the provision of breakfasts to students attending Department of Defense dependents' schools which are located outside the United States, its territories or possessions, the Secretary of Agriculture shall make available to the Department of Defense, from funds appropriated for such purpose, the same payments and commodities as are provided to States for schools participating in the school breakfast program in the United States.

(b) The Secretary of Defense shall administer breakfast programs authorized by this section and shall determine eligibility for free and reduced-price breakfasts under the criteria published by the Secretary of Agriculture, except that the Secretary of Defense shall prescribe regulations governing computation of income eligibility standards for families of students participating in the school breakfast program under this section.

(c) The Secretary of Defense shall be required to offer meals meeting nutritional standards prescribed by the Secretary of Agriculture; however, the Secretary of Defense may authorize deviations from Department of Agriculture prescribed meal patterns and fluid milk requirements when local conditions preclude strict compliance or when such compliance is highly impracticable.

(d) Funds are hereby authorized to be appropriated for any fiscal year in such amounts as may be necessary for the administrative expenses of the Department of Defense under this section and for payment of the difference between the value of commodities and payments received from the Secretary of Agriculture and (1) the full cost of each breakfast for each student eligible for free breakfast, and (2) the full cost of each breakfast, less any amounts required by law or regulations to be paid by each student eligible for a reduced-price breakfast.

(e) The Secretary of Agriculture shall provide the Secretary of Defense with technical assistance in the administration of the school breakfast programs authorized by this section. (42 U.S.C. 1789.)

FOOTNOTES TO CHILD NUTRITION ACT

[2]P. L. 91–295, 84 Stat. 336, June 30, 1970, authorized appropriations for years succeeding fiscal year 1970, substituted "June 30, 1969" for "June 30, 1966", and added "Guam." P.L. 93–347, 88 Stat. 341, July 12, 1974, substituted "such sums as may be necessary" for "not to exceed $120,000,000."

[3]Section 3 was redesignated as section 3(a) by section 813, P.L. 97–35, 95 Stat. 530, Aug. 13, 1981.

[4]Section 807, P.L. 97–35, 95 Stat. 527, Aug. 13, 1981 added the requirement that schools covered by this section may participate in the Special Milk Program only if the schools did not participate in any other program authorized under this Act or the National School Lunch Act.

[5]This sentence was amended by section 15(1), P.L. 94–105, 89 Stat. 522, Oct. 7, 1975, which inserted the words between "Guam" and "the District of Columbia."

[6]This sentence was added by P.L. 93–150, 87 Stat. 563, Nov. 7, 1973, amended by P.L. 95–166, 91 Stat. 1337, Nov. 10, 1977, and revised by section 5(a), P.L. 95–627, 92 Stat. 3619, Nov. 10, 1978, effective July 1, 1979.

[7]This sentence was amended by (1) P.L. 93–347, 88 Stat. 341, July 12, 1974, by adding provisions setting a minimum rate of reimbursement for a half-pint of milk served in schools and other eligible institutions and allowing for an annual adjustment of the minimum rate; (2) P.L. 95–166, 91 Stat. 1346, Nov. 10, 1977 to place the reimbursements on a school year rather than fiscal year basis, effective July 1, 1977; and (3) P.L. 95–627, 92 Stat. 3619, Nov. 10, 1978, which substituted "Producer Price Index for Fresh Processed Milk," for "series of food away from home of the Consumer Price Index," effective July 1, 1979.

[8]This sentence was added by section 3(b), P.L. 93–347, 88 Stat. 341, July 12, 1974.

[8a]Section 807, P.L. 97–35, 95 Stat. 527, Aug. 13, 1981, amended this section by deleting the eighth sentence which read "Notwithstanding any other provision of this section in no event shall the minimum rate of reimbursement exceed the cost to the school or institution of milk served to children."

[10]This subsection was added by section 813, P.L. 97–35, 95 Stat. 530, Aug. 13, 1981.

[11]P.L. 90–302, 82 Stat. 119, May 8, 1968, authorized additional appropriations, deleted pilot program authority, and added the last sentence. P.L. 91–248, 84 Stat. 214, May 14, 1970, increased the 1971 appropriation. P.L. 92–32, 85 Stat. 85, June 30, 1971, authorized 1972 and 1973 appropriations. P.L. 92–433, 86 Stat. 724, Sept. 26 1972, authorized 1973, 1974 and 1975 appropriations and substituted "in all schools which make application for assistance and agree to carry out a nonprofit breakfast program in accordance with this Act" for "in schools." Section 2, P.L. 94–105, 89 Stat. 511, Oct. 7, 1975, deleted the authorization of appropriations for the fiscal years ending June 30, 1973, June 30, 1974, and June 30, 1975. P.L. 95–961, 92 Stat. 2368, Nov. 1, 1978, added "and the Department of Defense."

*Section 509(b) of Public Law 96–88, 93 Stat. 695, Oct. 17, 1979, provides that any reference to the Secretary of Health, Education, and Welfare shall be deemed to refer to the Secretary of Health and Human Services.

[12]Subsection (b)(1) was completely revised by sec. 801, P.L. 97–35, 95 Stat. 522, Aug. 13, 1981.

[13]Section 801, P.L. 97–35, 95 Stat. 523, Aug. 13, 1981, substituted "on and annual basis each July 1" for "on a semiannual basis each July 1 and January 1."

[14]Section 801, P.L. 97–35, 95 Stat. 523, Aug. 13, 1981, substituted "twelve-month" for "six-month."

[15]Section 801, P.L. 97–35, 95 Stat. 523, Aug. 13, 1981, substituted "thirty" for "five."

[16]Section 819, P.L. 97–35, 95 Stat. 533, Aug. 13, 1981, deleted the words "financing the costs of."

[17]This sentence was substituted by P.L. 93–150, 87 Stat. 562, Nov. 7, 1973, for a provision authorizing assistance in financing the cost of obtaining food. P.L. 92–32, 85 Stat. 85, June 30, 1971, substituted "to assist such schools in financing the" for "to reimburse such schools for the."

[18]P.L. 92–32, 85 Stat. 85, June 30, 1971, added the last group of schools.

[19]This sentence was added by P.L. 93–433, 86 Stat. 725, Sept. 26, 1972.

[20]Section 801(c)(2), P.L. 97–35, 95 Stat. 523, Aug. 13, 1981, completely revised subsection (d).

[21]Original language was amended by P.L. 91–248, 84 Stat. 210, May 14, 1970, to prohibit identification of needy children; and P.L. 92–32, 85 Stat. 85, June 30, 1971, to insert additional language similar to that of National School Lunch Act. The present language was substituted by P.L. 92–433, 86 Stat. 725, Sept. 26, 1972.

[22]This subsection was added by section 3, P.L. 94–105, 89 Stat. 511, Oct. 7, 1975 and redesignated as (f) by section 817, P.L. 97–35, 95 Stat. 532, which also repealed the prior subsection (f) dealing with the provision of funds to nonprofit private schools.

[23]This section was repealed by section 805, P.L. 97–35, 95 Stat. 527, Aug. 13, 1981. Section 817, P.L. 97–35, 95 Stat. 532, Aug, 13, 1981, added a completely new section 5 authorizing appropriations to carry out school food service programs. The prior provision was amended by P.L. 91–248, 84 Stat. 208, May 14, 1970, to authorize appropriations for the 1971, 1972, 1973, and succeeding years; by P.L. 92–433, 86 Stat. 727, Sept. 26, 1972, to substitute the authorization for 1973 and succeeding fiscal years for the previous authorization; by section 5, P.L. 93–326, 88 Stat. 287, June 30, 1974, to change "$20,000,000" to "$40,000,000"; by P.L. 95–166, 91 Stat. 1332, Nov. 10, 1977, to change the heading "Nonfood Assistance Program Authorization" to "Food Service Equipment Assistance"; and by section 211, P.L. 96–499, 94 Stat. 2603, Dec. 5, 1980, to limit authorization to $15,000,000 for fiscal year 1981, $30,000,000 for fiscal year 1982, $35,000,000 for fiscal year 1983 and $40,000,000 for each succeeding year.

[24]This section was amended by P. L. 90–302, 82 Stat. 119, May 8, 1968, and P.L. 91–248, 84 Stat. 210, May 14, 1970. The section was completely revised by P.L. 95–166, 91 Stat. 1338, Nov. 10, 1977. Under the prior provision, funds were made available in amounts determined by the Secretary for additional child nutrition program activities undertaken by the States. Section 201, P.L. 96–499, 94 Stat. 2599, Dec. 5, 1980, for fiscal year 1981, reduced the national average payment rate under section 4 of the National School Lunch Act by 2½ cents in all schools where less than 60 percent of the lunches served were provided at no cost or at a reduced price. Section 201 further provided that the amount of state administrative expense funds available to States under this section not be reduced as a result of the 2½ cent rate reductions.

[25]This subsection was completely revised by P.L. 95–627, 92 Stat. 3621, Nov. 10, 1978.

[26]Section 819 of P.L. 97–35, 95 Stat. 533, Aug. 13, 1981 deleted references to section 5.

[27]See footnote 26, *supra*

[28]"September 30, 1981" was substituted for "September 30, 1978" by section 814, P.L. 97–35, 95 Stat. 531, Aug. 13, 1981.

[29]See footnote 26, *supra*

[30]Subsection (e) was completely revised by section 814, P.L. 97–35, 95 Stat. 531, Aug. 13, 1981.

[31]Sec. 201(b)(2), P.L. 96–499, 94 Stat. 2600, Dec. 5, 1980, extended the authorization for section 7 to September 30, 1984.

[32]P.L. 91–248, 84 Stat. 212, May 14, 1970, added the last portion of the first sentence beginning with "and the National School Lunch Act" and the last sentence.

[33]This sentence was added by P.L. 92–433, 86 Stat. 729, Sept. 26, 1972, except the phrase "approved by the Secretary" after "competitive foods" which was added by P.L. 95–166, 91 Stat. 1345, Nov. 10, 1977.

[34]Section 819, P.L. 97–35, 95 Stat. 533, Aug. 13, 1981, deletes references to section 5.

[35]This section was amended by section 17(b), P.L. 94–105, 89 Stat. 525, Oct. 7, 1975, which deleted paragraph (c), which had defined "nonprofit private schools" redesignated paragraphs (d) and (e) as (c) and (d), respectively, and amended the definition of "school"under the redesignated paragraph (c), P.L. 95–166, 91 Stat. 1346, Nov. 10, 1977, added the definition of "school year."

[36]Section 15(c), P.L. 94–105, 89 Stat. 522, Oct. 7, 1975, substituted "American Samoa, or the Trust Territory of the Pacific Islands" for "or American Samoa."

[37]Section 808, P.L. 97–35, 95 Stat. 527, Aug. 13, 1981 added the exception for schools whose tuition exceeds $1,500.

[38]Section 212, P.L. 96–499, 94 Stat. 2603, Dec. 7, 1980, added the phrase ", but excluding Job Corp Centers funded by the Department of Labor."

[39]Section 10(c), P.L. 95–627, 92 Stat. 3624, Nov. 10, 1978, amended the definition of school year from July 1 through June 30. P.L. 95–627 also added subsection (f).

[40]Section 16 was redesignated as section 16(a) by section 816, P.L. 97–35, 95 Stat. 531, Aug. 13, 1981.

[41]This subsection was added by section 816, P.L. 97–35, 95 Stat. 531, Aug. 13, 1981.

[46]This section was added by section 23, P.L. 94–105, 89 Stat. 528, Oct. 7, 1975.

[47]This section was added by P.L. 95–166, 91 Stat. 1340, Nov. 10, 1977.

*Section 509(b) of Public Law 96–88, 93 Stat. 695, Oct. 17, 1979, provided that any reference to the Secretary of Health, Education, and Welfare shall be deemed to refer to the Secretary of Health and Human Services.

[48]Subsection 6 was repealed by section 817, P.L. 97–35, 95 Stat. 532, Aug. 13, 1981.

[49]Section 213(a), P.L. 96–499, 94 Stat. 2603, Dec. 5, 1980, inserted the clause "For the fiscal year ending September 30, 1980, and for each succeeding fiscal year ending on or before September 30, 1984."

[50]The authorization for appropriations for fiscal year 1981 ($15,000,000 and $5,000,000 for all subsequent years) was added by section 806, P.L. 97–35, 95 Stat. 527, Aug. 13, 1981. The prior language authorized appropriations of $15,000,000 for fiscal year 1981 and all subsequent fiscal years.

[51]Section 20 was added by P.L. 95–561, 92 Stat. 2368, Nov. 1, 1978.

Appendix III

NATIONAL SCHOOL LUNCH ACT,[1]
AS AMENDED

AN ACT

To provide assistance to the States in the establishment, maintenance, operation and expansion of school-lunch programs, and for other purposes.

Be it enacted by the Senate and the House of Representatives of the United States of America in Congress assembled, That this Act may be cited as the "National School Lunch Act." (42 U.S.C. 1751, note.)

DECLARATION OF POLICY

SEC. 2. It is hereby declared to be the policy of Congress, as a measure of national security, to safeguard the health and well-being of the Nation's children and to encourage the domestic consumption of nutritious agricultural commodities and other food, by assisting the States, through grants-in-aid and other means, in providing an adequate supply of foods and other facilities for the establishment, maintenance, operation, and expansion of nonprofit school-lunch programs. (42 U.S.C. 1751.)

APPROPRIATIONS AUTHORIZED

SEC. 3.[2] For each fiscal year there is hereby authorized to be appropriated, out of money in the Treasury not otherwise appropriated, such sums as may be necessary to enable the Secretary of Agriculture (hereinafter referred to as "the Secretary") to carry out the provisions of this Act, other than sections 13, 17, and 19.[3] Appropriations to carry out the provisions of this Act and of the Child Nutrition Act of 1966 for any fiscal year are authorized to be made a year in advance of the beginning of the fiscal year in which the funds will become available for disbursement to the States. Notwithstanding any other provision of law, any funds appropriated to carry out the provisions of such Acts shall remain available for the purposes of the Act for which appropriated until expended. (42 U.S.C. 1752.)[4]

APPORTIONMENT TO STATES

SEC. 4.[5] (a) The sums appropriated for any fiscal year pursuant to the authorizations contained in section 3 of this Act shall be available to the Secretary for supplying agricultural commodities and other food for the program in accordance with the provisions of this Act.

(b)(1) The Secretary shall make food assistance payments to each State educational agency each fiscal year, at such times as the Secretary may determine, from the sums appropriated for such purposes, in a total amount equal to the product obtained by multiplying—

(A) the number of lunches (consisting of a combination of foods which meet the minimum nutritional requirements prescribed by the Secretary under subsection 9(a) of this Act) served during such fiscal year in schools in such State which participate in the school lunch program under this Act under agreements with such State educational agency; by

(B) the national average lunch payment prescribed in paragraph (2) of this section

(2) The national average lunch payment for each lunch served shall be 10.5 cents (as adjusted pursuant to section 11(a) of this Act) except that for each lunch served in school food authorities in which 60 percent or more of the lunches served in the school lunch program during the second preceding school year were served free or at a reduced-price, the national average lunch payment shall be 2 cents more.

Sec. 5. (Reserved)[6]

DIRECT FEDERAL EXPENDITURES

Sec. 6.[7] (a)[8] The funds provided by appropriation or transfer from other accounts for any fiscal year for carrying out the provisions of this Act, and for carrying out the provisions of the Child Nutrition Act of 1966, other than section 3 thereof, less—

(1) not to exceed 3½ per centum thereof which per centum is hereby made available to the Secretary for his administrative expenses under this Act and under the Child Nutrition Act of 1966;

(2) the amount apportioned by him pursuant to section 4 of this Act and the amount appropriated pursuant to sections 11 and 13 of this Act and sections 4 and 7 of the Child Nutrition Act of 1966; and[9]

(3) not to exceed 1 per centum of the funds provided for carrying out the programs under this Act and the programs under the Child Nutrition Act of 1966, other than section 3, which per centum is hereby made available to the Secretary to supplement the nutritional benefits of these programs through grants to states and other means for nutritional training and education for workers, cooperators, and participants in these programs, for pilot projects and the cash-in-lieu of commodities study required to be carried out under section 20 of this Act, and for necessary surveys and studies of requirements for food service programs in furtherance of the purposes expressed in section 2 of this Act and section 2 of the Child Nutrition Act of 1966, shall be available to the Secretary during such year for direct expenditure by him for agricultural commodities and other foods to be distributed among the States and schools and service institutions participating in the food service programs under this Act and under the Child Nutrition Act of 1966 in accordance with the needs as determined by the local school and service institution authorities.[10] Any school participating in food service programs under this Act may refuse to accept delivery of not more than 20 percent of the total value of agricultural commodities and other foods tendered to it in any school year; and if a school so refuses, that school may receive, in lieu of the refused commodities, other commodities to the extent that other commodities are available to the State during that year. The provisions of law contained in the proviso of the Act of June 28, 1937 (50 Stat. 323), facilitating operations with respect to the purchase and disposition of surplus agricultural commodities under section 32 of the Act approved August 24, 1935 (49 Stat. 774), as amended, shall, to the extent not inconsistent with the provisions of this Act, also be applicable to expenditures of funds by the Secretary under this Act. In making purchases of such agricultural commodities and other foods, the Secretary shall not issue specifications which restrict participation of local producers unless such specifications will result in significant advantages to the food service programs authorized by this Act and the Child Nutrition Act of 1966.[11]

(b) [12]Not later than May 15 of each school year, the Secretary shall make an estimate of the value of agricultural commodities and other foods that will be delivered during that school year to States for the school lunch program. If such estimated value is less than the total level of assistance authorized under subsection (e) of this section, the Secretary shall pay to each State educational agency, not later than June 15 of that school year, an amount of funds that is equal to the difference between the value of such deliveries as then programed for such State and the total level of assistance authorized under subsection (e) of this section. In any State in which the Secretary directly administers the school lunch program in any of the schools of the State, the Secretary shall withhold from the funds to be paid to such State under the provisions of this subsection an amount that bears the same ratio to the total of such payment as the number of lunches served in schools in which the school lunch program is directly administered by the Secretary during that school year bears to the total of such lunches served under the school lunch program in all the schools in such State in such school year. Each State educational agency, and the Secretary in the case of private schools in which the Secretary directly administers the school lunch program, shall promptly and equitably disburse such funds to schools participating in the school lunch program, and such disbursements shall be used by such schools to purchase United States agricultural commodities and other foods for their food service program. Such foods shall be limited to the requirements for lunches and breakfasts for children as provided for in regulations issued by the Secretary.

(c) [13]Notwithstanding any other provision of law, the Secretary, until such time as a supplemental appropriation may provide additional funds for the purpose of subsection (b) of this section, shall use funds appropriated by section 32 of the Act of August 24, 1935 (7 U.S.C. 612c) to make any payments to States authorized under such subsection. Any section 32 funds utilized to make such payments shall be reimbursed out of any supplemental appropriation hereafter enacted for the purpose of carrying out subsection (b) of this section and such reimbursement shall be deposited into the fund established pursuant to section 32 of the Act of August 24, 1935, to be available for the purposes of said section 32.

(d) [14]Any funds made available under subsection (b) or (c) of this section shall not be subject to the State matching provisions of section 7 of this Act.

LEVEL OF COMMODITY ASSISTANCE

(e) [15] The national average value of donated foods, or cash payments in lieu thereof, shall be 11 cents, adjusted on July 1, 1982, and each July 1 thereafter to reflect changes in the Price Index for Food Used in Schools and Institutions. The Index shall be computed using five major food components in the Bureau of Labor Statistics' Producer Price Index (cereal and bakery products, meats, poultry and fish, dairy products, processed fruits and vegetables, and fats and oils). Each component shall be weighted using the same relative weight as determined by the Bureau of Labor Statistics. The value of food assistance for each meal shall be adjusted each July 1 by the annual percentage change in a three-month simple average value of the Price Index for Foods Used in Schools and Institutions for March, April, and May each year.[16] Such adjustment shall be computed to the nearest one-fourth cent. Among those commodities delivered under this section, the Secretary shall give special emphasis to high protein foods, meat, and meat alternates (which may include domestic seafood commodities and their products).[17] Notwithstanding any other provision of this section, not less than 75 per centum of the assistance provided under this subsection (e) shall be in the form of donated foods for the school lunch program.[18]

(f) [19]Beginning with the school year ending June 30, 1981, the Secretary shall not offer commodity assistance based upon the number of breakfasts served to children under section 4 of the Child Nutrition Act of 1966. (42 U.S.C. 1755.)

PAYMENTS TO STATES

SEC. 7.[20] (a)(1) Funds appropriated to carry out section 4 of this Act during any fiscal year shall be available for payment to the States for disbursement by State educational agencies in accordance with such agreements, not inconsistent with the provisions of this Act, as may be entered into by the Secretary and such State educational agencies for the purpose of assisting schools within the States in obtaining agricultural commodities and other foods for consumption by children in furtherance of the school lunch program authorized under this Act. For any school year, the amount of the State revenues (excluding State revenues derived from the operation of the program) appropriated or used specifically for program purposes (other than any State revenues expended for salaries and administrative expenses of the program at the State level) is not less than 30 percent of the funds made available to such State under section 4 of this Act for the school year beginning July 1, 1980.

(2) If, for any school year, the per capita income of a State is less than the average per capita income of all the States, the amount required to be expended by a State under paragraph (1) for such year shall be an amount bearing the same ratio to the amount equal to 30 percent of the funds made available to such State under section 4 of the Act for the school year beginning July 1, 1980, as the per capita income of such State bears to the average per capita income of all the States.

(b) The State revenues provided by any State to meet the requirement of subsection (a) shall, to the extent the State deems practicable, be disbursed to schools participating in the school lunch program under this Act. No State in which the State educational agency is prohibited by law from disbursing State appropriated funds to private schools shall be required to match Federal funds made available for meals served in such schools, or to disburse, to such schools, any of the State revenues required to meet the requirements of subsection (a).

(c) The Secretary shall certify to the Secretary of the Treasury, from time to time, the amounts to be paid to any State under this section and shall specify when such payments are to be made. The Secretary of the Treasury shall pay to the State, at the time or times fixed by the Secretary, the amounts so certified.

STATE DISBURSEMENT TO SCHOOLS

SEC. 8. Funds[21] paid to any State during any fiscal year pursuant to section 4 shall be disbursed by the State educational agency, in accordance with such agreements approved by the Secretary as may be entered into by such State agency and the schools in the State, to those schools in the State which the State educational agency, taking into account need and attendance, determines are eligible to participate in the school-lunch program. Such disbursement to any school shall be made only for the purpose of assisting it to obtain agricultural commodities and other foods for consumption by children in the school-lunch program.[22] The terms "child" and "children" as used in this Act shall be deemed to include persons regardless of age who are determined by the State educational agency, in accordance with regulations prescribed by the Secretary, to be mentally or physically handicapped and who are attending any child care institution as defined in section 17 of this Act or any nonresidential public or nonprofit private school of high school grade or under for the purpose of participating in a school program established for mentally or physically handicapped: *Provided,* That no institution that is not otherwise eligible to participate in the program under section 17 of this Act shall be deemed so eligible because of this sentence.[23] Such food costs may include, in addition to the purchase price of agricultural commodities and other foods, the cost of processing, distributing, transporting, storing, or handling thereof. In no event shall such disbursement for food to any school for any fiscal year exceed an amount determined by multiplying the number of lunches served in the school in the school-lunch program under this Act during such year by the maximum per meal reimbursement rate for the State, for the type of lunch served, as prescribed by the Secretary.[24] In any fiscal year in which the national average payment per lunch determined under section 4 is increased above the amount prescribed in the previous fiscal year, the maximum per meal reimbursement rate for the type of lunch served, shall be increased by a like amount.[24a] Lunch assistance disbursements to schools under this section and under section 11 of this Act may be made in advance or by way of reimbursement in accordance with procedures prescribed by the Secretary.[25] (42 U.S.C. 1757.)

NUTRITIONAL AND OTHER PROGRAM REQUIREMENTS

SEC. 9.[26] (a) Lunches served by schools participating in the school-lunch program under this Act shall meet minimum nutritional requirements prescribed by the Secretary on the basis of tested nutritional research; except that such minimum nutritional requirements shall not be construed to prohibit the substitution of foods to accommodate the medical or other special dietary needs of individual students.[27] The Secretary shall establish, in cooperation with State educational agencies, administrative procedures, which shall include local educational agency and student participation, designed to diminish waste of foods which are served by schools participating in the school lunch program under this Act without endangering the nutritional integrity of the lunches served by such schools. Students in senior high schools that participate in the school lunch program under this Act (and, when approved by the local school district or nonprofit private schools, students in any other grade level[28]) shall not be required to accept offered foods they do not intend to consume, and any such failure to accept offered foods shall not affect the full charge to the student for a lunch meeting the requirements of this subsection or the amount of payments made under this Act to any such school for such lunch.

(b)(1)(A)[29] Not later than June 1 of each fiscal year, the Secretary shall prescribe income guidelines for determining eligibility for free and reduced-price lunches during the 12-month period beginning July 1 of such fiscal year and ending June 30 of the following fiscal year. For the school years ending June 30, 1982, and June 30, 1983, the income guidelines for determining eligibility for free lunches shall be 130 percent of the applicable family-size income levels contained in the nonfarm income poverty guidelines prescribed by the Office of Management and Budget, as adjusted annually in accordance with subparagraph (B). Beginning July 1, 1983, the income guidelines for determining eligibility for free lunches for any school year shall be the same as the gross income eligibility standards announced by the Secretary for any such period for eligibility for participation in the food stamp program under the Food Stamp Act of 1977. The income guidelines for determining eligibility for reduced-price lunches for any school year shall be 185 percent of the applicable family-size income levels contained in the nonfarm income poverty guidelines prescribed by the Office of Management and Budget, as adjusted annually in accordance with subparagraph (B). The Office of Management and Budget guidelines shall be revised at annual intervals, or at any shorter interval deemed feasible and desirable.

(B) The revision required by subparagraph (A) of this paragraph shall be made by
(i) the official poverty line (as defined by the Office of Management and Budget); by
(ii) the percentage change in the Consumer Price Index during the annual or other interval immediately preceding the time at which the adjustment is made.
Revisions under this subparagraph shall be made not more than 30 days after the date on which the consumer price index data required to compute the adjustment becomes available.

(2)(A) Following the determination by the Secretary under paragraph (1) of this subsection of the income eligibility guidelines for each school year, each State educational agency shall announce the income eligibility guidelines, by family-size, to be used by schools in the State in making determinations of eligibility for free and reduced-price lunches on or before the opening of school.

(B) Applications for free and reduced-price lunches, in such form as the Secretary may prescribe or approve, and any descriptive material, shall be distributed to the parents or guardians of children in attendance at the school, and shall contain only the family-size income levels for reduced-price meal eligibility with the explanation that households with incomes less than or equal to these values would be eligible for free or reduced-price lunches. Such forms and descriptive material may not contain the income eligibility guidelines for free lunches.

(C) Eligibility determinations shall be made on the basis of a complete application executed by an adult member of the household. The Secretary, States, and local school food authorities may seek verification of the data contained in the application. Local school food authorities shall undertake such verification of the information contained in these applications as the Secretary may by regulation prescribe and, in accordance with such regulations, make appropriate changes in the eligibility determinations on the basis of such verification.

(3) Any child who is a member of a household whose income, at the time the application is submitted, is at an annual rate which does not exceed the applicable family-size income level of

the income eligibility guidelines for free lunches, as determined under paragraph (1), shall be served a free lunch. Any child who is a member of a household whose income, at the time the application is submitted, is at an annual rate greater than the applicable family-size income level of the income eligibility guidelines for free lunches, as determined under paragraph (1), but less than or equal to the applicable family-size income level of the income eligibility guidelines for reduced-price lunches, as determined under paragraph (1), shall be served a reduced-price lunch. The price charged for a reduced-price lunch shall not exceed 40 cents.

(4) No physical segregation of or other discrimination against any child eligible for a free lunch or a reduced-price lunch under this subsection shall be made by the school nor shall there by any overt identification of any child by special tokens or tickets, announced or published lists of names, or by other means.

(5)[30] Any child who has a parent or guardian who (A) is responsible for the principal support of such child and (B) is unemployed shall be served a free or reduced-price lunch, respectively, during any period (i) in which such child's parent or guardian continues to be unemployed and (ii) the income of the child's parents or guardians during such period of unemployment falls within the income eligibility criteria for free lunches or reduced-price lunches, respectively, based on the current rate of income of such parents or guardians. Local school authorities shall publicly announce that such children are eligible for a free or reduced-price lunch, and shall make determinations with respect to the status of any parent or guardian of any child under clauses (A) and (B) of the preceding sentence[31] on the basis of a statement executed in such form as the Secretary may prescribe by such parent or guardian. No physical segregation of, or other discrimination against, any child eligible for a free or reduced-price lunch under this paragraph shall be made by the school nor shall there be any overt identification of any such child by special tokens or tickets, announced or published lists of names, or by any other means.

(c) School-lunch programs under this Act shall be operated on a nonprofit basis. Each school shall, insofar as practicable, utilize in its lunch program commodities designated from time to time by the Secretary as being in abundance, either nationally or in the school area, or commodities donated by the Secretary. Commodities purchased under the authority of section 32 of the Act of August 24, 1935 (49 Stat. 774), as amended, may be donated by the Secretary to schools, in accordance with the needs as determined by local school authorities, for utilization in the school-lunch program under this Act as well as to other schools carrying out nonprofit school-lunch programs and institutions authorized to receive such commodities. The Secretary is authorized to prescribe terms and conditions respecting the use of commodities donated under such section 32, under section 416 of the Agricultural Act of 1949, as amended, and under section 709 of the Food and Agriculture Act of 1965, as amended, as will maximize the nutritional and financial contributions of such donated commodities in such schools and institutions. The requirements of this section relating to the service of meals without cost or at a reduced cost shall apply to the lunch program of any school utilizing commodities donated under any of the provisions of law referred to in the preceding sentence. None of the requirements of this section in respect to the amount for "reduced cost" meals and to eligibility for meals without cost shall apply to schools (as defined in section 12(d)(6) of this Act which are private and nonprofit as defined in the last sentence of section 12(d)(6) of this Act)[32] which participate in the school-lunch program under this Act until such time as the State educational agency, or in the case of such schools which participate under the provisions of section 10 of this Act the Secretary certifies that sufficient funds from sources other than children's payments are available to enable such schools to meet these requirements.

(d)(1)[33] The Secretary shall require as a condition of eligibility for receipt of free or reduced-price lunches that the member of the household who executes the application furnish the social security account numbers of all adult members of the household of which such person is a member.

(2) No member of a household may be provided a free or reduced-price lunch under this Act unless—

(A) appropriate documentation, as prescribed by the Secretary, of the income of such household has been provided to the appropriate local school food authority; or

(B) documentation showing that the household is participating in the food stamp program under the Food Stamp Act of 1977 has been provided to the appropriate local school food authority. (42 U.S.C. 1758.)

DISBURSEMENT TO SCHOOLS BY THE SECRETARY

SEC. 10.[34] (a) The Secretary shall withhold funds payable to a State under this Act and disburse the funds directly to schools, institutions, or service institutions within the State for the purposes authorized by this Act to the extent that the Secretary has so withheld and disbursed such funds continuously since October 1, 1980, but only to such extent (except as otherwise required by subsection (b)). Any funds so withheld and disbursed by the Secretary shall be used for the same purposes, and shall be subject to the same conditions, as applicable to a State disbursing funds made available under this Act. If the Secretary is administering (in whole or in part) any program authorized under this Act, the State in which the Secretary is administering the program may, upon request to the Secretary, assume administration of that program.

(b) If a State educational agency is not permitted by law to disburse the funds paid to it under this Act to any of the nonpublic schools in the State, the Secretary shall disburse the funds directly to such schools within the State for the same purposes and subject to the same conditions as are authorized or required with respect to the disbursements to public schools within the State by the State educational agency. (42 U.S.C. 1759.)

SPECIAL ASSISTANCE

SEC. 11.[35] (a)(1) Except as provided in section 10 of this Act, in each fiscal year each State educational agency shall receive special-assistance payments in an amount equal to the sum of the product obtained by multiplying the number of lunches (consisting of a combination of foods which meet the minimum nutritional requirements prescribed by the Secretary pursuant to subsection 9(a) of this Act) served free to children eligible for such lunches in schools within that State during such fiscal year by the special-assistance factor for free lunches prescribed by the Secretary for such fiscal year and the product obtained by multiplying the number of lunches served at a reduced price to children eligible for such reduced-price lunches in schools within that State during such fiscal year by the special-assistance factor for reduced-price lunches prescribed by the Secretary for such fiscal year. In the case of any school which determines that at least 80 percent of the children in attendance during a school year (hereinafter in this sentence referred to as the "first school year") are eligible for free lunches or reduced-price lunches, special-assistance payments shall be paid to the State educational agency with respect to that school, if that school so requests for the school year following the first school year, on the basis of the number of free lunches or reduced-price lunches, as the case may be, that are served by that school during the school year for which the request is made, to those children who were determined to be so eligible in the first school year and the number of free lunches and reduced-price lunches served during that year to other children determined for that year to be eligible for such lunches. In the case of any school that (A) elects to serve all children in that school free lunches under the school lunch program during any period of three successive school years and (B) pays, from sources other than Federal funds, for the costs of serving such lunches which are in excess of the value of assistance received under this Act with respect to the number of lunches served during the period, special-assistance payments shall be paid to the State educational agency with respect to that school during that period on the basis of the number of lunches determined under the succeeding sentence. For purposes of making special-assistance payments in accordance with the preceding sentence, the number of lunches served by a school to children eligible for free lunches and reduced-price lunches during each school year of the three-school-year period shall be deemed to be the number of lunches served by that school to children eligible for free lunches and reduced-price lunches during the first school year of such period, unless that school elects, for purposes of computing the amount of such payments, to determine on a more frequent basis the number of children eligible for free and reduced-price lunches who are served lunches during such period.

(2)[36] The special-assistance factor prescribed by the Secretary for free lunches shall be 98.75 cents and the special-assistance factor for reduced-price lunches shall be 40 cents less than the special-assistance factor for free lunches.

(3)(A) The Secretary shall prescribe on July 1, 1982, and on each subsequent July 1, an annual adjustment in the following:

(i) The national average payment rates for lunches (as established under section 4 of this Act).

(ii) The special assistance factor for lunches (as established under paragraph (2) of this subsection).

(iii) The national average payment rates for breakfasts (as established under section 4(b) of the Child Nutrition Act of 1966).

(iv) The national average payment rates for supplements (as established under section 17(c) of this Act).

(B)(a) The annual adjustment under this paragraph shall reflect changes in the cost of operating meal programs under this Act and the Child Nutrition Act of 1966, as indicated by the change in the series for food away from home of the Consumer Price Index for all Urban Consumers, published by the Bureau of Labor Statistics of the Department of Labor. Each annual adjustment shall reflect the changes in the series for food away from home for the most recent 12-month period for which such data are available. The adjustments made under this paragraph shall be computed to the nearest one-fourth cent.

(b) Except as provided in section 10 of the Child Nutrition Act of 1966, the special-assistance payments made to each State agency during each fiscal year under the provisions of this section shall be used by such State agency to assist schools of that State in[37] providing free and reduced-price lunches served to children pursuant to subsection 9(b) of this Act. The amount of such special-assistance funds that a school shall from time to time receive, within a maximum per lunch amount established by the Secretary for all States, shall be based on the need of the school for such special assistance. Such maximum per lunch amount established by the Secretary shall not be less than 60 cents.

(c) Special-assistance payments to any State under this section shall be made as provided in the last sentence of section 7 of this Act.

(d)[38] In carrying out this section, the terms and conditions governing the operation of the school-lunch program set forth in other sections of this Act, including those applicable to funds apportioned or paid pursuant to section 4 or 5 but excluding the provision of section 7 relating to matching, shall be applicable to the extent they are not inconsistent with the express requirements of this section.

(e)[39] (1)[40] Each school participating in the school-lunch program under this Act shall report each month to its State educational agency the averge number of children in the school who received free lunches and the average number of children who received reduced price lunches during the immediately preceding month.

(2)[40] The State educational agency of each State shall report to the Secretary each month the average number of children in the State who received free lunches and the average number of children in the State who received reduced price lunches during the immediately preceding month.

(f)[41] Commodity only schools shall also be eligible for special-assistance payments under this section. Such schools shall serve meals free to children who meet the eligibility requirements for free meals under section 9(b) of this Act, and shall serve meals at a reduced price, not exceeding the price specified in section 9(b)(3) of this Act, to children meeting the eligibility requirements for reduced-price meals under such section. No physical segregation of, or other discrimination against, any child eligible for a free or reduced-priced lunch shall be made by the school, nor shall there be any overt identification of any such child by any means.

MISCELLANEOUS PROVISIONS AND DEFINITIONS

SEC. 12.[42] (a) States, State educational agencies, and schools participating in the school-lunch program under this Act shall keep such accounts and records as may be necessary to enable the Secretary to determine whether the provisions of this Act are being complied with. Such accounts and records shall at all times be available for inspection and audit by representatives of the Secretary and shall be preserved for such period of time, not in excess of five years, as the Secretary determines is necessary.

(b) The Secretary shall incorporate, in his agreements with the State educational agencies, the express requirements under this Act with respect to the operation of the school-lunch program under this Act insofar as they may be applicable and such other provisions as in his opinion are reasonably necessary or appropriate to effectuate the purposes of this Act.

(c)[43] In carrying out the provisions of this Act, neither the Secretary nor the State shall impose any requirement with respect to teaching personnel, curriculum, instruction, methods of instruction, and materials or instruction in any school.

(d)[44] For the purposes of this Act—

(1)[45] "State" means any of the fifty States, the District of Columbia, the Commonwealth of Puerto Rico, the Virgin Islands, Guam, American Samoa, or the Trust Territory of the Pacific Islands.

(2)[46] "State educational agency" means, as the State legislature may determine, (A) the chief State school officer (such as the State superintendent of public instruction, commissioner of education, or similar officer), or (B) a board of education controlling the State department of education; except that in the District of Columbia it shall mean the Board of Education.

(3)[47] "Participation rate" for a State means a number equal to the number of lunches, consisting of a combination of foods and meeting the minimum requirements prescribed by the Secretary pursuant to section 9, served in the fiscal year beginning two years immediately prior to the fiscal year for which the Federal funds are appropriated by schools participating in the program under this Act in the State, as determined by the Secretary.

(4)[48] "Assistance need rate" (A) in the case of any State having an average annual per capita income equal to or greater than the average annual per capita income for all the States, shall be 5; and (B) in the case of any State having an average annual per capita income less than the average annual per capita income for all the States, shall be the product of 5 and the quotient obtained by dividing the average annual per capita income for all the States by the average annual per capita income for such State, except that such product may not exceed 9 for any such State. For the purposes of this paragraph (i) the average annual per capita income for any State and for all the States shall be determined by the Secretary on the basis of the average annual per capita income for each State and for all the States for the three most recent years for which such data are available and certified to the Secretary by the Department of Commerce; and (ii) the average annual per capita income for American Samoa shall be disregarded in determining the average annual per capita income for all the States for periods ending before July 1, 1967.

(5)[49] "School" means (A) any public or nonprofit private school of high school grade or under, except private schools whose average yearly tuition exceeds $1,500 per child, (B) any public or licensed nonprofit private residential child care institution (including, but not limited to, orphanages and homes for the mentally retarded, but excluding Job Corp Centers funded by the Department of Labor), and (C) with respect to the Commonwealth of Puerto Rico, nonprofit child care centers certified as such by the Governor of Puerto Rico. For purposes of clauses (A) and (B) of this paragraph, the term "nonprofit," when applied to any such private school or institution, means any such school or institution which is exempt from tax under section 501(c)(3) of the Internal Revenue Code of 1954.

(6)[50] "School year" means the annual period from July 1 through June 30.

(7)[51] "Commodity only schools"means schools that do not participate in the school lunch program under this Act, but which receive commodities made available by the Secretary for use by such schools in nonprofit lunch programs.

(e)[52] The value of assistance to children under this Act shall not be considered to be income or resources for any purposes under any Federal or State laws, including laws relating to taxation and welfare and public assistance programs.

(f)[53] In providing assistance for school breakfasts and lunches served in Alaska, Hawaii, Guam, American Samoa, Puerto Rico, the Virgin Islands of the United States, the Trust Territory of the Pacific Islands, and the Commonwealth of the Northern Mariana Islands, the Secretary may establish appropriate adjustments for each such State to the national average payment rates prescribed under sections 4 and 11 of this Act and section 4 of the Child Nutrition Act of 1966, to reflect the differences between the costs of providing lunches and breakfasts in those States and the costs of providing lunches and breakfasts in all other States.

(g)[54] Whoever embezzles, willfully misapplies, steals, or obtains by fraud any funds, assets, or property that are the subject of a grant or other form of assistance under this Act or the Child Nutrition Act of 1966, whether received directly or indirectly from the United States Department of Agriculture, or whoever receives, conceals, or retains such funds, assets, or property to his use or gain, knowing such funds, assets, or property have been embezzled, willfully misapplied, stolen, or obtained by fraud shall, if such funds, assets, or property are of the value of $100 or more, be fined not more than $10,000 or imprisoned not more than five years, or, both, or if such funds, assets, or property are of a value of less than $100, shall be fined not more than $1,000 or imprisoned for not more than one year, or both.

(h)[55] No provision of this Act or of the Child Nutrition Act of 1966 shall require any school receiving funds under this Act and the Child Nutrition Act of 1966 to account separately for the cost incurred in the school lunch and school breakfast programs. (42 U.S.C. 1760.)

SUMMER FOOD SERVICE PROGRAM FOR CHILDREN

Sec. 13.[56] (a)(1) The Secretary is authorized to carry out a program to assist States, through grants-in-aid and other means, to initiate, maintain, and expand nonprofit food service programs for children in service institutions. For purposes of this section, (A) "program" means the summer food service program for children authorized by this section; (B) "service institutions" means public or private nonprofit school food authorities, local, municipal, or county governments, and residential public or private nonprofit summer camps, that develop special summer or school vacation programs providing food service similar to that made available to children during the school year under the school lunch program under this Act or the school breakfast program under the Child Nutrition Act of 1966; (C) "areas in which poor economic conditions exist" means areas in which at least 50 percent[57] of the children are eligible for free or reduced-price school meals under this Act and the Child Nutrition Act of 1966, as determined by information provided from departments of welfare, zoning commissions, census tracts, by the number of free and reduced-price lunches or breakfasts served to children attending public and nonprofit private schools located in the area of program food service sites, or from other appropriate sources, including statements of eligibility based upon income for children enrolled in the program; (D) "children" means individuals who are eighteen years of age and under, and individuals who are older than eighteen who are (i) determined by a State educational agency or a local public educational agency of a State, in accordance with regulations prescribed by the Secretary, to be mentally or physically handicapped, and (ii) participating in a public or nonprofit private[58] school program established for the mentally or physically handicapped; and (E) "State" means any of the fifty States, the District of Columbia, the Commonwealth of Puerto Rico, the Virgin Islands of the United States, Guam, American Samoa, the Trust Territory of the Pacific Islands, and the Northern Mariana Islands.

(2) To the maximum extent feasible, consistent with the purposes of this section, any food service under the program shall use meals prepared at the facilities of the service institution or at the food service facilities of public and nonprofit private schools. The Secretary shall assist States in the development of information and technical assistance to encourage increased service of meals prepared at the facilities of service institutions and at public and nonprofit private schools.

(3) Eligible service institutions entitled to participate in the program shall be limited to those that—

(A) demonstrate adequate administrative and financial responsibility to manage an effective food service;

(B) have not been seriously deficient in operating under the program;

(C) either conduct a regularly scheduled food service for children from areas in which poor economic conditions exist or qualify as camps; and

(D) provide an ongoing year-round service to the community to be served under the program (except that an otherwise eligible service institution shall not be disqualified for failure to meet this requirement for ongoing year-round service if the State determines that its disqualification would result in an area in which poor economic conditions exist not being served or in a significant number of needy children not having reasonable access to a summer food service program).

(4) The following order of priority shall be used by the State in determining participation where more than one eligible service institution proposes to serve the same area:

(A) local schools or service institutions that have demonstrated successful program performance in a prior year;

(B) service institutions that prepare meals at their own facilities or operate only one site;

(C) service institutions that use local school food facilities for the preparation of meals;

(D) other service institutions that have demonstrated ability for successful program operation; and

(E) service institutions that plan to integrate the program with Federal, State, or local employment programs.

The Secretary and the States, in carrying out their respective functions under this section, shall actively seek eligible service institutions located in rural areas, for the purpose of assisting such service institutions in applying to participate in the program.

(5) Camps that satisfy all other eligibility requirements of this section shall receive reimbursement only for meals served to children who meet the eligibility requirements for free or reduced-price meals, as determined under this Act and the Child Nutrition Act of 1966.

(6)[59] Service institutions that are local, municipal, or county governments shall be eligible for reimbursement for meals served in programs under this section only if such programs are operated directly by such governments.

(b)(1) Payments to service institutions shall equal the full cost of food service operations (which cost shall include the cost of obtaining, preparing, and serving food, but shall not include administrative costs), except that such payments to any institution shall not exceed (1) 85.75 cents for each lunch and supper served; (2) 47.75 cents for each breakfast served; or (3) 22.50 cents for each meal supplement served: *Provided,* That such amounts shall be adjusted each January 1 to the nearest one-fourth cent in accordance with the changes for the twelve-month period ending the preceding November 30 in the series for food away from home of the Consumer Price Index for All Urban Consumers[60] published by the Bureau of Labor Statistics of the Department of Labor: *Provided further,* That the Secretary may make such adjustments in the maximum reimbursement levels as the Secretary determines appropriate after making the study prescribed in paragraph (4) of this subsection.

(2)[61] Any service institution may only serve lunch and either breakfast or a meal supplement during each day of operation, except that any service institution that is a camp or that serves meals primarily to migrant children may serve up to four meals during each day of operation, if (A) the service institution has the administrative capability and the food preparation and food holding capabilities (where applicable) to serve more than one meal per day, and (B) the service period of different meals does not coincide or overlap. The meals that camps and migrant programs may serve shall include a breakfast, a lunch, a supper, and meal supplements.

(3) Every service institution, when applying for participation in the program, shall submit a complete budget for administrative costs related to the program, which shall be subject to approval by the State. Payment to service institutions for administrative costs shall equal the full amount of State approved administrative costs incurred, except that such payment to service institutions may not exceed the maximum allowable levels determined by the Secretary pursuant to the study prescribed in paragraph (4) of this subsection.

(4)(A) The Secretary shall conduct a study of the food service operations carried out under the program. Such study shall include, but shall not be limited to—

(i) an evaluation of meal quality as related to costs; and

(ii) a determination whether adjustments in the maximum reimbursement levels for food service operation costs prescribed in paragraph (1) of this subsection should be made, including whether different reimbursement levels should be established for self-prepared meals and vendored meals and which site-related costs, if any, should be considered as part of administrative costs.

(B) The Secretary shall also study the administrative costs of service institutions participating in the program and shall thereafter prescribe maximum allowable levels for administrative payments that reflect the costs of such service institutions, taking into account the number of sites and children served, and such other factors as the Secretary determines appropriate to further the goals of efficient and effective administration of the program.

(C) The Secretary shall report the results of such studies to Congress not later than December 1, 1977.

(c) Payments shall be made to service institutions only for meals served during the months of May through September, except in the case of service institutions that operate food service programs for children on school vacation at any time under a continuous school calendar.

(d) Not later than April 15, May 15, and July 1, of each year, the Secretary shall forward to each State a letter of credit (advance program payment) that shall be available to each State for the payment of meals to be served in the month for which the letter of credit is issued. The amount of the advance program payment shall be an amount which the State demonstrates, to the satisfaction of the Secretary, to be necessary for advance program payments to service institutions in accordance with subsection (e) of this section. The Secretary shall also forward such advance program payments, by the first day of the month prior to the month in which the program will be conducted, to States that operate the program in months other than May through September. The Secretary shall forward any remaining payments due pursuant to subsection (b) of this section not later than sixty days following receipt of valid claims therefor.

(e)(1) Not later than June 1, July 15, and August 15 of each year, or, in the case of service institutions that operate under a continuous school calendar, the first day of each month of operation, the State shall forward advance program payments to each service institution: *Provided,* That (A) the State shall not release the second month's advance program payment to any service institution that has not certified that it has held training sessions for its own personnel and the site personnel with regard to program duties and responsibilities, and (B) no advance program payment may be made for any month in which the service institution will operate under the program for less than ten days.

(2) The amount of the advance program payment for any month in the case of any service

institution shall be an amount equal to (A) the total program payment for meals served by such service institution in the same calendar month of the preceding calendar year, (B) 50 percent of the amount established by the State to be needed by such service institution for meals if such service institution contracts with a food service management company, or (C) 65 percent of the amount established by the State to be needed by such service institution for meals if such service institution prepares its own meals, whichever amount is greatest: *Provided,* That the advance program payment may not exceed the total amount estimated by the State to be needed by such service institution for meals to be served in the month for which such advance program payment is made or $40,000, whichever is less, except that a State may make a larger advance program payment to such service institution where the State determines that such larger payment is necessary for the operation of the program by such service institution and sufficient administrative and management capability to justify a larger payment is demonstrated. The State shall forward any remaining payment due a service institution not later than seventy-five days following receipt of valid claims. If the State has reason to believe that a service institution will not be able to submit a valid claim for reimbursement covering the period for which an advance program payment has been made, the subsequent month's advance program payment shall be withheld until such time as the State has received a valid claim. Program payments advanced to service institutions that are not subsequently deducted from a valid claim for reimbursement shall be repaid upon demand by the State. Any prior payment that is under dispute may be subtracted from an advance program payment.

(f) Service institutions receiving funds under this section shall serve meals consisting of a combination of foods and meeting minimum nutritional standards prescribed by the Secretary on the basis of tested nutritional research. Such meals shall be served without cost to children attending service institutions approved for operation under this section, except that, in the case of camps, charges may be made for meals served to children other than those who meet the eligibility requirements for free or reduced-price meals in accordance with subsection (a)(5) of this section. To assure meal quality, States shall, with the assistance of the Secretary, prescribe model meal specifications and model food quality standards, and ensure that all service institutions contracting for the preparation of meals with food service management companies include in their contracts menu cycles, local food safety standards, and food quality standards approved by the State. Such contracts shall require (A) periodic inspections, by an independent agency or the local health department for the locality in which the meals are served, of meals prepared in accordance with the contract in order to determine bacteria levels present in such meals, and (B) that bacteria levels conform to the standards which are applied by the local health authority for that locality with respect to the levels of bacteria that may be present in meals served by other establishments in that locality for that locality. Such inspections and any testing resulting there from shall be in accordance with the practices employed by such local health authority.

(g) The Secretary shall publish proposed regulations relating to the implementation of the program by November 1 of each fiscal year, final regulations by January 1 of each fiscal year, and guidelines, applications, and handbooks by February 1 of each fiscal year: *Provided,* That for fiscal year 1978, those portions of the regulations relating to payment rates for both food service operations and administrative costs need not be published until December 1 and February 1, respectively. In order to improve program planning, the Secretary may provide that service institutions be paid as startup costs not to exceed 20 percent of the administrative funds provided for in the administrative budget approved by the State under subsection (b)(3) of this section. Any payments made for startup costs shall be subtracted from amounts otherwise payable for administrative costs subsequently made to service institutions under subsection (b)(3) of this section.

(h) Each service institution shall, insofar as practicable, use in its food service under the program foods designated from time to time by the Secretary as being in abundance. The Secretary is authorized to donate to States, for distribution to service institutions, food available under section 416 of the Agricultural Act of 1949 (7 U.S.C. 1431), or purchased under section 32 of the Act of August 24, 1935 (7 U.S.C. 612c) or section 709 of the Food and Agriculture Act of 1965 (7 U.S.C. 1446a–1). Donated foods may be distributed only to service institutions that can use commodities efficiently and effectively, as determined by the Secretary.

(i)[62]

(j) Expenditures of funds from State and local sources for the maintenance of food programs for children shall not be diminished as a result of funds received under this section.

(k)(1)[63] The Secretary shall pay to each State for its administrative costs incurred under this section in any fiscal year an amount equal to (A) 20 percent of the first $50,000 in funds distributed to that State for the program in the preceding fiscal year; (B) 10 percent of the next $100,000 distributed to that State for the program in the preceding fiscal year; (C) 5 percent of the next $250,000 in funds distributed to that State for the program in the preceding fiscal year, and (D) 2½ percent of any remaining funds distributed to that State for the program in the preceding fiscal year; *Provided,* That such amounts may be adjusted by the Secretary to reflect changes in the size of that State's program since the preceding fiscal year.

(2) The Secretary shall establish standards and effective dates for the proper, efficient, and effective administration of the program by the State. If the Secretary finds that the State has failed without good cause to meet any of the Secretary's standards or has failed without good cause to carry out the approved State management and administration plan under subsection (n) of this section, the Secretary may withhold from the State such funds authorized under this subsection as the Secretary determines to be appropriate.

(3) To provide for adequate nutritional and food quality monitoring, and to further the implementation of the program, an additional amount, not to exceed the lesser of actual costs or 1 percent of program funds, shall be made available by the Secretary to States to pay for State or local health department inspections, and to reinspect facilities and deliveries to test meal quality.

(l)(1) Service institutions may contract on a competitive basis only with food service management companies registered with the State in which they operate for the furnishing of meals or management of the entire food service under the program, except that a food service management company entering into a contract with a service institution under this section may not subcontract with a single company for the total meal, with or without milk, or for the assembly of the meal. The Secretary shall prescribe additional conditions and limitations governing assignment of all or any part of a contract entered into by a food service management company under this section. Any food service management company shall, in its bid, provide the service institution information as to its meal capacity. The State shall, upon award of any bid, review the company's registration to calculate how many remaining meals the food service management company is equipped to prepare.

(2) Each State shall provide for the registration of food service management companies. For the purposes of this section, registration shall include, at a minimum—

(A) certification that the company meets applicable State and local health, safety, and sanitation standards;

(B) disclosure of past and present company owners, officers, and directors, and their relationship, if any, to any service institution or food service management company that received program funds in any prior fiscal year;

(C) records of contract terminations or disallowances, and healthy, safety, and sanitary code violations, in regard to program operations in prior fiscal years; and

(D) the addresses of the company's food preparation and distribution sites.

No food service management company may be registered if the State determines that such company (i) lacks the administrative and financial capability to perform under the program, or (ii) has been seriously deficient in its participation in the program in prior fiscal years.

(3) In order to ensure that only qualified food service management companies contract for services in all States, the Secretary shall maintain a record of all registered food service

management companies and their program record for the purpose of making such information available to the States.

(4) In accordance with regulations issued by the Secretary, positive efforts shall be made by service institutions to use small businesses and minority-owned businesses as sources of supplies and services. Such efforts shall afford those sources the maximum feasible opportunity to compete for contracts using program funds.

(5) Each State, with the assistance of the Secretary, shall establish a standard form of contract for use by service institutions and food service management companies. The Secretary shall prescribe requirements governing bid and contract procedures for acquisition of the services of food service management companies, including, but not limited to, bonding requirements (which may provide exemptions applicable to contracts of $100,000 or less), procedures for review of contracts by States, and safeguards to prevent collusive bidding activities between service institutions and food service management companies.

(m) States and service institutions participating in programs under this section shall keep such accounts and records as may be necessary to enable the Secretary to determine whether there has been compliance with this section and the regulations issued hereunder. Such accounts and records shall at all times be available for inspection and audit by representatives of the Secretary and shall be preserved for such period of time, not in excess of five years, as the Secretary determines necessary.

(n) Each State desiring to participate in the program shall notify the Secretary by January 1 of each year of its intent to administer the program and shall submit for approval by February 15 a management and administration plan for the program for the fiscal year which shall include, but not be limited to, (1) the State's administrative budget for the fiscal year, and the State's plans to comply with any standards prescribed by the Secretary under sub-section (k) of this section; (2) the State's plan for use of program funds and funds from within the State to the maximum extent practicable to reach needy children, including the State's method for assessing need, and its plans and schedule for informing service institutions of the availability of the program; (3) the State's best estimate of the number and character of service institutions and sites to be approved, and of meals to be served and children to participate fo the fiscal year, and a description of the estimating methods used; (4) the State's plans and schedule for providing technical assistance and training eligible service institutions; (5) the State's schedule for application by service institutions; (6) the actions to be taken to maximize the use of meals prepared by service institutions and the use of school food service facilities; (7) the State's plans for monitoring and inspecting service institutions, feeding sites, and food service management companies and for ensuring that such companies do not enter into contracts for more meals than they can provide effectively and efficiently; (8) the State's plan and schedule for registering food service management companies; (9) the State's plan for timely and effective action against program violators; (10) the State's plan for determining the amounts of program payments to service institutions and for disbursing such payments; (11) the State's plan for ensuring fiscal integrity by auditing service institutions not subject to auditing requirements prescribed by the Secretary; and (12) the State's procedure for granting a hearing and prompt determination to any service institution wishing to appeal a State ruling denying the service institution's application for program participation or for program reimbursement.

(o)(1) Whoever, in connection with any application, procurement, recordkeeping entry, claim for reimbursement, or other document or statement made in connection with the program, knowingly and willfully falsifies, conceals, or covers up by any trick, scheme, or device a material fact, or makes any false, fictitious, or fraudulent statements or representations, or makes or uses any false writing or document knowing the same to contain any false, fictitious, or fraudulent statement or entry, or whoever, in connection with the program, knowingly makes an opportunity for any person to defraud the United States, or does or omits to do any act with intent to enable any person to defraud the United States, shall be fined not more than $10,000 or imprisoned not more than five years, or both.

(2) Whoever being a partner, officer, director, or managing agent connected in any capacity with any partnership, association, corporation, business, or organization, either public or private, that receives benefits under the program, knowingly or willfully embezzles, misapplies, steals, or obtains by fraud, false statement, or forgery, any benefits provided by this section or any money, funds, assets, or property derived from benefits provided by this section, shall be fined not more than $10,000 or imprisoned for not more than five years, or both (but, if the benefits, money, funds, assets, or property involved is not over $200, then the penalty shall be a fine of not more than $1,000 or imprisonment for not more than one year, or both).

(3) If two or more persons conspire or collude to accomplish any act made unlawful under this subsection, and one or more of such persons do any act to effect the object of the conspiracy or collusion, each shall be fined not more than $10,000 or imprisoned for not more than five years, or both.

(p) For the fiscal years beginning October 1, 1977, and ending September 30, 1986,[64] there are hereby authorized to be appropriated such sums as are necessary to carry out the purposes of this section. (42 U.S.C. 1761.)

COMMODITY DISTRIBUTION PROGRAM

SEC. 14.[65] (a) Notwithstanding any other provision of law, the Secretary, during the period beginning July 1, 1974, and ending September 30, 1986, shall—

(1) use funds available to carry out the provisions of section 32 of the Act of August 24, 1935 (7 U.S.C. 612c) which are not expended or needed to carry out such provisions, to purchase (without regard to the provisions of existing law governing the expenditure of public funds) agricultural commodities and their products of the types customarily purchased under such section (which may include domestic seafood commodities and their products)[66] for donation to maintain the annually programmed level of assistance for programs carried on under this Act, the Child Nutrition Act of 1966, and title III[67] of the Older Americans Act of 1965; and

(2) if stocks of the Commodity Credit Corporation are not available, use the funds of such Corporation to purchase agricultural commodities and their products of the types customarily available under section 416 of the Agricultural Act of 1949 (7 U.S.C. 1431), for such donation.

(b)[68] Among the products to be included in the food donations to the school-lunch program shall be cereal and shortening and oil products.

(c)[69] The Secretary may use funds appropriated from the general fund of the Treasury to purchase agricultural commodities and their products of the types customarily purchased for donation under section 311(a)(4) of the Older Americans Act of 1965 (42 U.S.C. 3030(a)(4) or for cash payments in lieu of such donations under section 311(c)(1) of such Act (42 U.S.C. 3030(c)(1)).[70] There are hereby authorized to be appropriated such sums as are necessary to carry out the purposes of this subsection.

(d)[71] In providing assistance under this Act and the Child Nutrition Act of 1966 for school lunch and breakfast programs, the Secretary shall establish procedures which will—

(1) ensure that the views of local school districts and private nonprofit schools with respect to the type of commodity assistance needed in schools are fully and accurately reflected in reports to the Secretary by the State with respect to State commodity preferences and that such views are considered by the Secretary in the purchase and distribution of commodities and by the States in the allocation of such commodities among schools within the States;

(2) solicit the views of States with respect to the acceptability of commodities;

(3) ensure that the timing of commodity deliveries to States is consistent with State school year calendars and that such deliveries occur with sufficient advance notice;

(4) provide for systematic review of the costs and benefits of providing commodities of the kind and quantity that are suitable to the needs of local school districts and private nonprofit schools; and

(5) make available technical assistance on the use of the commodities available under this Act and the Child Nutrition Act of 1966.

Within eighteen months after the date of the enactment of this subsection, the Secretary shall report to the Congress on the impact of procedures established under this subsection, including the nutritional, economic, and administrative benefits of such procedures. In purchasing commodities for programs carried out under this Act and the Child Nutrition Act of 1966, the Secretary shall establish procedures to ensure that contracts for the purchase of such commodities shall not be entered into unless the previous history and current patterns of the contracting party with respect to compliance with applicable meat inspection laws and with other appropriate standards relating to the wholesomeness of food for human consumption are taken into account.

(e)[72] Each State educational agency that receives food assistance payments under this section for any school year shall establish for such year an advisory council, which shall be composed of representatives of schools in the State that participate in the school lunch program. The Council shall advise such State agency with respect to the needs of such schools relating to the manner of selection and distribution of commodity assistance for such program.

(f)[73] Commodity only schools shall be eligible to receive donated commodities equal in value to the sum of the national average value of donated foods established under section 6(e) of this Act and the national average payment established under section 4 of this Act. Such schools shall be eligible to receive up to 5 cents per meal of such value in cash for processing and handling expenses related to the use of such commodities. Lunches served in such schools shall consist of a combination of foods which meet the minimum nutritional requirements prescribed by the Secretary under section 9(a) of this Act, and shall represent the four basic food groups, including a serving of fluid milk. (42 U.S.C. 1762a.)

NATIONAL ADVISORY COUNCIL

SEC. 15.[74] (a) There is hereby established a council to be known as the National Advisory Council on Child Nutrition (hereinafter in this section referred to as the "Council") which shall be composed of nineteen[75] members appointed by the Secretary. One member shall be a school administrator, one member shall be a person engaged in child welfare work, one member shall be a person engaged in vocational education work, one member shall be a nutrition expert, one member shall be a school food service management expert, one member shall be a State superintendent of schools (or the equivalent thereof), one member shall be a supervisor of a school lunch program in a school system in an urban area (or the equivalent thereof), one member shall be a supervisor of a school lunch program in a school system in a rural area,[76] one member shall be a State school lunch director (or the equivalent thereof), one member shall be a person serving on a school board, one member shall be a classroom teacher, two members shall be parents of children in schools that particpate in the school lunch program under this Act, two members shall be senior high school students who participate in the school lunch program under this Act,[77] and four members shall be officers or employees of the Department of Agriculture specially qualified to serve on the Council because of their education, training, experience, and knowledge in matters relating to child food programs.

(b)[78] The fifteen members of the Council appointed from outside the Department of Agriculture shall be appointed for terms of two years, except that the appointments for 1978 shall be made as follows: Two replacements, one parent, and one senior high school student shall be appointed for terms of two years; and two replacements, one parent, and one senior high school student shall be appointed for terms of one year. Thereafter, all appointments shall be for a term of two years, except that a person appointed to fill an unexpired term shall serve only for the remainder of such term. Parents and senior high school students appointed to the Council shall be members of State or school district child nutrition councils or committees actively engaged in providing program advice and guidance to school officials administering the school lunch program. Such appointments shall be made in a manner to balance rural and urban representation between parents and students. Members appointed from the Department of Agriculture shall serve at the pleasure of the Secretary.

(c) The Secretary shall designate one of the members to serve as Chairman and one to serve as Vice Chairman of the Council.

(d) The Council shall meet at the call of the Chairman but shall meet at least once a year.

(e) Eight[79] members shall constitute a quorum and a vacancy on the Council shall not affect its powers.

(f) It shall be the function of the Council to make a continuing study of the operation of programs carried out under the National School Lunch Act, the Child Nutrition Act of 1966, and any related Act under which meals are provided for children, with a view to determining how such programs may be improved. The Council shall submit to the President and the Congress biennially[80] a written report of the results of its study together with such recommendations for administrative and legislative changes as it deems appropriate.

(g) The Secretary shall provide the Council with such technical and other assistance, including secretarial and clerical assistance, as may be required to carry out its functions under this Act.

(h) Members of the Council shall serve without compensation but shall receive reimbursement for necessary travel and subsistence expenses incurred by them in the performance of the duties of the Council: *Provided,* That members serving as parents, in addition to reimbursement for necessary travel and subsistence, shall, at the discretion of the Secretary, be compensated for other personal expenses related to participation on the Council, such as child care expenses and lost wages during scheduled Council meetings.[81] (42 U.S.C. 1763.)

ELECTION TO RECEIVE CASH PAYMENTS

SEC. 16.[82] (a) Notwithstanding any other provision of law, where a State phased out its commodity distribution facilities prior to June 30, 1974, such State may, for purposes of the programs authorized by this Act and the Child Nutrition Act of 1966, elect to receive cash payments in lieu of donated foods. Where such an election is made, the Secretary shall make cash payments to such State in an amount equivalent in value to the donated foods that the State would otherwise have received if it had retained its commodity distribution facilities. The amount of cash payments in the case of lunches shall be governed by section 6(e) of this Act.

(b) When such payments are made, the State educational agency shall promptly and equitably disburse any cash it receives in lieu of commodities to eligible schools and institutions, and such disbursements shall be used by such schools and institutions to purchase United States agricultural commodities and other foods for their food service programs. (42 U.S.C. 1765.)

SEC. 17. [Section 17 is omitted as not relevant to this book.]

NUTRITION PROGRAM STAFF STUDY

SEC. 18.[97] The Secretary is authorized to carry out a study to determine how States are utilizing Federal funds provided to them for the administration of the child nutrition programs authorized by this Act and the Child Nutrition Act of 1966, and to determine the level of funds needed by the States for administrative purposes. The study shall report on the current size and structure of State staffs, job descriptions and classifications, training provided to such staff, representation of minorities on staffs, and the allocation of staff time, training time, and Federal administrative dollars spent among each of the various child nutrition programs. The study shall assess State needs for additional staff positions, training, and funds, for each of the above areas, including additional State needs to implement adequately the provisions of this Act and the Child Nutrition Act of 1966. The study shall also determine State staffing needs and training program support required to conduct effective outreach for the purpose of reaching the maximum number of eligible children in the summer food service program and the child care food program. As part of this study, the Secretary shall also examine the degree and cause of plate waste in the school lunch program. The Secretary shall examine possible relationships between plate waste and (1) lack of adequate menu development, (2) the service of competitive foods, and (3) the nature of the type A lunch pattern. The Secretary shall review the study design with the appropriate congressional committees prior to its implementation, and shall report his findings together with any recommendations he may have with respect to additional legislation, to the Congress no later than March 1, 1976. (42 U.S.C. 1767.)

APPROPRIATIONS FOR THE TRUST TERRITORY OF THE PACIFIC ISLANDS

SEC. 19.[98] There is hereby authorized to be appropriated (a) for each of the fiscal years beginning July 1, 1975, and October 1, 1976, the sum of $500,000 and (b) for the period July 1, 1976, through September 30, 1976, the sum of $125,000, to enable the Secretary to assist the Trust Territory of the Pacific Islands to carry out various developmental and experimental projects relating to programs authorized under this Act and the Child Nutrition Act of 1966 to (1) establish or improve the organizational, administrative, and operational structures and systems at the State and local school levels; (2) develop and conduct necessary training programs for school food service personnel; (3) conduct a thorough study of the children's food and dietary habits upon which special meal and nutritional requirements can be developed; and (4) establish and maintain viable school food services which are fully responsive to the needs of the children, and which are consistent with the range of child nutrition programs available to the other States, to the maximum extent possible. (42 U.S.C. 1768.)

PILOT PROJECTS

SEC. 20.[99] (a) The Secretary shall conduct pilot projects with respect to local school districts or other appropriate units, or groups of program participants, for the purpose of determining whether there may be more efficient, healthful, economical, and reliable methods for operating school lunch, school breakfast, and summer feeding programs under this Act and the Child Nutrition Act of 1966, and methods for operating such programs that will result in improved delivery of benefits thereunder in accordance with the purposes of such Acts. Such projects shall, notwithstanding any other provision of law, include (1) not more than ten projects providing participating schools or other institutions the option of receiving all or part cash assistance in lieu of commodities under such Acts for such nutrition programs operated in such schools or institutions, (2) projects designed to streamline or reduce reporting requirements by local school districts, and (3) projects using the United States Department of Agriculture Extension Service to aid in nutrition training and education in schools and other institutions.

(b) The Secretary shall conduct a study to analyze the impact and effect of cash payments in lieu of commodities. The study shall be limited to a comparison between a State that phased out its commodity distribution facilities prior to June 30, 1974, and elected to receive cash payments in lieu of donated foods, and a State not eligible for cash payments in lieu of donated foods. Such study shall include an assessment of the administrative feasibility and nutritional impact of cash payments in lieu of donated foods, the cost savings, if any, that may be effected thereby at the Federal, State, and local levels, any additional costs that may be placed on programs and participating students, the impact on Federal programs designed to provide adequate income to farmers, the impact on the quality of food served, and the impact on plate waste in school lunch and breakfast programs.

(c) The Secretary shall report to Congress, not later than eighteen months after the date of the enactment of this section, on the results of the pilot projects and study conducted under this section except for the pilot projects conducted under subsection (d) of this section.[100] In connection with such pilot projects, such report shall include an assessment of the methods employed in such projects, for operating school lunch, school breakfast, and summer feedings programs, in terms of the following factors—

(1) the administrative feasibility and nutritional impact;

(2) the cost savings that may be effected at Federal, State, and local levels;

(3) the impact on Federal programs designed to provide adequate income to farmers;

(4) the impact on the quality of food served; and

(5) the impact on plate waste.

(d)(1)[101] The Secretary may conduct pilot projects in not more than fourteen school districts (or other appropriate units), of which not more than two may be located in any administrative region of the Food and Nutrition Service of the Department of Agriculture, for the purpose of determining the feasibility, cost, and other consequences of providing lunches free to all children, without regard to the income of the children's families, during the school year beginning July 1, 1979.

(2) The Secretary shall reimburse school food authorities participating in a pilot project under this subsection for all lunches served to children on the same basis that the Secretary normally provides for lunches served to children meeting the eligibility requirements for free lunches under section 9 of this Act.

(3) The Secretary shall submit to the appropriate committees of the Senate and the House of Representatives a report on the pilot projects conducted under this subsection not later than six months after the conclusion of such projects.

(4) There are hereby authorized to be appropriated such sums as are necessary for the fiscal year beginning October 1, 1978, for the purpose of conducting an evaluation of pilot projects conducted under this subsection and for the purpose of making additional payments for lunches served to children (beyond what the school food authorities would otherwise receive under sections 4 and 11 of this Act) to school food authorities participating in pilot projects. (42 U.S.C. 1769.)

REDUCTION OF PAPER WORK

SEC. 21.[102] In carrying out functions under this Act and the Child Nutrition Act of 1966, the Secretary shall reduce, to the maximum extent possible, the paperwork required of State and local educational agencies, schools, and other agencies participating in child nutrition programs under such Acts. The Secretary shall report to Congress not later than one year after the date of enactment of this section on the extent to which a reduction in such paperwork has occurred. (42 U.S.C. 1769a.)

DEPARTMENT OF DEFENSE OVERSEAS DEPENDENTS' SCHOOLS

SEC. 22.[102] (a) For the purpose of obtaining Federal payments and commodities in conjunction with the provision of lunches to students attending Department of Defense dependents' schools which are located outside the United States, its territories or possessions, the Secretary of Agriculture shall make available to the Department of Defense, from funds appropriated for such purposes, the same payments and commodities as are provided to States for schools participating in the National School Lunch Program in the United States.

(b) The Secretary of Defense shall administer lunch programs authorized by this section and shall determine eligibility for free and reduced-price lunches under the criteria published by the Secretary of Agriculture, except that the Secretary of Defense shall prescribe regulations governing computation of income eligibility standards for families of students participating in the National School Lunch Program under this section.

(c) The Secretary of Defense shall be required to offer meals meeting nutritional standards prescribed by the Secretary of Agriculture; however, the Secretary of Defense may authorize deviations from Department of Agriculture prescribed meal patterns and fluid milk requirements when local conditions preclude strict compliance or when such compliance is impracticable.

(d) Funds are hereby authorized to be appropriated for any fiscal year in such amounts as may be necessary for the administrative expenses of the Department of Defense under this section and for payment of the difference between the value of commodities and payments received from the Secretary of Agriculture and (1) the full cost of each lunch for each student eligible for a free lunch, and (2) the full cost of each lunch, less any amounts required by law or regulation to be paid by each student eligible for a reduced-price lunch.

(e) The Secretary of Agriculture shall provide the Secretary of Defense with the technical assistance in the administration of the school lunch programs authorized by this section. (42 U.S.C. 1769b.)

STUDY OF MENU CHOICE

SEC. 22.[104] As a means of diminishing waste of foods without endangering nutritional integrity of meals served, the Secretary shall conduct a study to determine the cost and feasibility of requiring schools to offer a choice of menu items within the required meal patterns. This study shall, as a minimum, include different needs and capabilities of elementary and secondary schools for such a requirement. The Secretary shall develop regulations designed to diminish such waste based on the results of this study. (42 U.S.C. 1769c.)

FOOTNOTES TO NATIONAL SCHOOL LUNCH ACT

[1]P.L. 79–396, 60 Stat. 230, June 4, 1946. For other child feeding programs, see also the Child Nutrition Act of 1966 (p. 87) and section 416 of the Agricultural Act of 1949 (p. 133).

[2]Section 3 was amended by P.L. 87–823, 76 Stat. 944, Oct. 15, 1962, to delete "beginning with the fiscal year ending June 30, 1947," following "fiscal year" and to add the phrase "other than section 11." The section was further amended by P.L. 90–302, 82 Stat. 117, May 8, 1968, to add the reference to section 13. The final two sentences were added by P.L. 91–248, 84 Stat. 207, May 14, 1970.

[3]P.L. 93–326, 88 Stat. 287, June 30, 1974, substituted "13" for "11 and 13." P.L. 94–105, 89 Stat. 529, Oct. 7, 1975, substituted "13, 17, and 19" for "13."

[4]P.L. 90–302, 82 Stat. 117, May 8, 1968, requires that appropriations be considered Health, Education and Welfare functions for budget purposes.

[5]Section 4 was substantially amended by P.L. 92–433, 86 Stat. 726, Sept. 26, 1972, effective July 1, 1973. The initial provisions for apportionment of funds among the States were amended by P.L. 82–518, 66 Stat. 591, July 12, 1952, to change apportionments to territories and possessions: P.L. 87–689, 76 Stat. 587, Sept. 25, 1962, to include American Samoa; and P.L. 87–823, 76 Stat. 944, Oct. 15, 1962, to change the apportionment factors, specify transitional formulas, and make several other changes. Section 201(a) of P.L. 96–499, 94 Stat. 2599, Dec. 5, 1980, reduced for fiscal year 1981 the national average payment per lunch provided from general cash assistance funds by 2½ cents for any school food authority under which less than 60 percent of the lunches were served free or at a reduced price during the second preceding school year. Section 4 was again substantially amended by P.L. 97–35, 95 Stat. 521, Aug. 13, 1981 effective September 1, 1981. Section 801 of P.L. 97–35 added an "(a)" after "Sec. 4." and eliminated the reference to section 5 and the language which authorized the Secretary to establish a national average payment factor for lunches "determined by the Secretary to be necessary to carry out the purposes of this act". Subsection (b) was added, which fixed the national average lunch payment at 10.5 cents (adjusted annually) and 2 cents per lunch more for schools which in the second preceding school year served 60 percent or more of the lunches in the program free or at a reduced price.

[6]Section 5, which authorized the food service equipment assistance program, was repealed by section 805 of P.L. 97–35, 95 Stat. 527, Aug. 13, 1981.

[7]Section 6 was amended by P.L. 87–823, 76 Stat. 945, Oct. 15, 1962, to refer to section 11; and P.L. 90–302, 82 Stat. 117, May 8, 1968, to refer to section 13, P.L. 91–248, 84 Stat. 209, May 14, 1970, substituted the first sentence for provisions appearing earlier, adding, in particular, references to the Child Nutrition Act of 1966 and the use of funds for nutritional training and education and for surveys and studies. P.L. 95–166, 91 Stat. 1335, 1336, Nov. 10, 1977, added the choice of commodities option for not more than 20 percent of commodities tendered to a school and the authorization of funds for pilot projects and studies under the new section 20 of this Act.

[8]This paragraph was designated subsection (a) by P. L. 93–13, 87 Stat. 10, March 30, 1973.

[9]Section 819 of P.L. 97–35, 95 Stat. 533, Aug. 13, 1981 removed references to sections 5 of the National School Lunch Act and the Child Nutrition Act of 1966.

[10]See section 404 of the Agricultural Act of 1949, as amended, authorizing the use of the services and facilities of Commodity Credit Corporation in carrying out programs under section 6.

[11]This sentence was added by P.L. 94–105, 89 Stat. 515, Oct. 7, 1975.

[12]This subsection was completely revised by P.L. 95–166, 91 Stat. 1334, Nov. 10, 1977.

[13]These subsections were substituted by P.L. 93–150, 87 Stat. 562, 563, Nov. 7, 1973, for similar provisions, effective for the fiscal year 1973, added to section 6 by P.L. 93–13, 87 Stat. 10, 11, March 30, 1973. P.L. 94–105, 89 Stat. 511, Oct. 7, 1975, deleted references to "nonprofit private" schools in subsection (b).

[14]See footnote 13, supra.

[15]Subsection (e) added by P.L. 93–326, 88 Stat. 286, June 30, 1974. P.L. 95–166, 91 Stat. 1345, Nov. 10, 1977. Section 202(a), P.L. 96–499, 94 Stat. 2600, Dec. 5, 1980, reduced for fiscal year 1981 the national average value of donated foods or cash payments by 2 cents. Section 802 of P.L. 97–35, 95 Stat. 524, Aug. 13, 1981, amended the first sentence to fix the national average value of donated foods or cash payments at 11 cents, adjusted July 1, 1982 and annually thereafter.

[16]Section 5(b) of P.L. 95–627, 92 Stat. 3619, Nov. 10, 1978 (effective July 1, 1979) amended subsection (e) by deleting from the first sentence "the series for food away from home of the Consumer Price Index published by the Bureau of Labor

Statistics of the Department of Labor," and inserting in lieu thereof "the Price Index for Food Used in Schools and Institutions. The Index shall be computed using five major food components. . ." and all of the material down through the end of the fourth sentence.

[17]Added by section 12(a) of P.L. 95–627, 92 Stat. 3625, Nov. 10, 1978, which provides as follows: "SEC. 12. (a) Section 6(e) of the National School Lunch Act is amended by inserting in the second [sic] sentence '(which may include domestic seafood commodities and their products)' after 'alternatives' [sic]."

[18]This sentence was added by P.L. 94–105, 89 Stat. 515, Oct. 7, 1975.

[19]Subsection (f) was added by section 202(b) of P.L. 96–499, 94 Stat. 2600, Dec. 5, 1980, to discontinue inclusion of breakfasts in the determination of commodity entitlements.

[20]This section was completely revised by sec. 804 of P.L. 97–35, 95 Stat. 526, Aug. 13, 1981.

[21]Section 819 of P.L. 97–35, 95 Stat. 533, Aug. 13, 1981, eliminated the reference to section 5.

[22]P.L. 92–433, 86 Stat. 729, Sept. 26, 1972, substituted the phrase "assisting it to finance" for "reimbursing it for" Section 819 of P.L. 97–35, 95 Stat. 533, Aug. 13, 1981, amended this sentence by substituting the phrase "to obtain" for "to finance the cost of obtaining" and eliminated a reference to the food service equipment program.

[23]This sentence was added by section 10(d)(1) of P.L. 95–627, 92 Stat. 3624, Nov. 10, 1978.

[24]Section 819 of P.L. 97–35, 95 Stat. 533, Aug. 13, 1981, amended this sentence by substituting the phrase "per meal reimbursement rate" for "Federal food cost contribution rate."

[24a]This sentence was added by P.L. 93–150, 87 Stat. 560, Nov. 7, 1973. Section 819 of P.L. 97–35, 95 Stat. 533, Aug. 13, 1981, amended this sentence by substituting the phrase "per meal reimbursement rate" for "Federal food-cost contribution rate."

[25]This sentence was added by P.L. 92–433, 86 Stat. 729, Sept. 26, 1972.

[26]Section 9 was substantially amended by P.L. 91–248, 84 Stat. 210, May 14, 1970. Among changes made were those which provided for determination of eligibility for free and reduced-price lunches on the basis of publicly announced criteria and for establishment by the Secretary of income poverty guidelines with free or reduced-price lunches for children from families with an annual income below such guidelines, P.L. 92–433, 86 Stat. 726, Sept. 26, 1972, designated the subsections; substituted new wording for (b) requiring that children from households whose income is not above the applicable family size income level in the Secretary's income poverty guidelines be served a free lunch and that State educational agencies prescribe income guidelines by family size to be used by schools in the State in determining eligibility for free and reduced-price lunches; and amended (c) to extend the provisions with respect to certain nonprofit private schools to all such schools. P.L. 94–105, 89 Stat. 512, Oct. 7, 1975, amended and expanded this section to make reduced-price meals more widely available, to provide for the reduction of food waste in high schools, and for other purposes.

[27] Exception added by P.L. 90–302, 82 Stat. 117, May 8, 1968.

[28]Section 811 of P.L. 97–35, 95 Stat. 529, Aug. 13, 1981, eliminated the words "in any junior high school or middle school."

[29]Subsection (b) was completely revised by section 803 of P.L. 97–35, 95 Stat. 524, Aug. 13, 1981.

[30]This paragraph was amended by Public Law 94–105, 89 Stat. 513, Oct. 7, 1975.

[31]Section 803(a) of P.L. 97–35, 95 Stat. 525, Aug. 13, 1981 eliminated the word "solely" from this sentence.

[32]Subsection (c) was amended by P.L. 94–105, 89 Stat. 514, Oct. 7, 1975, to refer to amended definition of "school."

[33]Subsection (d) was added by section 803(b) of P.L. 97–35, 95 Stat. 531, Aug. 13, 1981.

[34]Section 10 was completely revised by section 817 of P.L. 97–35, 95 Stat. 531, Aug. 13, 1981.

[35]Section 11 was extensively amended by P.L. 93–150, 87 Stat. 561, Nov. 7, 1973. As inserted by P.L. 97–823, 76 Stat. 946, Oct. 15, 1962, the section provided an apportionment formula. Amendments made by P.L. 91–248, 84 Stat. 211, May 14, 1970, deleted provisions limiting special assistance to schools drawing attendance from areas in which poor economic conditions exist, based the apportionment of funds upon number of children instead of number of lunches, and deleted provisions relating to the selection of schools on the basis of economic factors. P.L. 92–153, 85 Stat. 420, Nov. 5, 1971, added provisions for a base factor of 40 cents for free lunches and 40 cents, less the highest reduced price charged, for reduced price lunches. Section 801 of P.L. 97–35, 95 Stat. 521, Aug. 13, 1981, amended this section by redesignating subsection (a) as (a)(1) and clauses (1) and (2) as (A) and (B) respectively, and deleting obsolete language concerning adjustments of rates.

[36]Subsections (a)(2) and (a)(3) were added by section 801 of P.L. 97–35, 95 Stat. 522, Aug. 13, 1981.

[37]Section 819 of P.L. 97–35, 95 Stat. 533, Aug. 13, 1981 removed the words "financing the cost of."

[38]This subsection was changed from (g) to (d) by P.L. 93–150, 87 Stat. 561, Nov. 7, 1973.

[39]Added by P.L. 91–248, 84 Stat. 212, May 14, 1970, and changed from (h) to (e) by P.L. 93–150, 87 Stat. 561, Nov. 7, 1975. P.L. 94–105, 89 Stat. 514, Oct. 7, 1975, amended this subsection to change planning from a fiscal to a school year basis, and placed the date of the plans' submission at the discretion of the Secretary. This section was amended by section 812 of P.L. 97–35, 95 Stat. 520, Aug. 13, 1981 to eliminate former paragraph 1 which required that States file State plans.

[40]Sec. 812 of P.L. 97–35, 95 Stat. 530, Aug. 13, 1981, redesignated paragraphs (2) and (3) to (1) and (2) respectively and eliminated the requirement that schools and States provide an estimate of the number of children eligible for free or reduced meals.

[41]This subsection was added by section 813 of P.L. 97–35, 95 Stat. 530, Aug. 13, 1981.

[42]Section 12 was section 11 until renumbered by P.L. 87–823, 76 Stat. 945, Oct. 15, 1962.

[43]P.L. 87–823, 76 Stat. 945, Oct. 15, 1962, deleted a requirement of equitable distribution of funds in States maintaining separate schools for minority and majority races.

[44]P.L. 94–105, 89 Stat. 514, Oct. 7, 1975, deleted a definition of "nonprofit private school" and renumbered paragraphs 3–6.

[45]Amended by P.L. 82–518, 66 Stat. 591, July 12, 1952, to include Guam; P.L. 87–688, 76 Stat. 587, Sept. 25, 1962, to include American Samoa; P.L. 87–823, 76 Stat. 945, Oct. 15, 1962, to recognize Alaskan and Hawaiian statehood; and by P.L. 94–105, 89 Stat. 514, Oct. 7, 1975, to include the Trust Territory of the Pacific Islands.

[46]P.L. 87–823, 76 Stat. 945, Oct. 15, 1962, deleted an exception applicable to the District of Columbia and obsolete language.

[47]P.L. 87–823, 76 Stat. 945, Oct. 15, 1962, added this paragraph. P.L. 91–248, 84 Stat. 207, May 14, 1970, provided for the use of data from a different fiscal year. Section 819 of P.L. 97–35, 95 Stat. 533, Aug. 13, 1981 changed this paragraph from (4) to (3) and eliminated the preceding paragraph that referred to food service equipment.

[48]Added by P.L. 87–823, 76 Stat. 945, Oct. 15, 1962. Changed to (4) from (5) by section 819 of P.L. 97–35, 95 Stat. 533, Aug. 13, 1981.

[49]This definition was transferred from section 4 by P.L. 87–823, 76 Stat. 946, Oct. 15, 1962. P.L. 94–105, 89 Stat. 514, Oct.

7, 1975, expanded this definition to include nonprofit private residential child care institutions. P.L. 96–499, 94 Stat. 2601, Dec. 5, 1980, amended this definition to exclude Job Corp Centers funded by the Department of Labor. Section 808 of P.L. 97–35, 95 Stat. 527, Aug. 13, 1981 changed the definition to exclude private schools whose average yearly tutition exceeds $1,500.00 per child.

[50]This definition was added by section 12(b), P.L. 95–627, 92 Stat. 3624, Nov. 10, 1978 and the paragraph changed from (7) to (6) by section 819 of P.L. 97–35, 95 Stat. 533, Aug. 13, 1981.

[51]This definition was added by section 813, P.L. 97–35, 95 Stat. 530, Aug. 13, 1981.

[52]This subsection was added by P.L. 94–105, 89 Stat. 515, Oct. 7, 1975.

[53]This subsection was added by section 10(a) of P.L. 95–627, 92 Stat. 3623, Nov. 10, 1978.

[54]See footnote 53, *supra*.

[55]This subsection was added by section 6(a)(1) of P.L. 95–627, 92 Stat. 3620, Nov. 10, 1978 and amended by section 819 of P.L. 97–35, 95 Stat. 533, Aug. 13, 1981 to eliminate the requirement that reimbursement to school food authorities not exceed the cost of operating the lunch and breakfast programs.

[56]This section was completely revised by P.L. 95–166, 91 Stat. 1325, Nov. 10, 1977. The earlier section was enacted by P.L. 94–105, 89 Stat. 515, Oct. 7, 1975, replacing a section of the same number which provided for a special food service program for children.

[57]Section 809 of P.L. 97–35, 95 Stat. 527, Aug. 13, 1981 replaced the words "nonresidential public or private nonprofit institutions" with "public or private nonprofit school food authorities, local, municipal, or county governments," and substituted "50 percent" for "33⅓ percent."

[58]The phrase "or nonprofit private" was added by sec. 10(d)(2) of P.L. 95–627, 92 Stat. 3624, Nov. 10, 1978.

[59]Paragraph 6 was added by section 809, P.L. 97–35, 95 Stat. 527, Aug. 13, 1981.

[60]The phrase "for All Urban Consumers" was added by section 5(d) of P.L. 95–627, Nov. 10, 1978, effective July 1, 1979.

[61]This paragraph was amended by section 206, P.L. 96–499, 94 Stat. 2601, Dec. 5, 1980, to limit meal service to a lunch and either breakfast or a meal supplement, except in camps or institutions serving primarily migrants.

[62]Section 817, P.L. 97–35, 95 Stat. 532, Aug. 13, 1981 eliminated subsection (i) concerning the Secretary's authority to directly administer the program.

[63]This subsection was amended by section 7(b) of P.L. 95–627, 92 Stat. 2533, Nov. 10, 1978.

[64]Extended by section 207, P.L. 96–499, 94 Stat. 2602, Dec. 5, 1980.

[65]Added by P.L. 93–326, 88 Stat. 286, June 30, 1974, extended to Sept. 30, 1977, by P.L. 94–105, 89 Stat. 515, Oct. 7, 1975, extended to Sept. 30, 1982, by P.L. 95–166, 91 Stat. 1334, Nov. 10, 1977, and further extended to Sept. 30, 1984, by section 202, P.L. 96–499, 94 Stat. 2600, Dec. 5, 1980.

[66]This phrase was added by section 12(b) of P.L. 95–627, 92 Stat. 3625, Nov. 10, 1978.

[67]Section 819 of P.L. 97–35, 95 Stat. 533, Aug. 13, 1981 substituted "title III" for "title VII."

[68]This subsection added by P.L. 94–105, 89 Stat. 515, Oct. 7, 1975.

[69]This subsection added by P.L. 95–166, 91 Stat. 1334, Nov. 10, 1977.

[70]Section 819 of P.L. 97–35, 95 Stat. 533, Aug. 13, 1981 corrected the citations to the Older Americans Act from the old title VII references to the current title III references.

[71]This subsection added by P.L. 95–166, 91 Stat. 1335, Nov. 10, 1977.

[72]See footnote 71, *supra*.

[73]This subsection was added by section 813, P.L. 97–35, 95 Stat. 530, Aug. 13, 1981.

[74]This section was added by P.L. 91–248, 84 Stat. 213, May 14, 1970, as section 14. It was renumbered as 15 by P.L. 93–326, 88 Stat. 286, June 30, 1974.

[75]P.L. 93–150, 87 Stat. 564, Nov. 7, 1973, substituted "fifteen" for "thirteen." P.L. 95–166, 91 Stat. 1344, Nov. 10, 1977, substituted "nineteen" for "fifteen."

[76]P.L. 93–150, 87 Stat. 564, Nov. 7, 1973, added the two clauses referring to school lunch program supervisors.

[77]The last four members were added by P.L. 95–166, 91 Stat. 1344, Nov. 10, 1977.

[78]This subsection was completely revised by P.L. 95–166, 91 Stat. 1344, Nov. 10, 1977.

[79]P.L. 93–150, 87 Stat. 564, Nov. 7, 1973, substituted "eight" for "seven."

[80]The frequency of the report was changed from "annually" to "biennially" by section 819. P.L. 97–35, 95 Stat. 533, Aug. 13, 1981.

[81]The proviso was added by P.L. 95–166, 91 Stat. 1344, Nov. 10, 1977.

[97]Section 18 was added by P.L. 94–105, 89 Stat. 527, Oct. 7, 1975.

[98]Section 19 was added by PLL 94–105, 89 Stat. 527, Oct. 7, 1975.

[99]Section 20 was added by P.L. 95–166, 91 Stat. 1336, Nov. 10, 1977.

[100]Exception added by section 11 (1) of P.L. 95–627, 92 Stat. 3624, Nov. 10, 1978.

[101]This subsection was added by section 11(2) of P.L. 95–627, 92 Stat. 3624, Nov. 10, 1978.

[102]Section 21 was added by P.L. 95–166, 91 Stat. 1338, Nov. 10, 1977.

[103]Section 22 was added by P.L. 95–562, 92 Stat. 2366, Nov. 1, 1978.

[104]This section was added by section 9 of P.L. 95–627, 92 Stat. 3623, Nov. 10, 1978.

Appendix IV

MILK BID SAMPLE

This milk bid form is an example of how to write specifications.[1]

MILK BID (SAMPLE)

A. Sealed bids will be received by the Director of Food Service of the _____ Independent School District # _____ at the Administration Building or School Office until 9:00 A.M. on _____.

B. All bids shall be submitted on this prepared proposal blank. Bidder should retain a copy and return the original and one copy as his bid.

C. The Board of Education reserves the right to reject any or all bids and to terminate the contract at any time if the bidder fails, neglects, or refuses to comply with the terms of the bid.

D. Standards and specifications for milk to be delivered to the _____ School cafeteria(s) in quantities "more or less" as set forth herein for the period _____ through _____.

E. All milk products must be produced, handled, and pasteurized in conformity and in accordance with the provisions of the Standard Milk Ordinance and Code, 1953 revision, recommended by the United States Public Health Service and in accordance with any future upward revisions of the above recommended ordinance and code. In addition to compliance with the Standard Milk Ordinance and Code, all milk and chocolate milk must comply with the following specifications:

1. *Milk—Grade A*
   a. All milk products shall be date coded according to milk code regulation 1003.18. The milk shall have at least seven (7) days remaining on date code when delivered.
   b. Shall show a bacterial count of not more than 30,000 per cubic centimeter at any time of delivery or coliform count exceeding 10 per milliliter in any of 3 or 4 samples examined.

[1]Adapted from the Oklahoma State Department of Education form and Fairfax County (VA) Schools bid specifications.

c.   Shall contain no added water, preservatives, oils, coloring matter, or any foreign matter.

d.   Shall be pasteurized at not less than 143°F for not less than 30 minutes or at not less than 161°F for not less than 15 seconds.

2. *Price Adjustment*

a.   Price adjustment allowances based on "Milk Only" will be considered. Upward and downward adjustments in the delivered price of milk products will be considered, according to the provisions of Article 21, as amended by Chapter 383 of the Laws of 1937 of the Agricultural Marketing Agreement Act, and/or the Washington, D.C., Milk Marketing Order. Adjustments in the price paid for Class I Milk may be made when the price is increased or decreased by twenty cents ($0.20) or more per hundred weight, and published by the Federal Milk Market Administrator in the Market Administrator Bulletin, Federal Order No. 1.

b.   Price change will not be automatic. Any request for price adjustment must be initiated by the contractor in writing and supported by Applicable Milk Market Administrator Bulletin.

c.   Price adjustment(s) will only be authorized by contract amendment approved by the contracting authority and the effective date of the change will be the date of the amendment.

3. *Delivery*

a.   Deliveries are to be made daily, Monday through Friday, to the school sites listed below.

b.   Times of delivery shall be between 7:30 A.M. and 2:30 P.M.

c.   It is to be understood by each bidder that deliveries will be discontinued during regular school vacation periods as shown by a school calendar which will be provided to the successful bidder. In cases of variation from this calendar, ample notice shall be given the supplier.

d.   Milk is to be delivered in refrigerated trucks and placed in the refrigerated box provided by the school district. At the time of each delivery, all milk in the box is to be on top of the milk delivered that day.

e.   The dairy agrees to be responsible for damage to the milk boxes that are a direct result of carelessness of the delivery man.

Description (Quote Lowest Net Prices Including All Delivery Charges)	Insert Unit Price and Extension Against Each Item for Which You Are Bidding			
	Quantity	Unit	Unit Price	Extension
	8/25/85			
Pricing Schedule 1. *Milk,* Lowfat, Class I, Pasteurized, 8-ounce containers, 2.0% milk fat. Homogenized, Vitamin A and Vitamin D fortified. Milk shall not be fortified with additional milk solids. Number of Containers per case: _____ Net Weight per case: _____ Maximum elapsed time between Production Date and Delivery Date: _____		8 oz	$_____	$_____
2. *Milk,* Class I, Pasteurized, 3.25% milk fat. Homogenized, Vitamin D fortified. 8-ounce containers, packaged for vending machines in standard gable-top Pure-Pak cartons. Number of Containers per case: _____ Net Weight per case: _____ Maximum elapsed time between Production Time and Delivery Date: _____		8 oz	$_____	$_____
3. *Chocolate-Flavored Milk,* Lowfat, Class 1, pasteurized, 8-ounce containers, 2% milk fat. Homogenized. Chocolate shall not exceed 1% of the total solids. Product must be non-setting and noncreaming. Artificial flavorings or additives are unacceptable. Milk shall not be fortified with additional milk solids. Number of Containers per case: _____ Net Weight per case: _____ Maximum elapsed time between Production Date and Delivery Date: _____		8 oz	$_____	$_____
4. *Chocolate-Flavored Milk,* 3.25% milk fat, Grade A pasteurized. 8-ounce containers, packaged for vending machine in standard gable-top Pure-Pak cartons. Number of Containers per case: _____ Net Weight per case: _____ Maximum elapsed time between Production Date and Delivery Date: _____		8 oz	$_____	$_____

SCHOOL SITES TO WHICH DELIVERIES
ARE TO BE MADE

Schools   Addresses

_____   _____
_____   _____
_____   _____
_____   _____

The aggregate amount of milk to be delivered each day will be approximately _____ half pints. The contractor will also deliver other commonly marketed dairy products not included under this contract at regular wholesale prices as needed by the individual schools.

In the event of failure of the contractor to make deliveries of the milk products in such quantities as may be required in accordance with the specifications herein set forth, the authorized agent of the Board of Education, _____ School District, reserves the right to cancel this contract to purchase milk in the open market or to make new contracts with other bidders. Any excessive costs resulting from purchases under this provision will be charged to the supplier under this contract.

Bond: The successful bidder will be required to furnish a $5,000 performance bond.

CONTRACT SECTION

The undersigned firm agrees to furnish dairy products according to the preceding specifications in approximate quantities as stated, at the price shown, and for the period as stated in this proposal. Bids may be made on the entire quantity of milk to be delivered to the schools listed.

Name of Firm _____

Signed by _____Title _____

Date _____

The above bid proposal is hereby accepted and becomes a contract according to specifications and conditions stated herein.

Food Service Director _____Date _____

INDEX